Colección Tá

SERIE A: MONOGRAFÍAS, 262

A COMPANION TO *DON QUIXOTE*

Tamesis

Founding Editor
J. E. Varey

General Editor
Stephen M. Hart

Editorial Board
Alan Deyermond
Julian Weiss
Charles Davis

ANTHONY CLOSE

A COMPANION TO *DON QUIXOTE*

TAMESIS

© Anthony Close 2008

All Rights Reserved. Except as permitted under current legislation no part
of this work may be photocopied, stored in a retrieval system,
published, performed in public, adapted, broadcast,
transmitted, recorded or reproduced in any form or by any means,
without the prior permission of the copyright owner

The right of Anthony Close to be identified as
the author of this work has been asserted in accordance with
sections 77 and 78 of the Copyright, Designs and Patents Act 1988

First published 2008
by Tamesis, Woodbridge
Paperback edition 2010

Transferred to digital printing

ISBN 978-1-85566-170-7 hardback
ISBN 978-1-85566-208-7 paperback

Tamesis is an imprint of Boydell & Brewer Ltd
PO Box 9, Woodbridge, Suffolk IP12 3DF, UK
and of Boydell & Brewer Inc.
668 Mt Hope Avenue, Rochester, NY 14620, USA
website: www.boydellandbrewer.com

A CiP catalogue record for this book is available
from the British Library

This publication is printed on acid-free paper

CONTENTS

PREFACE

All translations from Spanish, except where indicated, are mine.

Non-English titles in the text are translated on first mention of the work, except when the title consists of a name or the sense is self-evident.

In referring to Cervantes's works, I have used the editions specified in the Preliminary Note of the Bibliography at the end of the book.

Abbreviated references to the text of *Don Quixote* conform to the following example: *DQ* I, 32; p. 373 or I, 32; p. 373, where the first two numbers correspond to Part and Chapter, and the third to the page.

In referring to works of modern criticism in the text, I have used the author/date or author/date/page system, keyed to Section C of the Bibliography. For example, the abbreviation '(Riley 1986: 100)' would refer to page 100 of the book by E.C. Riley published in 1986. 'Murillo (1975)', would refer to the book by L.A. Murillo published in 1975, and so on. Where the Bibliography lists two or more works by the same author published in the same year – for example, 2004 – references to the first work that is listed would have the form 2004a, to the second, 2004b, and so on.

In referring to pre-modern texts other than those by Cervantes, I have used a rather fuller abbreviated system, consisting of author's name, brief title, editor's name, date of edition if helpful, page number. Full publication details may be found in section B of the Bibliography.

1

Introduction

My purpose in this book is to help the English-speaking reader, with an interest in Spanish literature but without specialised knowledge of Cervantes, to understand his long and complex masterpiece: its major themes, its structure, and the interconnections between its component parts. I approach *Don Quixote* from the premise that it is essentially a work of comedy, and see no justification for seeing it in any other way, since all Cervantes's explicit comments on it insist on this aspect, specifically on its gaiety and risibility. It is plainly contradictory to acknowledge, as not a few Cervantine critics do, that Cervantes was an intelligent, self-critical writer who knew what he was doing, yet at the same time to turn a blind eye to this aspect of his novel. To avoid misunderstanding, I take for granted that great comedy is capable of pathos and thought-provoking profundity. *Don Quixote* has both of these, particularly the latter, as is shown by the fact that since the first half of the eighteenth century, it has probably exercised a greater impact on Western culture than any other literary classic. In my view, the profundity lies in its conception of character, particularly the two central ones, and in the outlook on life implied by it, not, as has often been claimed, in some portentous philosophical, political or ethical message.

What kind of story is it and what's it about? What evidence is there for its enduring impact, and, most puzzling of all, what are the reasons for it? In this introduction, I propose to sketch a preliminary answer to these questions.

Cervantes published *Don Quixote* in 1605, and following its immediate success, brought out a second part in 1615.[1] The action concerns an *hidalgo* from a village somewhere in La Mancha: that is, the flat, featureless, farming

---

[1] Though I shall give references later to more specialised studies, the following offer useful introductory guides from a variety of viewpoints: Riley (1986), Murillo (1988), Close (1990), Martín de Riquer (2003), Martínez Mata (2008). The fourth centenary of the publication of *DQ* I – that is, 2005 – was the stimulus for numerous volumes of collected essays. One might single out the ones edited by González Echevarría (2005), for classic essays by Riley, Spitzer, Menéndez Pidal, Auerbach, Wardropper, Haley, and by Egido (2005) for some substantial treatments of the hero's personality. Older, though still useful anthologies are those

and grazing region of southern Castille, scorchingly hot in summer, bounded
on its southern rim by the Sierra Morena, which separates it from Andalucía.
This character goes mad through excessive reading of chivalric romances,
and, despite his fifty years of age and rusty, makeshift armour, resolves to
become a knight-errant like those described in *Amadís de Gaula* and its
numerous sequels. The chivalric genre, satirically ridiculed in *Don Quixote*,
was hugely popular in sixteenth-century Spain, and was an offshoot of the
medieval *Lancelot*; it offered a fabulous version of medieval chivalry, telling
of the exploits of heroic knights-errant in a legendary world of forests, seas,
palaces, castles, tourneys, peopled by bloodthirsty giants, enchanters good and
evil, monsters, beautiful princesses, damsels-in-distress, dwarves, emperors
and what have you. *Hidalgos* – the class to which don Quijote belongs –
occupied the lowest rung of the Spanish nobility, and typically lived off the
proceeds of lands inherited from their warrior ancestors, struggling dowdily
to keep up appearances. So our hero's origins connote precarious clinging to
social status and nostalgia for faded medieval glory: a very prosaic backdrop
for the delusions of grandeur about to fill the stage.

Accompanied by a simple-minded peasant from his own village, who acts
as his squire, and has a down-to-earth, unheroic outlook quite different from
his own, the self-styled don Quijote de la Mancha rides through the coun-
tryside on his bony nag Rocinante, misinterpreting chance encounters with
wayfarers, animals and mechanical objects as marvellous chivalric adventures, and forcing these third parties willy-nilly to participate in them. To
this insane, gratuitous interruption of their pursuits, they react variously with
rage, panic, mischievous mockery or obtuse non-compliance, thus provoking
cross-purpose altercation with the choleric madman, followed by farcical
mayhem, which results, normally, in physical humiliation for him. Alternatively, he is subjected to *burlas* – hoaxes, practical jokes – in which clever
characters take advantage of his madness to enact some ridiculous chivalric
masquerade that plays up to it.

Like the romances of chivalry that it parodies, Cervantes's narrative
purports to be a chronicle of the hero's successive adventures in the course
of his wanderings in quest of fame; these, in chivalric literature, take him
through fields, forests, and across seas, leading him now to encounters in
some lonely glade with an arrogant knight or bloodthirsty giant who challenges him to do battle, now to palaces of – for Spanish readers – exotic,
legendary kingdoms like Celtic Britain or Scotland or Cornwall, where he is

by Avalle-Arce and Riley (1973), Haley (1980), El Saffar (1986). Several of these books are
in English.

entertained by a noble king with a beautiful daughter and defeats all rivals in a tourney (cf. Don Quixote's outline of his future career in I, 21), now to idyllic bowers of some seductive enchantress like Alcina in Ariosto's *Orlando furioso* Canto VI, who has ensnared and keeps captive scores of brave knights by her magic spells. Contemporary readers would have been keenly aware of the ironic contrast between settings such as these and the physical and social context of the *hidalgo*'s doings, evoked specifically enough to be quite familiar to them: for example, the shimmering, dusty plains of La Mancha in mid-July, traversed by migrating flocks of sheep, the occasional group of travellers mounted on mules or donkeys, or if higher up the social scale, on horseback, with only the occasional copse of stunted oaks or abject roadside inn to provide shade.

My previous use of the term 'farcical' to describe the adventures is potentially misleading, since it does little justice to their archetypal resonance and to the artistry of Cervantes's narration. Also, my characterisation of them so far refers particularly to some of the best-known incidents in the novel, clustered in about the first half of Part I, such as the attack on the windmills and the flocks of sheep. They constitute the backbone of the action of Part I, and in modified form, of Part II. However, Cervantes augments them with various other elements; what these are, and how they are added, are questions to which we will turn later.

Now I come to the evidence of *Don Quixote*'s enduring popularity. In 2002, the Norwegian Book Club conducted an opinion poll among 100 prominent writers of different nationalities, asking them the question: which, in your opinion – leaving aside the Bible – has been the most significant literary work of all time? *Don Quixote* won the election with over fifty percent more votes than the nearest rival, ahead of such masterpieces as the epics of Homer, Shakespeare's *Hamlet* and *King Lear*, and Tolstoy's *War and Peace*. While one may reasonably doubt what this poll proves, since it is not evident what criterion of significance could determine the superiority of any one of those masterpieces to the others, it is nonetheless a revealing indicator of *Don Quixote*'s enduring impact, especially on the genre of the novel. As we shall see in the last chapter, it has been an exemplary paradigm for practising novelists and theorists of the genre since about the mid-eighteenth century.

However, its popularity and impact are not confined to the novel, nor to the literary sphere, nor even to the literate classes.[2] For the man-in-the-street of

---

[2] An excellent general survey of its impact on Western culture since 1605, which relates artistic creation to academic criticism, has been made by Canavaggio (2005).

the modern age, virtually from Tokyo to Timbuctoo, the famous Cervantine quartet of Don Quijote and Sancho, Rocinante and the ass, with their inseparable associates: Dulcinea, the barber's basin, the windmills, and so on, are icons as instantly recognisable as Donald Duck, Tarzan, Jesus Christ, Charlie Chaplin, President Clinton, Adolf Hitler and Marilyn Monroe. A fact all the more extraordinary if one remembers that Quixote and Sancho are in essence and origin literary characters, rather than creations designed for audio-visual consumption by the mass media, as are, arguably, all the other personages I have mentioned. To be sure, *Don Quixote* too has benefited from this kind of marketing. The exploitation of its powerful iconic appeal and archetypal suggestiveness long predate the late twentieth century, beginning almost immediately after the publication of Part I in 1605, as Cervantes himself notes in the second part of the novel. Sansón Carrasco, in reporting various aspects of the reception of Part I by contemporary Spanish readers, says:

> children thumb it, young lads read it, grown men appreciate it, and aged ones applaud it; in short, it's so familiar, read and re-read, and well known by all kinds of people, that as soon as they see a bony nag, they exclaim: 'There goes Rocinante' (Part II, Chapter 3).

In Spain and its American dominions, from the early years of the seventeenth century, figures representing Don Quixote and Sancho appeared in street-processions and tourneys on days of public festivity. In seventeenth-century France, Quixotic themes and scenes were a basis of court-masques, comedies, ballets and numerous paintings, beginning in 1625 with a series of thirty-four commissioned from the artist Jean Mosnier to adorn the dining-room and gallery of the castle of Chéverny on the Loire. Adaptations of motifs from *Don Quixote* abound in the plays of seventeenth-century Spanish dramatists, with Calderón, Tirso de Molina and Guillén de Castro being among Cervantes's greatest admirers. Insistently, from that century to the present day, the novel has been an inspiration for cartoonists; one of the earliest examples, dating from 1641 and conserved in the Hispanic Society of America, caricatures Philip IV of Spain and his powerful minister the count-duke of Olivares in the guise of Don Quixote and Sancho astride their respective mounts. In various periods from the mid-nineteenth century, the two heroes and their adventures have been turned into an endless medley of objects intended for amusement, ornament and advertisement: circus shows, cartoon strips, children's toys, ash-trays, statuettes, posters, signs, packaging of food and wine, and designs on porcelain, fashionable dresses, playing cards. With the advent of film and television, the scope of diffusion spread more widely. The first film version of Cervantes's novel came out in 1932, was directed by Georg Wilhelm Pabst and made use of the grandly imposing figure and voice of the Russian bass Chaliapin in the title role. The first TV series, *I, Don Quixote*, dates from 1959; its author, Dale Wasserman, subsequently turned it into the successful musical 'Man of La Mancha', translated into many languages, one of whose lyrics was adopted as a battle hymn by the rebels against President Marcos's regime in the Philippines in 1986. *Don Quixote* has also been a recurrent theme in highbrow art: three songs by Ravel entitled 'Don Quichotte à Dulcinée'; orchestral suites by Telemann, Manuel de Falla and Richard Strauss; operas by Massenet and Mendelssohn, scenes or characters in plays by Strindberg, Benavente and Tennessee Williams; illustrations and paintings by Hogarth, Goya, Daumier, Gustave Doré, Dalí and Picasso, in an immensely rich iconographic tradition stretching back to at least the mid-seventeenth century.

What are the reasons for *Don Quixote*'s enduring popularity? Others will be mentioned in the course of this book, but, for the moment, let us just note two, of which the first is less commonly cited than it should be. It is Cervantes's sheer skill as a story-teller, whatever the genre of the story: timing, suspense, irony, drama, vividness, you name it, he has it all. Scheherezade was the maiden who obtained a temporary reprieve from sentence of death by telling the Sultan a different story every night; and were I in the same predicament, and could choose someone to act as Scherezade on my behalf, I would pick Cervantes. But the fundamental reason surely lies in that 'archetypal resonance' to which I have already alluded. In a sense, posterity has done to Cervantes what he did to his precursors, only in reverse; he assembled his characters less from observation than by combining type-figures in rich and dense profusion, then endowing the result with individual life, beginning with sharp, visual definition, which is stamped on the reader's mind by continual reminders of the contrasted physical aspects of his two heroes. It is significant that confirmation of the alleged authenticity of Benengeli's manuscript (see below, p. 160) is provided for Cervantes in Chapter 9 by the naturalistic etchings of Don Quixote's battle with the Basque lackey, Rocinante's gaunt and spindly frame, and Sancho's matted locks and beard, small stature, large belly and long shanks. Taking its cue from him, posterity has turned the lifelike individuals into mythic archetypes, crystallised in familiar icons.

The pair's origins can identifiably be traced back to a medley of traditional duos of a more or less similar kind, established by folklore or literature, as we shall see in Chapter 4 (pp. 90, 96–99). The dense concentration of these traditional pairs in two individualised forms captures in a perennially efficacious way a fundamental opposition in human nature, which recurs in many guises: obsessive concern for respectability contrasted with indifference to it, gross appetite with abstemiousness, recklessness with pusillanimity. Ever since Baltasar Gracián, in his great prose-allegory of man's pilgrimage through life, *El Criticón* (1651–7) (The Censor), interpreted Cervantes's pair of heroes as representing too much ambition and too little, or posturing arrogance and lazy attachment to an easy life, posterity has seen them as universal symbols. Specific interpretations have varied with the ideological orientation of each succeeding age, but the process has never stopped.

Before going on to examine *Don Quixote* itself, we ought first to give attention to Cervantes's life and times, his other works, and the cultural context of his masterpiece.

Cervantes's Life, Times and Literary Career

Life and Outlook

Miguel de Cervantes Saavedra was born in Alcalá de Henares, near Madrid, in 1547.[1] His father was a poor surgeon with a large family. Little is known for certain about his education, save that he completed it at the humanist academy of Juan López de Hoyos in Madrid. In 1569, he suddenly left Spain for Italy, possibly in order to escape the legal consequences of having wounded a man in a duel. By 1571, he had enlisted in the allied expeditionary force being assembled by Venice, Spain and the Papacy for a major attack on the Turkish fleet. In that year, he fought in the historic sea-battle of Lepanto, which he describes in the prologue to *Don Quixote* Part II as 'the most exalted occasion seen by ages past, present or to come', and suffered wounds that permanently crippled his left hand. After more military action in the Mediterranean, he was captured by Berber pirates while returning from Naples to Spain by sea, and spent the next five years, from 1575 to 1580, in captivity in Algiers; contemporary records testify to his fortitude and kindness to fellow captives during that ordeal, and also to his defiant courage, displayed by four unsuccessful escape attempts. This 'heroic' decade of Cervantes's life, from 1570 to 1580, is recalled in the captive's story in *Don Quixote* I, 39–42.[2]

Ransomed in 1580, he returned to Spain, settled in Madrid and began a moderately successful literary career. He was one of a circle of well-known poets, and published a pastoral romance, *La Galatea* (1585), which, like other such romances, served partly as a framework for the author's poems. For that reason, the genre is designated as 'libros de poesía' (books of poetry) in the critical scrutiny of Don Quixote's library (*DQ* I, 6; p. 84). *La Galatea* is also typical of its genre by virtue of its self-referential character; beneath their pastoral guise, the shepherds stand for the author and his literary friends.

---

[1] There have been many biographies of Cervantes. The most authoritative is by Canavaggio (1986), whose Spanish version came out in 1987.
[2] There is a very good treatment of this subject in Garcés (2002).

Though the book was not a flop, going through two re-editions in Cervantes's lifetime, he felt that it did not receive the recognition that it deserved. This can plainly be deduced from the priest's comment upon it in the above-mentioned chapter of *Don Quixote*. Claiming to be an old friend of Cervantes – by implication, to speak for him – he characterises him with a rueful quip as 'más versado en desdichas que en versos' (p. 86) (more versed in reverses than in verses). Cervantes was also busy as a playwright in the 1580s, and had some twenty to thirty plays performed without, as he pleasantly puts it in the prologue to the *Ocho comedias y ocho entremeses* (1615) (Eight Comedies and Eight Farces), 'offerings of cucumbers or other throwable matter'. Of these plays, some of whose titles are given in the 'Adjunta' or appendix to Cervantes's *Viaje del Parnaso* (Voyage to Parnassus) – only two survive, *La Numancia* (The Tragedy of Numancia) and *El trato de Argel* (Life in Algiers). The latter play gives a poignant picture of the sufferings of Spanish captives in that stronghold of Barbary corsairs – a theme also treated in the later play *Los baños de Argel* (The Prisons of Algiers) and in the interpolated *novela* of the ex-captive, previously mentioned – and is based on Cervantes's own experience. *La Numancia*, a stirring tribute to the heroic refusal to surrender by a Spanish town besieged by Scipio's army in Roman times, is Cervantes's most famous play. One of its modern revivals took place in Madrid, in 1937, during the defence of the city by the Republican army against the Nationalists in the Spanish Civil War. It was directed by the poet Rafael Alberti. These two early plays are not to be confused with the eight comedies and eight farces that Cervantes published in 1615 and were mostly written after the interruption of his literary career.

The priest's jest about Cervantes's reverses no doubt alludes in part to his misadventures during the long interruption of his literary career. After marrying Catalina de Salazar in 1584 and settling with her in her home town, Esquivias, he left the conjugal home and the region of Toledo for Andalucía in 1587, and would spend at least the next ten years there, engaged in humdrum and aggravating occupations: first, as requisitioner of food supplies for the Armada expedition against England (1588), then, as tax-collector. The bankruptcy of the banker of Seville with whom Cervantes had deposited a sizeable sum of tax money led to his imprisonment for some months in 1597 while he endeavoured to justify the shortfall to the Spanish Treasury. He confesses near the beginning of the prologue to *Don Quixote* Part I to having 'engendered' the story in a prison, whatever that term means;[3] and tradition

3 Probably, to judge by Cervantes's metaphorical use of *engendrar* in similar contexts, it

has it that he refers to this period of internment, though it might also allude to an earlier imprisonment in Castro del Río (1592).

When, around 1600, Cervantes devoted himself full-time to writing once again, he undertook a wholly new project: a work of prose-fiction satirising the highly popular genre of chivalry books. At the same time as he was writing *Don Quixote*, he must have become painfully aware of the huge success of the school of drama led by Lope de Vega – the cause, by his own admission in the revealing prologue to the *Ocho comedias*, of the reluctance of the *autores*, actor-managers, to buy and stage his plays. In *Don Quixote* I, 48, the priest of the hero's village, speaking on Cervantes's behalf, delivers a stinging, though reasoned and measured, attack on the New Comedy's violations of the rules of art. Since he attributes them chiefly to the commercially motivated philistinism of the *autores*, one infers that Cervantes, in writing this passage sometime before 1605, had already suffered the rebuff from that quarter to which he alludes in the prologue of 1615. Not only must it have been mortifying to his pride to suffer rejection after having enjoyed success as a playwright in the 1580s, the setback would have been aggravated by financial loss, the sense of a cheapening of artistic standards and of opportunities lost to luckier rivals, all added to the aggravations suffered during his bureaucratic interlude in Andalucía. The resentment is reflected in the prologue to *Don Quixote* Part I, which wittily and maliciously satirises the snobbish and pedantic pretensions of contemporary writers, among whom Lope de Vega – author of the pastoral romance *Arcadia* (1599) and the Byzantine romance *El peregrino en su patria* (1604) (Pilgrim in his Own Land) – stands out as the obvious target.

Now, the censure of the *comedia* in *Don Quixote* I, 48 immediately follows the canon of Toledo's critique of chivalry books in the previous chapter; and the canon treats the errors of one genre as exactly equivalent to those of the other.[4] There is no coincidence in the symmetry; and it helps to explain the polemical motivation of Cervantes's novel and the nature of its parody. In modern times, critics have sometimes questioned that motivation. Why, they ask, should Cervantes have bothered to attack the chivalric genre, which, by around 1600, was virtually defunct in terms of composition if not consumption? The answer is that he saw in its combination of artistic lawlessness and massive popularity the threatening shadow of another genre – the *comedia* – which was very much alive and kicking, and he considered its influence on

---

means: 'to have the original idea of', rather than to write a preliminary draft. See the passage from *DQ* II, 32, referring to the hero's conception of Dulcinea, cited in Chapter 6, p. 211.

  4   For an extended version of this argument, see Close (2000: 106–14).

public taste as a threat to the kind of fiction – specifically, heroic romance, and more generally, the romantic *novella* – that he wanted to write. One should remember that the canon of Toledo speaks not of outright demolition of the chivalric genre, but of overhaul and reconstruction, and ends his critique by sketching the outlines of an ideal prose epic that might replace it. Cervantes's Byzantine romance *Persiles y Sigismunda*, published posthumously in 1617, is more or less a fulfilment of that blueprint. The *novelas* that Cervantes interpolates in *Don Quixote* Part I are homogeneous with *Persiles*, since similar ones constitute its episodes. In other words, Cervantes felt that public taste needed to be educated through parodic satire of the chivalric genre, so that the fate that had already befallen his well-crafted plays should not also overtake his well-crafted stories.

Generally speaking, in his writings – plays, *novelas*, *Don Quixote*, *Persiles* – he aspires to entertain a wide readership while respecting the rules of poetic art; essentially, these comprise: verisimilitude; the reconciliation of pleasure and profit; decorum or fittingness in its many aspects, including plausibility of character-portrayal and the matching of style to theme. The fundamental principle of the canon of Toledo's theory of the prose epic is verisimilitude, equated with respect for the reader's critical intelligence; and this involves striking a nice balance between the epic's inherent striving for the extraordinary and the bounds of rational possibility. It is not to be confused with realism in the nineteenth-century sense, and presupposes that the events and characters represented in epic, and more generally in kindred forms of romance, belong to a more marvellous and noble plane of experience than is typical of most people's daily lives. Hence the abundance of improbable vicissitudes in Cervantes's romantic fiction, such as those incredibly fortunate reunions at the inn in *Don Quixote* Part I, Chapters 36 and 42; hence too, the plastercast decorum of behaviour displayed by many of his heroes and heroines, who, whatever indiscretions they may commit, remain sensitive to what they owe to their noble status and are endowed with the associated attributes, like valour, beauty, integrity, discretion.

Cervantes's sense of the validity of the traditional poetics is related to something more deeply felt than respect for academic authority: a passionate conviction, repeatedly expressed, of the inventiveness and artistry of his own work. A revealing expression of this pride, which implicitly reflects his high opinion of *Don Quixote*, occurs in the moving prologue to *Persiles*, written when Cervantes was on his deathbed; it contains his farewell to life and, specifically, to laughter and friends. His priorities are revealing. The prologue also contains the salute to Cervantes by a student, an avid aficionado of his works, whom he met by chance on the road from Esquivias to Madrid just a few days previously: 'Sí, sí, éste es el manco sano, el famoso todo, el escritor alegre, y, finalmente, el regocijo de las Musas' (Yes, yes, it's the whole one-hander, the great celebrity, the merry writer, and lastly, the Muses' joy). No doubt Cervantes intended it as his literary epitaph.

The success of *Don Quixote* Part I was instantaneous; in the very year of its publication (1605), the figures of Don Quijote and Sancho appeared in public festivities held in Valladolid, and from henceforth, would pass into Spanish, then universal, folklore. The book's enthusiastic reception mellowed Cervantes, appeased his injured vanity, and spurred him to unchecked literary activity until his death – a gloriously creative old age in which he completed *Don Quixote* Part II, his collection of twelve *Novelas ejemplares* (1613) (Exemplary Short Stories), the collection of eight comedies and eight farces already mentioned (1615), and a long, burlesque fantasy in verse, the *Viaje del Parnaso* (1614), which is a satire of contemporary poetasters, not to mention works unfinished or unpublished at his death. One perceives in the prologues to these works a keen awareness of his public image, pride in his fame and the qualities that have secured it, and, in respect of poetry and the theatre, a concern to obtain full recognition for its merits. All this is explicit or implied in the autobiographical dimension of the *Viaje del Parnaso*.[5] In the year prior to the publication of *Don Quixote* Part II – that is, in 1614 – a man writing under the pseudonym Alonso Fernández de Avellaneda brought out a continuation of *Don Quixote* Part I.[6] Though copyright in the legal sense did not exist in those days, Cervantes's pride in the uniqueness of his creation, and his sense that it is his and his alone, are splendidly expressed in *Don Quixote*'s last chapter, especially the final paragraph; and three chapters of the second Part (59, 69, 72), together with its prologue, are devoted in whole or in part to mockery of the rival's version. The mockery, though disparaging, is jocular rather than virulent: the sign of a writer who is secure of his fame. After his death in 1616 his widow arranged the publication of his Byzantine romance *Persiles y Sigismunda* (1617). It enjoyed some success in the seventeenth century, being in accord with the contemporary vogue of romance. José de Valdivielso, who was a widely admired religious poet and dramatist, esteemed it highly, writing in the *aprobación*:[7] 'pues de cuantos

---

[5] See Canavaggio (2000: 73–83; and cf., in the same work, 65–72).

[6] There have been various attempts to solve the mystery of Avellaneda's identity (e.g. Riquer 1988; Martín Jiménez 2001), including some very recent ones that diverge from those just cited. None, in my view, is conclusive.

[7] From the late 1550s onwards, together with other measures of censorship, these warrants of inoffensiveness to morals and the faith, drafted by clerics or laymen with literary leanings, were a standard feature of the preliminaries of literature of entertainment.

nos dejó escritos, ninguno es más ingenioso, ni más culto, ni más entretenido' (of all the works he has left us, none is more ingenious, more learned, nor more entertaining). Cervantes, never slow to promote his own merits, would have amended the first bit to 'of all the works of Spanish literature written to date', since that is more or less what he says in the dedicatory of *Don Quixote* Part II.

In the period 1606–16, Cervantes lived in Madrid, famous, widely admired and prominent in literary academies. Towards the end, the patronage of the Count of Lemos and the Archbishop of Toledo, Bernardo de Sandoval, did something to alleviate his chronic poverty. The preliminaries of *Don Quixote* Part II include an *aprobación* by Francisco Márquez Torres, a chaplain of the archbishop; compared with the usual certificate of this kind, it is unusually long and personal, and, for all its limitations, is the most illuminating commentary on Cervantes written by a seventeenth-century Spaniard. Praising him for his continuation of the edifying project of demolishing chivalry books, the unaffected clarity of his style, the genial urbanity of his satire of customs, and generally, for his *decoro, decencia, suavidad, blandura* (decorum, decency, smoothness, mildness), Márquez Torres goes on to relate a return visit by the retinue of his master, the archbishop, to the French ambassador, then in Madrid to negotiate a royal wedding. When the conversation turned to literature, and Cervantes's name was mentioned, the well-read French courtiers expressed the most lively enthusiasm. One claimed to know *La Galatea* virtually by heart. The *Novelas ejemplares* and the first part of *Don Quixote* were also warmly appreciated. The anecdote is a revealing indicator of the qualities of Cervantes that were then particularly esteemed; these include his verse, his romantic fiction and the rhetorically elegant, witty prose in which it is written.

In general, Cervantes's outlook bears out the impression of humanity, tolerance and genial optimism that any reader picks up on reading *Don Quixote*.[8] The insistent ridicule of the hero's attempts to avenge chimerical wrongs is echoed by Cervantes's principled repudiation of the gruesome principle underlying much of the fiction and drama of the age: 'la mancha del honor solo con sangre del que ofendió se lava' (the stain of honour is only wiped out by blood of the offender). He rejects it both on the basis of the commandment 'Thou shalt not kill' and of commonsense pragmatism, and takes this attitude towards any kind of hot-headed resort to violence in honour's name, not just wife-murder. In keeping with this, while he was too much a man of his time

---

[8] For a fuller coverage, see my essay 'Cervantes: pensamiento, personalidad, cultura' in the preliminaries to Rico's edn of *DQ* (1998), pp. lxvii–lxxxvi.

to question the hierarchical structure of the society in which he lived and the paramount importance of honour in it, he puts more emphasis on virtue as a means to its attainment than on noble status or what public opinion may say. He shows the same humane rationality in racial matters. Though it would be absurd to attribute to him political correctness of a modern kind, since he regards Jews and Muslims straightforwardly as infidels, and, with his contemporaries, would no doubt have regarded many of their Christianised Spanish descendants as insincere apostates, nonetheless, his writings are mercifully free of the anti-Semitic jibes which were popular in the Spain of that age, and his portrayal of Christian slaves and their Moslem captors in Algiers or Constantinople presents a much more nuanced view of relations between the races than was then usual. It is obviously conditioned by his own experience of captivity, and involves a recognition of the potential humanity of infidels, the moral fallibility of Christians and the difficult compromises that the latter confront in the circumstances of captivity. Cervantes's distaste for malicious jibes extends to personally directed satire, which flowed freely and virulently from the pens of his famous contemporaries. One of the principal villains of *Persiles y Sigismunda* is a slanderer, Clodio, who dies a fitting death when an arrow intended for someone else pierces his mouth.

In political matters, despite the attempts by modern *cervantistas* to enlist his support for fashionable liberal causes, his explicit statements generally reveal a non-interventionist attitude, exemplified by the way in which he repeatedly brands as meddlesome busybodies those who feel free to address criticisms or alternative suggestions to their rulers.[9] The examples include his portrayal of the above-mentioned Clodio and the crackpot proponents of political reform (*arbitristas*) depicted in *El coloquio de los perros* (Dialogue of the Dogs). Confronted by an authoritarian regime and a strict system of censorship, contemporaries like Tirso de Molina, Quevedo, Góngora and the count of Villamediana were far readier to voice dissent or infringe moral or religious taboos than he was. This is not owing to timidity or innate conformism on his part, but rather to a combination of innate good taste and a greater interest in human psychology and ethics than public affairs. That said, some social or political questions clearly concerned him: including the effects of the mass expulsion of the *morisco* community (see Chapter 6, p. 189), and the corruption of Seville's judiciary and public administration, denounced in *El coloquio de los perros*. The arbitrariness of the law comes in for repeated censure in his writings, as may be inferred from the

---

[9] On this subject, and Cervantes's attitude to satire, see Close (2000: 26–30).

episode of Sancho's governorship, exemplary precisely because of his avoidance of this abuse. However, in the *novela* just mentioned – a sombre satire
on contemporary Spanish society and the human condition – Cervantes aims
at no institutions higher up the social scale than Seville's, and much of it is
directed at impostors, frauds and parasites far lower down: butchers, gipsies,
moriscos, a constable, a witch, an incompetent playwright, ambulant peddlers
and showmen.

Though Cervantes does not flaunt his religious piety, I see no reason to
doubt it: the exaltation of the Catholic faith is a principal theme of *Persiles
y Sigismunda*; and the veneration of saints expressed in passages of *El licenciado Vidriera* (Licentiate Glass), *Persiles* and *Don Quixote* Part II, Chapter
8, which have been interpreted by some critics as ironic, is amply confirmed
by the last act of his saints' play *El rufián dichoso* (The Blessed Ruffian),
which yields nothing in hagiographic treacliness to other *comedias de santos*
of that age. However, in general, Cervantes devotes more attention to how to
achieve contentment in this world than felicity in the next. While he shares
something of the pessimism of his age about the ravages of original sin,
and in *Persiles* projects a vision of life as a pilgrimage over an uncertain
sea of travails and misfortunes, with Catholic faith as the guiding beacon,
he does not espouse the bleak view of human malice and duplicity held by
contemporaries like Mateo Alemán, nor their gloomy insistence on the theme
of *desengaño*, disenchantment with worldy vanities. Rather, he tends to see
human fallibility as a subject of mirth, portraying it as the reckless pursuit of
chimerical ambitions in which people indulge through their own blindness.
That is the view of the human condition prevalent in the *Ocho comedias*, *Don
Quixote*, and the comic *novelas*, and it accords with his repeatedly expressed
preference for harmony, proportion and moderation, and with his Stoic Christian assumption that the ups-and-down of fate balance themselves out in the
end and are providentially designed to test the individual's moral fibre, with
the consequence that 'cada uno es artífice de su ventura', each man makes
his own fortune (*DQ* II, 66; p. 1168). His ironic insight into the impetuous
mentality described above implies a measure of self-identification with it, as
one may infer from the way in which he characterises himself in the *Viaje
del Parnaso*, Chapter 1, as the archetypally fantasising, vainglorious poet,
absorbed in his own dreams and impervious to repeated failure. Obviously,
one cannot take this self-portrait quite literally, since it is partly a pose of
burlesque self-deprecation. Yet the same character-type recurs over and over
again in his writings, the major example being Don Quixote. It takes one to
know one.

Works Other than *Don Quixote*

Let us return to *La Galatea*, which anticipates Cervantes's later prose-fiction in various ways. The genre of pastoral romance, launched by Jorge de Montemayor's influential *La Diana* (1559?), was fashionable in Spain in the second half of the sixteenth century; and Cervantes would always remain attached to it, promising in the preliminaries of his late works to bring out a second Part of *La Galatea* – a promise thwarted by his death in 1616.[10] The genre is an extension of the Classical tradition of pastoral poetry, and offers a conventionally idyllic picture of the loves of shepherds and shepherdesses in an Arcadian setting, where sheep graze in green meadows by crystalline brooks, charmed by the melodious laments of tearful lovers to the accompaniment of pipe and rebec. Montemayor's innovation consists in giving a narrative background to the sentiments so exquisitely expressed in the verse; the characters tell the stories of their amatory misfortunes, importing the themes and form of the Italian novella. The principal interpolated narrative of *La Galatea*, Silerio's story, begun in Book II and not completed until Book V, opens a window on a world very different from idyllic Arcadia: the dilemmas of love and honour of minor aristocrats in an urban and courtly setting, involving a bitter feud between knights, a duel, riot, imprisonment, escape from execution, a raid by Moors on the coast of Barcelona, and other such vicissitudes. It shows Cervantes as an accomplished exponent of the kind of *novela* that he will cultivate throughout his career, either as independent story or as interpolated episode.

His enthusiasm for pastoral romance may strike us as puzzling in view of his ironic mockery of it and of literary implausibility in general in *Don Quixote*. The paradox is explained by his ambivalence towards the genre, which also extends to other florid and idealised literary modes. On the one hand, he is strongly drawn to it as a poetically heightened medium for the expression of the sentiments of love and the discussion of its ethics, psychology and metaphysics; on the other hand, his suspicions about literary inverisimilitude, precious excess and disregard for functional relevance in prose narrative cause him to mock it both in *Don Quixote* and in *El coloquio de los perros*, precisely because these works are primarily concerned to censure such failings. That does not mean that Cervantes's handling of the pastoral theme in the continuation of *La Galatea* would have differed radically from the way in which he treated it in 1585. The genre carries implicitly a poetic

---

[10] For a general survey of the genre, including *La Galatea*, see Avalle-Arce (1974), Solé-Leris (1980), Montero Reguera (1995: 157–66).

licence denied to other fiction, more strictly governed by the demands of verisimilitude; this, together with its appeal for a sophisticated readership, exempts it from the charge of fabulous nonsense that he makes against chivalry books. While the ridicule that he pours on these is radical, his ironic satire of pastoral preciosity in *Don Quixote* Part I, Chapters 12–14 and 50–51 is much less damaging.

Among his published works, only the *Novelas ejemplares* come anywhere near to rivalling *Don Quixote*'s enduring popularity.[11] In these, he exploits the thematic diversity and elastic size of the Italian short story derived from Boccaccio's *Decameron* (about 1350), and uses it as a form in which to synthesise plots and themes popular with Spanish readers. In so doing, he revolutionises the genre, gives it unprecedented depth and blends ingredients with startling audacity. For example, *El coloquio de los perros*, generally acknowledged as the masterpiece of the collection, takes from Apuleius' *The Golden Ass* (second century A.D.), the theme of man transformed by witchcraft into animal, who then experiences human nastiness at the hands of a succession of cruel masters. In this case the subjects of metamorphosis are the dogs Berganza and Cipión. The narrative of Berganza, who tells the story of his life, is also indebted to the picaresque, especially to Alemán's hugely popular *Guzmán de Alfarache* (1599, 1604), for its satiric denunciation of vices and abuses, its realistic attention to the social here-and-now, and for the *pícaro*'s moralistic meditations on his mis-spent past. Moreover, the *Coloquio* borrows the form of the Renaissance didactic dialogue, adapts some incidents from the fables of Aesop, and reflects the disenchanted, otherworldly vision of the human condition of the satires of Lucian of Samosata (second century A.D.). And since the fictitious author of the dogs' dialogue is the ensign Campuzano, protagonist of the *novela El casamiento engañoso* (The Deceitful Marriage) by which the dialogue is framed, all this is presented as the delirious invention of the chastened husband of that marriage, feverishly sweating out his pox on a sick-bed in hospital. The diversity of the *Coloquio*'s literary affiliations is matched by the complexity of its structure, since the narratives of Berganza and Campuzano are subjected to the reactions

---

[11] Among general studies devoted to the *novelas* I would recommend either as helpful or stimulating: El Saffar (1974), Forcione (1982, 1984), Laspéras (1987), Dunn (1993, Chapter 6), Johnson (2000), and the introduction to García López's edition of the *Novelas ejemplares* (2001). Zimic (2003) concentrates on the stories interpolated in *DQ*. See also the discussion of *El coloquio de los perros* and *Rinconete y Cortadillo* in Close (2000), Chapters 2 and 5. The term *novela* will be used henceforth in the sense that it had in the Spanish Golden Age: a short story. I will sometimes use the Italian novella, which has now become anglicised, in referring to Italian short stories.

of sceptical listeners, which constitute a critical meditation on the nature of satire and of story-telling, and a rational debunking of the supernatural. To contemporary readers, this thought-provoking manner of handling the *novela*, a genre hitherto solely concerned with telling a pleasing story, and also, notorious in Spain for its licentiousness, hence on both counts deemed somewhat frivolous, must have seemed extraordinary.

The principal reason for this unfavourable image was that among the leading themes of the Italian *novellieri*, headed by Boccaccio, were jolly, ribald stories about the sexual misdemeanours of randy friars, sexually frustrated wives of old or stupid husbands, hot-blooded youths and maidens, and so on. In such stories, morals go on holiday, and the reader's amused sympathy is invited for the clever circumvention of social or religious taboos. In Spain, from the mid-sixteenth century onwards, when the climate of state and religious censorship became severe, this kind of licentiousness was unacceptable; and Spanish translators of Italian novellas towards the end of the century become strident in their claims of having repudiated it. Cervantes's protestations of exemplariness in the prologue to his *Novelas* must be understood in that context. They are not mere lip-service to the censor. The avoidance of the amorality associated with the Italian genre can plainly be seen in the tragic dénouements, ironic reversals and final confessions of error by the husbands of both *El curioso impertinente* (The Impertinently Curious Husband, interpolated in *Don Quixote* Part I, Chapters 33–35) and *El celoso extremeño* (The Jealous Extremaduran), these being *novelas* which derive from Italian precedents on the theme of adultery. Both treat this subject as an occasion for serious meditation on the nature of marriage and of each spouse's responsibility for its success. And Cervantes's audacious blending of heterogeneous strands can be seen in the latter *novela*'s mix of farce and tragedy. The grotesquely exaggerated security measures of the pathologically jealous old husband, who turns the conjugal home into a combination of prison, convent, harem and kindergarten, are plainly reminiscent of farce; and so are the wiles of the seducer, the sanctimonious hypocrisy of the lewd *dueña* and the naïve credulity of the other servants. However, the fact that the outwitting of Carrizales is set in the context of his whole life, and culminates in his death-bed contrition and pardon of his wife, gives the story a tragic pathos quite untypical of this species.

Revolutionary experimentation with form is exemplified by the other well-known *novelas*. In *Rinconete y Cortadillo*, Cervantes reduces the *pícaro*'s autobiography to a brief slice of underworld life, told in the third person not the first; effectively, the story is about what Rinconete and Cortadillo, the two heroes, saw one day in the *patio* of the mafia boss of Seville after being inducted in his gang. In particular, what they heard, since the *novela*, which lacks a plot, is largely composed of dialogue and is focused on the barbarous mannerisms, the sanctimonious hypocrisy and the 'statutes and ordinances' of Monipodio and his underlings. In its dialogic form, it is indebted to comedies and farces about such personages; so here Cervantes synthesises picaresque novel with theatre, compressing them into a short story. He does something rather similar in *La ilustre fregona* (The Illustrious Kitchen Maid) and *La Gitanilla* (The Little Gipsy Girl). In the first, the picaresque, which normally paints an amusingly sordid picture of delinquent life, is astonishingly hybridised with romantic comedy and pastoral romance. The story is about two young noblemen who run away from their family homes in Burgos to lead the lives of *pícaros*, a project suspended when one of them falls in love with the beautiful, virtuous heroine, apparently a mere serving wench at an inn in Toledo. Despite its base setting, Avendaño's love for Costanza is reminiscent of the nobly spiritual love of Elicio for Galatea in Cervantes's pastoral romance. In the dénouement, Costanza turns out to have a noble pedigree; so a happy ending is achieved without violation of social decorum. Though this kind of theme has precedents in prose romance, it is treated over and over again in Lope's theatre: a model that Cervantes must have had in mind. *La Gitanilla* is similar in plot and theme to *La ilustre fregona*, with the difference that the sordid milieu with which the noble hero associates himself is not picaresque but a band of gipsies.

The *novelas* of a romantic nature like *La española inglesa* (The Spanish English Girl), *La fuerza de la sangre* (The Force of Blood-Ties), *Las dos doncellas* (The Two Damsels) and the interlinked stories of Cardenio and Dorotea, which is one of the major interpolations of *Don Quixote* Part I, used to be unpopular and relatively neglected. However, they have attracted a considerable amount of attention since the early 1970s, especially in the USA, largely because of their implications relating to gender. They constitute a literary species to which Cervantes was very attached, since he cultivates it throughout his career. Typically, they feature lovers of noble status or not far short of it, whose happiness is threatened by rivals, parental disapproval, abductions or other mishaps. The ethos is courtly and decorous, the tone sentimental and the discourse rhetorical. The plots are packed with extraordinary incident, including the improbable reunions and recognitions that unravel the tangled knots and reconcile estranged parties amid a flood of communal tears. Most of these *novelas* are ingeniously constructed so as to heighten the effect of suspense and drama by means of abrupt and mysterious beginnings, the delegation of narrative to the protagonists, the artful suspension and interleaving of narrative lines. These techniques were well established in

Ancient Byzantine romances, and were taken over by Spanish pastoral novelists in the second half of the sixteenth century. Cervantes's romantic *novelas* also have much in common with the Spanish theatre of the age, borrowing material from there and supplying a mine of themes to playwrights after him. They inspire writers of prose-fiction too, establishing the genre of the *novela cortesana*, the so-called courtly novel, which flourished in the first half of the seventeenth century.

By virtue of their roots in Byzantine romance, they are akin to Cervantes's prose-epic *Persiles y Sigismunda*.[12] The story concerns a pilgrimage by two chaste and faithful lovers of royal lineage from northern lands to Rome; they are packed off on that voyage by Persiles's mother, when she discovers his love for Sigismunda, in order to prevent her marriage to the hero's elder brother, Magsimino. The pilgrimage also has, of course, a religious purpose: the completion of the heroine's instruction in the Catholic faith. On their journey, which takes the protagonists from legendary Tile (supposedly somewhere near Norway), to Portugal, Spain, southern France, then Italy, they travel as brother and sister under the assumed names of Periandro and Auristela, and are joined by a succession of fellow travellers, all, like them, exiles or victims of misfortune. Each one of them narrates his or her sad story, and these interpolated narratives are of the kind already described.

Persiles is epic in length and design. It is largely grandiose and tragic in tone, and ingeniously complex in structure, with the episodes interlocking with the main action and each other like pieces of a jigsaw puzzle, which tantalisingly fall into place in such a way that links and identities are only gradually revealed. For instance, the origins and purpose of the hero and heroine remain shrouded in mystery until very near the end. The plot exemplifies a number of moral/religious themes, and overall, implicitly exalts the Catholic faith above pagan or heretical error. The novel applies with almost painstaking conscientiousness the rules of neo-Aristotelian poetics and bases itself on a Classical model, the *Aethiopic History* by Heliodorus, bishop of Thrace, written in Greek in the third century A.D., and much admired by Renaissance humanism for its verisimilitude, ingenious structure and exemplariness. *Persiles* is Cervantes's most carefully crafted work; and his esteem for it, and ambitious conception of it, have already been mentioned.

---

[12] Forcione (1972) is informative on the romance background, treating *Persiles* as a Christian allegory. His previous book (1970) supplements the coverage of the theoretical background by Riley (1962). Lozano Renieblas (1998) takes a very different point of view from Forcione's (1972), and offers a stimulating approach to *Persiles* from a Bakhtinian angle. Egido (2005) deals concisely and eruditely with the Ancient and Biblical antecedents of the pilgrimage of life theme. There is a good, recent edition by Romero (1997).

Of the collection of theatrical pieces,[13] the farces (*entremeses*) are justly celebrated, and are much more polished and carefully crafted than one might expect
from a genre dedicated to the arousal of uproarious laughter. The most famous
of them, *El retablo de las maravillas* (The Prodigious Mini-Theatre), is a variant
of the traditional story of the emperor's clothes, in which the showmen purport
to exhibit a succession of prodigies only visible to those untainted by bastardy
or Semitic blood. By means of a brilliant succession of situational ironies, based
on the spectators' collective fear of frankly avowing to each other that they can
see nothing whatever on the stage, it ridicules the Spanish peasantry's snobbish
pride in its old Christian ancestry. It was much admired in seventeenth-century
Spain; Baltasar Gracián bases an episode of his prose-allegory *El Criticón*
(1651–7) upon it, designed to show the psychological manipulation by which
fraudulent demagogues obtain the support of the mob. Other *entremeses* that
might be singled out are *El viejo celoso* (The Jealous Old Husband), *El juez
de los divorcios* (The Divorce-Court Judge), and *La guarda cuidadosa* (The
Jealous Guardian). In the first, the husband's domestic incarceration of his wife
is identical to that described in the novela *El celoso extremeño*, but the treatment
is purely farcical, and the wife has none of the submissive ingenuousness of
her counterpart in the narrative version. In the second, a succession of conjugal
misfits air their mutual grievances before the amused magistrate, who ends by
dismissing all their petitions for divorce, while the third, *La guarda cuidadosa*,
concerns the rivalry between a sacristan and a down-at-heel soldier for the love
of the maid Cristina, deriving its comic effect from the dog-in-the-manger attitude of the soldier, whose jealousy is such that he even turns tradesmen away
from the door of his beloved. Both these and the remaining *entremeses* are
remarkable for their dense interweaving of a variety of literary traditions, the
pace and wit of the dialogue, the exploitation of situational comedy, and the
finesse, even occasional pathos, of the characterisation.

The full-length comedies, however, are of more uneven quality, showing
an ambivalent relationship to the New Comedy of Lope de Vega and his
followers. While they sometimes poke fun at its conventions, they show extensive affinities with its themes, character-types and situations, handling these,
however, in a lighter and more ironic way than Lope does. Among the more
interesting ones are *La entretenida* (The Entertaining Comedy), *Pedro de*

---

[13] There is a competent general survey of the *Comedias* by Stanislav Zimic (1992), and a
collection of essays on different aspects of them by various specialists in *Theatralia* 5 (2003),
ed. Jesús Maestro. Riley, in Riley and Avalle Arce (1973: 302–10), covers Cervantes's theory
judiciously. On that subject, and the ethos of his theatre, see also Close (2000), Chapter 3.
Canavaggio's monumental book (1977) is scholarly and innovative, but dense. On the *entremeses*, see (apart from Zimic) Asensio's introduction to his edn (1970).

Urdemalas and *El rufián dichoso*. The first of these, a comedy of middle-class manners with a highly intricate plot, parodies, by its anti-climactic dénouement, the New Comedy's typical ending in multiple marriages, and exhibits in various other ways the tendency of Cervantine theatre to allude both to itself and to the genre's conventions. It is notable for its vigorous projection of the servants, whose doings are a sophisticated parody of the amatory entanglements of their foolish masters. The character of Pedro de Urdemalas, based on a legendary trickster and changeling of that name, is fascinating for what it reveals about Cervantes's love of the theatre and conception of the ideal actor. In Cervantes's play, the hero comes to realise that this is the profession for which he is destined; and the qualities that he reveals up to that point – quick-wittedness, eloquence, versatility, refusal of permanent attachments –show that Cervates has conceived his personality, from the beginning, in terms of that culminating self-discovery. The third of the plays named above is about a tearaway young ruffian of Seville, magnetically drawn to the company of cut-throats and prostitutes like Monipodio's gang, and showing something of Monipodio's misplaced religious devotion, though not his stupidity or dishonesty. At the end of the first act he realises the impiety of his ways, and vows to embrace the monastic life; in the next two acts we see him fulfilling that vow as a saintly friar of the Order of Preachers in Mexico. The portrayal of Lugo, subsequently Fray Cruz, is interesting as a study of a dissolute character who, nonetheless, is born to greatness; the perversely misdirected qualities that he reveals as a ruffian – recklessness, combativeness, chivalrousness, ambition, religious devotion – are continuous with the heroic virtues that he shows in Mexico. He is one of several Cervantine personages who have affinities with Don Quixote.

Golden Age Society and Culture

Something should be said about the society and culture in which *Don Quixote* was written. The political framework had been established by the Catholic Kings, Isabel of Castille and Ferdinand of Aragon, who united their kingdoms by their marriage in 1469, and laid the foundations of the absolutist monarchy by which Spain would be governed for the next three centuries.[14]

---

[14] Still the best general introduction to the history is Elliott (1963). On Spain in the years when *DQ* was published, see Pierre Vilar, in Haley, ed. (1980: 17–29) and Redondo in Anthony Close and others (1995: 257–93). On the structure of society, see Salazar Rincón (1986) and Domínguez Ortiz (1964 and 1970). Close (2000), Chapter 7 discusses the intersection of society and culture, including censorship. A concise general introduction to Spanish Golden Age literature is Gies, ed. (2004). For a full, general survey of the period –politics, society, literature, art – see Jover, ed. (1982, 1986).

They initiated its transformation into an early modern state, overhauling the legal system together with national and town government, turning the aristocracy into subservient collaborators with the crown while increasing their number and privileges, and, in general, imposing law, order and unity on a hitherto anarchic kingdom. Despite these innovations, the nation created by them retained its feudal character. Thus, the land was divided in myriad fiefdoms, owned either by crown or church or nobility, and society was stratified in three broad classes: the nobility, with a supposedly military vocation; the church and monastic orders; and the manual labourers, who, in this agrarian society, were mainly peasants. The burden of taxation, increasingly heavy with the acceleration of economic decline, fell entirely on this third, productive sector; the other two, among other privileges, were exempt from it. As part of their project of unification, the Catholic Kings required Spanish Jews, and subsequently Muslims, to convert to Christianity. To prevent backsliding among the *converso* Jews, they set up the Inquisition in 1480, which, armed with its formidable powers, was equipped to deal with the new heresies that presented themselves in the following century, including various forms of Protestantism. The Indies were discovered during the reign of Ferdinand and Isabel, and colonisation of South and Central America, and the southern tip of North America, would rapidly spread during their reign and the subsequent ones.

The monarchy's grip on the kingdom was strengthened by the reign of the Habsburg Emperor Charles V (1516–56), whose forces crushed a revolt of the towns against the crown in 1521. Charles launched the policy of aggressive defence of his sprawling European dominions, which chiefly comprised the Low Countries, southern Italy, Sicily and the Balearics, and assumed the related role of defender of the Catholic faith on several fronts simultaneously: against Islam in the Mediterranean and Protestantism in north Europe. That international strategy, continued by Charles's son Philip II (1556–98), was accompanied within Spain's borders by fierce repression of heresy and the vigorous implementation of the resolutions of the Council of Trent (1545–63), which formulated Catholicism's response to the Protestant schism. The series of man-made and natural disasters that overshadowed the last two decades of Philip II's reign – revolt in the Spanish Netherlands, rampant price-inflation, famine and plague, the rout of the Armada expedition, crippling debts to foreign financiers – induced recourse to a policy of détente, which began with the peace-treaty with France in 1598, the year of the king's death. This was followed in the reign of his successor Philip III by similar treaties with England (1604) and the Dutch Protestants (1609). Increasing awareness of the nation's economic and political decline was reflected in a profusion of projects of reform, including a programme of measures proposed by the government towards the end of Philip III's reign (1598–1621), amid the aura of sleaze and incompetence surrounding his administration, run by powerful court-favourites.

Such was the broad political context of Cervantes's life, and it had a direct effect on the cultural environment. Retrenchment and the suspension of military adventures abroad were accompanied in the early years of Philip III's regime by the opening of the floodgates of gaiety and festivity, and encouragement of the extravagance and ostentation of the court, in marked contrast with the solemn sobriety of the previous reign. In 1601 the court moved temporarily from Madrid to the northern town of Valladolid, and would stay there until 1606, when it returned. Cervantes's household moved to Valladolid sometime during this five-year period, following the court southwards subsequently; and life in that town was described by one intelligent observer as a perpetual comedy or farce in which dissolution was the norm. It is no accident that a spate of comic fiction and satire – including Mateo Alemán's *Guzmán de Alfarache* (1599, 1604), the brilliant sequel to it by Quevedo, *El Buscón* (c.1605) (The Sharper), and, of course, *Don Quijote* itself – were all written about that time, reflecting the prevailing festive mood. Another major stimulus to comic writing was the lifting on the ban on the theatre, which had been imposed for one year in 1597–8 after deaths in the royal family, including Philip II's. The temporary prohibition marked a phase in a fierce controversy, protracted into the seventeenth century, between the theatre's opponents, who objected to it on grounds of immorality, and its supporters, who pleaded the need for a popular medium of public entertainment and urged its value as a source of revenue for Madrid's hospitals (McKendrick, 1989: 201–8). As we have seen, Cervantes contributed prominently to that controversy by means of his attack on the New Comedy in *Don Quixote* I, 48. Though his invective might seem to make him one of the theatre's enemies, in fact his criticisms, while hard-hitting, are designed to save it, not to smother it.

Despite the religious fervour of the Counter-Reformation, and a spate of projects and books that aimed at social and moral reform, this was in many ways a corrupt society. Powerful court-favourites ran the country for the pious and colourless Philip III, enriching themselves in the process; and their spectacular rises and falls gave proof of the precariousness of fortune. Though, by its policy of enforced religious unity, Spain avoided the religious conflicts that shook its European neighbours, it experienced a different kind of dissension, originating from the socially stigmatised, hence disaffected, descendants of converted Jews and Moors. This was a society hyper-conscious of honour, caste and status, in which much of the large, hierarchically tiered class of the nobility –apart from those employed in national or municipal government or other honourable professions – pursued a life of dignified idleness, leaving commerce, manual labour and agriculture to the lower orders. Imported gold and silver from the Indies and the borrowed money that kept this society afloat had a harmful impact on the Spanish economy; at the same time, it created a new parvenu class, determined to buy access to nobility by hook or by crook. *Desengaño*, disenchantment with worldly vanities, and the precariousness of fortune, are dominant themes of the literature of the age.

They insistently run through the writings of Francisco de Quevedo (1580–1645), a prolific genius who attained literary greatness in diverse spheres at once: comic fiction, burlesque and satire, lyric verse, moral/religious poetry and prose.[15] His political and social attitudes, though more reactionary than those of some of his contemporaries, such as Cervantes, Góngora and Tirso de Molina, reflect significant aspects of the age's ideology, even though his mordant and irreverent expression of them got him into hot water with the government and the Inquisition. Born into a family originating from Santander in north-west Spain, he was a member of the minor rural nobility, and was educated at the Jesuit College of Madrid, where he acquired a good classical education, shown, later in life, by his translations of ancient Stoic texts. He frequented court circles in Madrid and Valladolid, becoming for a time an emissary of the Duke of Osuna, executor of Spanish foreign policy in Italy in the decade 1610–20. One side of his dual personality is shown in his picaresque novel *El Buscón*, coarse yet brilliantly witty, which testifies to intimate familiarity with the low life of court and university: brothels, taverns, student pranks, street-brawls, and the like. However, the other, less frivolous side concerns us here. It is typified by his political tract *España defendida* (1609) (Spain Defended), which coincided with the declaration of an armistice with the rebellious Flemish Protestant provinces, perceived by Quevedo as a national humiliation. In this apologetic piece, fiercely patriotic in tone, are revealed many of the political attitudes that emerge in later writings, such as the 'Epístola satírica y censoria' (Satiric and Censorious Epistle) addressed to the Count-Duke Olivares and written in the mid-1620s, the *Política de Dios* (1626) (God's Politics) and *La hora de todos* (1636) (Everyman's Hour). In that tract, he idealises the old Spanish virtues of honour, militarism, sobriety, toil, loyalty to king, law and faith – qualities seen at their best in the rude Middle Ages, but now, alas, debilitated by effeminate taste for foreign luxuries and fashions. He insists on Spain's

15 On Quevedo's life, see the introduction by Blecua to his edn of the poetry (1978).

sacred mission to defend the Catholic faith by force of arms against Islam and Protestantism, voices deep suspicion of foreignness, novelty and Arabic contamination of the Spanish language, biliously vents his hatred of Jews and phobia about the international Jewish conspiracy, linked to Machiavellianism in the brilliantly malign 'cuadro' (tableau) 39 of *La hora de todos*. Profoundly conservative, Quevedo was filled with a lifelong zeal to combat Spain's slide into decadence – by satiric ridicule, moral exhortation, political pamphleteering, diplomacy. However, he was incapable of seeing decadence as deriving from the inherent structure of Spain's society and economy and to its resistance to innovation. He blamed it instead on the weakness and corruption of rulers, the effeteness of his times, the proliferation and dishonesty of lawyers, the inability of the *nouveaux riches* to know their place, and saw international politics as a black-and-white struggle between the forces of the true faith and those of Satan.

People swarmed to the capital – that is, Madrid, except for the period 1601–6 – from the impoverished provinces in order to seek preferment at court or service in noble households; and the sharpers, beggars, prostitutes and diverse poseurs who came with them provided a rich quarry for satirists. Aristocrats, attracted by the prospect of power and enrichment, built expensive mansions there, neglecting their country estates. Another important provider of livings in a country of declining industry and commerce was the church, rich with its land and tithes. Convents and churches, built with the help of large donations, sprouted in the capital. The rapid expansion of Madrid, mirrored by that of towns in other parts of the country, created opportunities for literature, which was favoured by a combination of factors: royal, aristocratic and church patronage; academies; the proximity of writers to each other; and, above all, the emergence of a mass market of readers and theatre-goers. Consequently, it flourished in a variety of forms. Though the church made strenuous efforts to impose norms of decency upon it, and the Inquisition rigorously monitored it for any signs of unorthodoxy, irreverence or blasphemy, neither of them checked literary creativity, whose quality and quantity have earned that age – that is, from about 1580 to the mid-seventeenth century – the epithet 'golden'. Cervantes's active career occupies the first half of it.

The increasing urbanisation of Spanish society affects literary production in all sorts of ways. The picaresque novel, which flourishes following the publication of the first part of *Guzmán de Alfarache* in 1599, and purports to be the autobiography of a shamelessly disreputable character who drifts from one menial occupation to the next, acquiring the habits of swindler, scrounger, drop-out and thief, tends to favour urban settings, and reflects the proliferation of mendicancy and criminality mentioned above, while exaggerating the squalor for comic effect. A quite different social sector is represented in two other genres of the seventeenth century: first, the romantic *novela*, launched by Cervantes's collection of exemplary tales (1613), and second, the comedy of intrigue involving conflicts of love and honour in a contemporary setting, including such famous plays as Lope de Vega's *La dama boba* (The Nitwitted Lady, 1615) and Calderón's *La dama duende* (The Phantom Lady, 1629). The noblemen and noblewomen who feature as protagonists in both these genres testify to the emergence in the towns of a large 'middle-class' community – minor nobility, government and municipal officials, and so on – which looked to literature and the theatre to provide an idealised reflection of its own aspirations. In these works, cities like Madrid, Seville, Toledo, Barcelona and Valencia, with their famous sights and landmarks, their calendar of festivals and the associated customs and occupations, typically provide the background of the plot.

The theatre was a massively popular form of entertainment; and the inhabitants of Madrid, from the highest to the lowest, flocked to its two major theatre-houses, the Corral del Príncipe and Corral de la Cruz.[16] Since the run of any given play seldom exceeded two weeks, there was constant demand by the managers of theatrical companies for playwrights to supply them with new material. This explains the prolific output of the age's great dramatists – Lope de Vega, Tirso de Molina, Calderón – particularly Lope, whose productivity was prodigious. In his dramatic manifesto, the 'Arte nuevo de hacer comedias en este tiempo' (New Art of Writing Comedies in this Age, published in 1609), he admits that popular demand and the need to take his public's taste into account led him to create a revolutionary kind of theatre, which deviates from Classical rules and models. Hence its wide-ranging repertoire of themes and styles of a predominantly nationalist and contemporary flavour: not just the urban comedies mentioned above, but also plays based on the lives of saints, significant moments in Spanish history, pastoral and Moorish romances, popular legends and ballads, Classical mythology, plots derived from Ariosto and the Italian novella, the theme of the revenge of marital honour, as well as the brief sacramental allegories performed in Corpus Christi week. The *comedia*, subjected to constant attacks from the late sixteenth century onwards, illustrates the ways in which literature adapted itself to the threat of censorship. The effect is seen in the increasing care for artistic polish revealed by the plays of Lope's maturity, accentuated by his

---

16 On this, McKendrick (1989: Chapter 3).

follower Calderón de la Barca, whose most famous plays, such as *La vida es sueño* (Life is a Dream), *El príncipe constante* (The Constant Prince) and *El mágico prodigioso* (The Prodigious Magician), reveal a characteristic sombre reflectiveness, enhanced by metaphoric and symbolic density and intricate thematic and formal patterning.

Another prominent example of urban influence on literature was satire, whose outstanding representative in the latter years of Cervantes's life was Quevedo, a thorn in the flesh of the regimes of Philip III and Philip IV. From about the date of publication of *Don Quixote* Part I (1605), he started writing his *Sueños*: dreams of hell, death and the Last Judgement, continued later in his life by *La hora de todos*. As in the Medieval Dance of Death, anonymous representatives of society's professions and the Seven Deadly Sins parade before the mouthpieces of Quevedo's wit – devils, Death, the personification of *Desengaño*, Disillusionment – and are stripped bare by a torrent of caustic conceits, or caricatured in grotesque images reminiscent of Bosch. Though the settings are visionary, the types exposed to the reader's derision are the typical impostors of Madrid society, enumerated in long lists in the preliminaries: corrupt government ministers, pastry-cooks, constables, courtesans, rich noblemen, widows and widowers, innkeepers, and so on. From Quevedo's perspective of Christian Stoicism, the society around him is a world upside down, ruled by Hypocrisy and enslaved to Vanity, where nothing is what it seems.

The proximity of writers to each other resulting from urban life, and the increasing influence of academies and academic thinking on their literary production, are reflected in the nature and impact of the two major poems of one of the greatest poets of the age, Luis de Góngora: I refer to his *Soledades* (Solitudes) and *Polifemo* (Polyphemus), which circulate in manuscript in Madrid in the years 1612–13.[17] The first is a long, unfinished pastoral poem and the second a reworking of the myth of the giant Polyphemus and the nymph Galatea. Both are sumptuously imaginative and original creations, which provoked a prolonged controversy by virtue of their dense, complex syntax and ornately figurative style, and spawned a succession of learned commentaries by the poet's apologists, dedicated to elucidating the recondite references. The seventeenth-century polemics for and against Góngora, and also, for and against the innovations of Lope, were precisely the themes expounded in learned addresses to literary academies; and this is reflected in

---

[17] The best general introduction to Góngora's poetry and its subsequent reception remains the one by Dámaso Alonso (1960).

the academic nature of the discussions on chivalry books and the contemporary theatre in *Don Quixote* Part I, Chapters 47 and 48.

Another consequence of the creation of local literary groups is the evolution of the so-called *romancero nuevo*, the new ballad corpus, in the late sixteenth century and early seventeenth.[18] Using the metres of the old traditional ballads, the leading poets of the period – Lope de Vega, Góngora, Cervantes and others – write in sophisticated modern style, and replace the old themes (epic, Carolingian, historical) with new ones attuned to contemporary literary fashions: the romantic sufferings of pastoral or Moorish characters, captives' laments and pervasive burlesque of these and other motifs. The prevalence of burlesque is to a considerable extent related to the self-consciousness of this poetry, as well as to its formulaic and precious character; the authors represent their own amatory experiences in those of their fictitious personages, and the melodramatic posing invites parodic retaliation. The ferment of crystallising and disintegrating poetic myths, enthusiastic literary role-play and ironic satire on its falsity was an indispensable precondition for the conception of *Don Quixote*. It involves a sharp awareness, incorporated as ingredient in the poetic artefact, of the presence of the self behind its masks and of the conventionality of the literary medium of expression.

So the evolution of the age's literary culture does not occur in a vacuum, but is thoroughly enmeshed with other aspects of social life. This is also true of *Don Quixote*, in ways already noted, though in one major respect it appears an exception to the trends mentioned above, particularly as they concern prose narrative. I mean that the action transpires in a rural, and in some ways, an escapist setting. In mocking imitation of the wanderings of knights-errant through fields and forests in remote, exotic lands, the action of Part I is set in the flat plains and undulating hills of prosaic La Mancha, separated at its southern extremity from Andalucía by the craggy wilderness of the Sierra Morena. La Mancha was a region associated with backward rusticity, thus a fittingly ironic context for the hero's idealised literary fantasies. By contrast, the Sierra Morena was a place of transgression, wild and desolate, the haunt of wolves and bandits, but also one that could be romanticised as a pastoral retreat or a craggy, romantic solitude. In Part II the hero revisits southern La Mancha, where he explores the Cave of Montesinos (Chapter 23), before heading north, to the banks of the Ebro, Aragón and finally Barcelona. His visit to Barcelona is the only time when he sets foot in a major town (II, 61–65). Though traditionally *Don Quixote* has been

18 On this, see the introduction by Carreño (1982) to his edn of Góngora's *romances*.

assumed to offer a comprehensive picture of Spain's life at its moment of historical crisis, it would be truer to say that the picture is glowingly – and in some ways nostalgically – genial and picturesque, corresponding to a holiday parenthesis in which reality's harsh contours and ugly blemishes are softened, without being blurred beyond recognition. For example, Cervantes's portrayal of Sancho Panza tells us nothing about the abject poverty and squalor in which the mass of the peasants of New Castille led their lives, yet his story of Sancho's and his master's pursuit of archaic literary illusions can easily be read as symbolic of a collective mentality, diagnosed by Cervantes's perceptive contemporary, González de Cellorigo, as that of men 'bewitched, living outside the natural order of things'.[19]

---

[19] Cited in Elliott (1963: 305).

3

The Adventures and Episodes of *Don Quixote* Part I

The Black/White Dichotomy

The opening chapter of *Don Quixote* makes such a deft and confident beginning of a novel that one might expect it to derive from well-established precedents. Yet to my mind none of those that have been adduced, more or less plausibly, go very far towards explaining its genesis. I refer, first, to the social and domestic setting in which the hero is originally presented to us. It is the tranquil, sheltered life of a fifty-year-old country *hidalgo*, a bachelor, who lives with a housekeeper and his niece, consuming, week after week, the same frugal diet, wearing the same clothes, pursuing the same pastimes: now a spot of hunting with nag and greyhound, now a chat with the village priest and barber on politics or literature. Contemporaries of Cervantes would have recognised the type, evoked in Antonio de Guevara's *Menosprecio de corte y alabanza de aldea* (1539) (Disparagement of Court and Praise of Country) and an early ballad by Góngora.[1] However, the specific detail of this benignly satiric portrait, and its use as a way of contextualising the destiny of a fictional protagonist, are quite new.

The salient feature of it is the character's compulsive addiction to chivalry books, consumed day and night until they drive him mad, and making him lose all sense of the distinction, first of all between history and fiction, then between literary imitation and real doing or being. This is the impulse for his resolve to become a knight-errant and embark on the adventures to be studied in this chapter. Beyond saying that he was idle for most of the year, as most *hidalgos* of his class were, Cervantes does not explicitly draw a cause-and-effect relationship between his life-style and his mental condition. He does not say, for example, that he was driven mad by a combination of screaming boredom and nostalgia for the bygone military vocation of his class, still less that his retreat into fantasy was a way of sublimating an incestuous

---

[1] See the ballad 'Ahora que estoy despacio ...' (1582), in *Obras completas*, ed. Millé y Giménez, pp. 50–3, and the introduction to Rallo's edn (1984) of Guevara's *Menosprecio*.

passion for his niece.[2] It is typical of his mutely suggestive characterisation that it continually supplies hints that might prompt such hypotheses, without, however, making their consequences explicit. While there are contemporary reports or anecdotes about conditions like our hero's, the flat, take-it-or-leave-it way in which it is introduced, together with its sheer extremity, marks it as a burlesque device. Despite this, the portrayal of this crazy make-believe in the rest of the novel is rounded, particularised and – with exceptions to be noted later – consistent, and in these respects, comes entirely from Cervantes's own head.

For example, the belief in the historical truth of those books, exemplified specifically in the first chapter, is splendidly demonstrated much later by his attempted refutation of the contrary arguments by the judicious canon of Toledo (I, 49–50). In this debate, the *hidalgo* puts on the same level of reality a historic tourney of 1434, the love of Tristan and Isolde, and the peg with which – according to him – Pierres of Provence magically guided his wooden horse through the air (pp. 565–6).[3] Again, since, for him, this fabulous world of chivalry was once real, so must its personages have been: hence he claims almost to have seen Amadís with his own eyes, and on the strength of that, offers a precise description (II, 1; p. 636). Logically, since he implicitly believes other people's fictions, he believes his own; so he is able simultaneously to admit that Dulcinea is an idealised figment and to request Sancho to deliver a love-letter to her (I, 25; pp. 276 and 285–6).

Another basic habit of thought established in the first chapter is the Edenic process of renaming by which he transforms his own obscure identity, together with those of his steed and mistress, into new and more exalted ones.[4] Take, for example, the name Don Quijote de la Mancha. 'Quijote' is the name of a thigh-piece of a suit of armour, rhymes with heroic 'Lanzarote' (Lancelot), and plays on the hero's surname, whose variant forms – Quijada, Quesana, Quijana (I, 1) – eventually yield to the definitive version, Quijano (II, 74; p. 1217). So far so good. Yet the suffix '-ote' is pejorative in Spanish; as a mere *hidalgo*, the hero usurps the title *don*, reserved for the class of *caballeros*; and the linking of the name with the province of La Mancha, in attempted imitation of Amadís de Gaula, has a comically homely, not a noble, effect.

---

[2] For the first of these interpretations, see the introductory comments by Rico and Forradellas on the first chapter of *DQ* in vol. 2 of Rico's edn (1998); for the second, Carroll Johnson (1983).

[3] In fact, the horse which carried the fleeing lovers in *La historia de la linda Magalona* (The History of Fair Maguelone) moved under its own steam. Cervantes is confusing this with another romance.

[4] On this, see Rosenblat (1971: 168–75), also Redondo (1998: 213–21).

Dulcinea, rhyming with the names of famous heroines like Melibea or Chari-
clea, is a treacly enhancement of the plain Jane rusticity of Aldonza, of medieval origin, equivalent to modern 'la dulce', the sweet. The Spanish proverb
says: 'A falta de moza, buena es Aldonza' (if you haven't a wench, Aldonza
will do). Rocinante attempts to ennoble the bony nag in Don Quixote's stable:
that is, 'rocín' (nag) 'antes' (before), but now a steed, though alternatively, it
could be read as 'ante-rocín', supernag.

The second and third chapters show him applying this mental process to
the external world and seeking confirmation from it. Thus, we are told that
after leaving home and riding all day beneath the burning sun, he arrived
at dusk at an inn, which seemed to him a castle with four towers, spires
of gleaming silver, drawbridge and deep moat (I, 2). Presumably, his over-
heated wits and the evening gloom helped him to jump to these conclusions.
The two prostitutes at the door, travelling to Seville with some mule drovers,
seemed to him like beautiful damsels or gracious ladies taking solace at the
castle gate. The innkeeper offers *truchuela* for supper, meaning salt cod, and
is misunderstood to mean little trout: food fit for a knight. Clinching proof is
provided during the repast thus (I, 2; p. 54):

> Estando en esto, llegó acaso a la venta un castrador de puercos, y así como
> llegó sonó su silbato de cañas cuatro o cinco veces, con lo cual acabó
> de confirmar don Quijote que estaba en algún famoso castillo y que le
> servían con música y que el abadejo eran truchas, el pan candeal y las
> rameras damas y el ventero castellano del castillo, y con esto daba por
> bien empleada su determinación y salida.

> At this juncture, a swine castrator happened to arrive at the inn, and as he
> reached it, blew his reed whistle four or five times, as a result of which
> Don Quixote became fully convinced that he was in some famous castle,
> that they were serving him to the accompaniment of music, that the salt
> cod were trout, the bread was finest white, the prostitutes ladies and the
> innkeeper the warden of the castle, and so he considered his original
> resolve and sally well worth while.

The mental disposition displayed by this passage is defined, earlier in
Chapter 2 (p. 49), by Cervantes when he says: 'a nuestro aventurero todo
cuanto pensaba, veía o imaginaba le parecía ser hecho y pasar al modo de
lo que había leído' (all that our adventurer thought, saw or imagined seemed
to him to be done or to happen in the way that he had read), and much later,
in II, 10 (p. 703), by Sancho, who describes his master's madness as such
that it 'juzga lo blanco por negro y lo negro por blanco, como se pareció

cuando dijo que los molinos de viento eran gigantes, y las mulas de los religiosos dromedarios, y las manadas de carneros ejércitos de enemigos' (takes white for black and black for white, as was shown when he said that the windmills were giants, and the friars' mules were dromedaries, and the flocks of sheep enemy armies). By symmetrically highlighting how this mode of perception works in relation to the inn, the innkeeper, the prostitutes, the bread, the salt fish and the swineherd's whistle, Cervantes lays the basis for later chapters, where he expects the reader to take this mind-set for granted. His irony hinges on this kind of tacit understanding. This inn is the setting for the dubbing ceremony – a grotesque travesty of that sacrosanct ritual (Riquer, 2003: 127–30). The innkeeper who performs it is a thieving rascal who, instead of the traditional formulae, reads out gibberish from a book of fodder accounts; the inn conforms to the black legend of stereotype, a place of wretched discomfort, mockery and trickery; a drinking-trough for animals serves as altar for the vigil; a prostitute girds on the sword.

Cervantes does not classify his novel generically, wavering in the prologue to Part I between *libro* and *historia* (story or history), and designating it thereafter by this last, ironically ambiguous term. Though he does not call it a satire, he acknowledges its polemical purpose in that prologue by insisting on the idea of demolition of chivalric romances: 'una invectiva contra' (an invective against), 'deshacer la autoridad y cabida' (undoing the authority and sway), 'derribar la máquina mal fundada destos caballerescos libros' (knock down the ill-founded apparatus of those chivalric books), an idea firmly repeated in the final sentence of the novel. And while he never describes it as 'parody' or 'burlesque',[5] he nevertheless repeatedly asserts that his hero imitates chivalry books in a way that is both scrupulously detailed and ridiculous, and treats the imitation as involving those grotesque conjunctions of high and low deemed intrinsic to that literary mode by *Don Quixote*'s many eighteenth-century English admirers. They are fully exemplified by his idealising transformation of a squalid inn into a castle at the beginning of his first sally, and his capacity to do the same to subsequent inns remains a basic indicator of the vigour of his madness. Even when it disappears in Part II (see *DQ* II, 24, p. 835; II, 59, pp. 1108–9; and II, 71, p. 1202), his attitude to Dulcinea continues to exhibit the same kind of grotesque misappropriation.

---

[5] While the term *parodia* was known to Spanish prescriptive theorists, it was not much used, and never by Cervantes. He occasionally uses *burlesco* (e.g. *DQ* II, 22; p. 812), though in his own and contemporary usage it had a broader sense than English 'burlesque', that of jocose, jesting.

It has rightly been pointed out that *Don Quixote* is an unusual form of parody, since instead of purporting to be a work of the same kind as the genre that it sends up, while ridiculing it by exaggeration, degradation and other incongruities, it presents ordinary characters in a contemporary setting, very different from the heroic and fabulous world of chivalry books (Riley, 1986: 36).[6] However, an authentic effect of parodic imitation is achieved by ironically contrasting that setting with the hero's scrupulous attempt to relive *Amadís de Gaula* and its kind by thought, word and deed. As Vicente de los Ríos pointed out in his 'Análisis del Quijote', which forms the introduction to the Royal Spanish Academy's edition of *Don Quixote*, published in 1780, Cervantes succeeds in putting two kinds of work and two perspectives side by side within the same story, and starkly yet quite plausibly opposing them. He treats one of those perspectives as subjective illusion and the other as reality. This is how de los Ríos puts the matter (vol. i, p. 56):

> Cada aventura tiene dos aspectos muy distintos respecto al Héroe y al lector. Este no ve más que un suceso casual y ordinario en lo que para Don Quijote es una cosa rara y extraordinaria, que su imaginación le pinta con todos los colores de su locura ... Así en cada aventura hay por lo regular dos obstáculos y dos éxitos, uno efectivo en la realidad, y otro aparente en la aprehensión de don Quijote, y ambos naturales, deducidos de la acción, y verosímiles, sin embargo de ser opuestos.

> Each adventure has two very different aspects for the hero and the reader, who sees nothing other than a banal and natural occurrence in something which the hero's imagination paints in all the wonderful colours of his madness. So in each adventure there are two crises and two resolutions, one real and effective, and the other merely imagined by Don Quixote, yet both natural, derived logically from the action, and plausible, despite being opposed to each other.

And he concludes that the adventures that in books like *Amadís* become wearisome because of their implausibility are nothing of the sort in *Don Quixote*.

The passage makes a shrewd point, but also exaggerates it. For a start, Don Quixote's imitation does not exactly reproduce the behaviour of Amadís and Company, since he spoils the effect by exaggeration (e.g. the ridiculous names that he attributes to the warriors in the armies described in I, 18),

---

6 Genette makes a similar point (1982: 201–2), but his argument that, for precisely that reason, *DQ* is not properly speaking a parody, seems to me mere hair-splitting.

; my horses fault !

arrogance and bombast (defects shunned by Amadís, an epitome of modesty), and lapses into vulgarity or banality (freely displayed in his story of the Cave of Montesinos). Moreover, the very fact that we know that he is merely imitating, and that he and the chosen stage are quite unsuitable for the role, make his behaviour absurdly different from his models. Nonetheless, his mad seriousness, elegant style and evident familiarity with the chivalric genre imaginatively recreate that fictional world for us, all the more effectively since, as the philosopher Ortega y Gasset observed, his mental state of compulsive make-believe represents in extreme form that of any reader of novels, including ours, as readers of his story.[7] There is another sense in which Vicente de los Ríos goes too far, and it concerns verisimilitude. In original conception, Don Quixote's madness is less a realistic pathological condition than a literary device designed to caricature the chivalric genre's alienation from reality, at once exaggerating its insistence on the superlative and applying it to objects and persons of a degradedly contrasted kind. This madness has an implicitly symbolic and aesthetic significance, equivalent to the monstrous implausibility that Cervantes perceives in chivalry books; significantly, he uses the same word, *disparates* (nonsense), for both.

In the adventures following the hero's dubbing, Cervantes makes a greater effort to choose external phenomena that, by their ambivalence, plausibly stimulate his fanastic misconceptions. However, in the inn-scenes in Chapters 2 and 3, the split perspective identified by de los Ríos is a stark opposition, which well merits Sancho's black/white analogy. The narrator's sarcastic judgements are obtrusive and coincide with the innkeeper's mockery and the mirth of the prostitutes, inciting us to share their detachment. By implication, we are included in the knot of spectators gazing in astonishment at the self-absorbed figure keeping vigil in the moonlight (I, 3; pp. 57–8). The conception of the hero is powerfully suggestive, but external and limited. His discourse is stiffly imitative, bristling with chivalric literature's archaisms, for example, *mostredes, fuyan, fecho, membraros, atended, ca, al, non*,[8] which are archaic forms of *mostréis, huyan, hecho, acordaros, esperad, pues, otra cosa, no*) and trite formulae, such as *enderezar tuertos, deshacer agravios, otorgar un don, no por culpa mía sino de mi caballo*, meaning to right wrongs, repair offences, grant a boon, no fault of mine but of my steed. The imitation leads

[7] In his *Meditaciones del* Quijote (Meditations on *Don Quixote*), published in 1914. See Ortega y Gasset (1961: vol. i, pp. 380–1).

[8] These being or meaning respectively the second-person plural subjunctive of *mostrar* (show), the third-person plural subjunctive of *huir* (flee), done (past participle) or fact, remember (vocative plural), wait, for or since, anything else, not.

to virtual loss of identity in passages of Chapters 2 and 5, where he identifies himself, respectively, with Lancelot and the wounded Baldovinos in old
Spanish ballads about them, and in the latter case, goes on to see himself as
the captured Moorish hero Abindarráez in a well-known prose-romance. In
these early chapters, there is little communication between him and others;
such as it is, it is based on crossed purposes, misunderstanding on his side,
mocking irony on the other.

The stark opposition between the Quixotic viewpoint and the sane one
soon undergoes refinement, through a combination of factors: Cervantes's
conception of 'common nature' (below, pp. 45–53); his empathetic form of
parody (pp. 53–61); the interpolation of romantic episodes, which add a new
dimension to the central character by mirroring it in somewhat similar ones,
viewed compassionately rather than comically (pp. 61–79); the introduction
of Sancho in *Don Quixote* II, 7, which launches the dialogue between the
pair (Chapter 4); the abandonment of a sarcastic, judicial attitude in favour
of a light, playful and non-committal one (Chapter 5). All these developments
are part of the progressive evolution of Cervantes's original conception of his
story, which will be discussed in the next four sections of this chapter. The
sixth and final one will examine the galley-slaves adventure, as a culminating
example of the comic ethos of Part I.

Structure and Evolution of Part I

Part I is confusingly subdivided in four internal 'parts', which disappear in
Part II. They respectively comprise Chapters 1–8 inclusive, 9–14, 15–27 and
28–52. From the outset, *Don Quixote* exhibits the primitive, archaic structure typical of many long works of fiction until the late eighteenth century:
not only chivalry books, but also picaresque and Byzantine novels.[9] That is,
it has the loosely articulated form of a string of beads of somewhat similar
shape and colour, the string being the hero's quest or career, and the beads the
individual incidents and meetings between him and strangers, which mostly
happen by chance, in a potentially endless series of 'and then's and 'when
suddenly's. This disjointed form favours Cervantes's improvised composition
of the story: he adds new components to the assembly as he goes along,
which sometimes modify it significantly.

First of all, he profits by it to vary the nature of the 'beads'. These, in
Part I, are basically of three kinds: the hero's adventures, interspersed from

---

[9] See the essay 'Forms of Time and Chronotope in the Novel' in Bakhtin (1981:
84ff.).

Chapter 7 onwards by his conversations with Sancho; critical discussions of the romances of chivalry (in I, 6, 32, 47–50); episodes, mainly of a romantic kind. Secondly, he gives a kind of unity and shape to his story by locating these incidents in four recurrent types of setting, each with its distinctive associations: (a) the hero's home and native village; (b) the plains of La Mancha traversed by a *camino real* (royal highway); (c) roadside inns; (d) the wooded uplands near Puerto Lápice, then later, of the Sierra Morena. Adventures have a natural link with all these scenarios save home; something like the reverse is true of the critical discussions, which stand directly opposed to them. Two of the locations are ambivalent. Juan Palomeque's inn – I, 16–17 and 32–46 – serves, in the second and longer series of chapters, both as a degraded mock-castle and as an equivalent to the enchanted castles of romance where love's maladies are cured, for example, the palace of the enchantress Felicia in Montemayor's *La Diana* Books IV and V. The *sierra* is both a theatre of romantic interludes and of chivalric adventures. Thirdly, a further kind of unity is provided by grouping the incidents in cycles, which coincide with the duration of a journey by a given group of travellers to a particular destination, or else, by what happens to a company of guests at an inn or other dwelling. This means of organising the narrative is traditional: well known examples are Chaucer's *The Canterbury Tales* and Boccaccio's *Decameron*, where stories are told, respectively, by travellers on a pilgrimage to Canterbury and by a group of young ladies and gentleman who take refuge in a pleasant villa near Florence during the plague of 1348.

The hero undertakes three sallies in the novel. The first begins in Chapter 2, and abruptly ends in Chapter 5; the second, in which he is now accompanied by Sancho, begins in Chapter 7 and ends in Chapter 52, which closes Part I; the third begins in Part II, Chapter 8 and ends in the penultimate chapter. All three sallies describe a loop consisting in the hero's escape from home in search of adventure, followed by his return. All three returns are inglorious, the first being on the back of an ass, after he is discovered prostrate on the ground as a result of the thrashing that he suffers at the hands of the lackey of the Toledan merchants (end of Chapter 4, continued in Chapter 5). Within the major loop described by the second sally – that is, the hero's outward journey and his enforced return home in a cage mounted on an ox-cart – there are three minor journeys of a somewhat similar kind, with the difference that home is replaced either as the starting-point or the end-term or both by Juan Palomeque's inn.[10]

---

[10]   The first journey corresponds to Chapters 7–15 inclusive; the second, to Chapters 18–31; and the third, to Chapters 46 to the end.

The coordinates of time and space are handled with considerable haziness (cf. Murillo, 1975). Master and squire set forth from 'a place – i.e. village – in La Mancha' somewhere in the triangle formed by El Toboso (north), Argamasilla de Alba (south), and Puerto Lápice (west). They reach the pass of Puerto Lápice (91 km south of Toledo, according to the Michelin Guide) at three in the afternoon on the second day of their expedition, and on the fifth day are in the wilds of the Sierra Morena, heading, one gathers, in the general direction of Almodóvar del Campo and El Viso (I, 23; p. 249). How they managed to cover the intervening 100–150 kilometres on their slowly ambling beasts, with frequent halts for a series of jarring physical encounters, some of them sufficient to put lesser men in hospital, is not explained. Nor do we know which precise *camino real* they followed, what towns or villages they passed by, if any, nor where Juan Palomeque's inn was located. When Don Quixote suggests enchantment as the obvious explanation for the speed of Sancho's return journey between the *sierra* and El Toboso (I, 31; p. 360), one is inclined to agree.

So, like a piece of jazz, *Don Quixote* improvises within regulatory patterns. Of such improvisation there is plentiful evidence: signs of revision, omissions, happy afterthoughts, changes of plan, and much of it occurs in the first half of Part I;[11] it is related, clearly enough, to Cervantes's changing conception of the length, form, and nature of his story in the course of composition. This evolution does not stop in Part I, but affects the second Part too, whose design shows considerable modification of its precursor's, and is generally more coherent. Since the signs of Cervantes's revisions of the primitive draft(s) of Part I, are mostly inconclusive and contained in the text, with little solid complementary evidence external to it, the ingenuity of critics has had free rein in reconstructing the process and chronology of composition. The hypotheses vary in the degree of their persuasiveness, though few are incontestable.

The hypothesis about when Cervantes decided to divide his story into chapters almost certainly is: there are various indications that the first eighteen chapters originally formed a continuous whole, and that Cervantes only decided on the systematic use of chapter-divisions when on the brink of chapter nineteen. Their insertion in the first eighteen chapters, together with the respective chapter-headings, was evidently done retrospectively, and

---

11 For a general survey of this subject, see the essay by Anderson and Pontón Gijón, in the edn of *DQ* by Rico (1998: pp. clvi–cxci), and the review of criticism by Montero Reguera (1997: 124–33). Much of the critical debate goes back to a seminal essay by Stagg (1959); cf. also Murillo (1975: 72–117) and Flores (1979).

in some cases, quite arbitrarily: for example, the beginning of Chapter 6 is a relative clause ('who was still asleep') dependent on the last sentence of the previous chapter, and the same applies to Grisóstomo's ode (beginning of Chapter 14). It has been argued that the decision to divide the continuous narrative into internal 'parts' was also retrospective (Rico, 2004), though Cervantes may have originally conceived it in that form, which is that of *La Galatea*. However, his pastoral romance, like most other long fiction of the age, is divided in 'libros', books, not 'partes'. *La Galatea* clearly influences his choice of a pastoral episode, based on a theme treated in Book V, to round off internal 'part' two.

I doubt whether Cervantes had any very clear idea precisely where his story was heading or how far it was going when he wrote the early chapters, except that it was intended to satirise chivalric romances, and, in general, imitate their form. In 1920 the great medievalist Menéndez Pidal argued that Cervantes received the original stimulus from an anonymous brief farce, the *Entremés de los romances*, which parodies the contemporary vogue of ballads and shows remarkable similarities to what happens to the hero in his encounter with the merchants of Toledo and its immediate sequel (Chapters 4 and 5). Even if one grants this hypothesis about who influenced whom,[12] it does not alter the fact that the conception of Don Quixote's madness as a means of parodying chivalry books, established in the first three chapters of the novel, goes way beyond its rudimentary equivalent in the *entremés*. Just like one of those books, the story tells of the hero's origins, his resolve to become a knight-errant, his vigil and dubbing, and looks forward to a series of adventures stretching ahead (see, e.g., I, 2; p. 48). As we have already noted, the conception in Chapter 1 of the hero's fervent addiction to this genre, his reading-habits, the features of it which obsessed him, and the precise nature of the confusion in his brain that tipped him into insanity, are fraught with possibilities of future development of which Cervantes clearly had some inkling at a very early stage, since he explicitly anticipates them; they will be fleshed out in the rest of the novel, and are precisely what make this a *novel* rather than a more short-winded piece.

This conception, for which I know no literary precedent, tends by itself to belie another, related hypothesis about Cervantes's evolving view of his story: namely, that it emerged from the chrysalis of what was originally a *novela*, written by him in the early or mid-1590s, then picked up sometime towards

---

[12] Menéndez Pidal's hypothesis is not unproblematic and has been contested. See the retrospective review of the debate in Stagg (2002), and the interesting recent study by Rey Hazas (2006), which supports the hypothesis.

1600, dusted down and expanded. According to this traditional hypothesis, the primitive *novela* would have ended with the burning of the hero's books and walling-up of his library, drastic measures put into effect by the priest, the barber and Don Quixote's housekeeper in early Chapter 7 in an attempt to eliminate the original cause of his madness. However, the abrupt, undignified termination of the first sally in Chapter 5 seems less a confirmation of this theory than a pretext for putting into effect a happy afterthought: the introduction of Sancho. It is with the intention of acting on the innkeeper's advice to him to equip himself with a squire and other necessaries that the hero resolves to return home after the vigil and dubbing (beginning of Chapter 4). Certainly, if the narrative was originally conceived as a short *novela*, it is not at all clear why it should be scattered with loose ends waiting to be picked up and developed in later chapters, nor is it clear where it would have ended, since even while his two friends and the housekeeper are engaged in putting into effect their preventive measures, the patient shows signs – books or no books – of a flare-up of his delirium, and, after a fortnight of relative calm, busies himself with preparations for the new expedition, which include persuading Sancho to accompany him. If the hypothesis about a primitive *novela* were valid, it would seem logical for its conclusion to coincide with the end of internal 'part' one, which instead, by a brilliant stroke of anti-climactic comedy, comes bang in the middle of the hero's battle with the Basque squire, at its most gripping juncture (end of Chapter 8), after the second sally has got well under way. In any event, all hypotheses about a radical overhaul of a primitive draft conflict with the assumption, generally held by the very scholars who advance them (e.g. Stagg, 1959: 347), that Cervantes had careless habits of composition and was very reluctant to revise what he had already written. Since the pattern of the first sally, in which a sequence of violently punishing adventures is brought to an end by a forcible, humiliating return home for a period of rest and recuperation, is repeated by the second sally (I, 7–52), then by the third, which occupies the whole of Part II, it seems more probable that Cervantes envisaged his story from the beginning as the open-ended repetition of the same basic cycle of events.

The scrutiny of Don Quixote's library in Chapter 6 is evidently a comic version of the examination and censure of books by the Spanish Inquisition, which, in the case of books found objectionable, resulted either in their expurgation or outright prohibition. Prohibited books, when found, were regularly burned. Here the priest acts as inquisitorial censor, and the housekeeper, who makes a bonfire of the condemned tomes, is referred to as 'the secular arm', as though they were heretics to be burned at the stake. Her first, naïve reaction on entering the library is to fetch a basin of water and a hissop, treating them as demonically possessed and in need of exorcism.

As the barber picks the books from the shelves and hands them to the priest, the latter passes judgement on each one; taken together, these remarks represent the first instalment of Cervantes's censure of chivalry books in Part I; it is followed by a second in Chapter 32, arising from the innkeeper's revelation of his enthusiasm for them, including a belief, like Don Quixote's, in their historical truth. In this case, the belief is not a matter of madness but of ignorance, which proves obstinately impervious to the priest's reasoned correction. Juan Palomeque's ingenuousness is shared by his daughter's taste for the sentimental love-scenes of the romances, and Maritornes's for their eroticism, and these reactions, depicted with humorous objectivity, are evidently regarded as typical of the lowbrow reading-public. The third and final instalment comes in Chapters 47 and 48, where the canon of Toledo, starting from orthodox neo-classical principles, makes the case against the romances systematically, and outlines an ideal alternative to them (see above, p. 10). These three discussions constitute the novel's theoretical backbone.

The scrutiny in Chapter 6 is notable for various reasons. First, the effervescent wit of the priest's comments, in keeping with the comical extravagance of the entire proceedings, results occasionally in such whimsical exaggeration that it is difficult to perceive the serious intention behind it. The opinion on the chivalry book *Tirante el Blanco* is notoriously inscrutable: it is simultaneously praised as excellent, while its author is said to deserve condemnation to the galleys in perpetuity for '*not* having committed so many absurdities deliberately' (pues no hizo tantas necedades de industria) [my italics]. Secondly, despite the connotations of implacable prosecution of heresy attaching to the scrutiny, the priest's verdicts reveal judicious discrimination and balance, and in one or two cases, enthusiastic appreciation. This is true to a greater or lesser degree of four chivalry books (*Amadís de Gaula, Palmerín de Inglaterra, Tirante el Blanco* and *Belianís de Grecia*), which are considered meritorious and are spared the condemnation attaching to the mass. There is surely no need to take this as a sign of the inconsistency of Cervantes's censure of the genre as a whole, but rather of a capacity to make intelligent discriminations. Thirdly, the books singled out for judgement by the priest represent an odd assortment: not only chivalric romances and books akin to them about the exploits of Charlemagne's paladins, but also sundry Spanish epics, pastoral romances and poetry anthologies, which are treated as distinct from the chivalric genre and, for the most part, praised. The diversity suggests that Cervantes uses the scrutiny of the library partly as a pretext for a general survey of Spanish works of entertainment that lay on the fringes of that genre or caught his attention for personal reasons, such as friendship with the authors. Fourthly, given the date of the completion of composition of *Don Quixote* Part I (1604), the selection reveals some curious omissions: no mention of any book whose first edition comes after 1593, not even Pérez de Hita's extremely popular *Guerras civiles de Granada* (1595) (Civil Wars of Granada) and Lope de Vega's *Arcadia* (1599), which, as a Moorish romance and a pastoral romance respectively, correspond to the types of literature chosen for comment by the priest. This has given rise to speculation, to my mind dubious, that the composition of this chapter, hence the conception of *Don Quixote* itself, preceded 1593.

Internal 'part' two begins with the discovery of Cide Hamete Benengeli's manuscript in Chapter 9, after Cervantes has reported that, to his chagrin, his original sources of information have run out (end of Chapter 8). Now, this again must be deemed a happy afterthought, since the logical place for telling us about this manuscript would be the prologue – where the author of *Amadís de Gaula* informs us about the alleged source of *his* story – or alternatively, the first paragraphs of the opening chapter. The reason why one expects to be told about Benengeli before anything else is that the Moor, after his introduction into the narrative, supposedly provides the evidential basis for all that follows, and underpins the pretence that it is based on facts recorded in contemporary chronicles. I postpone until a later stage (pp. 159–60) the discussion of Chapter 9. Let us simply note at this point that, having solidly established the life and deeds of Don Quixote as the principal subject of his story in this chapter, Cervantes almost immediately veers away from it by introducing the episode of Marcela and Grisóstomo, pastoral in nature, at the end of Chapter 11. It will occupy most of the last three chapters of internal 'part' two, with Vivaldo's ironic interrogation of the hero on the way to Grisóstomo's funeral providing a momentary return to the main theme.

Another theory concerning Cervantes's revision of a primitive draft concerns this particular episode and needs to be mentioned because it has received much support from *cervantistas*. According to it (Stagg, 1959), the Marcela/Grisóstomo episode was originally sited in the middle of Part I, then relocated to its present position. The argument is attractive because it appears to resolve difficulties concerning, first, the anomalous heading of Chapter 10, which refers in part to the contents of Chapter 15 and would thus suggest that these two originally formed a single chapter, and, second, the principal, famous inconsistency of the first Part: Cervantes's failure to mention the theft of Sancho's ass, reported as present near the beginning of Chapter 25, then as missing soon afterwards, with no intervening explanation as to the cause. The beast reappears in Chapter 42 just as mysteriously as it disappeared seventeen chapters previously. In the second edition of *Don Quixote*, Cervantes attempted to put things right by means of opportune insertions in the text, but only managed to compound confusion. Puzzled readers of the first edition had to wait until Sancho's amusing but inadequate explanation in Part II, Chapter 4 of what went wrong and why. However, in accounting quite satisfactorily for these problems, the theory about the relocation of the pastoral episode creates others, including the one that has already been mentioned, and is its premise: Cervantes's endemic aversion to applying Horace's precept about ninefold revision.

To sum up the argument so far, what Cervantes has given us in the first two internal 'parts' of his story, that is, Chapters 1 to 14 inclusive, is a miscellaneous hotch-potch: a brief string of adventures that parody the opening of a knight-errant's career; a satirically burlesque critique of some well-known romances in the form of a jocular inquisitorial tribunal; the spoof discovery of the story's arcane source; a partly ironic, partly tragic pastoral interlude to provide a variation of mood and style from the foregoing. This medley is probably just what he intended, and gives every sign of having been assembled piecemeal. The narrative only seems to head along a definite track towards more distant horizons from Chapter 15 onwards.

The way in which the story evolves from the beginning, and expands from the end of internal 'part' two onwards, exemplifies a fundamental principle of Cervantes's composition, which has two related aspects: first, the repetition of motifs as in a musical fugue, resulting in their variation and enrichment each time they recur; second, variation resulting from the importation of new motifs into the novel from outside it, or their transference from one zone of the novel to another, or from one character to another. This phenomenon is partly explained by *Don Quixote*'s incorporation of the disjointed, reiterative structure common to other primitive story forms (chivalric, Byzantine, the picaresque).[13] It also exhibits something like the substitutions and transformations of fairy tales, which, as Vladimir Propp observed (1984: 82–3), present a limited number of basic functions recurring in multiple variations. The principle may be observed in two major happy afterthoughts: the introduction of Sancho in Chapter 7 and the account of the discovery of Cide Hamete Benengeli's manuscript in Chapter 9, and in various other

---

[13] On this, apart from Bakhtin (1981: 84ff.), see Lázaro Carreter (1972).

ways besides, including the manifold repetition on an expanded scale of the outward-and-return loop established rudimentarily by the first sally.

Before Sancho emerges in Chapter 7, he has been preceded, like the Messiah, by signs and prefigurations. One of them is Pedro Alonso, the neighbour from Don Quixote's village, who discovers him prostrate and delirious on the ground following the ill-fated encounter with the Toledan merchants, and, like the good Samaritan, tends him and bears him home athwart the rump of an ass. His role precisely anticipates that of Sancho in Part I, Chapter 15, after the thrashing that he and his master suffer at the hands of the Galician mule-drovers, save that the destination on this occasion is not home but a roadside inn. Another of these precursors is Don Quixote's niece, who, in Chapter 7, admonishes her uncle with prudent proverbs about the advisability of staying quietly at home, instead of roaming the world in quest of wool with the likelihood of returning shorn. Sancho, near the nadir of his disillusion after the blanketing at the inn, gives his master the benefit of very similar proverbial wisdom in Part I, Chapter 18 (p. 187). However, the character who most nearly plays St John the Baptist to Sancho's Messiah – though in another respect the divine analogy is scarcely apt – is the rascally innkeeper featured in Chapters 2 and 3 of the novel, who, after agreeing to perform the dubbing ceremony, learns that his lunatic protégé has no money on him and promptly gives him a piece of advice: to go no further until he has equipped himself with the necessaries for his journey, which include saddle-bags, a change of shirts, a first-aid kit consisting of a small chest with curative salves, a well-stuffed purse and a squire. Don Quixote promises to comply at the first opportunity. This character's sly precepts contain in embryo, not just Sancho, but several themes closely associated with him that are destined to reverberate in several later chapters of Part I.

The same process of recycling is at work in the emergence of Benengeli. Though the story begins emphatically in the first person (In a village in La Mancha, whose name I do not choose to recall ...), leaving us in no doubt who is really in charge, Cervantes, tongue-in-cheek, subsequently pretends to defer to unspecified 'autores', authors, for his information about the variant versions of the hero's surname (Quijada, Quesada, Quijana), and, like a historian judiciously sifting the available evidence, tells us that the most plausible conjecture points to the last one, Quijana (Chapter 1, pp. 36–7). That is the name used by Pedro Alonso, on the occasion mentioned above. The *autores* vaguely invoked in Chapter 1 later become *the autor desta historia* (the author of this history), who could find nothing more recorded about the doings of Don Quixote, and had to leave the battle with the Basque suspended at its most interesting point (end of Chapter 8). However, the *segundo autor desta obra* – the second author of this work, that is, Cervantes himself – not content to leave matters there, had the good fortune to stumble on Cide Hamete's manuscript in a street-bazaar in Toledo, got it translated by a bilingual Moor, and edited and published the result (Chapter 9). This fiction establishes the trinity of narrators responsible for the rest of the narrative, whose respective roles are more clearly demarcated by this description than they are in practice.

Cervantes's pretence about the authorship complements and mirrors the hero's own make-believe, since, as soon as he embarks on his first sally (Chapter 2), he fantasises about the florid dawn-description with which the future chronicler of his deeds will extol his early morning ride over the plain of Montiel, and addresses to the nameless scribe watching over him an apostrophe in which he begs him not to fail to mention his steed Rocinante, 'eternal companion to me in all my wanderings' (Chapter 2, pp. 46–7). From Don Quixote's fantasy the theme is transmitted to our *segundo autor*, who in early Chapter 9, expresses his perplexity that there should appear to be no more information to be had about his hero, 'since each one of them [i.e. knights-errant] had one or two sages, made to measure, who not only wrote down their deeds, but who depicted their every tiny thought and whim, however recondite'. That statement not only leads immediately into the report of the discovery of Benengeli's manuscript, but also, in an important sense, defines his, and Cervantes's, future attitude to their subject-matter in the novel (see below, pp. 160–62). On later occasions in Part I (Chapter 19, p. 205; Chapter 31, p. 361), the hero will refer again to the beneficent sage watching over him like a guardian angel. For example, he attributes the epithet 'el Caballero de la Triste Figura' (The Knight of the Sorry Countenance), coined for him by Sancho, to the sage's supernatural inspiration. The ironic complementarity of Cervantes's flippant fiction about the story's authorship and his hero's ingenuous assumption about a sage chronicler will merge in Part II and become a fundamental feature of it.

We need to keep in mind this twin-faceted principle of composition – that is, repetition with variations, transference of motifs from zone A to zone B – since it is fundamental to the characterisation of Don Quixote and Sancho.

Literary Stylisation versus Common Nature

I take the phrase 'common nature' from the canon of Toledo's splendid invective against chivalry books in Part I, Chapter 49 (p. 562), where he says that he would throw even the best of them into the fire for being 'fuera del trato que pide la común naturaleza' (outside the bounds of common nature).

What he means by the phrase is exemplified by the priest's judgement on
Tirante el Blanco in the scrutiny of Don Quixote's library (I, 6; p. 83):

> Dígoos verdad, señor compadre, que por su estilo es este el mejor libro
> del mundo: aquí comen los caballeros, y duermen y mueren en sus camas,
> y hacen testamento antes de su muerte, con estas cosas de que todos los
> demás libros deste género carecen.

> I tell you, kinsman, that after its fashion this is a splendid book: here
> knights eat and sleep and die in their beds, and make their wills before
> dying, with other such things lacking in other books of this genre.

The words have thematic significance in *Don Quixote*, which begins by
describing what the hero ate and wore on weekdays and weekends, and ends
by telling how he died in bed and made his will before dying. They are specifically recalled by the scribe's comments on the manner of his death. Thus,
Cervantes's critical attitude to the fabulous implausibility of chivalry books
leads him ironically to highlight the normal, banal nature of Don Quixote's
world, and thus to discover a revolutionary kind of literary representation, focused on homely ordinariness. It is the very opposite of the typical
emphasis on extraordinary degradation in contemporary picaresque novels,
and is superbly exemplified by the hero's parochial routine of life, as depicted
in the first chapter, and by the characters of his family and friends: the silly
housekeeper fussing over her master like a hen over an errant chick; the
ploddingly sensible niece; the merry, judicious village-priest and his friend
the barber; the mischievous, cocksure graduate Sansón Carrasco. These are
the ancestors of similar groups in the great English novels of the eighteenth
century: Fielding's *Joseph Andrews*, Sterne's *Tristram Shandy*, Smollett's *The
Expedition of Humphrey Clinker*.

Yet Cervantes's attention to 'common nature' in *Don Quixote*, though
persistent, is not systematic. First, though not absent from his romantic, heroic
or tragic fiction, represented by the novel's interludes, it is not a predominant
tendency of them, for reasons considered in the previous chapter. Secondly,
even in a comic context, it contends and blends with a quite different tendency,
pinpointed by the French Hispanist Maxime Chevalier in the following
comment about the 'realism' of the comic folk-tales of the Spanish Golden
Age, which he extends to its comic literature in general:

> It was not, and could not be, that of the methodical observation and system-
> atic reconstruction of reality ... the method of Flaubert, the Goncourts,
> Galdós, that is, of men nourished by positivism ... The realism which pulses

in the pages of the picaresque novel and Cervantine fiction is second-degree realism, which constantly refers to commonly admitted truths enshrined in popular tales. It ... had a long life in Western literature and was perfectly effective, since it seduced intelligent minds of the nineteenth century into seeing the picaresque as the legitimate ancestor of contemporary Spanish literature's depiction of social customs.[14]

Though one may quibble about whether realism in *Don Quixote* is primarily mediated by folk-tales, the observation that it is mainly one of second degree is incontestable, despite the fact that the psychological, social and geographic world that Cervantes pits against his hero's illusions is more 'realistic', by nineteenth-century criteria, than anything to be found in the works of his contemporaries. Cervantes's commitment to 'common nature' set him firmly on the road that would eventually lead to Flaubert, the Goncourts and Galdós, but he travelled only part of the way along it.

This is very evident in Cervantes's representation of the inns of Part I, particularly the first. According to the black legend about inns perpetuated by Spanish folklore, they are places of wretched discomfort and ludicrous mishap, where the innkeeper, an ex-thief, is a purveyor both of ribald badinage and of the proverbial cat masquerading as hare, the hostess is typically an ex-prostitute driven by the necessity of age to practise a less active profession, and the daughter is a teasing siren who entices male travellers to lodge at the inn, without, however, going to bed with them (Joly, 1982: part II). In the two inns portrayed in Part I – the first in Chapters 2–3, and the second in Chapters 16–17 and 32–46 – Cervantes freely modifies these stereotypes, and in respect of the second inn, greatly refines them, yet their influence is still plainly discernible. So, the first innkeeper, introduced as 'no less a thief than Cacchus, nor less given to pranks than a page well versed in his office' (I, 2; p. 51), confirms these credentials by his *curriculum vitae* and by his unremittingly jocose and burlesque attitude to his insane guest. The sketch of his former 'chivalric' exploits that he offers Don Quixote as justification for assuming the role of patron in the dubbing ceremony establishes him as an archetypal *pícaro*, who has frequented every corner of the 'picaresque map of Spain', that is, visited all its legendary red-light districts, criminal ghettoes and other places of ill repute, and is expert in all the associated malpractices (I, 3; pp. 55–6). For Cervantes, these haunts are associated with the picaresque genre, and specifically with its classic, *Guzmán de Alfarache*.[15] At the same time, the CV's ironic form as the recapitulation of a heroic chivalric

14 For the original Spanish text, Chevalier (1978: 152).
15 See, e.g., *La ilustre fregona*, in *Novelas*, ed. García López, pp. 372–5.

career, in which its protagonist 'had exercised the nimbleness of his feet and the dexterity of his hands, done many wrongs, wooed many widows, and deflowered not a few damsels', carries clear echoes of Fra Cipolla's burlesque sermon to a rustic congregation on the supposedly legendary places that he passed through on his pilgrimage to the Holy Land, and of the long list of bogus miracle-working relics that he saw there (*Decameron* VI, 10). Among the other literature and folklore recalled by those early inn-scenes are: folk-tales, farce, Fernando de Rojas's *La Celestina*, various hoaxes of Boccaccio's *Decameron* besides Fra Cipolla's, above all, the first part of *Guzmán de Alfarache* (1599), which treats squalid inns as the site of initiation of the *pícaro*'s delinquent career, and in so doing, establishes a precedent exploited not just by the picaresque novelists who follow Mateo Alemán, but also, in a different way, by Cervantes in *Don Quixote*.[16] The reality that is opposed to Don Quixote's illusion by that first inn is thus, in a very full sense, realism of the second degree.

The ingredients that go into the conception of the second inn at which the hero stays are just as dense and seamlessly compressed as those of the first, and in Chapters 16 and 17, derived mostly from the same sources. However, Cervantes offers a more particularised and nuanced portrait of the inn's personnel than before: for example, by the already noted differentiation of the reactions to the reading of chivalry books by the innkeeper, his wife, the daughter and Maritornes (I, 32). Furthermore, he transforms the inn of traditional stereotype by borrowing from contemporary comedy its characteristically two-tier contrast between a serious romantic plot and the parodic counterpoint to it provided by the servants. One finds it in almost all his own *Ocho comedias*, and also in contemporary comedies by Lope de Vega, including those like *La noche toledana* (Night in Toledo) or *La ilustre fregona* (The Illustrious Inn-Maid), which use an inn setting for part of the action.

Of course, the serious romantic plot in Chapter 16 exists only in the imagination of the bruised and battered knight, who, lying on his wretched pallet in the inn's hay-loft, feverishly imagines that he is in a castle, that his wounds have been tended by the chatelain's wife and their fair daughter, and that the daughter is so smitten with him that she intends to come to his bed that night, emulating (among other precedents) Elisena's nocturnal visit to the bed of King Perión, from whose coupling Amadís is born. Meanwhile, in the real world, the hideously deformed Maritornes, who is the inn's skivvy, and so promiscuous that she would never fail to keep a vow such as this, has

---

16 On this, see Joly (1982: 333–7), also Close (2000: 40, note).

promised to lie with a Moorish mule-drover that night, whose bed happens to be adjacent to the hero's. Don Quixote, for whom make-believe is reality, intercepts Maritornes on the way to her paramour, believing her to be the fair chatelain's daughter, and mentally transforms each of the wench's coarse physical attributes into its opposite: the glass beads on her wrists into precious oriental pearls, the hair like a horse's mane into delicate strands of purest Arabian gold, the breath that stinks of rotten cold meat into delicate aromatic perfume, and so on. Cervantes gets the idea of this idealising transformation of a repulsive slut into a radiantly beautiful heroine, together with that of the chaotic general mêlée triggered by Don Quixote's error, from the short stories of Bandello.[17]

At this stage of the novel, the two-tier division of the action is merely potential. However, from Chapter 32 onwards, the potential is fulfilled, and romantic novelas are systematically interleaved with the hero's comic doings, including his ill-fated flirtation with Maritornes and the innkeeper's daughter (Chapter 43), in which he is left suspended by his wrist from the aperture of the hay-loft. Nothing better illustrates the hybrid nature of Cervantes's novel, poised between comic farce and serious romance, than his partial transformation of Juan Palomeque's inn in the latter half of Part I. Even while making it conserve the associations of the traditional black legend, he turns it into an equivalent of the magic castles or palaces of pastoral and chivalric romance where love's maladies are cured.

Though in the depiction of the first inn, traditional stereotypes easily outweigh 'common nature', the balance is restored to some extent by the adventures in open country. This is related to Cervantes's need to invent encounters that might plausibly stimulate his hero's fantasy by their resemblance to those in chivalry books, as well as to the critical impulse to seek a deflatingly likely explanation for them. The two factors are clearly at work in Don Quixote's first adventure as an armed knight (Chapter 4), where Cervantes anticipates the ambivalent strategy of initial presentation that he will adopt in the famous five adventures clustered from Chapters 18 to 22 inclusive: the battles with the sheep and with the funeral cortège (Chapters 18–19), the discovery of the fulling-mills (20), the capture of the barber's basin (21), the liberation of the galley-slaves (22).

Hearing piteous cries, Don Quixote rides into a wood, and sees, tied to a tree, a lad of about fifteen being lashed by a burly man with his belt. To the hero, these outward appearances naturally augur a chivalric adventure, and

---

[17] See Bandello, *Novelle*, Part II, *novella* 47; cf. also II, 11, in the edn by Flora (1952).

he assumes without further ado that this is a grievous wrong that needs to be righted. However, the more we find out about the case, the less well founded this view proves to be (cf. Redondo, 1998: 307–23). The hero's arrogant challenge to the man, confusedly perceived now as a knight and now as a *villano* (peasant, churl), elicits the meek explanation that the boy has charge of a flock of sheep and is being punished for negligence: he loses them at the rate of one a day. Against that, the boy, Andrés, alleges that the beating is just an excuse for his master's refusal to pay his wage-arrears: nine months at seven *reales* monthly. However, he does not deny the loss of the sheep. The boy's carelessness or dishonesty – the two possibilities are left open – induces one to compare him with the dishonest shepherds of Cervantes's *El coloquio de los perros*, who spend their day delousing themselves, mending their sandals and giving tuneless renderings of ditties like 'Cata el lobo do va Juanica' (See where the wolf runs Joanie), while at night they prey on the very flock that they are meant to guard. In this *novela*, the brutal reality of country life is ironically contrasted with the idyllic, sentimentalised picture of it offered by pastoral romances. In the chapter of *Don Quixote* something similar happens: the stereotypes of chivalric fiction are mocked by being measured specifically against a slice of 'common nature'. The level of Andrés's wages, Juan Haldudo's claim that the cost of two blood-lettings and three pairs of shoes should be deducted from them, his demeanour before Don Quixote, at first cowed, later shifty and evasive – all this would have seemed to contemporary readers drawn from life, and, given the circumstances, they would not have regarded the summary whipping of the servant as outrageous.

Mid-way through the dialogue the peasant's initial meekness turns to evasiveness and mockery (clearly he doubts his adversary's sanity), while the boy takes alarm at Don Quixote's rash confidence in the peasant's promise to pay the debt as soon as he can return home for the money. Don Quixote declares superbly: 'My mere command is enough to ensure his respect; provided that he swears to pay by the order of knighthood he has received, I will let him go free and will guarantee the payment.' After he rides off, the peasant, having been humiliated before his servant, naturally thirsts for revenge, but first he savours the moment by unctuously inviting him to come so that he may be paid what he is owed. The description of how he is tied to a tree and left for dead is laconic. When, much later (end of I, 31), Andrés runs into Don Quixote again, he heaps reproaches on his self-imagined liberator, humiliating him before his friends, the priest and barber, and tells him what would have happened had he not intervened. After a few more blows, his rage spent, Juan Haldudo would have untied his servant and paid him. The lessons of the adventure are paradigmatic in *Don Quixote*: the folly of trying to drive out

Nature with a pitchfork (Horace, *Epistles* I, x, 24), of judging by appearances, of meddling where one is not called. They are also mediated by folklore: first, by the traditional stereotype of the sly, deceitful peasant; secondly, by Aesopic fables about not trusting the fair words of rogues; thirdly, by the brutal initiation in human perfidy suffered by young Lazarillo, in the first chapter or *tratado* of *Lazarillo de Tormes*, when invited by the blind man to place his head against the stone bull of Salamanca. Cervantes underscores the caustic effect of his satire by leaving the chief dupe, Don Quixote, immune to this awakening.

Compared with other adventures along the road, the one just discussed is unusually specific in its reference to social circumstances. In some of the later ones, the enraged or panic-stricken reactions of Don Quixote's adversaries, or their non-human nature, preclude the dialogue that elicits the informative allegations and counter-claims of Juan Haldudo and Andrés. In others, the reactions to him take the form of mockery of what he says and does, rather than of self-revelation. In all cases, however, the clarification of who or what his imagined adversaries really are, whether offered by them or by Cervantes as narrator, are sufficient, however brief, to place them firmly in the sphere of 'common nature': that is, to assign them to a realistic social context and sketch the outlines of their individual history. They achieve the effect all the more because the hero's vivid yet false suppositions stimulate the reader's imagination to fill in the blanks. This is, I think, what Flaubert was getting at in his comment on 'those roads of Spain that one sees everywhere in *Don Quixote* though they are nowhere described'.[18]

For example, we are told that the retinue of merchants on horseback intercepted by the hero in Chapter 4, and peremptorily commanded to confess that the Empress Dulcinea del Toboso is the most beautiful damsel in the world, are on their way from Toledo to Murcia to buy silk. The detail, though cursorily mentioned, is eloquent; it marks them as frequent travellers along this road and implies something about their daily life. Murcia was the principal silk-producing region of Spain; Toledo was a busy mercantile city, known for its manufacture of textiles and swords, and was connected by the Tagus to Lisbon. We have another example of this suggestiveness in Part I, Chapter 8. Don Quixote sees a couple of Benedictine friars, mounted on huge mules, and equipped with face-masks and parasols – normal protective gear for travellers – to shield them from the dust and sun, and a little way behind them a coach with an escort of riders and lackeys, which is a sign that the

---

[18] Quoted in Canavaggio (2005: 148).

occupant is of noble status. Whereas Don Quixote assumes the friars are enchanters abducting a princess, we learn that they have nothing to do with the coach behind them, bearing a lady from the Basque country to Seville to join her husband, just appointed to a prestigious office in the Indies. The prosperous sea-port of Seville was the main embarcation point for trans-Atlantic journeys; ships would sail from there in convoy bearing travellers and merchandise; one such traveller is Juan Pérez de Viedma, whose career resembles that of the husband of the Basque lady. In the course of his reunion with his brother Ruy Pérez in *Don Quixote* I, 42, we learn that he has just been appointed to the Supreme Court in Mexico, and is travelling to Seville with his eighteen-year-old daughter, Clara, to join the fleet, due to sail in one month's time. Since the ex-captive has just told his lengthy story, we are left wondering about his brother's. What else –apart from studying law at Salamanca – did he do in the twenty-two years since leaving the parental home? What became of him in Mexico? How was Doña Clara's liaison to Don Luis eventually resolved? *Don Quixote* keeps prompting questions like these.

In his choice of the physical background – the settings of the adventures and the objects and animals on which Quixotic fantasies are projected – Cervantes is guided partly by likelihood and partly by symbolic associations. The craggy solitudes of the Sierra Morena are a real, inhospitable place and, traditionally, the kind of romantic setting for meetings with despairing lovers. The fulling-mills discovered by master and servant in the foothills of the *sierra* (I, 20) served, in that textile-producing region, to clean the raw material for the weavers and dyers and make it workable, though the idea of that encounter was also suggested by the word *batanear*, to pummel someone physically or morally, an idea evocative of the hero's blind insistence. The windmills featured in the hero's most famous adventure (I, 8) were introduced quite late in the sixteenth century, but by the time Don Quixote was published, had become familiar landmarks. Yet they also have symbolic significance, since, as Sancho points out, windmills connote wind in the head. In the case of the sheep mistaken for armies (I, 18), realism intertwines with literary reminiscences. The plains of La Mancha were frequently traversed by flocks on their seasonal migrations from the uplands around Cuenca southwards towards Murcia. At the same time, the encounter may also echo Sophocles' tragedy *Ajax*, where the hero, driven mad by Minerva, slaughters a flock of sheep imagining them to be his enemies of the house of Atraeus, then, coming to his senses, is overcome by shame and kills himself.

In the adventures that involve dialogue between Don Quixote and his adversaries, the reactions of the latter are not just conditioned by the demands of parody but also by the influence of the comic types of literature and folklore.

Since we will come across several examples in the galley-slaves adventure (below, pp. 79–87), there is no need to offer any at this stage.

Empathetic Parody

In relation to other burlesque styles of that age, the distinguishing feature of Cervantine parody in *Don Quixote* is its internal and complicit relationship to its target. Besides affirming his intention to overhaul and renew rather than destroy the chivalric genre (I, 47–48), Cervantes assiduously cultivates throughout his career types of prose fiction more or less akin to it: his pastoral romance *La Galatea*, his Byzantine epic *Persiles y Sigismunda*, numerous romantic novelas and interpolated stories featuring courtly characters. His mockery of the chivalric genre therefore stems from an insider's empathy with it. Hence, in *Don Quixote*, he portrays a madly serious and ingeniously inventive hero who is intimately familiar with it, and who embroiders his imitation of it with echoes of a host of other more or less kindred genres, rendering all this absurd not so much by the degraded nature of his behaviour as by its exuberant excess, as well as by his own physical inadequacy for the role and the incongruity of the chosen stage. Hence too Cervantes's frequent tendency to use scenes of his own romantic fiction and its characteristic styles as the implicit model on which to base Don Quixote's adventures and his typically florid, high-flown discourse. This is a feature of his writing in *Don Quixote* that is not often remarked, yet it has important implications for other aspects of the novel.

Here is an example of it: a passage that comes after the capture of the barber's basin and the ensuing discussion between master and squire; it contains still-lingering echoes of the altercation between them provoked by the discovery of the fulling-mills (I, 21; p. 228):

> Y luego, habilitado con este permiso, hizo *mutatio capparum y puso su asno a las mil lindezas, dejándole mejorado en tercio y quinto*. Hecho esto, almorzaron de *las sobras del real que del acémila despojaron*, bebieron del agua del arroyo de los batanes, sin volver la cara a mirallos; tal era el aborrecimiento que les tenían, por el miedo en que les habían puesto. *Cortada, pues, la cólera, y aun la malenconía*, subieron a caballo, y sin tomar determinado camino, por ser muy de caballeros andantes el no tomar ninguno cierto, *se pusieron a caminar por donde la voluntad de Rocinante quiso, que se llevaba tras sí la de su amo, y aun la del asno*, que siempre le seguía por dondequiera que guiaba, en buen amor y compañía. Con todo esto volvieron al camino real, y siguieron por él a la ventura, sin otro disignio alguno.

With this authorisation, Sancho performed the robe-changing ceremony, which left the ass as pretty as you like, enriched with the lion's share of the other one's estate. After that, they made a picnic from the left-overs of the booty got by the raid on the funeral cortège, and drank from the stream that flowed by the fulling-mills, without turning to look at them, such was their detestation of them because of the fear they had provoked. With pangs of hunger appeased and gloom dispelled, they mounted, and without heading in any particular direction, because knights-errant rarely did, they rode wherever Rocinante might lead, since his will ruled his master's and also that of the ass, always ready to follow the nag in good and loving fellowship. And so they returned to the highway, and followed it taking pot-luck, without any definite destination in mind.

The narrative is sprinkled with jests, some less apparent in translation than in the original,[19] where they are marked with italics: the comparison of Sancho's despoliation of the country barber's ass with the ritual changing of robes by Roman cardinals at Easter, and with the right of testators to leave over a third of the estate to favoured heirs; the use of a military metaphor – the plundering of a military camp – to refer to the seizure of the provisions of the funeral cortège; the play with the set phrase 'cortada la cólera', to cut or check the excess of the choleric humour by eating something, which permits, by the juxtaposition of *cólera* with *malenconía* (melancholy), the insinuation of another sense of *cólera*, anger; the ironic placing of Don Quixote and the two animals on the same level, emphasised by the rhyme of *amo* (master) and *asno*. Much of the verbal humour serves to bring out the underlying comedy of the exaggerated, still-smarting effect upon master and squire of the discovery of the fulling-mills. We are very far from the tragic pathos of the preamble to Book I, Chapter 21 of *Persiles*, which, however, is linked in various respects to the one just discussed, serving essentially as a bridge

---

[19] I shall return to this point in Chapter 5. By way of comparison with my own effort, here is how the passage is translated by John Rutherford, whose translation of *DQ* in Penguin is, I think, the best available in modern English (Penguin edition, p. 170):

'And now that he'd been granted official permission, he performed the *mutatio capparum* [footnote reference inserted] and refurbished his donkey, a very great change for the better. Then they breakfasted on the left-overs of the camp-provisions plundered from the priests' supply-mule, and they drank from the stream that powered the fulling-mill, taking care not to look in that direction, so great was the loathing inspired by the fear it had struck into them. Once they'd dulled the pangs of hunger, and even the pangs of melancholy, they mounted, and not taking any particular direction, as is appropriate for knights-errant, their progress was dictated by Rocinante's will, which carried along with it that of his master, and even that of the ass, which always followed wherever Rocinante went, in love and good fellowship.'

between one significant event and another, and covering the same topics in the same order, without, of course, a hint of humour. The pilgrims think back painfully to the recent adversity; a mood of friendship and a shared meal restore their morale; they set sail without setting any definite course, putting themselves at the mercy of fortune.[20]

Cervantes's facility for transposing passages originally written in a serious key into a comic one, or vice-versa, is demonstrated by the virtuoso set-pieces of florid rhetoric in Part I, all uttered by the hero: the dawn-description in Chapter 2 (pp. 46–7); the Golden Age speech (I, 11; pp. 121–3); the praise of Dulcinea's physical charms (I, 13; pp. 141–2); the description of the two imaginary armies (I, 18; pp. 190–3), the apostrophe to the sylvan creatures and spirits (I, 25; pp. 278–9); the imaginary adventure of the Knight of the Lake (I, 50; pp. 569–71). Cervantes may say of that dawn-description that the hero is imitating the style of chivalry books; in fact, the soliloquy is a congested pastiche of the tropes used in similar passages in *La Galatea*.[21] He makes the same assertion about the description of the two armies; yet the second half of it is a clear parody of the description of Turnus' host in Virgil's *Aeneid*.[22] The Golden Age speech is an eclectic medley of umpteen precedents in Ancient and Renaissance literature (Stagg, 1985), including a poignant soliloquy by Aurelio, hero of Cervantes's play *El trato de Argel*.[23] As this example shows, in writing such parody, he is capable of drawing indiscriminately on his own works and those of other, admired authors; and he probably saw little difference between the two sources, since in both he is conscious of dealing in elegant, conventionalised topics, characteristic of a certain kind of literary context rather than of a particular writer.[24] Common to all the above-mentioned passages is his ambivalently intimate relationship to the target texts; one can sense him savouring the familiar literary clichés, yet, conscious of their triteness, he mocks them by pouring them out with lush and precious excess.

---

[20] *Persiles*, ed. Schevill and Bonilla, vol. i, p. 137.

[21] On this see Close (1985: 91–4).

[22] Book VII, ll. 641ff.

[23] *Comedias y entremeses*, vol. v, pp. 53–5.

[24] So, when Don Quixote offers his hyperbolical description of Dulcinea's charms: hair like gold, forehead like Elysian fields, and so on, he characterises them as 'los imposibles y quiméricos atributos de belleza que los poetas dan a sus damas' (I, 13; p. 141) (the impossible and chimerical attributes of beauty that poets ascribes to their ladies). In a serious context, the hero of the novela *El amante liberal* accompanies a very similar, if less exuberant, description of Leonisa's beauty with an acknowledgement that it was a common object of praise by poets, without describing the praise as chimerical and impossible (*Novelas*, ed. García López, pp. 113–14).

Empathetic parody involves the naturalisation of the hero's style and the broadening of its range, a result to which the introduction of Sancho in Chapter 7 contributes by making Don Quixote's language more natural, supple and idiomatic (see below, pp. 110–13). The chivalric archaisms, formulae and quotations that spattered his discourse in the first five chapters of Part I diminish in the rest of it; at the same time, the scope of his imitation becomes much more eclectic, absorbing a host of elevated styles and topics, some more or less akin to chivalry books, such as pastoral, epic, history, ballads, Ariosto's *Orlando furioso*, and others unrelated to them, including the Bible, various lyric poets, Aristotle and other classic authors, themes of Renaissance humanism, learned anecdotes and sayings, and so on. Furthermore, his discourse intertwines or collides with registers of very different origin – ruffian's slang, coarse oaths, notarial and commercial jargon – sometimes articulated by other characters, at other times, disconcertingly, by him. The bewildering breadth of reference is illustrated by his proposal to enact a penance for Dulcinea in the Sierra Morena (I, 25; pp. 274–87), unfolded with the following repertoire of wit and erudition: an elegant exposition of the Renaissance doctrine of literary imitation; Aristotle's concept of poetic universality; rehearsal of the precedents of his penance in *Amadis* and *Orlando furioso*; echoes of Albanio's farewell to the natural world in Garcilaso's Second Eclogue; satire of the indecipherable script of scribes, the affectations of love-poets, the faking of lineages; the amusingly vulgar anecdote of the merry widow and her lover; an edifying maxim about the nature of true love, adduced to justify the choice of low-born Aldonza as mistress; the drafting of two letters, one to Dulcinea couched in the archaic convolutions of chivalric novels, the other authorising the gift of three donkey-foals to Sancho in the wooden jargon of commercial bills of sale. Though the effect is absurd, the range of reference is dazzling in its scope, and latent seriousness is perceptible in the absurdity. Thus, the doctrine of imitation is central to Cervantes's own theory of the epic romance (*Don Quixote* I, 47–48); Garcilaso, though unwittingly parodied by Don Quixote, is Cervantes's favourite poet; that same maxim about true love is cited with perfect seriousness by the priest in urging Don Fernando to take Dorotea, a mere commoner, as his wife (I, 36; p. 431; cf. I, 25; p. 285).

Empathetic parody affects not just style, but the handling of the adventures: their settings, their anti-climactic irony; the narrator's and reader's viewpoint. From the outset, Cervantes shows a tendency, as narrator of *Don Quixote*, to harmonise his style closely with the thoughts and typical turns of phrase of his hero, in a way that comes near to 'style indirect libre'; by this means he creates the illusion of citing what the hero says or thinks while signalling ironic detachment from it. So, in the first chapter, we find numerous expressions like 'he would say to himself that', 'it seemed to him that', couched in a style that both mimics Don Quixote's self-satisfied make-believe and mocks it. This complicity is related to his strategy of presentation of the hero's adventures, which is an ironic equivalent of the means employed in his romantic fiction to maximise the illusion of dramatic immediacy. A good example of it is the way the reader is drawn into the interwoven and interrelated stories of Cardenio and Dorotea, which are developed by a series of partial instalments, separated by interruptions, from Chapter 23 to Chapter 36. Don Quixote is directly involved in the initial stages of this process.

In his romantic fiction Cervantes tends, at various stages of the story's unfolding plot, to identify implicitly with the perceptions of one or other of the characters, who typically becomes involved in events as an interested outsider, without being privy to the background,[25] and serves, in effect, as a kind of proxy for the reader, creating the illusion that reading is equivalent to direct observation. This witness becomes curious about some tantalising feature of the protagonist's behaviour, indicative of harrowing affliction or of having undergone a remarkable experience, and incites him or her to tell the story which lies behind these mysterious appearances. It is in just this way that we are introduced to Cardenio's misfortunes (Chapters 23–24), and, in the first instance, Don Quixote is the witness whose perceptions and reactions serve as a guide to ours. It is he who first spots the half-rotten suitcase lying on the ground in the wilds of the Sierra Morena, tells Sancho to investigate the contents, correctly guesses that the author of the notebook is an unhappy lover of noble status, and identifies him with the savage, ragged figure leaping from crag to crag, whose appearance he notes in graphic detail. At this stage, there is no suggestion that his impressions are tainted by madness; one reason why he is treated as an apt witness in this case is his temperamental curiosity about anything that smacks of romantic adventure, coupled to his affinity with this particular character (see below, pp. 73–74). It is he, moreover, who gets preliminary but limited information about Cardenio from a goat-herd, then comes face to face with him, and hears the first part of his story from his own lips.

However, Don Quixote's mad obsession with chivalry books eventually blocks his access to the full facts of the case (end of Chapter 24), and the role of principal witness then passes to the priest, who meets Cardenio in

---

[25] On this, Close (2000: 68–9, 168–9), and, in greater detail, Close (1990).

another part of the *sierra* and hears the second instalment of the story from him (I, 27). Cardenio has hardly finished recounting it, when he, the priest and the barber encounter Dorotea and hear *her* story (beginning of I, 28); as it unfolds, Cardenio discovers its vital connection with his own, to which it adds important new information. He learns that their misfortunes stem from the same cause, the perfidious Don Fernando, who first seduced Dorotea under a vow of marriage, then, tiring of this rich farmer's daughter, became infatuated with Cardenio's fiancée, Luscinda, and, taking advantage of his ducal rank and betraying Cardenio's friendship, secretly betrothed himself to her. Later, in Chapter 36, the priest observes the crisis as it is played out and resolved. It is triggered by the unexpected reunion of Cardenio and Dorotea with Don Fernando and Luscinda at Juan Palomeque's inn; the reunion involves a dramatic moment of recognition (*anagnorisis*), the most memorable scene of this kind in Cervantes's fiction.

At first the four characters are unaware of their proximity to each other, but then masks or veils slip from faces, Cardenio hears Luscinda's voice and emerges from an inner room, and they are all left staring at each other. This is the prelude to the confrontation between Dorotea and Fernando, in which she, by her skilful pleading, persuades him to fulfil his original vow of marriage to her and leave Luscinda to Cardenio. In this dénouement the priest takes an active role as mediator, and it is typical of many others in Cervantine fiction, where lovers are restored to each other, lost status is recovered, family-bonds are retied and parental origins revealed, amid tears of rejoicing and the benign approval of the witnesses, whose status and moral authority imply society's blessing on the outcome.

We are thus led, as in a Who Dun It, via a chain of clues and revelations, not completed until the mutual recognition between Cardenio, Dorotea, Luscinda and Fernando in I, 36, to an increasingly complete grasp of the interlocking parts of the affair, and each link is interpreted from the viewpoint of a witness more qualified than the previous ones to obtain the information, either because of greater perceptiveness, or more direct involvement. In this graduated approach to the whole truth, the increasing engagement of the witnesses stands implicitly for that of the reader. They are proxies for us within the fiction; the keenness of their interest and insight represents ours. Although, so far as concerns the interpolated tales of *Don Quixote* Part I, the process is most fully and systematically exemplified by the interlinked stories of Cardenio and Dorotea; it is also observable, to a significant extent, in the ex-captive's story (Chapters 39–42) and that told by Doña Clara (Chapter 43).

In the mock-chivalric adventures of the mad *hidalgo* Cervantes exploits the method for comic effect by inverting it. The phenomena, as they initially appear to him and are presented to the reader, fire the hero's expectation of adventure and invite investigation of their true cause. However, as we have already seen in the encounter with Andrés and Juan Haldudo (pp. 49–51 above), the clues and signs are deceptive and provoke him to jump to false conclusions; further enquiry into them is conducted on a basis of comic crossed-purposes and obstinate casuistry; and the final discovery brings bathetic anti-climax, which Don Quixote typically blames on enchantment. As in Cervantes's romantic fiction, there is tantalising inflation of the balloon of suspense, but the objective is ironic, and empathetic parody is essentially involved in the process. The adventure of the fulling-mills is a good example of it.

The setting in which he and Sancho find themselves at the beginning of Part I, Chapter 20, after going further into the *sierra* in search of water, is eerily suggestive: a wood of tall trees with leaves rustling softly in the breeze, a dark and moonless night, and from somewhere nearby the mighty crash of a cascade, accompanied by dreadful pounding and creaking of chains 'que les aguó el contento del agua' (p. 208) (which cast a wet blanket over their joy at finding water). But Don Quixote 'with his intrepid heart, leapt on Rocinante, and clasping his shield, tilted his lance and ...' (acompañado de su intrépido corazón, saltó sobre Rocinante, y embrazando su rodela, terció su lanzón, y ...) launched into a pompously self-glorifying speech. Cervantes's empathetic method is well illustrated by the words just quoted; the hero's actions are painted just as he would wish. Moreover, Cervantes's description of the physical setting has a vividness unmatched by any comparable passage in his serious works of fiction, let alone in chivalric romances, even though Don Quixote's situation here resembles the preamble to Amadís's battle with a monster in *Amadís de Gaula*, Chapter 73. In fact, the details of Cervantes's description are modelled on his own pastoral romance, *La Galatea*, where thick woods often serve as the scene of some dramatic event or else as sympathetic backdrop for the shepherds' sufferings, enhanced by moonlight, flowers, soft breezes. While the wood described in *Don Quixote* I, 20 lacks these soothing charms, it nonetheless shares with those of *La Galatea* a function dictated by the so-called pathetic fallacy: that of harmonising with the characters' sentiment, which in this case is exaggerated fear. The atmosphere conjured here is spookily sombre; only the casual pun: 'que les aguó el contento del agua' betrays the ironic intention behind it.

Cervantes's empathetic method is shown not just by his style and attitude as narrator, but also by the knight's above-mentioned speech. Since it is long, I quote it in abridged form (I, 20; pp. 208–9):

Bien notas, escudero fiel y legal, las tinieblas desta noche, su estraño silencio, el sordo y confuso estruendo destos árboles, el temeroso ruido de aquella agua en cuya busca venimos, que parece que se despeña y derrumba desde los altos montes de la Luna, y aquel incesable golpear que nos hiere y lastima los oídos, las cuales cosas todas juntas y cada una por sí son bastantes a infundir miedo, temor y espanto en el pecho del mesmo Marte, cuanto más aquel que no está acostumbrado a semejantes acontecimientos y aventuras.

Well do you mark, my good and faithful squire, the darkness of this night, its strange silence, the muffled and confused din of these trees, the roar of that water in search of which we come, apparently precipitating itself and crashing down from the high mountains of the moon, and that incessant pounding which pierces and afflicts our ears, all of which, taken separately and together, is sufficient to strike fear, dread and horror in Mars himself, let alone anyone unused to such hazardous adventures.

Here, the knight echoes the very circumstances mentioned by the narrator in his setting of the scene. So, apparently the hero's speech and the narrator's presentation are in harmony with each other; the intrepid response is equal to the sinisterness of the surroundings. However, there is a considerable amount of stylistic touching up. The general effect of grandiloquence achieved by solemn and sonorous vocabulary, amplification of circumstances, artful internal rhymes, and so on, is compounded by notes of high pomposity and absurd arrogance: the description of Sancho with epithets normally applied to scribes in legal documents ('fiel y legal', true and trusty), the pretentious references to Mars and the mountains of the moon, and above all, the speech's opening – not quoted above – with its triumphant first-person fanfare (I was born to ... I am ... I am) and announcement of Don Quixote's destined revival of an age of gold in the present age of iron. This echoes both Virgil's fourth eclogue and chivalry books where similar portentous forecasts are made; but the effect is ruined by the fact that here it is the hero himself who makes it – boastfulness condemned by his own precept: 'la alabanza propria envilece' (self-praise is demeaning; I, 16; p. 170). The speech carries forward his eccentric version of the history of chivalry and of his own place in it (Chapters 5, 11 and 13), which treats the mythic Golden Age and the legends of the Round Table as historical fact.

Amadís's squire, Gandalín, on hearing his master's resolve to do battle with the monster in the above-mentioned chapter of *Amadís de Gaula*, bursts into tears and begs him to desist. Sancho does likewise here, but unlike Gandalín, is primarily concerned to save his own skin. His response is a travesty of the rhetoric of entreaty by virtue of the baseness and spuriousness of the motives: e.g., nobody will be any the wiser if we take another road; I shall die if you leave me here; I left wife and children to better my lot and now you do *this* to me. Here begins the long process of deflating the balloon of suspense created by Cervantes's original scene-setting and the hero's intrepid reaction: it continues with Sancho's sly trick of hobbling Rocinante; his rambling shaggy-dog story; his contorted efforts to rid himself of his fear-induced burden while not leaving his master's side; and, above all, by the discovery of the banal cause of the din on the following dawn: the rhythmic beating of the fulling-mill paddles. So, Cervantes's empathetic method should not be confused with identification: it is an ironist's tactic designed to make mockery more effective by adopting an initial pose of awed suspense, in accord with the maxim 'the bigger they come, the harder they fall'.

This is made evident by the manner in which the discovery is related, the very opposite of dramatic anagnorisis. After master and squire emerge from the wood at dawn and apprehensively approach the cause of the terrifying noise, 'pareció descubierta y patente la misma causa, sin que pudiese ser otra, de aquel horrísono y para ellos espantable ruido, que tan suspensos y medrosos toda la noche los había tenido. Y eran – si no lo has, ¡oh lector!, por pesadumbre y enojo – seis mazos de batán que con sus alternativos golpes aquel estruendo formaban' (I, 20; pp. 218–19) (there, patent and exposed to view was the very unmistakable cause of that horrendous and dreadful noise, which had kept them in such fearful suspense all night. It was, if it doesn't irritate and upset you, reader, six fulling-mill paddles, which caused the din by their alternate blows). That wink of complicity at the reader implies playful apology for having promised so much and delivered so little; and Cervantes, at the very moment of revelation, reminds us just how much was promised by echoing, in a tone of mock-awe, the solemnly eery terms of his original scene-setting.

Episodes

The episodes of the novel – that is, the interpolated tales and other matter not directly connected with the hero's chivalric mania – are not much to the taste of modern readers, and moreover, seem to them a diversion from its main theme, an opinion shared, as we learn in Part II, by many of Cervantes's contemporaries. To some extent, he shares these reservations about relevance, yet in Part I, they succumb to his conviction, common to the literature and literary theory of his age, that 'for the ornamentation and beauty of a praiseworthy work, not only are the variety of digressions and length of collo-

quies defensible, but strictly necessary'.[26] Cervantes had no doubt that the
interpolated *novelas* of Part I offered such enhancement, since he proclaims
their artistry in every statement that he makes about them. It had been customary to include one or more interpolated tales in lengthy works of prose-
fiction since Classical Antiquity. The examples include the fable of Cupid and
Psyche, narrated in Book IV of Apuleius's *The Golden Ass* (second century
A.D.), the Moorish romance of Abindarráez and Jarifa, inserted at the end of
Book IV of the 1561 edition of Montemayor's pastoral romance *La Diana*,
and, in the two Parts of *Guzmán de Alfarache*, four *novelas*, which by virtue
of the courtly settings or poignant themes contrast with the rumbustious low
comedy of the *pícaro*'s adventures. In short, Cervantes would have considered it very odd *not* to resort to this kind of expedient.

Whether he realised it clearly or not, episodes are integral to his novel's
design because of its peculiarly internal and intimate relation to the genre that
it parodies. Since he measures the defects of chivalry books by the standards
of an ideal romance that might replace them, his hero's comically ineffectual efforts to revive knight-errantry call forth a positive complement, having
the same relation to them as Life to Literature, or lifelike representation to
escapist fantasy. Though this justification does not exactly coincide with the
grounds on which he asserts their relevance, it overlaps with them.

In the Renaissance, the rationalisation of episodes came mainly from
Aristotelian poetics, which regarded them as accesssories to the main action
of an epic poem, designed to provide the grandeur, ornament and variety
essential to its appeal. According to Giraldi Cinthio's discourse on the heroic
romance (1554), they should give proof of the poet's rhetorical virtuosity
and of his capacity to treat of everything under the sun: 'unexpected events,
deaths, exequies, lamentations, recognitions, triumphs, rare battles, jousts,
tournaments, catalogues and other such things'.[27] Bernardo de Balbuena's
epic poem *Bernardo* (1624), which aimed to compete with the variety of
Ariosto's *Orlando furioso* (1516) itself, exemplifies this vast range: descriptions of palaces, castles, caverns, the heavens, the earth, hell; mytholo-
gical fables; hunting scenes; transformations and enchantments; not least,
the flashback narratives by which each new personage gives an account of
himself. However, episodes and digressions – terms used interchangeably
by Cervantes and Renaissance theorists – were not confined to epics, but

---

[26] From the prologue to Suárez de Figueroa's pastoral romance *La constante Amarilis*
(Constant Amaryllis) (1609). Quoted in Close (2000: 130). For the following discussion of
episodes, see pp. 128–42 of the book just cited.

[27] Quoted in Close (2000: 130).

appeared in all sorts of other lengthy works: history, satire, even didactic treatises. Though, in prose-fiction, they consisted primarily of interpolated tales, they often included other matter, which in the two Parts of *Guzmán de Alfarache* (1599, 1604) and the apocryphal continuation of the first Part by Juan Martí (1602) consists of sermons, burlesque set-pieces, panegyric orations and much else. In *Don Quixote* Part I, Cervantes repeats more or less what he did in his pastoral romance *La Galatea*, where the doings of the shepherds and shepherdesses were interleaved with romantic *novelas* featuring courtly characters. Yet though, in *Don Quixote*, he tends to associate episodes or digressions primarily with *novelas*, he implies that they have a wider scope, without precisely defining it. This doubtless included the orations uttered by the hero in his 'lucid intervals', which in Part I are the discourses on the Golden Age (I, 11) and on Arms and Letters (I, 37–38). Cervantes refers to both with terms synonymous with digression, describing the first sarcastically as 'toda esta larga arenga que se pudiera muy bien escusar' (p. 123) (all this prolix, impertinent discourse that one could well have done without) and referring to the second as 'todo este largo preámbulo' (p. 449) (all this lengthy digression).[28]

His thinking on the subject is formulated in the preambles to *Don Quixote* I, 28 and II, 44. Both passages pose considerable difficulties of interpretation owing to the vagueness of the terminology, compounded in the later one by whimsy and confused expression. They need to be considered together, since the premises of the first are articulated more fully by the second, which explains Cervantes's change of policy towards episodes in Part II.

At the beginning of Part I, Chapter 28 he says that thanks to Don Quixote's resolve to revive knight-errantry

> gozamos ahora en esta nuestra edad, necesitada de alegres entretenimientos, no solo de la dulzura de su verdadera historia, sino de los cuentos y episodios della, que en parte no son menos agradables y artificiosos y verdaderos que la misma historia, la cual, prosiguiendo su rastrillado, torcido y aspado hilo, cuenta que …

> we are able to enjoy in our own age, sorely in need of cheering entertainment, not only the pleasure of his true history, but also that of its tales and episodes, which are in part no less agreeable, well-crafted and true than the history itself, which, pursuing its combed, twisted and stretched-out thread, relates that …

---

[28] I translate in accord with definitions of *arenga* and *preámbulo* given in the *Diccionario de Autoridades*.

The timing of this statement is significant: it occurs at the beginning of internal 'part' four, and is sandwiched between the end of Cardenio's story and the beginning of Dorotea's. A large proportion of 'part' four will be taken up by episodes, all but one narrated at the inn; and it is considerably larger than the proportion devoted to the doings of Don Quixote. The preamble to I, 28 is obviously designed to defend the notable shift in balance from one type of subject-matter to the other, with the consequent reduction of attention to the novel's main theme. The concluding jocular metaphor about the story's tangled skein alludes to this lop-sided effect, and also, given the timing, to the intricate complexity of the intermeshing of Cardenio's story with Dorotea's, and of both with the main action.

This includes, from Chapter 26 onwards, the leisurely execution of the burlesque charade designed to bring Don Quixote home from the wilds of the Sierra Morena. It involves the witty and beautiful Dorotea masquerading as a damsel-in-distress, the Princess Micomicona, who begs the famous Don Quixote to accompany her to her kingdom and restore her to her rightful throne, usurped by a wicked giant (Chapter 29). This hoax culminates, from the end of Chapter 46 onwards, in the Don's confinement to a cage mounted on an ox-cart, the means by which he is conveyed back to his village. Thus, Cervantes has concentrated most of the episodes of the first Part, together with Don Quixote's enforced return home, within the second leg of the outward-and-return loop described by the second sally. This entails a notable slackening of the hectic pace that the action has sustained heretofore, with its spate of farcically violent adventures. The leisureliness is symbolised by the long halt at Juan Palomeque's inn and the tardy progress of the ox-cart, which create ample opportunity for attention to other matters than the demolition of chivalry books: stories, orations, conversations about literature, meetings with strangers and enquiry into their lives. All this is symptomatic of Cervantes's impulse not to bring his story to a hasty conclusion, and establishes the diversified focus that will be sustained in Part II.

The passage quoted above implies this diversification by the suggestion that episodes are to some extent digressive, that is, supplementary to the novel's main business, which is the 'true history' of Don Quixote. It does so, first, by its 'not only ... but also' structure, and second, by claiming that the episodes are *in part* no less agreeable, well-crafted and true than the history itself. This implies that in part they are just that: in particular, less 'true'. Despite this, their inclusion is justified on grounds mentioned earlier in the passage, the present age's sore need of cheerful entertainment.

The modern reader is likely to be puzzled by the use of the term 'verdadero', true, which occurs twice in the passage; it is linked to the similarly confusing concept of 'la verdad de la historia', the truth of the history, fundamental in *Don Quixote*. On its first occurrence, 'verdadera', as applied to *historia* (history or story), carries an obviously ironic sense, yet also a residually positive and figurative one, since Benengeli's mock-history relates events that resemble the truth and could happen, quite unlike the hero's chimerical delusions, nourished by a genre that peddles impossibilities. On its second occurrence, however, 'verdadero' has a different sense, which is also recurrent in the novel: essential, relevant. It is related to a meaning often attributed to *verdad* in *Don Quixote* and derived from contemporary historiography: those true matters that are the historian's essential concern, as distinct from irrelevance or embroidery, which falls outside it. So, in the chapter relating the discovery of Benengeli's manuscript, Cervantes says of it: 'otras algunas menudencias había que advertir, pero todas son de poca importancia, que no hacen al caso a la verdadera relación de la historia, que ninguna es mala como sea verdadera' (I, 9; p. 110) (there were other trifles to be noted in it, but they are all of little importance, and do not affect the true relation of the history, for there is none that is bad provided it is true).

This second – to us very peculiar – sense of *verdad*, *verdadero* provides the key to the flippantly, and also confusedly, worded preamble to Part II, Chapter 44 (pp. 979–80), which, for sake of intelligibility, I both quote and freely paraphrase. It takes the form of a complaint by Cide Hamete Benengeli about having undertaken 'so arid and limited a history as this' (tan seca y limitada como esta de don Quijote), which imposes on him the intolerable and profitless burden of speaking always of Don Quixote and Sancho, 'without daring to branch off into more serious and entertaining digressions and episodes' (sin osar estenderse a otras digresiones y episodios más graves y más entretenidos). In Part I, to avoid such monotony, he resorted to the device of interpolating certain *novelas*, like *El curioso impertinente* and the story of the ex-captive, 'which are as if separated from the history, though the other *novelas* related there are cases which befell Don Quixote himself and could not be omitted' (que están como separadas de la historia, puesto que las demás [novelas] que allí se cuentan son casos sucedidos al mismo don Quijote, que no podían dejar de escribirse). At the same time, he thought that many readers, engrossed in the doings of Don Quixote and Sancho, might skip cursorily over the *novelas*, without appreciating their artistry, which would be clearly apparent if they were published independently, without being linked to the affairs of the two heroes. He continues: 'So, in this second Part, he decided not to introduce loose, detachable *novelas*, but certain episodes resembling them, born of the very events that the truth proposes, and only in just sufficient words to relate them' (Y así, en esta segunda parte no quiso ingerir novelas sueltas ni pegadizas, sino algunos episodios que lo pareciesen, nacidos de los mesmos sucesos que la verdad ofrece, y aun estos limitadamente y con solas las palabras que bastan a declararlos). And he ends, jocularly attributing to himself the inexhustible inventive genius associated conventionally with the epic poet, by craving the reader's praise not for what he has written but for what he has omitted to write, despite 'having ability, talent and wit enough to deal with everything under the sun'.

The criterion of relevance that is established by this passage may be inferred from the virtual equivalence of 'cases that befell Don Quixote himself and could not be omitted' and 'born of the very events that the truth proposes'. In the mock-history of Benengeli, the hero's career is 'the truth' with which the chronicler is essentially concerned. The two *novelas* explicitly identified as loose and detachable, however meritorious in themselves, fall outside this sphere. Yet even the other *novelas*, whose inclusion in Part I is considered defensible by the above criterion, are implicitly treated as open to criticism on grounds of excessive length; this may be inferred from the insistence on the brevity of exposition adopted in Part II, and on the need for *novelas* to be even more closely integrated with the main theme than they were in Part I. The passage gives to understand that Cervantes's change of policy was mainly motivated by a spontaneous calculation about the likely reactions of readers. In fact, as may deduced from the discussion between Don Quixote, Sansón Carrasco and Sancho about the reception of Part I (II, 3), the point was borne in upon him by the objections of many readers to the interpolation of *El curioso impertinente* (p. 652), and more generally, by the massive evidence of the popularity of his two heroes, which persuaded their creator that the continuation of the story would have self-sufficient appeal if centred primarily on their affairs, without the prop of masses of ancillary entertainment. That realisation was the spur for the change of policy, but not the principle underlying it. This was his sense, already apparent in Part I, that his novel should concern itself with a single 'truth', and it is allied to his concern for another principle: decorum. Both motives are responsible for the highly unusual way – as it would have seemed then – in which the episodes of Part I are intertwined with the main action.

To see how and why decorum affects the handling of episodes it is necessary to turn to the prologue to *Don Quixote* Part I, which contains Cervantes's chief statement on the principles underlying its composition. The prologue, which is mostly a brilliant satire on the pretentious posturing and didacticism of contemporary literature,[29] contains, near the beginning, Cervantes's description of himself in his study, paralysed with doubt as to how to present his novel to the public without the customary sheaf of laudatory verse tributes from distinguished acquaintances, and without the usual learned apparatus of marginal notes, indices and quotations. A friend finds him in this condition, and on learning the reason for it, proceeds to pour ridicule on these literary fashions by suggesting a series of bogus remedies for the omissions. To make up for the absence of verse tributes, he suggests that Cervantes invents his own, ascribing them to fictitious personages like Prester John of the Indies or the Emperor of Trebizond; and this is indeed what Cervantes does. The preliminaries of *Don Quixote* Part I carry a sheaf of laudatory poems, attributed not to the author's distinguished acquaintances but to famous chivalric personages (Amadís, Belianís, Oriana, and so on), who mostly address their eulogies to their counterparts in *Don Quixote*. They are all wittily burlesque, and unlike the usual poetic tributes, are great fun to read. As for the lack of erudite marginalia and indices, the friend impudently recommends solutions of an off-the-peg kind, such as citing any familiar classical tag that might be appropriate to the topics that arise in the story, or ensuring that there is a giant in it called Goliath, which will permit the footnote: 'the giant Goliath was a Philistine slain by the shepherd David with his sling in the vale of Terebinth, as is told in the book of Kings'.

The satire starts from this jibe by Cervantes (pp. 11–12), which shows that the principle of decorum is its fundamental premise:

> pues ¿qué cuando citan la Divina Escritura? No dirán sino que son unos santos Tomases y otros doctores de la iglesia, guardando en esto un decoro tan ingenioso, que en un renglón han pintado un enamorado destraído y en otro hacen un sermoncico cristiano, que es un contento y un regalo oílle o leelle.

> And what about their quotations of Divine Scripture! They must take themselves for St Thomases or other doctors of the church, for they observe so ingenious a decorum that in one line they have painted a distracted lover, and in the next they deliver a pretty Christian sermon, which is a pleasure and delight to hear or read.

Towards the end of the prologue, switching into more serious vein, the friend tells Cervantes that since his novel just aims to ridicule the vogue of chivalry books 'no hay para qué andéis mendigando sentencias de filósofos, consejos

---

[29] For a fuller discussion, see Close (2000: 96–7, 114–16).

de la Divina Escritura, fábulas de poetas, oraciones de retóricos, milagros de santos' (p. 18) (there's no need for you to go scrounging maxims of philosophers, precepts of Holy Scripture, poetic fables, rhetorical orations, saints' miracles). The only objectives that need concern him are verisimilitude, clarity and plainness of diction combined with elegance, and persistent incitement to laughter, so that his story appeals to all types of reader and fulfils its corrective purpose. These principles bring *Don Quixote* firmly into the sphere of the Classical art of comedy, which aims to purge the emotions through laughter, as distinct from the pity and terror provoked by tragedy, and portrays, in easy and familiar language, the ridiculous foibles of ordinary folk in order to teach them prudence in the conduct of their private lives.[30]

Now, these principles should pose difficulties for the interpolation of episodes in the novel, since the types of subject-matter excluded by Cervantes's friend are prominent among those to which writers turned in search of such material. Episodes based on poetic fables are rife in the epic tradition from Homer onwards. Rhetorical orations – for example, sermons – and precepts of Holy Scripture are found in *Guzmán de Alfarache*. Saints' miracles abound in Lope de Vega's *El peregrino de su patria*. Avellaneda, clearly considered it improper to incorporate such serious matter in his own version of Don Quixote's career, since, in Chapter 11, he begins to describe the witty devices on the shields of the contestants in a joust in Zaragoza, then abruptly breaks off 'por no hazer libro de versos el que solo es corónica de los quiméricos hechos de don Quijote' (so as not to turn into a book of verse what is merely the chronicle of Don Quixote's chimerical deeds).[31] Cervantes felt the same scruples in respect of the Golden Age speech (*DQ* I, 11), which may be considered both a 'poetic fable' and a 'rhetorical oration'. However, instead of suppressing it, he chooses another option, which minimises its incongruity with the main theme, and enables him to harmonise one with the other.

The hero delivers the speech to his hosts, a company of simple and hospitable goat-herds, who have just shared their supper with him: goats' meat stew, cheese harder than plaster, and a dessert of shrivelled acorns, with a wine-skin freely passed from hand to hand. The Don, seated on an upturned tub, and oblivious of the unsuitability of this learned lecture to its illiterate audience, is moved to utter it merely because the acorns remind him of that idyllic vegetarian age, while the goat-herds listen with stupefied incomprehension. Moreover, he adapts it to his chivalric obsession by concluding that the transition from the age of gold to one of iron gave birth to knight-errantry,

---

[30] For documentation of this point, Close (2000: 74–5).
[31] Avellaneda, *Don Quijote*, ed. Riquer, vol. i, p. 207.

in response to the need to protect innocent virgins from sexual predators. As we have already noted, Cervantes treats the hero's bookish eloquence as impertinently superfluous, and to highlight this, emphasises its stilted, literary preciosity. Despite this sarcasm, the speech is the first of the hero's 'lucid intervals', which will later be presented in a more positive light, and it provides a model for all the subsequent ones, to the extent that they are always to some extent nuanced by his mania, and by this means avoid an effect of heavy didacticism. Thus does Cervantes square the circle of introducing edifying matter into his novel without appearing to lecture or preach. Though he infringes the letter of his merry counsellor's advice in the prologue to Part I, he respects the spirit.

The principal 'lucid interval' in Part I is the Arms and Letters speech in Chapters 37 and 38, and is handled very differently from the discourse on the Golden Age, while showing significant continuities with it. These consist, first, in the premise of the speech, which links the hero's otherwise judicious exposition of this learned topic to his mania by treating knight-errantry as a supreme example of the nobility of Arms. Secondly, they consist in the way in which he holds forth uninvited and impromptu during a meal, addressing his comments to the other diners, who in this case are the ladies and gentlemen seated round the table at Juan Palomeque's inn (I, 37; p. 442). Yet the differences between the two orations are even more significant. Cervantes tells us that the gentlemen, because of their innate military vocation, listened with silent approval to the hero's arguments for the superiority of Arms, only regretting that so fine an intellect should be blighted by an absurd monomania (I, 38; p. 449). So, the sarcastic attitude that Cervantes showed on the previous occasion has been replaced by a more compassionate and admiring one. Obviously, about mid-way through the composition of Part I, he must have begun to perceive positive potential in his hero's bookish intelligence, beyond its comic aspect of inopportune pedantry or the crazy misapplication of edifying principles. Faced with the prospect of introducing a cluster of serious interpolated *novelas* from Chapter 33 onwards, he evidently decided to take advantage of it in order to introduce an episode matched in gravity to the *novelas*, though of a different kind: not a courtly tale of love, but an elegant set-piece oration. The comparison of Arms and Letters was, like the speech on the Golden Age, a consecrated humanistic topic, and, like that speech again, as we shall see soon, is used by Cervantes as a thematic prelude to the episode that follows. The evolution in Cervantes's handling of the hero's lucid intervals continues in Part II. It is a notable example of the compositional principle of repetition with variations, permitting him to ascribe to his hero, despite his insanity, the seriously instructive and mora-

listic function typical of his other protagonists, like Elicio of *La Galatea*, or
Periandro in *Persiles y Sigismunda*.

The difficulties that Cervantes faced in linking rhetorical orations to the
main theme also apply to interpolated tales of a kind too noble and serious
to be compatible with unpretentiously comic subject-matter. It is on these
grounds, by means of the doctrine of the division of styles, that Classical
literary theory prescribed the separation of comedy and tragedy. No doubt
Cervantes's respect for the precept explains why, for the first and only time
in *Don Quixote*, he resorts to the 'juxtapositive' method when he interpolates the tragically exemplary *novela* of *El curioso impertinente* in it.[32] This
was the traditional method of interpolating tales in a long work of prose-
narrative, and it consisted in inventing pretexts for one of the characters to
tell a story to the others. The pretexts are conventional. In Don Juan Manuel's
fourteenth-century story-collection *El Conde Lucanor*, tales are told by a
preceptor to his pupil to illustrate a moral point; in *Guzmán de Alfarache*,
they serve as relief from the boredom of a journey, an antidote to care, or
pleasant relaxation after a meal; *El curioso impertinente* is read aloud by the
priest to while away the siesta-hour, at the request of other characters, whose
curiosity is aroused by a manuscript found in a suitcase containing books
and papers. In all these cases, the main action is suspended while the story is
told, and this is marked by the circumstances of the telling: a period of leisure
or inactivity. Consequently, the story, whose plot is obviously independent
of that of the work in which it is interpolated, may exhibit a quite different
character from it, as occurs in the case of *El curioso impertinente*, whose
tragic exemplariness contrasts starkly with the comic antics of Don Quixote
and Sancho. This may be a reason why Avellaneda uses the juxtapositive
method in interpolating two *novelas* in his version of *Don Quixote*; the other
reason, no doubt, is its sheer traditionalism. One of them is a gruesome tale
of revenge (Chapters 15–16), and the other is a miracle of the Virgin (Chapters 17–20); both therefore are incompatible with the unremittingly risible,
often coarse, light in which he depicts Don Quixote and Sancho.

However, this is not how Cervantes does things in the rest of the episodes
of his novel. The normative pattern is fixed quite early in Part I by the
pastoral interlude of Marcela and Grisóstomo (I, 12–14), which, as a pastoral
tragedy, might have been expected to pose the same kind of problems as *El
curioso impertinente*. It is preceded in Chapter 11 by the Golden Age speech,
whose Arcadian theme makes it a natural gateway to the pastoral world; and

---

[32] On the juxtapositive method and the distinction between it and the coordinative one,
Close (2000: 137–8).

Cervantes's ironic treatment of one has much in common with his treatment of the other.

The episode is an example of the 'coordinative' method, which differs from the 'juxtapositive' one by virtue of the fact that its plot, though it may begin by being independent of the main action, eventually intertwines with it. Cervantes derives it from Byzantine and pastoral romance, including his own *La Galatea*, where it serves to link independent story-lines. The revolutionary aspect of its use in *Don Quixote* is his adaptation of it to combine incongruous strands: romantic fiction with the comic doings of Don Quixote and Sancho, instead of with more fiction of a romantic kind.

The episode concerns the unrequited love of Grisóstomo, ending in his death, for the cold, beautiful and wilful Marcela. The story is told by Pedro, a lad from Grisóstomo's village, to an audience consisting of Don Quixote and Sancho, plus the goat-herds who have just entertained them to supper (I, 12). On the following morning, master and squire, together with their hosts, travel to the site chosen for Grisóstomo's funeral; on the way, they meet a party of riders bound for the same destination; one of them is Vivaldo, who submits Don Quixote to ironic interrogation about his chivalric vocation (I, 13).

Before the funeral begins, Vivaldo reads out Grisóstomo's ode (beginning of I, 14), whose style and sentiments mark him as one of the obsessively morbid, suicidal lovers of the Spanish pastoral tradition. Almost as soon as it is finished, Marcela makes a dramatic appearance on a crag above the grave, and in a robustly rational and eloquent speech, rebuts the accusations of cruelty made against her by Grisóstomo and his friends, especially the implication that simply by virtue of being the object of a man's love she is obliged to reciprocate it. The scene is based on one in Book VI of Cervantes's *La Galatea*, where the cruel and lovely Gelasia – her very name connotes ice – smilingly looks down from a hill above the Tagus upon the attempt by Galercio to drown himself for love of her. She then flees from the formerly loveless Lenio, as he toils up the hill to plead his suit. Though Gelasia is not a particularly nice piece of work, Cervantes attributes to her a sonnet whose concluding tercet is one of the noblest in the Spanish language: 'Del campo son y han sido mis amores; / rosas son y jazmines mis cadenas;/ libre nací, y en libertad me fundo' (the country is and always has been my true love; my chains are the flowers of rose and jasmine; I was born free, and freedom is my watchword).[33] These are Marcela's sentiments too, though she amplifies them with the morally persuasive claim to her right to live independent of

---

[33] *La Galatea*, ed. Schevill and Bonilla, vol. ii, pp. 266–7.

men's attentions, in communion with Nature and God. That kind of retreat from society is a recurrent ideal of the age's country-praising poetry.

For most of the episode, until her intervention at the funeral, we see Marcela through the eyes of her critics, including Pedro, whose story sets the background to the affair. From his viewpoint, Marcela's resolve to adopt a life of rural solitude, and Grisóstomo's to become a love-lorn shepherd for her sake, are equally eccentric, and this view of their behaviour brings its literary conventionality down to earth with a bump. They, implicitly members of the country gentry, are living a kind of pastoral romance; he treats this as irrational escapism, judging it by the standards of common opinion of the village to which he, and they, belong. His viewpoint, therefore, is rural and parochial, and so is his style. Though he tells his story well, he mispronounces learned words and is corrected by Don Quixote with tiresome pedantry. Describing the village's astonishment at Marcela's sudden escape from home, he lapses into colloquialism: 'Pero hételo aquí, cuando no me cato, que remanece un día la melindrosa Marcela hecha pastora' (p. 132) (but lo and behold, when you'd least expect, up pops flighty Marcela turned into a shepherdess). His account of Grisóstomo's contribution to the running of his father's farm and to village festivities contains realistic touches that one would never find in the bland, idyllic context of pastoral romance. For example, he reveals that Grisóstomo, a student from Salamanca, would compose the carols for the village's Christmas festivities and the short mystery plays for the Feast of Corpus Christi. In describing the extravagant affectation of Grisóstomo's friends, all of whom have become shepherds for Marcela's sake, Pedro is wittily satiric (I, 12; p. 134):

> Aquí sospira un pastor, allí se queja otro; acullá se oyen amorosas canciones; acá desesperadas endechas. Cuál hay que pasa todas las horas de la noche, sentado al pie de alguna encina o peñasco, y allí, sin plegar los llorosos ojos, embebecido y transportado en sus pensamientos, le halló el sol a la mañana, y cuál hay que sin dar vado ni tregua a sus suspiros, en mitad del ardor de la más enfadosa siesta del verano, tendido sobre la ardiente arena, envía sus quejas al piadoso cielo.

> A shepherd sighs here, another laments there; amatory songs resound yonder, despairing dirges hither. One fellow spends all the hours of the night sitting at the foot of some oak or rock, and there, without having shut his tearful eyes, rapt and transported in his thoughts, he is discovered by the morning sun; another, without allowing his sighs respite or intermission, stretched on the sand in the full heat of summer's most oppressive siesta, directs his laments to merciful heaven.

It is a splendid example of Cervantes's anti-pastoral vein. Moreover, the extravagances of behaviour described above remind us of Don Quixote, notably his nocturnal vigils; we are thus induced to see him and Grisóstomo as tarred with a similar brush. Pedro's satire complements the moral thrust of Marcela's speech, which undercuts the courtly lover's cult of despairing recrimination. And Vivaldo's ironic insinuations in Chapter 13, on the way to Grisóstomo's funeral, about the unpracticality and idolatry of the chivalric code, anticipate the self-consciously literary paganism of the funeral in unhallowed ground, reflected in the artificiality of its staging: a procession of twenty mourners wearing black shepherds' smocks with wreaths of box and cypress on their heads; the body of Grisóstomo on a bier, covered with flowers, and surrounded by books and papers (I, 13; p. 143).

Yet Cervantes's treatment of the pastoral convention is not wholly negative. The death of the young and talented Grisóstomo is a human tragedy, even though he brought it on himself. Marcela's claim to liberty is noble and eloquently expressed. And Pedro is a perceptive informant about this drama, not merely a comic foil to it. He reacts with curiosity, wonderment and regret; and his homeliness provides an appropriately rural bridge between Don Quixote's world and the literary theatricality of the funeral.

As in the adventure of the shepherd-boy Andrés, and again, in the Golden Age speech, Cervantes has given us in this episode a version of the ironic contrast between Life and Literature, in which low rusticity, realistically drawn, mocks literary escapism. In this case, pastoral romances, not chivalry books or Classical myth, are the target; and the satire aimed at them is not unsparing in its ridicule. The close coordination of low rusticity with high pastoral is essential to this ambivalent effect, and enables Cervantes to incorporate his two heroes in both worlds simultaneously. He can thus legitimately claim of the episode that it is a 'case which befell Don Quixote himself and could not be omitted'

Coordination is taken even further in the next episode in Part I, the interlinked stories of Cardenio and Dorotea (see above pp. 57–58). The process of a tantalisingly graduated approach to the crisis becomes protracted and elaborate, with Cardenio's story being broken up into at least five separate instalments (contained in Chapters 23, 24, 27, 36), the last three being interleaved with other matter to increase the effect of suspense. Don Quixote is not merely the recipient of the first instalment, told by a goat-herd, but is himself a principal instigator, witness and interpreter of the second. The relation between the planes of comedy and romance is further emphasised by the symmetrical epithets ironically applied to the two madmen at the end of Chapter 23, 'The Ragged Knight of the Ill-favoured Countenance'

(Cardenio) and 'The Knight of the Woeful Countenance' (Don Quixote), and by the thematic interconnections between the two cases of amatory despair, which derive from the same literary precedents. These are: Orlando's jealous fury on discovering the evidence of Angelica's affair with Medoro (Ariosto, *Orlando furioso*, Canto 23), and Amadís's despairing penance on a lonely island hermitage after being banished by Oriana from her presence (*Amadís de Gaula*, Chapters 45 and 48). The action of Dorotea's story is enmeshed not only with Cardenio's but also with Don Quixote's, which to some extent it mirrors.[34] Her burlesque role as the Princess Micomicona is a fictional version of the real predicament in which the faithless Fernando placed her; Don Quixote, as she herself acknowledges, is the unwitting means of its resolution (I, 37; p. 437); she repays the compliment by motivating his return home.

For reasons already considered, Cervantes abandons coordination in the case of *El curioso impertinente* (I, 33–35). Though set in Italy and akin in theme and sombre mood to the tragic novelle of Bandello and Giraldi Cinthio, it illustrates the intellectual and moral seriousness of Cervantes's *novelas*, compared with their Italian precursors. It is based on the story told by the melancholy host of Rinaldo in Cantos 42–3 of Ariosto's *Orlando furioso*, about the disillusioning discovery that he made when he put his beloved wife's fidelity to the test by means similar to Anselmo's in the Cervantine *novela*. When she fails, he heaps reproaches on her for her inconstancy, provoking her to such scorn that she abandons him for her rival. Since then, his only consolation has been to get other husbands to drink of a golden goblet made by the enchantress Morgana, which has the property of spilling its wine on the chest of cuckolds who put it to their lips. No husband has drunk from it so far without getting splashed. But when the goblet is offered to Rinaldo, he masters his own curiosity and prudently refuses to drink. Upon this, his host bursts into tears, lamenting that he lacked Rinaldo's wisdom.

Cervantes turns this amusingly cynical fable into a sternly moral thesis about the potential fragility of a woman's virtue, and what this entails for the husband anxious to preserve the integrity of his marriage and thus respect its sanctity. The action of the *novela* turns on Anselmo's foolishly capricious wish to test the virtue of his wife Camila by getting his best friend Lotario to try to seduce her. Guillén de Castro, in his dramatic adaptation of it, also

---

[34] Both Cardenio's predicament, with its roots in the theme of Roland's jealousy, and Dorotea's, were popular subjects in the contemporary *comedia*. It is therefore not surprising that their interlinked stories inspire a comedy by the contemporary Valencian dramatist Guillén de Castro, entitled *Don Quijote de la Mancha*.

entitled *El curioso impertinente*, sought to provide a stronger motivation for Lotario's passion for Camila by depicting them as lovers prior to her marriage to Anselmo. His experiment rekindles their love for each other and drives her back into Lotario's arms. By contrast, Cervantes, to reinforce his moral point, makes Lotario and Camila start virtually from zero. Lotario vehemently and eloquently opposes Anselmo's project, expounding all the moral, psychological and theological reasons why, if he persists, he courts disaster, having nothing to gain and everything to lose. This prudent discourse on the obligations of the conjugal state yields little in respect of weighty earnestness to the age's principal tract on the subject, Fray Luis de León's *La perfecta casada* (1583) (The Perfect Wife), though in the Cervantine *novela* the slant is moral/psychological rather than theological, and the emphasis falls primarily on the worldly imperatives of honour. However, Anselmo is deaf to rational advice, and insists on going through with the experiment. In its initial stages, both Lotario and Camila behave, respectively, as a true friend and a loyal and loving wife should do. However, Anselmo's persistent goading of his friend into undertaking the seduction in earnest, and his ill-advised abandonment of Camila to Lotario's advances, lead them from initial indifference to each other into passionate complicity, setting off a chain of consequences that eventually result in Anselmo's discovery of their adultery. The narrative is punctuated with ironically sententious comments and rhetorical questions that highlight the logical inevitability of this process and Anselmo's blindness to it until the dénouement, which, as a result, has the air of a *quod erat demonstrandum* appended to a geometrical theorem.

Though the ex-captive's story (Part I, Chapters 39–42) is coordinated to the main action by being related by its protagonist to the other characters at the inn, and the priest is the instigator of its dénouement, Don Quixote is virtually marginalised from it. Though present when it is told and when Ruy Pérez de Viedma is reunited with his brother, he shows none of the lucidity with which he reacted to part of Cardenio's story, and attributes all that he sees and hears to 'quimeras de la andante caballería', fantasies of knight-errantry (Chapter 42; p. 499). He is even more detached from the reading of *El curioso impertinente*, during which he is fast asleep. This is why, in Part II, Chapter 44, Cervantes treats both *novelas* as being 'as if separate from the history'. The reason for the segregation of the ex-captive's story from Don Quixote's doings is its heroic nature, including its basis in a real, recent – and for Cervantes, glorious – period of Spain's military history, a theme too serious to be associated with the fabulous world of chivalry books.

Nonetheless, despite this segregation, the story has been immediately preceded by Don Quixote's oration on the contrasted merits of Arms and

Letters and the question which is superior (Chapters 37–38). The juxtaposition of the speech and the story is no coincidence. The *hidalgo* interprets 'letters' not as 'literature' in general, but as academic studies, and even more specifically, as university education, which for many students in Cervantes's age meant either the study of theology or law. The emphasis of the speech falls implicitly on law, and this reflects the bureaucratisation of national and local government during the reign of Philip II (1556–98), which created golden opportunities for the rise of the *letrado*, the professional with a law degree, capable of exercising as a lawyer, judge or civil servant. The significance of this for Ruy Pérez's story is that it begins with his father's decision, reminiscent of traditional fable, to curb his spendthrift impulse by dividing his inheritance between his three sons, and telling each of them to use his share in order to establish himself in his chosen career. He makes the gift conditional on their choice of one of three career-paths, defined by the old Spanish proverb: 'Tres cosas hacen al hombre medrar: iglesia y mar y casa real' (There are three ways of getting on in the world: church, sea and royal household). Ruy Pérez, the eldest brother, chooses the last option, deciding to serve the king as a soldier. The middle son opts to go to the Indies, and there becomes a wealthy merchant. The youngest of the three, Juan Pérez, prefers to continue his education at Salamanca, where he studies law. Since we hear little more of the merchant, the dénouement of the story, which brings about the reunion of the eldest brother and the youngest at Juan Palomeque's inn, highlights the outcome of the destinies of these two in particular. At the moment of reunion, Juan Pérez has reached the summit of his profession (see above, p. 52). So, the two destinies offer a contrast between a heroic life of Arms and a successful career of Letters. The venerable literary topic articulated by Don Quixote comes to life in two concrete, historically realistic illustrations.

Ruy Pérez's story, autobiographical in form, relates in its first part his experiences as a soldier and as a captive of the Turks in the eastern and southern Mediterranean during the period 1570–80, including his participation in the battle of Lepanto in October 1571. The experiences are based in detail on historical events, and overlap with Cervantes's own; his proud identification with the story is implicit in Ruy Pérez's confident personal judgements on strategic decisions and his detailed references to real individuals, battles, ships, and forts, including an oblique allusion to Cervantes's own heroism in captivity in Algiers (I, 40; p. 463). Such historical specificity makes this *novela* unique within the genre. When the narrative gets to Ruy Pérez's Algerian captivity, it blends those references with pious fable, reworking the traditional legend of the Moorish princess secretly devoted to the

Virgin Mary who flees to Christian lands, chaperoned by a chivalrous Spanish knight. The young Tirso de Molina wrote a play based on the legend, *Los lagos de San Vicente* (The Lakes of St Vincent), virtually contemporaneous with the publication of *Don Quixote* Part I.

The last two interpolated *novelas* of Part I are briefer and lighter in tone than the ones just discussed; both are excellent, though in different ways. The first, told in Chapter 43, is a story of teenage love; Cervantes characterises the amusing ingenuousness of Doña Clara's account of how she and Don Luis fell for each other merely by looks and signs exchanged across the street, and of his adoption of the demeaning disguise of a mule-boy in order to follow her on her journey south. The plot, derived in part from a novella by Bandello,[35] anticipates another play by Tirso, *Desde Toledo a Madrid* (From Toledo to Madrid), and more indirectly, Cervantes's novela *La ilustre fregona*, where the hero becomes a stable-hand at the inn to court the kitchen-maid of the title. The ballad sung by Luis at the beginning of Chapter 43, 'Marinero soy de amor' (I'm one of love's sailors), is one of Cervantes's finest poems. The *novela* is coordinated with Don Quixote's affairs by means of theme and plot, since the conflict between Don Luis and his servants over whether he should return immediately to his father's home mirrors, and partly intertwines with, the farcical dispute over the barber's basin and pack-saddle (Chapters 44–45).

The last interpolated *novela* in Part I, Eugenio's story, told in Chapter 51, is pastoral, and resembles the Marcela/Grisóstomo episode in its partly ironic and satiric treatment of the genre, while inverting its plot. Leandra, like Marcela, is legendarily beautiful, steadfastly indifferent to offers of marriage, and modestly secluded from men's attentions. Like Marcela again, she astonishes the inhabitants of her village by suddenly escaping from home. But in this case, the motive is not virtuous but scandalous: elopement with the flashy soldier Vicente de la Rosa, who up to that point has impressed the locals with his guitar-playing and his boasts of dubious military exploits. Three days after her disappearance Leandra is found in a cave, naked and without her jewels, but with her virtue improbably intact. She is packed off by her father to a convent; and her many admirers, in despair, become shepherds and take to the hills to vent their grief, each one finding a different cause for lamentation. Once again Cervantes satirically mocks the pastoral genre's gratuitous wallowing in sentimental misery, lyrically and fantastically exaggerating its scale (p. 581):

---

[35] Bandello, *Novelle* Part II, *novella* 41: 'Uno di nascoso piglia l'innamorata per moglie …'.

No hay hueco de peña, ni margen de arroyo, ni sombra de árbol que no
esté ocupada de algún pastor que sus desventuras a los aires cuente; el eco
repite el nombre de Leandra dondequiera que pueda formarse; Leandra
resuenan los montes, Leandra mumuran los arroyos, y Leandra nos tiene
a todos suspensos y encantados.

There is not a hollowed-out rock, nor stream-bank, nor tree-shadow which
is not occupied by some shepherd lamenting his misfortune to the skies.
Echo repeats Leandra's name wherever it may be voiced; Leandra resounds
from the hills, Leandra murmur the brooks, and Leandra has us all captive
and bewitched.

The episode is thoroughly coordinated with the main theme by means of
the undignified brawl that breaks out between Don Quixote and Eugenio
following the knight-errant's ridiculous reaction to the goat-herd's story; the
spectators, including even the priest and the canon of Toledo, whoop on the
two contestants as though they were dogs locked in combat.

Just prior to this *novela*, we have had the discussion between the canon
of Toledo and the priest about the chivalric genre, followed by the priest's
censure of the contemporary *comedia* (Chapters 47–48). Probably Cervantes
would have considered these passages episodic, since, like the captive's tale
or *El curioso impertinente*, they take place in a halt in the action, and Don
Quixote and Sancho are excluded from them. Also, like the discourses on
the Golden Age and Arms and Letters, they consist of two lengthy orations
of an academic nature. However, despite the hero's exclusion, they are coordinated with his career, not just thematically, but actively, since the canon
takes it upon himself to try to convince the *hidalgo* of his error by rational
argument (Chapter 49; pp. 562–4)), and is met by a splendidly vehement
and casuistical refutation (I, 49–50; pp. 564–72), including the exuberant
story of the Knight of the Lake, designed to convince the interlocutor of
the pleasure and profit to be had from the genre. The ironic objectivity with
which Cervantes presents this rebuttal, and his pleasure in characterising
his hero's idiosyncratic mania, are well illustrated by his refusal to take
the didactic option of highlighting his error by obvious means. Instead,
Don Quixote defends himself with eloquent casuistry, speciously jumbling
together historical fact and falsehood, and telling his story with enthusiastic
vividness. The canon is left astonished by these 'concertados disparates' (I,
50; p. 573), well-ordered nonsense, a phrase that evokes the perverse but
inventive ingenuity alluded to by the novel's title: *El ingenioso hidalgo don
Quijote de la Mancha*.

The principle underlying the degree of linkage between episodes and main theme is therefore clear: the more their content approximates to the hero's chivalric mania or to the satire of chivalry books, whether thematically or by virtue of their kinship to the genre of comedy, the higher the degree of coordination, and vice-versa. We shall see in Chapter 6 how Cervantes applies this principle in Part II.

The Galley-Slaves Adventure (*DQ* I, 22)

In the Introduction, I briefly characterised the abrasive humour of the hero's chivalric adventures clustered in the first twenty-two chapters of Part I, and alluded to their archetypal resonance. The adventure of the galley-slaves, which rounds off this series, exemplifies both aspects.

When Sancho sees the procession of chained men approaching, accompanied by armed guards, he states the obvious straight off: 'Esta es cadena de galeotes, gente forzada del rey, que va a las galeras' (p. 236) (This is a chain of galley-slaves, the king's forced men, on their way to the galleys). To this Don Quixote replies: '¿Cómo gente forzada ... es posible que el rey haga fuerza a ninguna gente?' (What do you mean, the king's forced men ... how can the king do violence to anybody?). The question twists the legal sense of 'gente forzada del rey', galley-slaves, equivalent to the French *forçats*, into a literal, emotive channel that fits the Quixotic preconception of the chained men as unfortunate victims of duress. Sancho scrupulously corrects this perversion of meaning: 'No digo eso ... sino que es gente que por sus delitos va condenada a servir al rey en las galeras, de por fuerza' (I'm not saying that, but rather that these are people who have been condemned for their crimes to serve the king in the galleys, and are going there by force). But the knight insists: 'comoquiera que ello sea, esta gente, aunque los llevan, van de por fuerza, y no de su voluntad' (However that might be, these people, since they are being led there, are going by force and not of their own free will). The phrase 'de por fuerza, no de su voluntad' recurs like a refrain later in the adventure, and constitutes the grounds for Don Quixote's intervention: a world-upside-down view of the relation of prisoners to the law underpinned by a casuistical pun.

The Quixotic adventures of Part I, including this one, are saturated with echoes of robustly comic species of previous literature and folklore: farcical interludes and other motifs of theatre, *fabliaux* and novellas, popular jests, the picaresque novel. Don Quixote's interrogation of the galley-slaves, which occupies about two-thirds of Chapter 22, and has the aim of eliciting from them evidence to confirm his *a priori* notion of their undeserved ill-fortune, is fundamentally indebted to the genre of farce, particularly to the species that has the form of a burlesque tribunal,[36] such as Cervantes's own *El juez de los divorcios*. But the indebtedness to farce doesn't end there. In the prologue to Cervantes's *Ocho comedias y ocho entremeses*, he recalls having seen as a boy performances by Lope de Rueda, the famous dramatist and theatre director active in the mid-sixteenth century, and remembers his excellence in several farcical roles: ruffian, negress, fool, Basque and others. In one of Lope's farcical interludes (*pasos*), a thieving braggart (Madrigalejo) boasts about past exploits to a sceptical lackey (Molina), who challenges him to deny that he once suffered the ignominy of being given a hundred lashes as a thief. The dialogue proceeds thus:

> *Madrigalejo*: ¿Contaron vuestras mercedes los azotes que me dieron?
> *Molina*: ¿Para qué se habían de contar?
> ......
> *Madrigalejo*: Pues voto a tal, que no daba vez vuelta o corcovo con el cuerpo que no le echase el verdugo un azote de clavo. Mire vuestra merced si es ciento si no fueron más de quince de menos.
> *Molina*: No hay duda de que es ansí.
> *Madrigalejo*: ... Tampoco lo quel hombre no sufre por su voluntad no se puede llamar afrenta. Comparación: ¿qué se me da a mí que llamen a uno cornudo, si la bellaquería está en su mujer, sin ser él consentidor?
> *Molina*: Tenéis razón.
> *Madrigalejo*: Pues ¿qué afrenta recibo yo que me azoten, si es contra mi voluntad y por fuerza?[37]

> *Madrigalejo*: Did you count the number of lashes?
> *Molina*: What need was there to count them?
> *Madrigalejo*: Because I swear to God, every time I twisted or jerked my body, the man with the whip miscued his stroke. So how can you say it was a hundred if it was at least fifteen less?
> *Molina*: You have a point there.
> *Madrigalejo*: And another thing: one can't call it an affront if what a man suffers is inflicted on him by force, not freely consented to. For example, what's it to me if they say I'm a cuckold, when the mischief is in my wife and not in me?

---

[36] I take tribunal in a broad sense, as referring to any kind of burlesque cross-examination, whether of criminals (e.g. the *paso* by Lope de Rueda quoted below in the text, which ends with a constable interrogating the two personages), or cranks and misfits (e.g. the anonymous *El hospital de los podridos* [Hospital of Chronic Whingers], sometimes attributed to Cervantes), or candidates for an election (e.g. Cervantes's *La elección de los alcaldes de Daganzo* [Election of the Mayors of Daganzo]). On the reasons for the popularity of this kind of farce, see Asensio (1965: 85–8 and 114–17).

[37] Rueda, *Pasos*, ed. Canet Vallés, pp. 174–5.

Molina: I grant you that.
Madrigalejo: Well then, what affront is it if the whipping is done to me by force, not by my consent?

This comic casuistry, and particulary the last few words, must have stuck in young Cervantes's mind because years later he adapted them to his own purposes in the galley-slaves adventure. He also exploits a kind of verbal humour that occurs in several *pasos* by Lope, arising either from the situation in which novice thieves ask an old lag to explain the meaning of criminal slang to them, or alternatively, that in which the fool takes in a literal sense euphemistic allusions to shameful punishments to be inflicted on his nearest and dearest, like being pilloried, whipped, tortured, and assumes they refer to honours that will be conferred upon them.[38] Don Quixote's interrogation of the galley-slaves is based on both kinds of double-entendre. When he asks the first convict the reason for his punishment he is surprised to learn that it is merely because this individual was *enamorado*. The convict goes on to explain what the nature of this love was: 'quise tanto a una canasta de colar, atestada de ropa blanca, que la abracé conmigo tan fuertemente, que a no quitármela la justicia por fuerza, aún hasta agora no la hubiera dejado de mi voluntad' (p. 237) (I loved this basket of washing so much, and grasped it to me so tightly, that had not the police taken it from me by force, I would never have consented to let it go). Note the mocking echo of the Don Quixote's dichotomy 'de por fuerza' / 'de su voluntad', and also the parody of his sentimental conception of the villains as unfortunate victims.

Another genre from which Cervantes draws inspiration is the newly established picaresque novel, effectively launched by *Guzmán de Alfarache*. To go into Cervantes's ambivalent relation to the picaresque, which oddly combines fascination and detachment, and into the sophisticated metafictional games that he plays in this chapter with *Guzmán de Alfarache* and its superb little precursor *Lazarillo de Tormes*, would take us too far from our track. Suffice to say that both here and in one of his most famous novelas, *Rinconete y Cortadillo*, he alludes playfully to its conventions, and in a loose sense, parodies them, while using them as a trampoline to launch off in different directions. The most famous convict of the chain-gang, Ginés

---

[38] See, in the same edition, the second *paso* of *Registro de representantes*, included in an appendix among those of doubtful authenticity (pp. 295–303), and the fifth *paso* of *El deleitoso* (pp. 146–53) (Book of Delights) where two thieves intercept a simpleton carrying a pot of food for his wife in prison, 'por cosas de aire, dicen malas lenguas que por alcahueta' (for mere trifles, though according to gossip, for being a go-between).

de Pasamonte, is, among other things, a personification of the arch-*pícaro*, Guzmán de Alfarache, since, like Guzmán, he has written his own memoirs, and intends to finish them on the galleys, which is where Guzmán writes his.[39] In this adventure, the picaresque mainly serves Cervantes as a model of pedigree criminal traits: cynical contempt for the law, stoical defiance, truculence, and a characteristic style, including ruffian's slang and the already mentioned euphemisms. All this is intended as a mocking antithesis of Don Quixote's idealistic altruism, and can be exemplified by convict number five, who has much in common with Guzmán de Alfarache, since he is a student, a glib talker and a competent Latinist. Let us recall that Guzmán, besides having the fluency and wit of an ex-court jester, also studied theology at the university of Alcalá de Henares where he displayed considerable ability until he fell for an innkeeper's daughter and abandoned his studies. Moreover, the crime of the Cervantine convict – promiscuity with two female cousins of his, and simultaneously, with two sisters who weren't related to him, such that the resulting illegitimate brood thoroughly muddied the genealogical trees of the families in question – brings to mind the serial infidelities of Guzmán's grandmother, who managed to tangle up a hundred lineages by persuading each one of her swarms of lovers that her illegitimate daughter, Guzmán's mother, was his and his alone.[40] The unabashed *donjuanismo* of convict number five is compounded by the laid-back, laconic style of his account of his trial and sentence, with its nonchalant assumption that had he been able to pull strings and grease palms, he would have got off scot-free: 'Probóseme todo, faltó favor, no tuve dineros, víame a pique de perder los tragaderos, sentenciáronme a galeras por seis años, consentí; castigo es de mi culpa, mozo soy: dure la vida, que con ella todo se alcanza' (p. 241) (All the charges against me were proven, there was no protector I could turn to, I had no cash, my neck was on the line, they sentenced me to six years in the galleys, I took it on the chin; it's a fair cop, I'm still young, as long as there's life, there's hope). Guzmán de Alfarache, Cervantes's Rinconete and Cortadillo, and Quevedo's Pablos de Segovia exhibit the same staccato succinctness, and the same shoulder-shrugging cynicism and stoicism,

---

[39] Traditionally, the well-known passage of dialogue in which Ginés de Pasamonte refers to his memoirs, destined to eclipse *Lazarillo* and 'todos cuantos de aquel género se han escrito o escribieren' (p. 243) (all those of that genre which have been or may be written), has been interpreted as implying Cervantes's negative attitude towards the new genre. To my mind, this interpretation attributes excessive subtlety to a casual and jocular allusion to what was then perceived as one of the genre's novel and prominent features. See Guillén (1971: 156) and (1966); also, Dunn (1993: 213–15).

[40] *Guzmán de Alfarache*, I, i, 2, ed. Gili Gaya, vol. i, p. 98.

in similar circumstances.[41] Cervantes clearly saw these qualities as intrinsic to the *pícaro*'s brand image.

The Don Quixote of Part I – the character, not the book – is a loose cannon; one never knows into what he will crash next. One aspect of this is his blind tenacity. When involved in an imaginary chivalric adventure, he becomes madly impervious to dissuasion; the least aggravation inflames his choler and provokes aggression. Apart from one major lucid interval – the Arms and Letters speech – his immersion in chivalric fantasy is virtually total, and precludes the affable discretion that will mark much of his dealings with others in Part II. To all intents, the only person with whom he establishes human contact in Part I is Sancho.

The knight is a loose cannon in the further sense of being psychologically unpredictable. While his character derives a basic consistency from his attempt to imitate on a real-life stage the chivalric heroism of Amadís and Company, his madness serves Cervantes as an alibi for ascribing to him arbitrary shifts of attitude. The unqualified devotion that he professes to Dulcinea in I, 13, 25 and 31 does not prevent him from fantasising opportunistically about marrying some beautiful *infanta* and by this means inheriting her father's kingdom (I, 21); his stiff and solemn identification with a haughty stereotype of knightly behaviour, and the imitation of the corresponding style, yields disconcertingly to witty badinage with the first innkeeper about the prospect of *truchuela* (salt cod) for supper (I, 2), and soon after, with the sheep farmer Juan Haldudo about the blood-lettings and shoe-leather owed to him by his servant Andrés (I, 4). His alert and lucid reaction to the first instalment of Cardenio's story (I, 23–24) contrasts with his autistic immersion in chivalric fantasy when the ex-captive recounts his (I, 39–42). So, in the galley-slaves adventure, his ingenuous idealism is disconcertingly belied by his perversely witty apology for the social utility of the shameful office of *alcahuete*, go-between, this being one of the crimes of which convict number four – a tearful, self-pitying ancient with a long white beard – has been found guilty. According to Don Quixote, it is not a criminal activity at all, but rather 'an office most necessary in a well regulated republic, only to be exercised by intelligent, well-born persons, and there should even be an inspector and tribunal charged with testing their suitability and qualifications, as for other trades and offices ... to obviate the regrettable consequences of entrusting the job to imbeciles, like silly women plucked from heaven knows where, page-boys and buffoons of tender years and no experience' (pp. 239–40). The

---

[41] Cf., for example, the style in which Rinconete tells of the whipping and sentence of exile imposed on him as a thief: *Novelas*, ed. García López, p. 166.

Spanish Golden Age, with its fixation on keeping up appearances, derived
endless amusement from the burlesque eulogy of vile occupations, or from
the portrayal of characters who exercise them and, despite that, impudently
lay claim to honour and nobility. The praise or self-praise of the *alcahuete*
or pimp was a topic of the tradition of comedies-in-prose deriving from *La
Celestina*,[42] with their richly diversified cast of ruffians, bawds and whores,
and then becomes popular in seventeenth-century theatre and poetry.[43] In
making Don Quixote articulate it, Cervantes lands us with the problem of
interpretating his motives. Innocently misplaced compassion? Scarcely.
Caustic wit? But how would that square with the innocent idealism shown
elsewhere in the adventure? Clearly, for Cervantes, madness cuts the Gordian
knot of such dilemmas.

A similarly disconcerting impression is caused, after the interrogation is
over, by the speech with which our self-appointed attorney for the defence
pleads with the guards to let their captives go free (pp. 244–5). It is, like the
praise of the *alcahuete*, a world-upside-down defence of the indefensible;
though here the comic inversion of rational normality is not an effect of wit,
but of an incongruous mix of unctuous compassion, naïve casuistry, messianic
arrogance, supplication, threat and emotive maxims. The latter, in particular,
contribute to the speech's ambivalence, which led the essayist Ángel Ganivet
is his *Idearium español* (Spain's Ideology) and the philosopher Miguel de
Unamuno in his *Vida de don Quijote y Sancho* (1905) (Life of Don Quixote
and Sancho), to see it as upholding ideal justice against the cold, institutio-
nalised process of the law.[44] So, for Unamuno, Don Quixote's liberation of
the galley-slaves is consistent with his – also God's, Nature's and the Spanish
people's – preference for hot-blooded, spontaneous punishment followed by
forgiveness. Unamuno's idealised conception of Don Quixote as a modern
version of Christ is, as he well knew, quite unCervantine; it is at odds with the
burlesque effect of the knight's speech, signalled by the unctuous 'hermanos
carísimos' (dearest brethren) with which it begins, grotesquely inappropriate
to the villains whom he has just interviewed. Yet Unamuno's reading is not
wholly off-beam. Don Quixote's maxims, which Unamuno quotes extensi-
vely and are the basis of the knight's plea, would be moving and persuasive
if only the application took account of the circumstances. In pleading for the

[42] It is launched by Celestina herself, who in Act III of Rojas's tragi-comedy, in talking
of her mastery of her profession, boasts of the honourable reputation it has won her. See *La
Celestina*, ed. Cejador y Frauca, vol. i, p. 133. On the figure of the go-between, Redondo (1998:
347–61 and 251–63).

[43] *Don Quijote*, ed. Rodríguez Marín, vol. ii, pp. 173–4 (note).

[44] Ganivet (1933: 68–9), and Unamuno, *Vida*, commentary on Chapter 22, pp. 87–93.

prisoners' freedom he invokes the principle of natural law that was basic to scholastic philosophy's debate about the legitimacy of political authority: 'me parece duro caso hacer esclavos a los que Dios y la naturaleza hizo libres' (It seems to me very harsh to make slaves of persons created free by God and nature).[45] He invokes Christ's 'Judge not that ye be not judged', or a Spanish proverb that expresses basically the same idea: 'Allá se lo haya cada uno con su pecado; Dios hay en el cielo que no se descuida de castigar al malo, ni de premiar al bueno' (Each man's sin is his own affair; God's in heaven, and he doesn't fail to punish the wicked nor to reward the good). He asks the guards, what's in it for you?, or, to put it in his words: 'No es bien que los hombres honrados sean verdugos de los otros hombres, no yéndoles nada en ello' (It's not right for men of honour to inflict punishment on other men, without any personal incentive to do so). This is a principle of clemency that Don Quixote will enjoin on governor-elect Sancho in these terms: 'Cuando pudiere y debiere tener lugar la equidad, no cargues todo el rigor de la ley al delincuente, que no es mejor la fama del juez riguroso que la del compasivo' (II, 42, p. 971) (When clemency can and should be applied, don't come down with all the rigour of the law on the delinquent, for the reputation of a harsh judge is no better than that of a compassionate one). As this quotation shows, in that largely lucid discourse, the injunctions to be merciful carry significant qualifications about taking account of the circumstances and the rights of the other party. By contrast, the exhortation to the guards to show clemency to the impenitent scoundrels in their custody is ridiculous. So, when Don Quixote, after having assaulted the guards and released the prisoners more by luck than by his own efforts, gathers them in a circle around him and arrogantly orders them to go loaded in chains to pay homage to Dulcinea, he gets what he deserves: instead of admiring gratitude, an ignominious pelting with stones.

The chapter ends with a brilliantly evocative image of two vertical figures and two horizontal ones in the now-deserted *sierra*: Don Quijote and Rocinante stretched on the ground side by side; Sancho stripped of his cloak beside his ass, which stands pensive, with head lowered, its ears still twitching in reflex response to the now-ended shower of stones. Those ears are the nearest thing to a comment on the moral of the affair, since Cervantes, characteristically, offers none, save to describe Don Quixote as 'mohinísimo de verse tan malparado por los mismos a quien tanto bien había hecho' (p. 248) (most dejected to find himself so ill used by the very persons to whom

[45] Hamilton (1963: 35–6).

he had done such a good turn). That phrase, I think, carries an echo of the
moral of the Aesopic fable about the man who nurtured a snake and then
complained when it bit him. In the Spanish versions available to Cervantes
it reads: 'El que faze bien y ayuda al malo ingrato sepa que sera del desa-
gradecido y en lugar de le responder con buena obra le contrariara' (He who
does good to the ungrateful evil-doer will receive no thanks from him, and
will get the very opposite of good deeds in return).[46]

So, one can read the adventure as a right-wing fable about the folly of
doing good to the undeserving, an idea that the Spanish proverb expresses
with succinct savagery: 'Cría cuervos y te sacarán los ojos' (Nurture crows
and they will peck your eyes out). Or, with Unamuno, you can read it as a
Christian fable about charity being its own reward, sole consolation for its
inevitable defeat in a mean and nasty world. Or, with the author of *Moby
Dick*, you could take it as yet another example of Don Quixote's defence of
the oppressed and down-and-out, hence as a heart-warming affirmation of the
democratic ideal of the brotherhood of man.[47] This open-ended virtuality of
meaning, characteristic of myth, is typical of *Don Quixote* and is furthered
by Cervantes's playfully ironic detachment.

In this respect it is instructive to compare the galley-slaves adventure
in his novel with its imitation in Avellaneda's sequel to Cervantes's Part
I. In Chapter 8 of Avellaneda's *Don Quijote*, the hero, in Zaragoza, sees a
prisoner being paraded through the streets on an ass while being subjected to
a public whipping. Imagining some fantastic story about a knight abducted
by wicked enemies, he tries to rescue the felon, is overcome by a crowd of
guards and bystanders, and is clapped into prison with the imminent prospect
of suffering the same fate as the man he tried to liberate. He only avoids this
thanks to the intervention of his aristocratic protector, Don Álvaro Tarfe, who
persuades the magistrate to release him on grounds of insanity. That is to
say, Avellaneda treats Don Quixote's intervention as chimerically ineffectual
from a perspective of law-abiding common sense, and quite suppresses the
subversive and thought-provoking implications of the Cervantine adventure.
In Cervantes's version, these arise from a combination of factors: Don Quixote's appeal to principles of clemency and forgiveness; the passing allusions,
however tendentious, to the arbitrariness and corruption of the law; the brutal
disproportion between the prisoners' retaliation and Don Quixote's offence;
above all, the fact that, however mad his intervention, it succeeds. Avellaneda

---

46 *Fábulas de Esopo*, fols xxix–xxx, 'del ombre y de la culuebra'.
47 Levin (1947: 260, 263–6).

upholds conventional poetic justice; Cervantes turns it upside down, and in so doing, appears to be trying to tell us something.

But what precisely? In trying to answer that question, we must not exaggerate the novel's subversiveness. The Quixotic adventures of Part I are rooted in farce, or in neighbouring genres, and partake of farce's licence to turn the normal, respectable world topsy-turvy. When Cervantes, in his prose-epic *Persiles y Sigismunda*, handles situations somewhat similar to the galley-slaves adventure, as he does on three occasions (Book III, Chapters 6, 10, 13), the treatment is more serious and less out of tune with conventional proprieties. The same consideration applies to Don Quixote's lucid precepts of government to Sancho in Part II, Chapters 42 and 43, where some of the edifying principles that are madly misapplied by the liberator of the galley-slaves – particularly those about tempering justice with mercy – are reaffirmed in an ideological context that no contemporary reader would have considered revolutionary. The merry chaos unleashed by Don Quixote's madness permits Cervantes to provide a dénouement which, while castigating his error, satisfies various impulses of his own that are at variance with Avellaneda's conventional solution: his characteristically Spanish suspicion, still alive and kicking today, of the corruption of the law, with accompanying sympathy for the astute outwitting of the legal apparatus;[48] his habitual preference, well exemplified by Sancho's governorship in Part II, for justice of a humane, informal, commonsensical kind that cuts through legalities and tempers harshness with mercy.[49]

So, the galley-slaves adventure cannot plausibly be cited as corroboration of the postmodernist view of *Don Quixote* as a radical questioning of established ideology. All the same, one must avoid minimising this adventure's, and the novel's, potential suggestiveness, similar to the effect of a heavy stone being cast into a deep pool, with ripples of implication spreading out in ever-widening circles from the point of impact. Ever since Baltasar Gracián, in his mid-seventeenth-century prose-allegory of man's pilgrimage through life, *El Criticón* (The Censor), took Don Quixote and Sancho as archetypes of two contrasted moral failings, vain self-importance and selfish pusillanimity, or too much ambition and too little,[50] Cervantes's story, and particularly its

---

[48]   Cf. *El licenciado Vidriera*, in *Novelas*, ed. García López, pp. 188–9; *La ilustre fregona*, in *Novelas*, p. 397; cf. also the dénouement of the interrogation of the two false ex-captives in *Persiles*, Book III, Chapter 10.

[49]   See, apart from the precepts of government to Sancho and his performance as governor in Barataria, *DQ* II, 32, p. 900, *El amante liberal*, in *Novelas*, p. 128 and Periandro's advice to the vengeful husband Ortel Banedre in *Persiles*, Book III, Chapter 6.

[50]   On this, see Close (2004a: 181–2).

central character, have appeared to each succeeding age as symbols of the
human condition, which that age interprets in terms of its own leading preoc-
cupations. We shall examine this historical process in the final chapter and
also try to deal with the question that naturally arises from it: what explains
this book's capacity to mean something different to each succeeding age?
Here, I offer a preliminary answer based on the adventure that has just been
discussed.

The first reason for *Don Quixote*'s open-ended significance – and here lies
its revolutionary novelty in relation to the prose-narrative of its age – has to
do with its ambivalent alternation between the modes of heroic or romantic
adventure and critical parody of them, which often results in the fusion of
these two things. In Don Quixote, liberator of those felons, one perceives a
frustrated and abortive version of Periandro, the hero of Cervantes's Byzantine epic *Persiles y Sigismunda*, much more interesting to us than Periandro
because, unlike that priggish paragon of virtue, he, and the novel about him,
are not set in the plastercast mould of the neo-classical epic and courtly
decorum; rather, he is an individualised, quirkily deluded personality, absurdly
at odds with respectable, commonsense behaviour, who nonetheless violates
these norms from a standpoint that strikes a chord with rational ethical principles. From that paradoxical blend of contraries derives the thought-provoking
resonance of the galley-slaves adventure, giving it simultaneously the stark
exemplariness of a moral fable and the open-ended virtuality of myth.

The second reason, which compounds that original ambivalence, stems
from the original strategy adopted by Cervantes to deal with a dilemma posed
by Spanish Counter-Reformation didacticism. The age's literature of entertainment, *Guzmán de Alfarache* being a major example, either emphatically
identified with it, as Alemán's novel did, or felt obliged to justify its failure to
do so. However, turning a work of light fiction into a pulpit was an infraction
of decorum, as much for post-Tridentine piety as for Classical aesthetics;
and that kind of pretentiousness comes in for wittily malicious satire in the
prologue to *Don Quixote* Part I. Cervantes solved the dilemma of how to
avoid frivolity without sermonising by incorporating in his novel the learned
topics and moral wisdom of his age, while treating them in a manner that
is light, humorous and idiosyncratic. So, the liberator of the galley-slaves
invokes Christian forgiveness, scholastic natural law, the Classical definition
of prudence, and the juridical principle of clemency – all in support of a
comically crazy case. From this clash of persuasively argued unreason and
the established order, Cervantes stands back with amused, ironic detachment.
As a result, ever since about 1700, when temporal distance began to blur
the cultural and ideological premises that Cervantes's contemporaries took

for granted, readers have been asking themselves what he is getting at and whose side he is on. The reactions to his novel by the philosopher Ortega y Gasset and the novelist Milan Kundera, cited towards the end of Chapter 7, are eloquent in this respect.

The third, and related reason for Don Quixote's suggestiveness is its archetypal quality, deriving mainly from the way in which the hero's and Sancho's characters are conceived as a concentrated, seamless synthesis of literary and folkloric types. If Baltasar Gracián in the mid-seventeenth century perceived Don Quixote as the personification of vain self-importance, this was because Cervantes smoothly blends into the character, without advertising the quotations, traits taken from well-known models of boasting and bravado: the *miles gloriosus* of Latin comedy, the braggart lackeys and ruffians of its Spanish Renaissance continuations, the hectoring paladins of the Ariostan tradition, the pathologically snobbish squire of *Lazarillo de Tormes*. If Herman Melville and Unamuno see the liberator of the galley-slaves as an epitome of idealistic altruism, this is because he continually nourishes his conception of knight-errantry with motifs drawn from the Utopian discourses of his epoch: the poetic myth of the Golden Age, the topical contrast of rugged medieval virtues with the degeneracy of the present times, Platonic love, the ideal of a just ruler and of a society of primitive justice.[51] We shall see more examples of such wide-ranging eclecticism in the next chapter. Cervantes's novel is like a giant sponge passed over preceding literature and folklore, absorbing its motifs almost imperceptibly; posterity, in squeezing out the sponge's contents, detects the allusiveness but no longer perceives the specific references, and so supplies any that takes its fancy. Madame de Pompadour's 'Après nous, le déluge' might be Cervantes's fitting epitaph.

---

[51] See Scaramuzza Vidoni (1998: 90–8).

4

The Personalities of Don Quixote and Sancho: Their Genesis, Interrelationship and Evolution

Basic Patterns and Themes of the Dialogue

In the intervals between adventures the knight and his squire talk, and their conversations make up a significant proportion of the novel, representing a radical shift in the development of narrative fiction from incident to dialogue and from action to character. Cervantes's motive in giving the conversations such prominence is clearly attested by those who overhear them and comment on them (e.g. II, 2; p. 641, and II, 7; p. 684): he comes to see the two central figures as extraordinary characters, whose delusions and mannerisms, including their changing attitude towards each other and the world around, constitute the main focus of interest of his story. In Part II, this conception of them supersedes, without totally supplanting, the original motive for pairing Sancho with his master: parody of the knight/squire relationship in chivalry books.

A related, if implicit, motive for the introduction of Sancho in Chapter 7 is the need to complement the solitary, self-absorbed protagonist of the first sally, solemnly engrossed in imitative role-play, with a comic foil of a quite different kind, and the rustic nitwit (*bobo*) of sixteenth-century comedy provided a convenient model. Sancho embodies the stock traits of this type: foolishness, forgetfulness, talkativeness, greed, cowardice, sloth, proneness to solecisms. His arrival in the story logically causes the exchanges with Don Quixote to slot into the standard patterns of master/servant dialogue in sixteenth-century comedy, a high/low antiphonal in which the nobleman's lyrical effusions and posturings of love and honour are met by the commoner's quips, complaints, objections, and concern for skin and creature comforts. In Fernando de Rojas's comedy-in-prose *La Celestina* and its continuations, and in the plays of Lope de Rueda, Juan de Timoneda and the early Lope de Vega, one finds fragments of dialogue that closely prefigure the attitudes of Cervantes's famous pair (Close, 1981). Another early model, though outside the theatre, is the relation of young Lazarillo to his third master, the snobbish, down-at-heels squire, in the third *tratado* or chapter of the first picaresque novel, *Lazarillo de Tormes* (1554).

Such are the basic models of Cervantes's conception of his pair of heroes, though in the course of the story they are augmented by a host of others. The archetypal suggestiveness of the two personalities is explained by a combination of factors: the seamless synthesis of these diverse, traditional traits; the finesse with which they are given life and nuance in specific contexts; and the stark, simple antithesis of two basic tendencies in human nature

In Part I, the theme of the conversations is Don Quixote's chivalric mission. In response to his servant's questions, doubts and mockery, he expounds its rules and practices, his future projects, and, after yet another adventure has ended in humiliation, the reason for the gap between aspiration and outcome. In Part II, where such explanation is no longer deemed necessary, the focus falls on major themes, like the enchantment of Dulcinea and the merits or failings of 'Benengeli's chronicle' (i.e. Part I); also, thanks to major changes in the nature of the story, the subject-matter becomes more diversified and less subservient to the ridicule of chivalry. Though madness effectively isolates Don Quixote from others in Part I, and even in Part II, prevents any genuine intimacy with them, it constitutes no such bar between him and Sancho, to whom he is tied by a bond of increasing affection, the frank exchange of confidences, frequent slippage of the chivalric mask, and a wavelength of colloquial familiarity. With marvellous insight, Cervantes grounds the intimacy between them, which remains immune to the friction between their opposed temperaments and to their differences of rank and education, on a shared attitude of childish make-believe, stemming from the Don's dreams of endless conquests, fame, romance with Dulcinea, and a kingdom, and Sancho's of governorship of an island. This was the aspect that caught Mark Twain's imagination in *The Adventures of Huckleberry Finn* and *Tom Sawyer* (Wonham, 2005: 163). In both Parts, the comedy of their exchanges lies in our perception of the ironic incongruity between the hero's attempt to live on an escapist plane of heroism and his servant's naïve, base pragmatism, coupled with their unawareness both of this incompatibility and of the chimerical nature of their project.

The traits that Don Quixote reveals in that attempt include such things as principled abstemiousness, precious sentimentality, impetuous rashness, overbearing arrogance, trying to keep face in humiliating circumstances, steadfast refusal of inconvenient evidence and, above all, inflexibly treating books as a viable rule of life. Although, thus defined, they are obviously not unique to him, he carries them to a mad extreme, and also, because of the particular nature of his madness, compensates for them with wisdom on matters other than chivalry, wide learning, high moral principle and, lastly, well-meaning innocence. In deflating contrast with his master's high-mindedness, Sancho exhibits a spontaneous reflex of self-preservation, plaintive insistence on painful indignities, stubborn tendency to state the obvious, eagerness to fill his pockets or his belly, and indifference to military glory or nice points of honour. On both sides, this richly ironic counterpoint is constantly enhanced by the style: elegant metaphors and symmetries, word-play, incongruously applied registers, quotations, adages. It abundantly fulfils comedy's perennial mission as Aristotle conceived it: to explore the undignified, but not odious, weaknesses of human nature.

The introduction of Sancho at once lifts the novel to a new plane, transforming Don Quixote from the monomaniac of the early chapters into an individual personality. The exchange of confidences with his servant elicits from him a wide spectrum of traits and moods and the elaboration of the idiosyncratic rationale of his mission. Furthermore, Sancho's presence confronts the knight's fabulous and literary view of things with a reaction of practical reason and instinctive impulse, which, though expressed in ingenuous form, anticipates the objections that common sense would make, forces him to respond to them, and thus to display the absurdity of his convictions all the more effectively.

A passage of dialogue near the beginning of I, 21 (pp. 223–4), humming with acrimonious undertones of the discovery of the fulling-mills in the previous chapter, illustrates these functions well. As he rides away from the melancholy scene of that incident, the hero, over-eager to recover lost face, announces with qualified confidence that he can see a man coming towards them with the helmet of Mambrino on his head. Sancho, wary after the chastisement that met his mirth upon that discovery, including the admonition to talk a lot less in future, expresses scepticism with sly innuendo: *if* he could talk as freely as before, he *might* adduce reasons that *might* cause his master to recognise his error. Naturally, this goads his master to pass from qualified confidence to irate certainty:

> '¿Cómo me puedo engañar en lo que digo, traidor escrupuloso ... Dime, ¿no ves aquel caballero que hacia nosotros viene, sobre un caballo rucio rodado, que trae puesto en la cabeza un yelmo de oro?'
>
> 'Lo que yo veo y columbro ... no es sino un hombre sobre un asno pardo, como el mío, que trae puesto sobre la cabeza una cosa que relumbra.'
>
> 'Pues ese es el yelmo de Mambrino ... Apártate a una parte y déjame con él a solas; verás cuán sin hablar palabra, por ahorrar del tiempo, concluyo esta aventura y queda por mío el yelmo que tanto he deseado.'

'Yo me tengo en cuidado el apartarme … mas quiera Dios, torno a decir, que orégano sea y no batanes.'

'Ya os he dicho, hermano, que no me mentéis ni por pienso eso de los batanes … que voto, y no digo más que os batanee el alma.'

'How can I be wrong in what I say, you quibbling traitor? … Tell me, don't you see that knight coming towards us, on a dappled grey horse, wearing a golden helmet on his head?'

'All I can see … is a man on a greyish donkey like my own with something that shines on his head.'

'Well, that's the helmet of Mambrino … move to one side, and leave him to me; just see how soon I conclude this affair, without wasting time on words, and win the helmet I've wanted for so long.'

'I'll take good care to move aside, and pray to God you strike gold this time and not more fulling-mills.'

'Have I not told you, sir, never, ever to mention fulling-mills to me again, or else I swear to … well, I won't say it – but I swear it will be you that's put through the mill.'

The dogmatism, exasperation and arrogance of the initial question are absurdly punctured by the reply: wary, laconic, factual, matching it point by point. The last part of the altercation contains word-play and a shift of register that are impossible to translate literally, conveying, on Sancho's part, mocking allusions to the humiliating discovery of those fulling-mills, and on his master's side, menacing anger provoked by the reminders. 'Quiera Dios … que orégano sea y no batanes' facetiously alters the proverb '¡A Dios plega que orégano sea y no se nos vuelva alcaravea!' (pray to God it's oregano and doesn't turn into caraway), used to express the hope that there will be a good outcome rather than a bad one. The *hidalgo*'s anger is reflected in the shift from familiar 'tú' (thou) to disdainful 'vos' (you), used by noblemen when addressing very lowly inferiors, and in the half-checked oath 'voto a Dios' (I swear to God), with the subsequent threat of inflicting yet more violence on his impertinent servant. The irony of these exchanges is enhanced by Cervantes's neutrality, since so far he has not revealed who the distant figure and what the object is. Sancho's wariness points to an outcome that common sense expects, but must as yet infer. Cervantes supplies it while Don Quixote prepares to charge: the alleged wearer of the helmet is a country barber who has put a basin on his head to protect his new hat from a shower of rain.

When Don Quixote triumphantly returns with the captured spoils, abandoned by the terrified barber as soon as he sees the armed rider bearing down upon him, the altercation resumes with a different tone and resolution.

Sancho, still wary after the adventure of the fulling-mills, checks his laughter on hearing the object described as a helmet, and comes up with an explanation for its appearance that meets Don Quixote half-way: 'Ríome ... de considerar la gran cabeza que tenía el pagano dueño deste almete, que no parece sino una bacía de barbero pintiparada' (pp. 225–6) (I'm laughing at the thought of the huge head the pagan owner of the helmet must have had; it looks just like a barber's basin). Don Quixote, perhaps mollified by this moderation, or magnanimous after victory, or mindful of his mistake over the fulling-mills, comes up with his first acknowledgement that the prosaic aspect of marvellous things is no insignificant accident to be brushed aside, but a permanent aspect that requires explanation. The one that he suggests is quite barmy: the helmet must have fallen into the hands of an ignoramus, who, ignorant of its true worth, and seeing it to be of pure gold, melted down the lower half for the money, turning the upper half into 'this, which looks like a basin, as you say'. It is another significant turning-point in Don Quixote's evolution, portrayed with exquisite humour and finesse. It also confirms the wisdom of Dr Johnson's remark about this novel's universal truth to human nature. Every day in the real world one observes disputes – personal, professional, political – that follow the pattern of this one, from heated altercation through prudent concession to amicable compromise; it is the fantastic dottiness of the premises, coupled to that resemblance, that makes this manifestation so appealing.

Character-Construction

I now want to consider how Cervantes constructs his two central characters: that is, how he invents, combines and develops the traits of each. Though their evolution over the course of the novel anticipates one of the major themes of the future genre: the forging and loss of illusions, thoughts of supplying their relationship with this kind of unifying thread were no doubt remote from Cervantes's mind in Part I, which ends with the heroes' illusions firmly intact. They crystallise in Part II, more in relation to Don Quixote than to Sancho, though even in this Part, the progress of both towards enlightenment is halting and checked by frequent regression. Indeed, their psychological development, from beginning to end, is a contradictory process: logically evolutionary in one aspect, circular, irregular and arbitrary in another, resulting from the improvised way in which the original model is modified and enriched.

Among Cervantes's fictional characters, Don Quixote and Sancho are alone in undergoing this peculiar form of development, and this is owing to factors unique to them. First, though Cervantes's notions of characterisation, like those of his contemporaries, are generally guided by what was then called 'decoro', decorum, which in a primary aspect refers to common expectations about how a person of a given age, sex and status would or should typically behave, his conception of one of the heroes as mad and the other as simple-minded liberates him to a considerable extent from the constraints of stereotype. Not only does he depict their delusions as extraordinary; he also often attributes to them behaviour that seems inconsistent or capriciously unexpected, leaving the reader to guess at the motivation. Secondly, there is a fundamental conflict in Cervantes's motives in composing his story. In one way, the fundamental logic of Don Quixote's and Sancho's experience, in which optimistic but illusory expectations are repeatedly dashed on the rocks of 'common nature', demands that both, particularly the hero, should progress towards rational enlightenment. To some extent, this is indeed what happens; for example, in Part II, chastened by previous humiliations, the hero no longer sees inns as castles. However, definitive recovery of sanity by him would put an end to the story, and a logic just as powerful as the one just mentioned, reflected in the delight of other characters in humouring his madness, results in indefinite postponement of the moment of truth. That delight is eloquently attested by the fervent protest of Don Antonio Moreno, Don Quixote's host and chaperone in Barcelona, when he hears Sansón Carrasco explain why he has pursued his mad friend to that city in order to provoke a joust with him, defeat him and impose on him the condition of returning home and renouncing chivalry for one year (II, 65; p. 1162). Consequently, the steady erosion of illusions is continually checked, though not totally reversed, by reconfirmation of them. For example, even after Sancho's abdication from the governorship of Barataria (II, 53), which one might suppose to be a definitive moment of enlightenment, he still dreams of acquiring a noble office that will be more lucrative and less demanding (see the endings of II, 55 and II, 64).

The third factor relates to the fundamental principle of composition noted above (pp. 43–45): continuous recycling of motifs with new variations on each new occurrence. So far as concerns the pair's conversations, it can partly be seen as a natural process. For example, since Don Quixote assumes *a priori* that he is an all-conquering knight-errant, it is logical, if crazily absurd, that in the face of repeated undignified mishaps he should continually refuse the evidence of his senses and resort to the excuse of being thwarted by envious enchanters. Moreover, his sensitivity to recent and accumulated experience entails that the excuse does not remain static, but evolves in response to circumstances. However, explanations in terms of verisimilitude and logical consistency only explain so much. Often, the variations of recurrent behaviour-patterns involve an unpredictable departure from them, resulting either from the importation of motifs from an external source, or their arbitrary transfer from one character to another, or from one context to a quite different one.

This improvisatory method of composition is integral to the assembly of Don Quixote's and Sancho's characters, and endows them with disconcerting ambiguity. It has been overlooked by a long tradition of modern Cervantine criticism, from Salvador de Madariaga's *Guía del lector del* Quijote (1926)[1] to much more recent essays or books of a Freudian or post-Freudian bent, which take for granted that Don Quixote's and Sancho's personalities are determined by notions of realistic psychology. To see why the assumption is misleading in this case, it is instructive to contrast Cervantes's procedure with that typical of a novelist like Galdós, active in the heyday of nineteenth-century positivism.

In the prologue to *Misericordia* (1897), Galdós speaks like an anthropologist of the months spent in observing and documenting the behaviour of the residents of Madrid's poor quarters; and the effects of this empiricism are readily observable in his fictional characters, who give the impression of being shaped in accord with psychological principles and socio-economic circumstances established from the beginning. Whereas their development exhibits the logic of a biological organism, those of Don Quixote and Sancho resemble a haphazard process of DIY, in which an original framework is continually modified by the addition of new pieces or the alteration of existing ones.

Let us see how this applies to Sancho. Instead of adopting Galdós's procedure – that is, placing the character in a well-defined social context, endowing him with realistic, consistent mannerisms, and baptising the result with a plausible proper name – Cervantes introduces him in Part I, Chapter 7 as a generic type – 'un labrador vecino suyo ... de muy poca sal en la mollera' (a peasant from the same village, with very little grey matter in his noodle) – baptising him with a partly symbolic name.[2] The sources from which he draws his traits include the proverb tradition, popular jests, student folklore, *Amadís de Gaula*, contemporary theatre and sixteenth-century comedy. Thus, the rustic associations of the name and Sancho's friendship with his ass are anticipated by the proverbs 'Topado ha Sancho con su asno' (Sancho has bumped into his donkey) and 'Allá va Sancho con su rocino' (there goes

---

1 The English translation is listed in the Bibliography. See Madariaga (1948).

2 On Sancho Panza's genesis, see Hendrix (1925); Rosenblat (1971: 173–4); Márquez Villanueva (1973: 20–94); Molho (1976: 248ff.); Urbina (1991); Redondo (1998: 191–203).

Sancho with his nag), which refer to inseparable friends, and his former job as swine-herd is evoked by 'Sancho, cochino o puerco, todo es uno' (Sancho, pig or swine it's all the same). The popular jest-tradition contains alternating and contradictory images of the peasant as a credulous fool and a sly rogue (Chevalier, 1978: 145ff.). Sancho combines them both, and, as already noted, various traditional attributes of this type as portrayed in the theatre, including sturdy, plain-speaking integrity, whose most famous embodiment in Spanish Golden Age literature is Pedro Crespo, the hero of Calderón's *El alcalde de Zalamea* (The Mayor of Zalamea). At carnival time in the university of Salamanca, the students called the patron-saint of their feasts, Panza, belly; as applied to Sancho, the name signifies his gluttony (Redondo, 1998: 196). As for *Amadís de Gaula*, Sancho's affectionate loyalty towards his master repeats, and also parodies, that of Amadís's squire, Gandalín, who is rewarded by governorship of an island for his service: the model of Don Quixote's promise to Sancho in I, 7.

Now let us consider his style. Here again, Cervantes's procedure is very different from Galdós's systematic documentation of the speech-habits of Madrid's urban proletariat. For a start, he avoids the use of *sayagués* – the Leonese rural dialect conventionally used by the rustics of the theatre – and the crude, rustic solecisms that spatter the discourse of Avellaneda's version of Sancho. Instead, he creates a stylised, literary illusion of rusticity by means of rambling, unstructured syntax, and comparisons, exclamations, and turns of phrase of a plebeian and colloquial, but not specifically rustic, flavour. The most obvious example of this is Sancho's habit of citing proverbs in torrential profusion, first revealed in Part I, Chapter 25. This trait was treated in the *Celestina* tradition as typical of low-class, underworld characters of *urban*, not rustic, origin; and in Quevedo's satiric writings the mindless and inconsequential overuse of proverbs is regarded as a habitual defect of vulgar speech regardless of the speaker's origin.[3] Moreover, Sancho's style frequently goes far beyond the capacities of an ignorant peasant, embracing legal and commercial jargon, Italianisms and Latinisms, reminiscences of Garcilaso, Jorge Manrique, Petrarch, ruffian's slang, sophisticated word-play and not infrequent rhetorical elegance (Rosenblat, 1971: 205–42). In short, if one took Sancho's discourse as a norm, one would obtain a very peculiar notion of the speech-habits of the peasantry of New Castile around 1600.

Furthermore, the original reason for Sancho's existence has just as little to do with empirical reality as the sources on which his character is modelled;

---

[3] Close (2004b: 28, 30, 32–3).

rather, it consists in his essential function in relation to his master: to provide
an ironically negative counterpoint to the latter's chivalric posturing. In all
these ways Sancho is the product of an archaic art-form, the term archaic
being used in the neutral, non-derogatory sense of typical of an age prior to
the contemporary one. The foregoing considerations about his genesis apply,
with suitable variations in each case, to Monipodio and his criminal gang
in Cervantes's *Rinconete y Cortadillo*, the bawd Celestina in Fernando de
Rojas's tragi-comedy *La Celestina*, Lazarillo de Tormes, Lope's jesting servants.

The same considerations apply to Don Quixote. I do not mean to suggest
that the conception of his character is not influenced to a certain degree
by Cervantes's knowledge of the behaviour of madmen, either acquired by
direct observation or mediated to him by medical treatises on the melancholic
condition (cf. below, p. 174).[4] Although the hunt for real-life models of Don
Quixote has long since been abandoned, nobody could dispute Cervantes's
keen interest in the types of ingeniously inventive madness described by Juan
Huarte de San Juan in his *Examen de ingenios para las ciencias* (Enquiry
into mental aptitudes for various intellectual disciplines),[5] and later portrayed
by Lope de Vega in the fourth book of his *Peregrino en su patria* (1604)
(The Pilgrim in his own Land). But for the most part the original ingredients of Cervantes's mad *hidalgo* do not derive from observation but from
sources of a folkloric, literary, theatrical and anecdotal nature: the madly
boastful, fantasising soldier known as El Capitano in the *commedia dell'arte*
(Roca Mussons, 2003), the allegorical figure of Lent contrasted with Carnival
satiety (Redondo, 1998: 206–9), anecdotes about obsessive readers of chivalry
books whose addiction anticipates Don Quixote's,[6] the bombastic knights of
the tradition stemming from Ariosto's *Orlando furioso*,[7] the braggart lackeys
and ruffians of sixteenth-century Spanish comedy,[8] Amadís de Gaula and his

---

4 Such as Cristóbal de Vega, *De arte medendi*, 1564. For a more detailed list, see the catalogue of the sources of Robert Burton's *The Anatomy of Melancholy* (1621), drawn up by Paul
Jordan Smith (1931: 43–9). Renaissance ideas on melancholy, documented by Babb (1951) and
by Redondo (1998: 121–46), also influence treatises on laughter, such as Gómez de Miedes, *De
sale libri quatuor* (1572)

5 In Chapter 4 of the 1575 edition, which becomes Chapter 7 of the 1594 edition. On this,
see the chapter by Redondo just mentioned.

6 See Riley (1986: 42–3); also López Pinciano, *Philosophia antigua poetica*, ed. Carballo
Picazo, vol. i, pp. 170–2.

7 It is a characteristic trait of paladins featured in Spanish plays derived from Ariosto and
Boiardo; cf. the boastful paladins Roldán and Reinaldos of Cervantes's own comedy *La casa
de los celos*, which belongs to this family (Close, 2003: 338–41).

8 Such as the ruffian Centurio in Rojas's *La Celestina*, whose vainglorious panegyric to

progeny, the madly besotted Calisto of Rojas's *La Celestina*,[9] the emotional and stylistic preciosity of shepherds of pastoral romance,[10] the paranoid obsession with honour of Lazarillo's third master,[11] the romantic lovers of Lope de Vega's theatre, whose relation to their servants is a primary model of the Quixote/Sancho relationship (Close, 1981). As for Don Quixote's style, we have already noted its vast eclecticism, which not only embraces a host of elevated literary registers but also incongruously combines them with others of a very different origin: the colloquial familiarity of his discourse with Sancho, vulgar oaths, witty word-play, comic proverbial sayings, and so on. The explanation that is implied within the story for this impressive linguistic scope consists in the bookishness and ingenious inventiveness of the hero's madness; however, one could scarcely consider this to be a realistic idiosyncracy of character. To a large extent, its origin lies in Don Quixote's function as an instrument of parody. Furthermore, the particular nature of Don Quixote's madness must be attributed to a similar cause: his role as vehicle for the ridicule of chivalry books, which leads Cervantes to visualise him as a sort of living embodiment of the genre. His tendency to take black for white – inns as castles, sheep as armies, and so on – is designed to highlight, by its burlesque exaggeration, the genre's fabulous perversion of 'la común naturaleza', common nature (I, 49; p. 562). For Cervantes, his madness is, by definition, a condition that negates normality as well as rationality.

the lethal properties of his sword in Act XVIII of the tragi-comedy anticipates Don Quixote's indignant tirade about the exemptions and privileges of knight-errants whose 'ley es su espada, sus fueros sus bríos, sus premáticas su voluntad' (I, 45; p. 529) (whose law is their sword, their charter of rights their valour, their edicts their own will). Both passages consist of a passionate torrent of rhetorical questions beginning with '¿quién?' or '¿qué?' (who or what?).

[9] Apart from stylistic anticipations of Cervantes's novel, the way in which Calisto humiliates himself before the shameless bawd Celestina in Act I of *La Celestina*, praising her as though she were a saint, constitutes an evident model for Don Quixote's attitude towards the prostitutes at the inn (I, 2), Maritornes (I, 16), Aldonza Lorenzo (I, 25 y 31).

[10] An analogy suggested by Cervantes himself, through the niece's suggestion in the scrutiny of Don Quixote's library that the pastoral romances should be burnt alongside the chivalry books (I, 6; p. 84). See also the discussion of the Marcela/Grisóstomo episode in Chapter 3, pp. 70–73.

[11] See the passage of the third *tratado* (chapter) of *Lazarillo de Tormes*, in which the squire's boasts about the sharpness of his sword blade, supposedly capable of cutting a ball of wool, provoke young Lázaro to reflect sarcastically how well his teeth could cut a loaf of bread (*Lazarillo de Tormes*, ed. Cejador y Frauca, pp. 160–1). It prefigures numerous exchanges between Don Quixote and Sancho in which the military enthusiasm of the former is deflatingly contrasted with the cautiously pragmatic response of the latter.

Character-Development: the Dulcinea Theme

So much for the models on which Cervantes bases the two protagonists.
Let us now see how he develops them in the course of the story, taking as
example the hero's conception of Dulcinea. Once again, we need to be wary
of applying modern notions of psychological realism to *Don Quixote*. The
Dulcinea theme has a burlesque function; and burlesque, as Henry Fielding
notes in the preface to *Joseph Andrews* (1742), involves 'appropriating the
manners of the highest to the lowest' and vice-versa, and by this means,
presents monstrous incongruities alien to 'the just imitation of [Nature]'.[12]
While the theme complies fully with the first part of Fielding's diagnosis, it
only partly confirms his comment about inverisimilitude; nonetheless, it does
so to the extent that in order to sustain those grotesque misappropriations,
Cervantes causes the two principal characters to perform functions instru-
mental to his purpose, often with scant regard for consistency. Modern criticism, taking advantage of the often unexplained arbitrariness of the hero's
attitude to Dulcinea, which leaves ample scope for the reader's imagination,
tends to treat it without further ado as psychologically lifelike, and furthermore, as nobly idealised, hence essentially independent of its coarse rustic
antitheses, originating mainly from Sancho.[13] This makes possible a compassionate interpretation of it, according to which its degradation in Part II is
symptomatic of a traumatic, poignant contamination of the hero's chivalric
ideal, resulting from his conscious or subconscious recognition that it does
not conform to reality's laws.[14] Yet to interpret it mainly from the perspective of his subjectivity falsifies it: first, because Cervantes, like Sancho and
other characters around Don Quixote, always treats it with detached levity,
unlike the seriously compassionate attitude that he shows towards the sentiments of a true romantic hero; and, secondly, because one cannot separate
the high strand of the theme from the low one with which it is deliberately
intertwined from the beginning. Their conjunction is a sign of the extremity

---

12 Fielding, *Joseph Andrews* and *Shamela*, ed. Hawley, p. 50.

13 Much of this line of interpretation goes back to Chapters 9 and 10 of the book by Madariaga (1948) originally published in 1926, and centres on the story of the Cave of Montesinos.
Apart from him, the critics to whom I particularly refer are: Percas de Ponseti (1975: vol. ii, pp.
407–583); Avalle-Arce (1976: 173–214); Parker (1984: 113–17); Riley (1982: 105–19; 1986:
135–43). See also on this much-discussed episode, Dunn (1973); Torrente Ballester (1975:
178–84); Gethin Hughes (1977); Aurora Egido (1986–91); Redondo (1998: 403–20).

14 For example, Parker, referring to the story of the Cave, notes: 'everywhere there is an
atmosphere of psychological and physical decline ... When ideals come to this, disillusion is
pathetically sad and no longer funny' (1984: 115).

of Don Quixote's infraction of decorum – in the sense of appropriateness to circumstances; it is a principle instinctively ingrained in Cervantes, and much less evident and strongly felt in our age than it was then. Rather than some kind of tragi-comic romance, the relation of Don Quixote to Dulcinea constitutes a story of a quite different kind, essentially comic in nature though not without pathos towards the end.

It plays an unusual variation on the habitual opposition between Quixotic illusion and some kind of debased reality, which the knight seeks to explain away by enchantment. Here, what is opposed to his ideal is just as fictitious as it is, and originates in Sancho's description of Dulcinea in mid-Part I, conjured out of his own fantasy. With an irony of which Don Quixote is never aware, he trustingly depends on Sancho, a broken reed, to act as honest broker between his poetic make-believe about his mistress and her counterpart in the real world. Cervantes evidently delights in the complex spiral of embarrassing dilemmas and face-saving subterfuges in which Sancho's original fibs land him, accompanied by his master's tortuous attempts to reconcile the Sanchopanzine versions of Dulcinea with his own idealised image of her. It is a grotesque collision of opposed mirages, which brings into play an interlinked series of situational ironies: 'the tables turned', 'hoist with own petard', 'standing on the evidence and failing to see it', 'treating damning evidence as positive proof'. If Don Quixote is originally the deceived party, and Sancho the deceiver, their common credulity ends up by reducing them to the same level. In the protracted evolution of the Dulcinea saga, the repetition or recycling of motifs, with the various types of variation previously noted, plays a fundamental role.

Our starting-point is Don Quixote's conversation with Sancho about his projected penance for Dulcinea in the *sierra* (I, 25), in the course of which he casually lets slip the information that she is Aldonza Lorenzo, daughter of Lorenzo Corchuelo and Aldonza Nogales, thus fleshing out the narrator's original information that a good-looking wench of that name from El Toboso, whom the *hidalgo* had once fancied, is the real-life basis for Dulcinea (I, 25; pp. 282–3; cf. I, 1; p. 44). Don Quixote adds that their relationship has always been platonic, never having gone beyond a chaste exchange of looks, a revelation immediately qualified in such a way as to imply that 'platonic' means virtually non-existent. Sancho pounces on this disclosure, claiming to know Aldonza well, and proceeds to offer a shatteringly degraded portrait of a coarse, suntanned, brawny, loud-voiced and promiscuous village lass, whose typical pursuits are carding flax or threshing wheat. In reply, Don Quixote defends his choice of mistress and his idealised conception of her with a tissue of sophistry (pp. 284–5) – a crazy blend of sly vulgarity, cynical candour and high-minded principle – the gist of which is the admission that he merely pretends she is a princess, while justifying the pretence with the argument that beauty and virtue, not rank, are the true causes of love. This would be more persuasive if he did not admit in the next breath that the beauty and virtue are poetic figments too: 'Y para concluir con todo, yo imagino que todo lo que digo es así, sin que sobre ni falta nada, y píntola en mi imaginación como la deseo, así en la belleza como en la principalidad, y ni le llega Elena, ni la alcanza Lucrecia, ni otra alguna de las hermosas mujeres de las edades pretéritas, griega, bárbara o latina' (And to conclude, I imagine that all is as I say, no more and no less, and I depict her in my imagination as I wish her to be, both in beauty and in princely rank, so that neither Helen nor Lucrece nor any other beautiful woman of the past, Greek, Latin or barbarian, comes near her). The confession should not lead us to see his attitude to Dulcinea as deliberate fraud: the nature of his madness is such that, for him, there is no difference between make-believe and being. Even so, at the back of his mind there lurks the realisation that Dulcinea's status is not what he claims, since when interrogated it by Vivaldo (I, 13), and again by the Duke and Duchess (II, 32), he takes refuge in evasions that revealingly imply what he is ashamed to admit.

From the moment of his confession to Sancho in I, 25, his attitude to Dulcinea, and others' response to it, will chiefly consist in variations on this juxtaposition of idealised fantasy and crude rusticity, accompanied by his attempts to explain away the discrepancy. In origin, this situation blends two burlesque motifs derived from early sixteenth-century theatre: the contrast between the nobleman's idealised attitude to his mistress and the servant's degraded version, which the lover indignantly corrects, and the scene where an impudent rustic describes his sexual encounter with a girlfriend who is the epitome of unladylike rusticity.[15] So, in I, 25, we have the first major modification of the original dichotomy Aldonza Lorenzo/Dulcinea, and it involves importation of motifs from an external source. How does the Dulcinea theme evolve subsequently?

Six chapters later (I, 31), Sancho is debriefed by his master concerning his alleged embassy to Dulcinea, in which he was supposed to deliver a love-letter to her and give an account of his penance for her sake in the *sierra*. In fact, Sancho never went to El Toboso, for his mission was thwarted by the priest and barber before he got beyond the inn (I, 26); there, they bullied him into leading them back to his master so that they could bring him home and

---

[15] E.g. Torres Naharro, *Comedia Ymenea, Comedia Calamita* and *Comedia Aquilana*, in *Propalladia*, ed. Gillet, vol. ii, pp. 271–6, 369–71 and 458–63.

cure him. When, after being reunited with Don Quixote, Sancho is subjected to his eagerly curious questions about what transpired in the interview with Dulcinea, he is forced to tell a pack of lies, endeavouring to keep consistency with his portrayal of Aldonza in I, 25. He improvises a picture of a muscular, sweaty wench winnowing wheat in the yard of her house, and reacting to the delivery of the letter in a suitably prosaic, if well-meaning way. The dialogue runs on parallel but incompatible tracks, high and low, one obtusely and serenely at odds with the other, like this:

'Todo eso no me descontenta; prosigue adelante,' dijo don Quijote. 'Llegaste, ¿y qué hacía aquella reina de la hermosura? A buen seguro que la hallaste ensartando perlas, o bordando alguna empresa con oro de cañutillo poara este su cautivo caballero.'

'No la hallé,' respondió Sancho, 'sino ahechando dos hanegas de trigo en un corral de su casa.'

'Pues haz cuenta … que los granos de aquel trigo eran granos de perlas, tocados de sus manos. Y si miraste, amigo, el trigo ¿era candeal o trechel?'

'No era sino rubión,' respondió Sancho.

'Pues yo te aseguro,' dijo don Quijote, 'que ahechado por sus manos, hizo pan candeal, sin duda alguna. Pero pasa adelante; cuando le diste mi carta, ¿besóla? ¿Púsoselo sobre la cabeza? ¿Hizo otra ceremonia digna de tal carta, o qué hizo?'

'Cuando yo se la iba a dar,' respondió Sancho, 'ella estaba en la fuga del meneo de una buena parte de trigo que tenía en la criba, y díjome: "Poned, amigo, esa carta sobre aquel costal, que no la puedo leer hasta que acabe de acribar todo lo que aquí está."'

'All that doesn't displease me; carry on,' said Don Quixote. 'You arrived, and what was that queen of beauty doing? No doubt you found her stringing pearls or embroidering some device with gold thread for this captive knight of hers.'

'I just found her winnowing some bushels of wheat in a yard of her house,' replied Sancho.

'Then imagine that the wheat was grains of pearls, touched by her hands … And did you look to see if the wheat was *candeal* [the finest quality] or *trechel* [also esteemed]?'

'It was just *rubión* [coarser reddish grain],' answered Sancho.

'Then I assure you,' said Don Quixote, 'that winnowed by her hands it made the very whitest bread, without a doubt. But continue: when you gave her my letter, did she kiss it? Did she place it on her head? Did she perform some other ceremony worthy of it, or what did she do?'

'When I was about to give it to her,' replied Sancho, 'she was vigorously shaking a large quantity of wheat in her sieve, and said to me: "Put it there on that sack for I can't read it until I've finished what I'm doing."'

One notes that Don Quixote does not, as he will later do, reject Sancho's account as a delusion caused by enchantment, but benignly and quite incongruously accepts the essentials while combining them with his own idealised conception of how the interview should have gone. He does not, for example, dispute that she, a princess, was winnowing wheat, he just quibbles about the quality and fantasises about its transformation into pearls. Furthermore, Sancho's version of events, though more or less consistent with his previous portrayal of Aldonza, contradicts it in one important respect. On this occasion Cervantes comments that Sancho was relieved when his master's interrogation was over, since, though he knew her to be a country girl from El Toboso, he had never seen her in his life. On the previous occasion Sancho claimed to know her well and gives clear evidence of doing so. The reason for this flagrant inconsistency, I believe, is that in the earlier chapter, Cervantes, influenced by his theatrical sources, attributes to him the impudent wit of the clowns featured in them, whose burlesque portrait refers to a wench whom they know. In the later chapter, he makes Sancho revert to his more usual ingenuousness, reflected in the pedestrian banality of his account, and to his familiar habit of lying to save face or get out of a scrape.

The next major manifestation of the Dulcinea theme comes in Part II, Chapters 8 to 10 inclusive, a sequence of events precipitated by Don Quixote's announcement that he intends to go to El Toboso to seek Dulcinea's blessing for the new sally. This puts Sancho in an awful pickle: how is he to avoid discovery of the lies that he told in I, 31 about having delivered a message to Dulcinea at her home? After the pair have blundered about the town at dead of night (II, 9), at ridiculous cross-purposes over the nature and whereabouts of her dwelling, which for Don Quixote must be a noble palace and for Sancho a small house with a yard enclosed by mud walls, the master agrees to wait outside the town, letting his servant return in daylight to find Dulcinea. Their search is all the more absurd because by this stage, for both of them, she has lost all contact with anybody in the real world; Sancho has forgotten about her equivalence to Aldonza Lorenzo (though he remembers again in a letter to his wife in II, 36), and nitwittedly supposes her to be a noble lady of El Toboso, while Don Quixote, even less in touch with reality, claims never to have seen Dulcinea, and to have fallen in love with her merely 'de oídas', by hearsay, despite his previous contrary assertion in I, 25. Cervantes offers no explanation for these inconsistencies.

Left to his own devices (II, 10), Sancho hits on a ruse to get himself out of his scrape. He returns to his master claiming that three peasant-girls mounted on donkeys who emerge by chance from the town are the radiantly beautiful Dulcinea accompanied by two ladies-in-waiting, and ceremoniously presents her to him, relying on Don Quixote's credulity about enchantment to do the rest.

In this encounter, the uncouth, brawny Dulcinea previously engendered by Sancho's inventive fantasy now materialises in the shape of a rather similar wench of flesh-and-blood accompanied by two others. So, the function of opposing a rustic Dulcinea to the Don's idealising expectations has been transferred from Sancho to Cervantes, as narrator and painter of the girls' appearance and language. In this famous scene, the hero kneels with bulging eyes and distraught gaze ('con ojos desencajados y vista turbada') before the girl before him, gracelessly snub-nosed and moon-faced ('carirredonda y chata'); and her and her companions' coarse reaction to this surprising interception befits their rustic status:

> A lo que respondió Sancho:
> '¡Oh princesa y señora universal del Toboso! ¿Cómo vuestro magnánimo corazón no se enternece viendo arrodillado ante vuestra sublimada presencia a la coluna y sustento de la andante caballería?'
> Oyendo lo cual otra de las dos, dijo:
> 'Mas ¡jo, que te estrego, burra de mi suegro! ¡Mirad con qué se vienen los señoritos ahora a hacer burla de las aldeanas, como si aquí no supiésemos echar pullas como ellos! Vayan su camino e déjenmos hacer el nueso, y serles ha sano.'

> To which Sancho replied:
> 'Oh princess and universal lady of Toboso! How can your magnanimous heart not melt when you see kneeling before your heavenly presence the column and pillar of knight-errantry?'
> At which one of the other two girls said:
> 'Fine words butter no parsnips, I'm sure.[16] See these toffs trying to take the mickey out of us village-girls, as if we couldn't repay their funny remarks with interest. Get on your way and let us go ourn, and it'll be the better for you.'

The scene involves the arbitrary transfer of motifs – apart from the one just mentioned – from one zone of the novel to another; and it affects both master

---

[16] The literal translation of the Spanish would be: 'Whoa, I'm rubbing you down, my father-in-law's donkey', and signifies 'Don't say thank you!' addressed to an ungrateful person. It was also a standard sarcastic retort by country-girls to the flirtatious compliments of wayfarers.

and squire. First, Sancho displays unprecedented wit and aplomb, not only deceiving his master, but doing so with a hyperbolic virtuosity that maliciously parodies his style. Also, Don Quixote's reaction to Sancho's trick shows a notable deviation from his previous attitude to women, including some quite as unattractive as these three. Previously, in potentially romantic encounters like this, his imagination never failed to transform them into exalted ladies; now, all fired by expectation, it fails. Why? An explanation based on natural verisimilitude suggests itself: in Part II, chastened by previous humiliations, he tends to see things as they are. Yet there is a more specific reason. The roles of master and squire in this adventure are prefigured by the practical joke in late Part I, modelled on a famous one in Folengo's macaronic epic *Baldus*, in which the guests at the inn support Don Quixote's claim that the barber's shaving-basin is the helmet of Mambrino (I, 44–5), to the consternation of its rightful owner. Don Quixote is not the principal butt of the joke on this occasion, yet, added to other imagined instances of enchantment, all involving the transformation of marvellous things into prosaic ones, it gives a new inflexion to his belief in it, thus predisposing him for the victim's role.

That belief is affirmed as a kind of general principle of relativity, in Part I, Chapter 25. With the example of the basin/helmet of Mambrino in mind, and also incidents like the blanketing and the assault on the sheep, he tells Sancho that it is the peculiar lot of knights-errant to be persecuted by envious enchanters who keep turning things from their true shapes into false ones, so that 'eso que a ti te parece bacía de barbero, a mí me parece yelmo de Mambrino, y a otro le parecerá otra cosa' (p. 277) (what seems like a barber's basin to you, is the helmet of Mambrino to me, and will be something different to somebody else). At a later stage of Part I, he sees the altercation at the inn over the basin/helmet as furnishing manifest proof of this principle, and, together with other occurrences of magical transformation at this imagined castle, leaves him incapable of identifying anything in it with certainty. It is no doubt memory of the metamorphoses of Part I, all involving the supposed conversion of noble things into abject ones, which leads to a further refinement of the principle in Part II, Chapter 8, which has specific reference to Dulcinea and remains basic to his outlook thereafter. On the way to El Toboso to see Dulcinea, he indignantly disputes Sancho's allegation that he saw Dulcinea winnowing wheat in the yard of her house during his visit to her. Denying that she could possibly have been engaged in activity so unbecoming, he claims that she must have been occupied in weaving tapestries in rich thread, like the nymphs described in Garcilaso's Third Eclogue 'sino que la envidia que algún mal encantador tiene a mis cosas, todas las que me han de dar gusto trueca y vuelve en diferentes figuras que ellas tienen'

(p. 688) (except that some evil enchanter's envious spite against me and the things dear to me, causes him to change them from their true shapes into quite different ones). So, not only do enchanters persecute him, like other knights-errant, by changing the world's appearance topsy-turvy, but also they maliciously contrive to hit him in particular where it hurts most.

The above-quoted remark puts into Sancho's head, or more probably, into Cervantes's, the seed of the subterfuge to which Sancho will soon resort. His implementation of it repeats his previous function of mediating to his master a rustic version of Dulcinea, with a variation that follows the lines of the practical joke played on the country-barber, and transfers to him the role of its clever perpetrators, and to his master that of their victim.

For the hero, the supposedly magical transformation of his beloved into a rustic wench is a deeply disturbing event, to which he will refer obsessively on later occasions; and Cervantes evidently delights in the absurd circularity, reminiscent of Joseph Heller's *Catch-22*, with which the various high points of the Dulcinea saga, together with other supposed instances of enchantment, appear to him mutually to corroborate each other, thus reinforcing the paranoid conviction of being persecuted by envious enchanters that sustains the card-castle of his self-belief.

Thus, though immediately after the supposed encounter with his lady outside El Toboso he believes that the enchanter's spell merely affected his eyesight, not her real appearance, he has changed his mind by the time he reports her enchantment to the Duke and Duchess (II, 32; pp. 899–900) because of his recollection of Sancho's report of his embassy to her. He reasons that if she, despite really being a beautiful princess, appeared as a rustic wench to Sancho on that occasion, and in a similar guise to him, Don Quixote, outside El Toboso, then it cannot be he who is under a spell. Further confirmation that she, rather than he, is the victim of enchantment is provided by his vision in the Cave of Montesinos (II, 23). These incidents become landmark precedents in his belief-system. So, in order to quash Sancho's suggestion that the vanquished Knight of the Wood and his squire were really Sansón Carrasco and Tomé Cecial, rather than two strangers transformed into that aspect by magical means, he triumphantly cites his squire's very recent experience of the power of enchanters outside El Toboso, little realising how unconvincing this argument must seem to his interlocutor (II, 16; pp. 749–50). Nonetheless, he is not the only victim of irony, since Sancho's ruse is neatly turned against him. If he contradicts his master by telling the truth about what happened on that occasion, he incriminates himself. So he is forced to keep silent. The major example of such irony again affects Sancho as much as his master. When the Duchess hears him tell of the trick that he played on his master outside El Toboso, she persuades him to believe that the wench in question really was Dulcinea in enchanted form (II, 33; pp. 905, 908–9). The way is now open for the adventure of the enchanted carts (II, 35), in which 'Merlin', impersonated by the Duke's majordomo and accompanied by a page-boy in the guise of Dulcinea, imposes on Sancho the conditions for Dulcinea's release from enchantment: 3300 lashes to be applied by Sancho to his own behind.

So, the wheel comes full circle for both heroes. Sancho is caught in the web of lies that he began to weave in mid-Part I. Don Quixote's attempts to be admitted to his lady's presence, which began at the same time amid burlesque self-mortification, bare buttocks and shirt tails, blackmail, lies and prosaic inducements (I, 25–26), ends in the same inglorious way. In the foregoing account of his attitude to Dulcinea's enchantment, I have only mentioned in passing an essential link: his vision of her in the Cave of Montesinos. Since that adventure is not solely concerned with her predicament, I shall postpone consideration of it to a later stage.

Yet Don Quixote's credulity over Dulcinea's enchantment is not merely treated as a farce. In his comments on the icons of four saints transported by peasants to adorn their village church (II, 58; pp. 1095–7), his melancholy over her misfortune blends with disillusion about the value of his own chivalric endeavours, a pessimism provoked by his reflection on the heavenly glory won by Saints George, Martin, James and Paul:

> Ellos conquistaron el cielo a fuerza de brazos, porque el cielo padece fuerza, y yo hasta agora no sé lo que conquisto a fuerza de mis trabajos; pero si mi Dulcinea del Toboso saliese de los que padece, mejorándose mi ventura y adobándoseme el juicio, podría ser que encaminase mis pasos por mejor camino del que llevo.

> They took heaven by force, for 'heaven suffereth force' [Matthew 11: 12], but I do not know as yet what I have won by force of my travails. Yet if Dulcinea del Toboso should escape from those that she suffers, with the consequent improvement of my fortune and my wits, perhaps my steps would be guided along a better road than the one I now follow.

The Spanish philosopher Unamuno, who treats Don Quixote as a latter-day Christ in his *Vida de don Quijote y Sancho* (1905), is deeply moved by this meditation on the vanity of the quest for temporal fame.[17] The conjunction of the hero's pious admission of self-doubt with his melancholy over

17 His commentary follows the order of the chapters of *DQ*. See his comments on II, 58.

Dulcinea's enchantment raises this theme, momentarily, to a new and more serious level. In talking of mental improvement in this passage he is more probably referring to a cure for grief rather than insanity.

On two further occasions in late Part II the Dulcinea theme is tinged with pathos. When Don Quixote is defeated by 'the Knight of the White Moon' – that is, Sansón Carrasco in that guise – in the joust on the beach of Barcelona (II, 64), and, with his opponent's lance at his visor, is commanded to confess that Dulcinea is inferior in beauty to the stranger's mistress, he heroically refuses to do her such dishonour; and his attitude, and in part his words, closely resemble the reaction of Renato, a knight featured in *Persiles y Sigismunda*, when he finds himself in similar circumstances.[18] While the similarity between the two contexts is significant, so too is the difference between them. Renato's poignant narration of his defeat and its harrowing impact on him is quite unlike the humorous objectivity with which Cervantes treats the equivalent scenes in *Don Quixote*. This is because in the first case the predicament and the suffering are real, while in the other, the predicament – though Don Quixote is not aware of it – is just the result of a hoax designed to make him return home and renounce chivalry for one year, and his reactions to it, including his defiance *in extremis*, issue from his imitative mania, as Sansón Carrasco notes in Chapter 65 (p. 1162) in predicting that he will scrupulously abide by the condition imposed on him. Another pertinent comment is the reflection of the brigand Roque Guinart on Don Quixote's profound melancholy on letting himself, a supposedly invincible knight-errant, be overpowered so easily by Roque's men: 'luego conoció que la enfermedad de don Quijote tocaba más en locura que en valentía' (II, 60; p. 1120) (he realised at once that Don Quixote's infirmity was more a sign of madness than of valour). This remark could as well be applied to Don Quixote's reaction to his defeat in the joust.

So, whereas Renato evokes the crushing sense of shame and dejection that he felt on his journey home, Cervantes, in Chapter 66, treats in much lighter vein Don Quixote's conversation with Sancho in the same circumstances. For example, when Sancho self-interestedly suggests that they remove his master's armour from the ass's back and hang it from a tree like a convicted felon so that he may be saved the long hike home on foot, Don Quixote initially warms to the proposal since it would allow him to imitate Roland's behaviour in a passage of *Orlando furioso* (Canto 24, stanza 57). Yet when Sancho facetiously adds that they should hang Rocinante there too, as being the cause

---

[18] *Persiles* Book II, Chapter 19; vol. i, p. 306.

of his master's defeat, Don Quixote rejects the idea of this 'execution', and changes his mind about the previous one, wittily citing the proverb: 'que no se diga a buen servicio mal galardón' (let it not be said loyal service met with poor reward). With such humorous meanders as these does the dialogue between the two heroes unfold: a clear sign that while Cervantes recognises the integrity of his hero's knightly behaviour in defeat, and no doubt feels fond sympathy for his resilience of spirit and innocent unawareness of having been tricked, he is far from mentally attributing to it, as the novelist Juan Valera did,[19] the accompanying mood-music of sobbing violins.

The other occasion to which I referred coincides with the defeated hero's return to his village. Just outside it he interprets two insignificant incidents, quite unconnected with Dulcinea, as bad omens for his chances of ever seeing her again (II, 73; pp. 1210–11): a remark by a boy quarrelling with another over possession of a cricket-cage and the fact that a hare, pursued by greyhounds, takes refuge beneath Sancho's donkey. Sancho consoles his master with judicious comments about the superstitious silliness of belief in omens. Yet the depression that is reflected in Don Quixote's reaction combines with the demoralising impact of defeat to bring him to his death-bed.

It would be going too far, however, to treat the erosion of his faith in the restoration of Dulcinea as some kind of tragedy. From beginning to end, she is a poetically fanciful mirage, mocked by her imaginary embodiments in the real world. In essence, his conception of her is, literally, much ado about nothing; the proof is that when he recovers his sanity on his death-bed, all thought of her flies out of his head.

Expansion of Don Quixote's Style and Personality

Cervantes's tendency to modify the original framework of the two central characters as he goes along has major consequences for them apart from those already mentioned. The introduction of Sancho in early Part I significantly affects the portrayal of Don Quixote. Up till then, his behaviour primarily conforms to an imitative mode (above, pp. 35–36, 56). Avellaneda's Don Quixote, like a mentally retarded child, scarcely gets beyond this stage of development. By contrast, one perceives in the Cervantine hero's very first words to Sancho a transition to a new mode, whose nature is at once explanatory, rationalistic, and familiar (I, 7; p. 93):

> *Has de saber*, amigo Sancho Panza, que fue costumbre muy usada de
> los caballeros andantes antiguos hacer gobernadores a sus escuderos de

---

[19] *Ensayos (Segunda Parte)*, p. 37. Cf. Allen (1969: 49–50) and Mancing (1982: 162–3).

las ínsulas o reinos que ganaban, y yo tengo determinado de que por mí no falte tan agradecida usanza, antes pienso aventajarme en ella: porque ellos algunas veces, y quizá las más, esperaban a que sus escuderos fuesen viejos, y, ya después de hartos de servir y de llevar *malos días y peores noches*, les daban algún título de marqués, de algún valle o provincia *de poco más a menos, pero si tú vives y yo vivo* bien podría ser que antes de seis días ganase yo tal reino, que tuviese otros a él adherentes que *viniesen de molde* para coronarte por rey de uno dellos. Y no lo tengas a mucho, que *cosas y casos* acontecen a los tales caballeros por modos *tan nunca vistos ni pensados*, que con facilidad te podría dar aun más de lo que te prometo.

You should know, Sancho Panza my friend, that it was a very common custom of knights-errant of old to reward their squires with the islands or kingdoms that they conquered, and I'm determined not to let this generous practice lapse; rather, I intend to go out of my way to fulfil it. I say this because some of those knights, perhaps most, would wait until their squires reached old age before palming them off with a title of Marquis of some obscure valley or province when they were already fed up with being in service and putting up with hardship day and night; but assuming nothing untoward happens to us, it might easily turn out that within a week I've won a kingdom so big that it has two others attached to it, which would suit us just nicely, for then I could crown you king of one of them. And don't think that would be in any way extraordinary, for such unheard-of and unforeseeable things keep happening to knights-errant that I could easily end up giving you even more than I've said.

Up to this point, Don Quixote's discourse has been predominantly literary. The novel feature of the above-cited passage is its familiar register, marked in various ways, above all, by the frequency of turns of phrase associated with humorous or colloquial contexts in Cervantes's works. They are italicised by me in the Spanish version of the passage.[20] This is the typical register of the dialogue between master and squire henceforth; and the participation of Sancho ensures that, despite being focused primarily on chivalry, it maintains a prosaic level.

The extract is typical not only because of the aspect just mentioned, but also because it shows the hero explaining and rationalising the code of chivalry, and his particular application of it, for Sancho's benefit. This involves a different perspective on chivalry books from the one that he adopts in the heat of

---

[20] For a list of other Cervantine contexts in which they occur, see Close (2007: 47). Cf. Lázaro Carreter's essay on the language of *DQ* in the preliminaries of Rico's edn, p. xxix.

an adventure: instead of imitating them directly, he discusses the how and the why of the imitation. So, he will detail the typical activities, objectives and social usefulness of his profession (I, 13), speculate on the future unfolding of his own career (I, 21), and above all, find pretexts and arguments to explain why the past adventure fell short of expectations (e.g. most of I, 15). In the course of all this, he adopts a reflective attitude towards his own project, and elaborates his idiosyncratic conception of it, which, though generally based on chivalry books, is destined to incorporate all kinds of erudite or technical topics unconnected with them: on lineages, the mythical Golden Age, duelling, honour, fame, poetry, government, taxes, imitation as key to mastery of the arts, true valour opposed to rashness. This crazy ideology incorporates a relativist epistemology, a history, an ethics, an autobiography, a justification of his attitude to his mistress, a concept of knight-errantry's privileges and exemptions, a defence of its usefulness, and much else besides. We know Don Quixote's mind, albeit mad, better than that of any other character of the Spanish Golden Age, except Sancho.

The imitative mode does not of course drop out, but alternates and intertwines with the conversational one. Also, by contrast with the detailed, insistent mimicry typical of the early chapters, it becomes more natural and spontaneous; and an obvious sign of this is the marked diminution of archaic forms after that stage. A more significant one is the amplification of its range far beyond the boundaries of the chivalric genre; and one of the earliest manifestations of this is the speech on the Golden Age (I, 11; see above, p. 55). Here, I simply wish to draw attention to one particular aspect of it. The nature of Quixotic imitation has changed, since the hero's model is no longer the chivalric genre but a theme treated by a multitude of poets from Hesiod to Cervantes's own contemporaries, and employed as a rhetorical exercise in humanist education. The speech is notable for the eclectic range of its sources: three have been identified as definite, six as probable, and over thirty as possible (Stagg, 1985).

We are soon given further examples of such eclecticism. On the way to Grisóstomo's funeral (I, 13), the hero is interrogated by the ironic Vivaldo about his chivalric mission, and when asked about the name, place of origin, status and beauty of his lady, he replies, first, with a eulogy of her physical charms, which consists in a flood of the commonplace hyperbolic attributes ascribed to their mistresses by poets within the Petrarchist tradition (pp. 141–41), and next, in reply to a probing supplementary question about her pedigree, he offers a suspiciously evasive list of all the ancient noble houses to which she does *not* belong, before concluding defiantly that the house of the Tobosos de la Mancha, though of modern date, is capable of generating a most illustrious succession. The answer shows his familiarity with the discourse of noble lineages, a subject to which, in that age, specialised treatises were devoted. From this point on, the repertoire of models of Quixotic imitation broadens indefinitely. In the examples just mentioned, Cervantes portrays the hero's learned eloquence in a comic light. However, by mid-Part I, he has discovered more positive potential in it, such as the chastened humility that Don Quixote shows after the battle with the sheep, marked by quotations from the gospel of St Matthew (I, 18; p. 197), and his elegant exposition of the doctrine of imitation as key to mastery of the arts, adduced as justification for his hairbrained penance for Dulcinea (I, 25; pp. 274–5). As we have noted (above, p. 69), the result of this mid-stream reappraisal of Don Quixote's character is the attribution to him of his first genuinely lucid 'lucid interval', the Arms versus Letters speech, which paves the way for Cervantes's radical alteration of the balance between madness and lucidity in him that we shall observe in Part II.

Functionalism versus Verisimilitude: the Question of Sancho's Salary

A theme of this chapter so far has been the conflict between verisimilitude and function in the portrayal of the two central characters, function being understood as any feature of the story determined by artistic necessity or convenience rather than by considerations of truth-to-life. The conflict is, of course, more apparent than real since literary art is functional through and through; yet appearances matter within the genre of the novel, which at a later stage of its development would seek more and more to disguise artifice as nature. They also matter in discussing *Don Quixote*, since criticism has traditionally seen it as a precursor of this tendency towards realism, or even as a full representative of it, overlooking its functionalism in the process.

Nonetheless, it is not at all my intention to deny the truth-to-life of Don Quixote and Sancho, which is the essential reason why they still interest us, but rather to explain how Cervantes achieves the effect despite the burlesque exaggeration inherent in the original conception of their characters and the makeshift, arbitrary manner of their assembly. Repetition with variants, a basic principle of composition of *Don Quixote*, makes an important contribution here, particularly to their psychological coherence.

Let us take as an example the hero's habitual resort to the excuse of enchantment. The idea is first put into his head by his niece who, coached no doubt by the priest and barber, ascribes the walling-up of his library and disappearance of the books to the work of a malign enchanter (I, 7; p. 90). He readily accepts this nonsense, and adduces it just one chapter later to acount for the frustrating transformation of giants into windmills, confidently predicting, however, that the enmity of the sage Frestón will avail little against the power of his sword (I, 8; p. 96). From this point on, the successive instances of the excuse (e.g. I, 15–18 inclusive, and notably I, 21) show a steady erosion of the initial arrogant confidence; the effects are perceptible, as we previously noted, in the theory of relativity improvised to explain the metamorphosis of Mambrino's helmet (I, 25), and later, in the paranoid conviction that enchanters have resolved to injure him through Dulcinea (II, 8). The belief crystallises in the defeatism that he expresses at the end of the adventure of the commandeered fishing-boat: 'Dios lo remedie, que todo este mundo es máquinas y trazas, contrarias unas de otras. Yo no puedo más' (II, 29; p. 874) (God help me; this world is riddled with contradictory plots and designs, cancelling each other out. I can do no more.). Though its premises are quite preposterous, the process of his disillusionment displays the kind of psychologically unified evolution typical of a real person; the excuse remains basically the same, yet its form at any stage is conditioned by the accumulated memory of previous setbacks, memory that is lived in the present moment of experience rather than a deliberate act.

His unique identity is constituted by this kind of continuity-in-change, and also by his explicit awareness of that identity, including his origins, how he is seen by others and the aspirations that motivate his own conduct. This very rounded consciousness of self is expressed in his dialogue with Don Diego de Miranda in II, 16 and other contexts. Sancho has it too.

The conflict between truth-to-life and artistic function is vividly exemplified by the theme of Sancho's salary. This is an aspect of the question of the eventual reward for his services, which runs through the dialogue between him and his master from beginning to end and is not definitively resolved until the *hidalgo* drafts his will on his death-bed. The prospect of governorship of an island – Don Quixote's original promise to Sancho –is, from the outset, a Utopian fantasy, ridiculous because of its fabulous nature and Sancho's utter unsuitability for any such role; and the absurdity is reflected in the alternative possibilities that are suggested in the course of the novel – king, husband of an *infanta*, count; elevation of his wife and daughter to a peerage – and in the ingenuous opportunism with which Sancho fantasises about them.[21] Even though he displays a greater moral maturity in discussing the prospect of a governorship in Part II (II, 4; p. 660, and II, 43; pp. 978–9), and most of all, in discharging the office of governor when, thanks to the

---

[21] See I, 21: pp. 233–4; I, 26: pp. 297–8; I, 29: p. 336; I, 47: pp. 545–6; I, 50: pp. 572–3.

Duke's caprice, it falls into his lap, the topic remains, in essence, an absurd chimera, reminiscent of the dreams of a Land of Cockaigne exhibited by the rustic fools of sixteenth-century comedy.

However, Sancho's salary, or the prospect of a legacy that would stand in lieu of it, is a quite different matter. This is because the topic reflects the real bond between master and servant as that society understood it: one in which servants were treated as part of the family, albeit inferior members of it. Their masters fed, clothed and lodged them, paid their wages, and, at the end of their services, would procure a job for them or find them a spouse or reward them with some kind of financial settlement.[22] In the royal household, these supplementary benefits were known as 'mercedes', gifts; their award was formally recorded and amounted to a significant charge on the household's budget (Close, 2001: 156).

To be sure, not all servants were so well treated. The fate of many is reflected in the bitter comments of the ex-page boy who, having quit the court in disillusionment to join the army, runs into Don Quixote and Sancho in II, 24. Though in his case, the stinginess of the social climbers whom he served is to some extent justified by their poverty, the frequent contemporary indictments of the treatment of servants by noblemen show that many lacked this excuse (Close, 2000: 219). So, when Don Quixote, in his first remarks to Sancho (I, 7), contrasts his own intended generosity with the meanness of knights-errant of bygone times who would let their squires grow old before fobbing them off with some nondescript title or office, the contemporary reader would have seen a clear social reference beneath the literary satire.

That is why, when Don Quixote recovers his sanity and prepares to meet his maker, the promise of the island to Sancho is the only one of his former delusions of chivalry that fails to vanish without trace. He remembers it because, from the outset, their relationship has involved an ambiguous mix of illusion and reality: beneath its make-believe aspect of a knight's association with his squire, it reflects his real obligations, moral and social, towards a faithful servant whom he originally enticed into his service on an illusory promise of reward.

The play between fiction and reality is thus inherent in the theme of Don Quixote's will, identified with the question of Sancho's remuneration should the promise of governorship of an island, or some other *merced*, remain unfulfilled. The subject is mentioned for the first time in the adventure of the fulling-mills (I, 20). When, after spending the night in a state of suspense

---

[22] On this, Domínguez Ortiz (1964–70: vol. i, pp. 277–9).

owing to the fearsome, incessant din, Don Quixote sets off at daybreak to
investigate the cause, he repeats his lugubrious last request to Sancho: that if
he should die in the battle that awaits him, his servant should go to El Toboso
to convey the sad news to Dulcinea. But this time he adds an unexpected
rider, implicitly prompted by Sancho's previous complaint that if that tragedy
were to befall his master, he would be left abandoned and unrewarded. Don
Quixote says:

> y que, en lo que tocaba a la paga de sus servicios, no tuviese pena, porque
> él había dejado su testamento antes que saliera de su lugar, donde se hallaría
> gratificado de todo lo tocante a su salario, *rata por cantidad*, del tiempo
> que hubiese servido; pero, que si Dios le sacaba de aquel peligro *sano y
> salvo y sin cautela*, se podía tener por muy más que cierta la prometida
> ínsula.

> and that, insofar as concerned the payment of his services, Sancho was not
> to worry, because he, Don Quixote, had made his will before leaving his
> village, and in it had made provision for Sancho to be fully remunerated
> in proportion to the time that he had served; but if God should deliver him
> safe and sound from the imminent danger, Sancho could confidently expect
> the award of the promised island.

This is the first we have heard of Don Quixote's will. Is this afterthought to
be understood as a mad invention on his part, or as a precautionary measure
that Cervantes forgot to tell us about?[23] We do not know. In another respect,
rata por cantidad, italicised by me in the Spanish original, is commercial
language; *sano y salvo y sin cautela*, also italicised, was a formula used in
the deeds of ransom of captives. The two expressions, typical of Cervantes's delight in parodying bureaucratic jargon, contrast incongruously with
the romantic pathos of the reference to the embassy to Dulcinea. Let us note
particularly the first expression, which like a refrain, will humorously accompany the theme of Sancho's remuneration on later occasions.

By this means, the *hidalgo* makes a significant concession to reality, undertaking to replace pie-in-the-sky, should it fail to materialise, with a tangible
pie on the table. For Spaniards of Cervantes's age, the preparation of a will
was a serious matter, since it gave the testator the opportunity to depart this

---

[23] The idea is possibly inspired by Cervantes's memory of Celestina's mention to young
Pármeno, in Act I of Fernando de Rojas's *La Celestina*, that she has been keeping a sum of
money on trust for him, bequeathed to him by his father (ed. Cejador, vol. i, pp. 99–100). The
disclosure is no doubt to be read as a lie by the bawd, designed to lure Pármeno into alliance
with her.

world with a clear conscience, having settled all obligations to his dependants and society, and to ensure that the heirs would go on saying masses for the soul of the departed after his demise (Nalle, 1992: 183ff.). Don Quixote alludes to these beliefs when he tells Sancho why he drafted that codicil: 'fue por lo que podía suceder, que aún no sé cómo prueba en estos tan calamitosos tiempos nuestros la caballería, y no querría que por pocas cosas penase mi ánima en el otro mundo' (I, 20; p. 222) (it was in case of contingencies, for I still do not know how chivalry may fare in this present calamitous age, and I would not want my soul to be tormented for trifles in the next world).

When, at the anti-climactic climax of the fulling-mills adventure, the two heroes discover the disillusioning cause of the din that so terrified them (I, 20; pp. 218–19), Don Quixote is mortified; Sancho, unable to control himself, bursts into laughter and even dares to parody his master's boastful speech of the previous night. The master vents his wounded vanity by striking his cheeky servant with his lance, then, controlling his temper, humanely asks for forgiveness. Sancho, taking advantage of the mood of reconciliation, returns to the theme of the salary, and asks how a squire's wages were computed in chivalry books, monthly, or on a daily basis, like those of builders' labourers. Don Quixote, concerned above all to make his squire talk less and show more respect, is little interested by the question, and answers that he has never read of squires being rewarded other than by *mercedes*. Thus, the question of the salary is temporarily shelved. Yet it will be raised on four subsequent occasions (I, 46; II, 7; II, 28; II, 74), and two of them (II, 7 and 28) repeat the pattern established in I, 20: the conflict between the master's imposition of authority and his servant's irreverent questioning of it; Sancho's preference for pie on the table, and Don Quixote's for pie-in-the-sky. This basic scheme will be modified in accord with the development of the pair's characters in Part II: the sophisticated humour shown by both and the awareness of their own and each other's mannerisms.

Let us look at the conversation in II, 28, which immediately follows Sancho's imprudent demonstration of his ability to bray like an ass to the army of the village of the braying aldermen (II, 27). His master flees the foreseeable consequences, which fall entirely on Sancho. When he rejoins Don Quixote, the thrashing he has just suffered provokes him to pour out a heartfelt expression of his disillusionment with his master's enterprise, the bitterest, wittiest and most elegant so far.[24] On those previous occasions in Part I, he talked of returning home; now, he mentions the possibility again,

---

[24] *DQ* II, 28: pp. 863–4; cf. I, 18: p. 187, and I, 25: p. 271.

though it is more talk than a firm intention. Don Quixote reacts with sardonic humour to this outburst, as he did in Part II, Chapter 7 (pp. 680–1), when his servant tried to renegotiate the terms of his service by putting it on the basis of a fixed wage rather than of the lottery of the promised *merced*. Then, Don Quixote mocked Sancho's mispronunciation of *rata_por cantidad* with a playful pun and, rubbing in the refusal with sarcastic parody of his strings of proverbs, dismissed the request as quite without precedent in chivalry books. Here, he takes a somewhat different tack, though once again, there is menace in his humour, implied by the replacement of informal *tú* with haughty *vos*. Taking Sancho's talk of returning home literally, he invites him to calculate the wages owed to him and pay himself at once from the purse that he carries on him. Now Sancho is forced to reply to his own original question: on what basis is a squire's wage calculated? On this occasion, he takes as a norm of comparison what he earned when he served Sansón Carrasco's father: two ducats monthly, plus food. In other words, twenty-two *reales* monthly. However, he calculates that he is entitled to an additional eight *reales* per month to compensate both for the hardship of the job and for the unfulfilled promise of the governorship. Total thirty *reales* per month, equivalent to over twelve thousand *maravedíes* a year.

Needless to say, Sancho exaggerates. Though he does not say in what capacity he served Sansón Carrasco's father, we can take for granted that his wage would have been equivalent to that of the shepherd-boy Andrés, whom Don Quixote tried to save from his master's fury in his first adventure as an armed knight (I, 4). Andrés earned seven *reales* monthly: a realistic figure by the standard of average wages in New Castille around 1600.[25] However, Don Quixote, for whom maths was never a strong point, seems impressed by Sancho's mastery of his brief; one notes in passing a return to informal *tú*. He now asks Sancho to calculate, on the basis of this exorbitant tariff, what he is owed *rata por cantidad* for the twenty-five days that have elapsed since the beginning of the third sally. At this crucial juncture, Sancho ruins his case, although it is unlikely that Don Quixote would have granted his claim, however reasonable the computation. Rightly insisting that the period for which payment is due should date from the very beginning of their association, Sancho estimates this as being twenty years approximately, three days more or less. Covetousness makes him inflate time even more extravagantly than madness distorts Don Quixote's notion of how long he spent down in the Cave of Montesinos (II, 23; p. 824).

---

25 See Close (2001: 160–1).

On hearing this, his master smites his brow, bursts out laughing, and delivers the furious reprimand that he has no doubt already prepared. With absurdly exaggerated reproaches, he scolds Sancho for turning the ordinances of chivalry upside down and laments the inopportuneness of his decision to quit: '¡Oh pan mal conocido! ¡Oh promesas mal colocadas! ... ¿Ahora te vas, cuando yo venía con intención firme y valedera de hacerte señor de la mejor ínsula del mundo?' (II, 28; p. 866) (Oh, what ingratitude to the bread so freely given! How misplaced my promises! Now you talk of going, when I had the firm and unshakeable intention of making you lord of the fairest island in the world?). The style is superb, but the accusations are ridiculous. Sancho has no cause whatever to thank Don Quixote for his promises about the island, which at this moment are as empty as they have always been and show no prospect of materialising. If, as it so happens, they are destined to be fulfilled quite soon, this startling turn of events will be owing to the Duke's whim, not to any initiative on Don Quixote's part. However, none of these considerations occur to Sancho. Bursting into tears, he humbly begs forgiveness for his insolence, accuses himself of being an ass and promises that he will faithfully serve his master in this capacity for ever more. As on the previous occasion (II, 7), when faced by his master's unshakeable resolve to offer nothing more than pie-in-the-sky common sense deserts him and his resistance crumbles. The step forward towards lucidity is cancelled by retreat into credulity. On both sides, the patterns of behaviour fixed in I, 20, despite surface variations, remain basically the same.

The next and final manifestation of this topic is the scene of Don Quixote's death (II, 74), where the tension between verisimilitude and function is very apparent. It might be formulated thus: should the hero's abrupt recovery of sanity be seen as the logical, traumatic outcome of previous setbacks, or merely a convenient means by which Cervantes puts a full-stop to the story? We could argue it both ways. We are told that after the defeat on the sands of Barcelona, the hero discoursed more lucidly on all subjects than before (II, 71; p. 1202), and this comment, while implying the chastening effect upon him of defeats in general, already noticeable in Part II, suggests an accelerating return towards sanity. Also, the demoralising effect of the enchantment of Dulcinea is evident from Chapter 58 onwards, and it is mentioned by the narrator, and also regarded by Don Quixote's friends, as a cause of his terminal illness. On the other hand, the familiar resilience of Don Quixote's madness has been apparent even after the defeat in Barcelona. For instance, in Chapter 67, on passing the wood where he met the ladies and gentlemen engaged in a pastoral masquerade, he fantasises enthusiastically about the pastoral life that he and Sancho might lead during his year's sabbatical from knight-errantry, thus fulfilling his niece's premonition that if he should ever be cured of his obsession with chivalry books, pastoral romances might provide an alternative outlet (I, 6). Moreover, the sheer abruptness of his transition from madness to sanity, with the consequent renunciation of chivalry, suggests the author's arbitrary resolve to bring things to a conclusion.

Though in forswearing chivalry books the hero seems brutally to cut the ties to his own past, the terms in which he does this give a strong impression of continuity with it. The effect is achieved by the recycling or transference of motifs that is the basic principle of composition of the story. Consequently, in the novel's final chapter, function prevails to a considerable extent over psychological verisimilitude, enabling Cervantes satisfactorily to tie up a number of loose ends. On various previous occasions, edifying alternatives to chivalry books have been proposed by the priest, the canon of Toledo and Don Diego de Miranda: history and the Bible (I, 32: pp. 371–2 and I, 49; p. 563), books of devotion and well-written works of entertainment (II, 16; p. 754). Now, on his death-bed, the hero himself espouses the suggestions that he has steadfastly rejected hitherto, deploring the time wasted on chivalric nonsense, and regretting that none is left to devote to reading books that might enlighten the soul ('leyendo otros que sean luz del alma'). Here, he echoes the title of a book of devotion, *Luz del alma*, which he leafed through approvingly in a printer's workshop in Barcelona (II, 62; p. 1145). Repeatedly he has been told to give up his chivalric wanderings, stay at home and concern himself with activities proper to his age and status: the first such injunction came from his niece (I, 7), and the last and most recent from his housekeeper, who tells him: 'Mire, señor, tome mi consejo … estése en su casa, atienda a su hacienda, confiese a menudo, favorezca a los pobres, y sobre mi ánima si mal le fuere' (II, 73; p. 1215) (Look, sir, take my advice, stay at home, look after your affairs, confess often, do good to the poor, and upon my soul it will do no harm). Now, on his death-bed, he follows this advice to the letter. In one way, his reversion to origins is perfectly consistent with the way in which he originally turned his back on them. When he resolved to become a knight-errant, he marked his change of life with a new name, calling himself Don Quijote de la Mancha. Now, in renouncing knight-errantry, he logically inverts that baptismal act, announcing that he has become Alonso Quijano, whose virtue earned him the epithet 'el Bueno'. That goodness of disposition marks the link between the sane and the mad personality: we are told that both when he was plain Alonso Quijano el Bueno, and, later, when he was Don Quijote de la Mancha, he was always even-tempered and agreeable, and for that reason was well liked by those of his own household and by all those who knew him.

The hero's death, the first such scene in the genre of the novel and one of the finest, not only ends with these satisfying symmetries but also strikes a marvellous balance between humour and pathos, fantasy and verisimilitude. Avoiding sentimentality, Cervantes describes the reactions of Sancho, the niece and the housekeeper to his demise as a mixture of grief and healthy conformity to the Spanish proverb 'el muerto al hoyo y el vivo al bollo' (the dead to the grave and the living to their crust of bread). The last will and testament that he drafts in the scribe's presence is in part burlesque, hence fantastic, since it imitates the language, form and content of real wills, while incorporating bizarre clauses and employing a colloquial register that would be inconceivable in them. It is the major example of Cervantes's habit of poking fun at notarial language.

What scribe of flesh-and-blood in the Spain of that age would have put in writing the following sarcastic jest at Avellaneda's expense, which brilliantly conveys an insult in the form of a meek request for forgiveness?:

> Ítem, suplico a los dichos señores mis albaceas que si la buena suerte les trujere a conocer al autor que dicen que compuso una historia que anda por ahí con el título de *Segunda parte de las hazañas de don Quijote de la Mancha*, de mi parte le pidan, cuan encarecidamente ser pueda, perdone la ocasión que sin yo pensarlo le di de haber escrito tantos y tan grades disparates como en ella escribe.

> I beseech my executors that if by good fortune they should make the acquaintance of the author who is said to have composed the work known as *Segunda parte de las hazañas de don Quijote de la Mancha*, to ask him on my behalf, as earnestly as they may, to pardon me the occasion that I unwittingly gave him to write all the nonsense that the said work contains.

On the other hand, it is conceivable that the scribe might have taken this down just as dictated since the formulation is perfectly adapted to the contrite tone conventionally used in such documents.[26] And what scribe of flesh-and-blood would have set down the legacy in favour of the hero's niece, which imposes the condition that if she should ever marry a man who knows what chivalry books are, then she forfeits it altogether? The restriction excludes virtually every marriageable male in the Spain of that age. However, albeit preposterous, the clause reflects what happened in real life to the extent that

---

[26] There are various examples of the wills of that epoch in González de Amezúa (1950).

legacies conditional on the beneficiary marrying a designated spouse were not unknown.

If, in these respects the dying Alonso Quijano speaks more with Cervantes's voice than with his own, this is not true of the legacy in favour of Sancho, which, sharply reversing the stance so far taken by Don Quixote, replaces pie-in-the-sky once and for all with pie on the table. It is couched in amusingly colloquial and affectionate terms, expressive of all the fondness and sense of obligation that he feels towards his credulous servant:

> Ítem, es mi voluntad que de ciertos dineros que Sancho Panza, a quien en mi locura hice mi escudero, tiene, que porque ha habido entre él y mí ciertas cuentas, y dares y tomares, quiero que no se le haga cargo dellos, ni se le pida cuenta alguna, sino que si sobrare alguno después de haberse pagado de lo que le debo, el restante sea suyo, que será bien poco, y buen provecho le haga; y si como estando yo loco fui parte para darle el gobierno de la ínsula, pudiera agora, estando cuerdo, darle el de un reino, se le diera, porque la sencillez de su condición y fidelidad de su trato lo merece.

> Regarding a sum of money of mine now held by Sancho Panza, whom I in my madness made my squire, and with whom I entered into reckoning and had some difference of opinion over the use of the said money, it is my wish that he should not be required to render any account of it, but that if any should be left over after he has paid himself what I owe him, which will be very little, then let him keep it and good luck to him; and if in my madness I was instrumental in giving him the governorship of an island, I could now, in my right mind, give him that of a kingdom, I would do so, because his candour and fidelity deserve it.

Yet, idosyncratic as this formulation is, this clause too keeps touch with reality. Though more tortuously and informally worded, it corresponds to a bequest made by the dramatist Calderón de la Barca to two faithful maids, many years after the publication of *Don Quixote* Part II.[27] Warm admirer of Cervantes though he was, Calderón can scarcely be supposed to have been thinking of the last chapter of *Don Quixote* when he drafted that clause. It is much more likely that his wording, like Don Quixote's, was based on the standard formulae of wills of that epoch, as prescribed in manuals for scribes.

My emphasis on the functionalism of Cervantes's portrayal of Don Quixote and Sancho has been a way of drawing attention to the kind of truth-to-life

---

[27] González de Amezúa (1950: 379–80).

embodied in them. As Aristotle observed, poetic truth is more universal than the historical kind; and the abiding claim on our attention of Cervantes's two heroes is related to that universality, or to put it in modern terms, to that archetypal scope, achieved by constant transcendence of mere empiricism.

5

Wit, Colloquialisms and Narrative Manner

Preliminary Observations

Nowadays, these are unfashionable subjects, seldom touched upon in introductory books on *Don Quixote*. Yet it has not always been so. Eighteenth-century French and English novelists were fascinated by what I call Cervantes's manner: his mock-solemn and casually flippant attitude to his story, which he treats as a burlesque blend of epic and history; it inspires a succession of seminally influential imitations, including two of the century's greatest novels: Fielding's *Tom Jones* (1749) and Sterne's *Tristram Shandy* (1759). While modern novelists and critics have continued to be interested in the pseudo-historical and metafictional aspects of this,[1] they have been less concerned with others, notably Cervantes's wit and his mock-grave irony. The latter in particular was much admired in the England of Shaftesbury, Addison, Pope, Fielding and Hogarth, and was seen as integral to his method of parody (Paulson, 1998: 40–1), while in Enlightenment Spain, men-of-letters regarded the naturalness, clarity and purity of his language, including its witty levity, as principal reasons for his elevation to classic status.[2]

The eighteenth century was right in considering these aspects of *Don Quixote* essential. The lack of interest shown by modern critics in how the story is told reflects an underlying indifference to what kind of story it is, by which I mean a disposition to ignore or downplay its predominantly comic aspect in order to elicit the supposed profundities that lie beneath. Cervantes clearly considers it paramount since he highlights it in every one of his general comments on his novel's import and purpose.[3] It fundamentally conditions his style and manner of narration, with logical implications for authorial viewpoint, characterisation and the metafictional nature of Part II. As one might

---

[1] Much of the critical discussion on these topics flows from Riley (1962). See Wardropper (1965), Haley (1965), Alter (1975).

[2] See, e.g., Antonio Capmany, *Teatro histórico-crítico*, vol. iv, pp. 426–7.

[3] See *Persiles*, ed. Schevill and Bonilla, vol. i, p. lviii; *Viaje del Parnaso*, Chapter iv, pp. 54–5; prologue to *DQ* I: p. 18; *DQ* II, 3: p. 653.

expect, he sheds this manner in contexts of the novel that are intended to be taken seriously, such as the tragic interpolated *novela El curioso impertinente* (I, 33–35). In Cervantes's works other than *Don Quixote*, we find the characteristics of the humorous mode only in those which have a predominantly comic purpose: passages of certain *novelas* such as *Rinconete y Cortadillo* and *La ilustre fregona*; the *Viaje del Parnaso*; the comic theatre, including, in particular, the *entremeses*. Its merrily effervescent ethos is well expressed by the lackey Ocaña in the comedy *La entretenida*:[4]

> Siempre la melancolía
> Fue de la muerte parienta,
> Y en la vida alegre asienta
> El hablar de argentería.
> Motes, cuentos, chistes, dichos,
> Pensamientos regalados,
> Muy buenos para pensados,
> Y mejores para dichos.

> Melancholy was always a relative of death; sparkling talk is based on a life of merriment. Witticisms, tales, jokes, sayings, brilliant ideas: good if they're thought, better if they're said.

In *Don Quixote*, this spirit of levity is common to the discourse of the narrator and the characters, and even affects the hero's, despite the unwavering solemnity that we might expect from his commitment to behave like Amadís.

So, without a proper understanding of *Don Quixote*'s humour, one arguably misses much of its point. Since this depends heavily on word-play, Hispanic readers are less handicapped than non-Hispanic ones in perceiving it. This can easily be exemplified by modern translations of *Don Quixote*; even the most competent find difficulty, as I shall too in what follows,[5] in successfully rendering Cervantes's verbal humour into another language: not only, for obvious reasons, the puns and double-meanings, but also the constant play with registers, commonplaces, set phrases and colloquialisms. Given this fact, one needs to explain the paradox of *Don Quixote*'s universal appeal, quite unaffected, apparently, by the story's transposition into Urdu, Russian, Chinese, or whatever, despite so much loss in the wash of transla-

---

[4] *Comedias y entremeses*, ed. Schevill and Bonilla, vol. iii, p. 6.

[5] A specific illustration of this difficulty is given above, pp. 53–54. Capmany commented in the late eighteenth century (see above, n. 2) that it is difficult for a foreigner, who only knows *DQ* through cold, insipid and faulty translations, to appreciate the 'frases burlescas, dichos festivos y voces graciosas, con que ameniza su locución' (jocular turns of phrase, witty jests and funny terms with which he spices his style).

tion. This puzzle is largely explained, I believe, by an underlying principle of the novel's composition: relevance.

I propose to divide the topic into three broad aspects: first, wit and verbal humour; second, colloquialisms and commonplaces; third, the narrator's personality.

Wit

We have already considered in Chapter 3 a principal aspect of the influence of Cervantes's romantic mode on his humour: empathetic parody. Three others will be considered in this section: word-play; means of intensification; means of attenuation.

(i) Word-play

In general, Cervantes's verbal humour is affected by his concern with the principle of relevance (see above, pp. 65–66), which is common to his comic and his romantic fiction, other than to the latter's high-flown modes, epic and pastoral, where licence is given to stylistic embroidery. In *Don Quixote*, relevance is an integral aspect of the 'truth of the matter' that is persistently opposed to the hero's subjective fantasy. It is reflected in the sacrosanct force of the phrase 'and that was the truth' (así era la verdad), which, in variant forms, becomes a recurrent refrain of the story.[6] Cervantes's adherence to this principle, which contrasts markedly with the attitude of contemporary picaresque novelists, such as Alemán, Quevedo and López de Úbeda (in *Guzmán de Alfarache*, *El Buscón* and *La pícara Justina* respectively), is shown in various ways: the curtailment of digression; the tendency to let dialogue prevail over narrative; the preference for describing scenes of robust physical comedy with graphic energy that eschews witty asides and embroidery; the concern to offer factual and sober explanations for potential mysteries, such as the identity of the ambulant puppeteer Maese Pedro (*DQ* II, 27) or the reason why that country barber wore a basin on his head (I, 21). In general, Cervantes's functional aesthetics is manifest in his preference for undemonstrative modes of humour: quiet irony, citational mock-seriousness, euphemism and understatement. Most of the word-play to be discussed in the following pages, like the jests in the passage of I, 21 cited in Chapter 3 (p. 53), is incidental to the narrative flow, rather than witty virtuosity to be appreciated for its own sake.

---

[6] E.g. the narrator's curt interjection at the end of the hero's florid soliloquy in *DQ* I, 2, p. 47; cf. other examples in I, 11: p. 127; I, 29: p. 335; II, 9: p. 698; II, 10: p. 700.

The compositional principles of repetition with variation and transference of motifs, discussed in the previous chapter, also affect the novel's tropes of verbal humour. Let us take as an example the play between 'andante' (errant, as in knight-errant, though literally, walking, as present participle) and 'por andar' (still to walk or to be walked). It revives the dead metaphor 'andante' by taking it in a literal sense, and also plays with a common grammatical structure that normally opposes the verb in past participle form to the same verb in the infinitive preceded by 'por'. Sancho is the first to coin the jest in his burlesque portrait of Aldonza Lorenzo (I, 25; p. 283): '¡Vive el Dador, que es *moza de chapa*, hecha y derecha y de pelo en pecho, y que puede sacar la barba del lodo a cualquier caballero andante, o por andar' (Praise the Lord! She's a lusty, upstanding wench who could get any knight-errant or about to err out of a jam). The narrator picks it up and modifies it many chapters later, playing with the set phrase 'por sus pasos contados' (by regular stages – literally, by their numbered steps): 'por sus pasos contados y por contar … llegaron don Quijote y Sancho al río Ebro' (II, 29; p. 867) (by regular – and still to be counted or recounted – stages Don Quixote and Sancho reached the river Ebro), and gives another variant on it at the end of the next chapter, saying that the Duke and Duchess considered it great good fortune to welcome to their castle 'tal caballero andante y tal escudero andado' (II, 30; p. 879) (such an errant knight and so well-travelled a squire). Sancho introduces a new modification on hearing Merlin's proposal that the flagellation designed to dissolve Dulcinea's enchantment might be administered by a hand other than the squire's own, 'aunque sea algo pesada' (even if it should be somewhat weighty). Sancho indignantly rejects the suggestion with 'ni ajena ni propia, ni pesada ni por pesar' (II, 35; p. 924) (neither another person's nor my own, nor weighty nor to be weighed). Finally, obliged to face the prospect of renouncing chivalry for one year, Don Quixote undertakes to support his dependants just the same, 'ahora sea caballero andante, o pastor por andar' (II, 73; p. 1215) (whether as a knight-errant or as a shepherd about to err).

To the modern reader, puns like the foregoing may seem somewhat puerile. However, they were appreciated then, and, in the context of Cervantes's prose, are more effective than they appear now, since they harmonise with its wit, opulence and cult of symmetry, repetition, alliteration and internal rhymes. Similar tropes, without humorous intent, were considered an elegant ornament of courtly style. We find them abundantly in Cervantes's lyric poetry and romantic fiction, to which the humorous word-play of *Don Quixote* is intimately related. This helps to create its characteristic urbanity of tone, which contrasts markedly with the coarseness – despite often sparkling ingenuity – that marks the humour of contemporaries such as Quevedo. Though this apparently surprising affinity between such dissimilar contexts is not unusual in Golden Age literature,[7] it is intensified in Cervantes's case by the close links between his romantic and comic modes. The reason for the affinity is that in the culture of the age, wit – basically, the ingenious coining of relationships between dissimilar things – was considered an elegant stylistic ornament and a source of pleasurable surprise. Though not assumed to be funny *per se*, it became so when combined with undignified or degrading associations.

Granted that Cervantes would consider rhetorically heightened language as acceptable in the heroic and lyric genres, his norm of good style basically corresponds to the ideal of correct and elegant plainness formulated by the student who guides Don Quixote to Camacho's wedding (II, 19; p. 787). I quote:

> El lenguaje puro, el propio, el elegante y claro, está en los discretos corte-sanos, aunque hayan nacido en Majalahonda; dije discretos, porque hay muchos que no lo son, y la discreción es la gramática del buen lenguaje, que se acompaña con el uso.

> Pure, correct, elegant and clear language is that spoken by courtiers of good judgement, even though born in Majalahonda; I said 'of good judge-ment' because there are many courtiers who lack it, the grammar of good usage being judgement backed up by long practice.

Courtly discretion, the touchstone of this ideal, rejects affectation and vulgarity alike. The censure of affectation is exemplified by the passage in which the pompous, flowery speech addressed by Don Quixote to the ex-captive is contrasted with the 'más llanos y más cortesanos ofrecimientos' (plainer and more courtly expressions of goodwill) with which he is welcomed to the inn by Don Fernando, Cardenio and the priest,[8] and is generally implied by the insistent mockery of preciosity, pedantry and pomposity in *Don Quixote*. As for vulgarity, a fair indicator is the attitude of characters like Sansón Carrasco, the Duke and Duchess towards Sancho's solecisms and other lapses, to be considered later in this chapter. By contrast with such fool-ishness, the orators and narrators of stories in Cervantes's works – characters like Dorotea, Lotario, Don Quixote in his lucid intervals, the ex-captive – are repeatedly praised for their discretion; and it is revealed in stylistic features such as sonorous and well-chosen vocabulary, symmetrically constructed

---

[7] On this, Close (2000: 187–8).

[8] *DQ* I, 42; p. 495; other contexts in which this linguistic norm is formulated are *DQ* I, 6: p. 82; II, 12: p. 720.

periods, and enhancement of style by ellipsis, antithesis, metaphor and other tropes that lend themselves naturally to the display of wit.

I offer below a brief list, with examples, of the devices of wit of Cervantes's courtly style, and will subsequently relate them to equivalent word-play employed for humorous effect in *Don Quixote*.

Wit in Cervantes's Courtly Style

a. *Double-meanings.* According to a major theorist of wit and the conceit, the Jesuit Baltasar Gracián, writing in the mid-seventeenth century, 'son poco graves los conceptos por equívoco, y así más aptos para sátiras y cosas burlescas, que para lo serio y prudente' (conceits based on double-meaning are somewhat frivolous, and thus more suited for satire and jesting, than for grave and prudent matters).[9] This admonition is amply confirmed by *Don Quixote*, in which humorous double-meanings abound, contaminating all other species of wit. Despite Gracián's disapproval, they pervade the serious poetry and prose of the age, including Cervantes's. So, Dorotea, in the course of her poignant narrative, refers to Don Fernando's persistent overtures to her as follows: 'en términos le veo que, no usando el que debe, usará el de la fuerza, y vendré a quedar deshonrada y sin disculpa de la culpa que me podía dar el que no supiere cuán sin ella he venido a este punto' (*Don Quijote* I, 28; p. 327) (I see him reduced to such terms [i.e. situation, state] that, casting aside those [forms of conduct] that befit him, he will resort to that [extremity] of force, and I shall be left dishonoured and without means of unburdening myself of the burden of guilt that could be laid on me by anyone ignorant of how guiltless I came to this pass). Here, double-meaning is based on ellipsis, achieved by substituting *términos* by pronouns that imply different senses of the same word. It can also be produced by simple repetition of the word, instead of substitution. Thus, a shepherdess in Cervantes's pastoral romance describes how she spent the night impatiently awaiting the dawn in order to be reunited with her lover: 'según deseaba la nueva luz, para ir a ver a la luz por quien mis ojos veían' (*La Galatea* II; vol. i, p. 86) (so eagerly did I desire the light of day, in order to be able to go to see the new light that gave sight to my eyes). In the next example, this kind of play between metaphorical and literal senses is achieved by antithesis. Referring to the beautiful, capricious Leandra, the goat-herd Eugenio says: 'que así se llama la rica que en miseria me ha puesto' (I, 51; p. 577) (for that is the name of the treasure who has reduced me to such wretchedness/poverty).

---

[9] *Agudeza y arte de ingenio*, discurso xxxiii; ed. Correa Calderón, vol. ii, p. 61.

Proper names were a particularly fertile source of double-meanings in that age. One of the strophes of Cervantes's verse eulogy of St Teresa's ecstasies plays with the metathesis between Ávila (her birth-place) and Alba (where she died), accentuated by the lack of differentiation between Spanish *v* and *b*. The lines also involve double-meaning (since *alba* means dawn) and repetition:

> Aunque naciste en Ávila, se puede
> decir que en Alba fue donde naciste,
> pues allí nace, donde muere el justo.
> Desde Alba, ¡oh madre!, al cielo te partiste,
> alba pura, hermosa, a quien sucede
> el claro día del inmenso gusto.[10]

Though you were born in Ávila one could say that you were born in Alba, since where the elect die is their true birth-place. From Alba, mother, you departed for heaven; pure and beautiful dawn, to be followed by the bright day of immense happiness.

In the second book of *La Galatea*, Silerio recites a poem that praises his lady, Blanca; it systematically plays with the ambiguities inherent in the name: the colour white, and a coin of small worth. Here is one of the stanzas:

> Blanca, sois vos por quien trocar querría
> De oro el más finísimo ducado,
> Y por tan alta posesión, tendría
> Por bien perder la del más alto estado.
> Pues esto conocéis, ¡oh Blanca mía!,
> Dejad ese desdén desamorado,
> Y haced, ¡oh Blanca!, que el amor acierte
> A sacar, si sois vos, Blanca, mi suerte.[11]

Blanca, it is you for whom I would wish to exchange the finest golden ducat, and for such exalted possession, would consider it a good to lose the highest estate. Since you know this, my Blanca, leave off this cold disdain, and let love succeed in drawing lots for me, as you are the colour of my good fortune.

b. *Continued metaphors.* These, exemplified by the above-cited word-play on *alba* and *blanca*, are prominent features of Cervantes's courtly style (cf. *DQ* II, 12; p. 720), and a certain elaboration of syntax involving witty symmetries

---

[10] In the edition of Cervantes's verse included in vol. vi of the *Comedias y entremeses*, ed. Schevill and Bonilla, p. 90.

[11] *La Galatea*, ed. Schevill and Bonilla, vol. i, pp. 150–1.

is integral to it. They are related to elaborate comparisons, of which Lotario's long, cautionary speech to Anselmo in the interpolated *novela El curioso impertinente* offers numerous examples. In trying to dissuade his friend from going through with his foolish experiment on Camila's virtue, he compares a chaste wife successively to a fine diamond, an imperfect animal, an ermine, a mirror, a relic, a garden, carefully drawing the moral from each analogy and applying it to Anselmo's project. Finally, he compares woman to glass, then to Danae secluded in her tower but ravished nonetheless by Jupiter in the form of a shower of gold (II, 33; p. 386). Here is another elaborate metaphor taken from a later stage of the same *novela*: 'Finalmente, a él le pareció que era menester … apretar el cerco a aquella fortaleza, y así, acometió a su presunción con las alabanzas de su hermosura, porque no hay cosa que más presto rinda y allane las encastilladas torres de la vanidad de las hermosas que la mesma vanidad, puesta en las lenguas de la adulación' (II, 34; p. 396) (Finally, he decided that he needed to tighten still further the siege around that fortress [i.e. Camila's chastity], and so, mounted an attack on her conceit by praising her beauty, for there is nothing which more quickly overthrows and levels the fortified turrets of vanity than vanity itself, entrusted to the tongues of adulation).

c. *Play between words that share the same root.* This and the next category are further aspects of the repetition favoured by the courtly style. Cf. the first example cited in (a) above, and, likewise from Dorotea's story: 'por quitalle a él la esperanza de poseerme, o a lo menos, porque yo tuviese más guardas para guardarme' (*Don Quijote* I, 28; p. 324) (to deprive him of the hope of possessing me, or at least, so that I should have about me more guards to guard me).

d. *Repetition of the same word, or play between its different grammatical inflexions.* We find these examples in *La Galatea*: 'Vesme aquí, desconocido Grisaldo, desconocida por conocerte …' (Book IV; vol. ii, p. 9) (You see me here, forgetful Grisaldo, quite unknown to myself for having known you), and 'Ví a Nísida, a Nísida vi, para no ver más, ni hay más que ver después de haberla visto' (Book II; vol. i, p. 133) (I saw Nísida, Nísida I saw, and would see no more and have nothing left to see after having seen her). In the first case, the key-term (*desconocido*) is used in two different senses.

e. *Antithesis.* Cardenio, addressing Dorotea, says: «sin acordarme de mis agravios, cuya venganza dejaré al cielo, por acudir en la tierra a los vuestros» (*Don Quijote* I, 29) (unmindful of the offences done to me, leaving it to heaven to avenge them on my behalf, so that I may repair on earth those done to you). In Grisóstomo's song of despair, there is this couplet: «que allí se esparcirán mis duras penas / en altos riscos y en profundos huecos» (*Don Quijote* I, 14) (for my harsh sufferings will be scattered amid lofty crags and deep hollows). See also the example from Eugenio's story cited in (a).

f. *Alliteration, assonance.* In *El curioso impertinente*, Camila's pretence of vengeful fury is described thus: «Se paseaba por la sala con la daga desenvainada, dando tan desconcertados y desaforados pasos ... que no parecía sino que le faltaba el juicio» (*Don Quijote* I, 34) (She paced the room with dagger drawn, taking such wild and extravagant steps that she seemed out of her mind). Here alliteration is achieved by the repeated play on the initial *d*, and assonance by the internal rhymes on *a*-consonant-*a*, and *a*-consonant-*o*. See also the examples in (a) and (d) above.

g. *Gradation, proportion.* Camila confides to her maid her worries about whether she has lowered herself in her lover's eyes by yielding so quickly, and Leonela reassures her with the proverb: 'el que luego da, da dos veces' (to give at once is to give twice), but Camila objects to this that 'lo que cuesta poco se estima en menos' (what costs little is esteemed even less) (II, 34; p. 401). So much for gradation. We have an elaborate example of proportion in the narrator's manner of underscoring the dramatic irony of Lotario's recital of his love-sonnets, seemingly addressed to Clori, though unbeknown to Anselmo, who hears and praises the sonnets, to his wife Camila: 'También alabó este segundo soneto Anselmo como había hecho el primero, y desta manera iba añadiendo eslabón a eslabón a la cadena con que se enlazaba y trababa su deshonra, pues cuando más Lotario le deshoraba, entonces le decía que estaba más honrado; y con esto todos los escalones que Camila bajaba hacia el centro de su menosprecio, los subía, en la opinión de su marido, hacia la cumbre de la virtud y de su buena fama' (II, 34; p. 401) (Anselmo praised the second sonnet just as he had praised the first, and thus he added link upon link to the chain with which he fastened and bound his own dishonour; with the result that all the steps by which Camila descended to the nadir of her shame, raised her, in her husband's eyes, to the summit of her virtue and good name).

Humorous Wit in Don Quixote

While all the species of wit characteristic of the courtly style recur in Cervantes's humorous mode, double-meaning predominates and tends to intertwine with the others, with the result that it would be laboriously repetitive to sort them into separate categories.

Especially frequent in *Don Quixote* are double-meanings that tinker with commonplace terms and expressions by reanimating their literal sense, or which acquire comically degraded connotations as a result of the word's alternative meaning. This is the kind of frivolity that the severe Gracián doubtless had in mind, and it is rare in Cervantes's courtly style. The reverse is true of his humorous mode. The antithesis 'caballero andante ... por andar' and its variants, as we have seen, furnish numerous examples, and these also illustrate two other species of word-play besides double-meaning [see categories (d) and (f) above]. Just as productive are the other key-terms relating to the hero's vocation: *deshacer agravios* (to undo offences), *enderezar tuertos* (right wrongs), *buscar las aventuras* (go in search of adventures). So the facetious member of the funeral cortège, unhorsed during Don Quixote's assault on it, counters his explanation that this was motivated by his mission to roam the world righting wrongs with this firework display of puns: 'No sé cómo pueda ser eso de enderezar tuertos ... pues a mí de derecho [cf. (a) and (c)] me habéis vuelto tuerto [(a) and (e)], dejándome una pierna quebrada, la cual no se verá derecha [(d)] en todos los días de su vida; y el agravio que en mí habéis deshecho ha sido dejarme agraviado [(c)] de manera que me quedaré agraviado [(d)] para siempre, y harta desventura ha sido topar con vos, que vais buscando aventuras [(c)]' (I, 19; p. 204) (I don't know so much about righting wrongs, since you've left me with this leg all wrong which was alright before, and I don't expect it to be right ever again, and the only injury to me that you've undone has been to injure me in such a way that I shall be left injured for ever, and it's been misadventure enough running into you who go looking for adventures).

Because the hero's chivalric escapade constitutes the nerve-centre of the novel's comedy, any major aspect of it is liable to elicit puns like the above. This applies to the familiar traits of the two central characters, which are the subject of the following amusingly elegant antithesis [(e)], compounded by the way in which 'desatado', unfettered, reactivates the dead metaphor 'sueño suelto', deep – literally, loose or unchecked – sleep: 'los cuales, el uno durmiendo a sueño suelto, y el otro velando a pensamientos desatados, les tomó el día y las ganas de levantarse' (II, 70; p. 1193) (who, buried in sleep and consumed by restless fancies respectively, were overtaken by a new day and the desire to get up). The hero's madness, in particular, is a mine of word-play, as in the following example, where jingling puns, italicised by me, highlight the priest's attempt to retrieve it from its murky labyrinth: 'dieron orden para que ... pudiesen *el cura* y el barbero llevársele como deseaban y procurar *la cura* de su *locura* en su tierra' (I, 46; p. 536, cf. a, d, f) (they made provision for the priest and barber to convey him thence, as was their plan, and arrange for the cure of his madness in his native village). The final example is a complex witticism upon the outcome of the joust between the Knight of the Wood (i.e. Sansón Carrasco) and Don Quixote: 'si no fuera por los pensamientos extraordinarios de don Quijote, que se dio a entender que el bachiller no era el bachiller, el señor bachiller quedara imposibilitado para siempre de graduarse de licenciado, por no hallar nidos donde pensó hallar pájaros' (II, 15; pp. 747–8, cf. a and d) (But for the extraordinary notions of Don Quixote, who took it into his head that the Bachelor of Arts was not the Bachelor of Arts, the Bachelor of Arts would have been left for ever incapable of graduating as Master, as a result of not even finding nests where he expected to find birds).[12] This way of saying that Sansón, by masquerading as the Knight of the Wood, might have got himself killed by Don Quixote gives an unexpected double-meaning to *bachiller* on its third repetition, and the concluding phrase cleverly plays with two proverbs by conflating them: 'no hay pájaros hogaño en los nidos de antaño' (there are no birds in yesteryear's nests) and 'unos piensan hallar tocinos y no hay estacas' (some go looking for sides of bacon and don't even find poles to hang them on).

The word-play considered so far is the product of wit. However, naïvely silly examples of it were also appreciated. So, we have the following manifestation of the housekeeper's alarm at the prospect of the hero's third sally. In reply to Sansón, who asks her what the matter is, she replies (II, 7; p. 678):

> 'No es nada, señor Sansón mío, sino que mi amo se sale; ¡sálese sin duda!'
> 'Y ¿por dónde se sale, señora? ¿Hásele roto alguna parte de su cuerpo?'
> 'No se sale ... sino por la puerta de su locura. Quiero decir, señor bachiller de mi ánima, que quiere salir otra vez.'

> 'It's nothing, Mr. Sansón, sir; it's only that my master's off again; no doubt about it, he's leaving.'
> 'Through what part is he leaking, madam? Is some bit of his body broken?'
> 'No, he's just leaving through the door of his madness. I mean, my dear Bachelor Sansón, he wants to be off again'.

---

[12] Though the editors of *DQ* do not comment on this passage, I believe that something is missing here. The sense demands something like 'si no fuera por haberse frustrado los pensamientos extraordinarios de don Quijote ...' (if it hadn't been for the timely frustration of the extraordinary thoughts of Don Quixote ...), since the *hidalgo*, convinced that this is not Sansón Carrasco but an enchanter who looks like him, is about to finish him off with his sword, when he is prevented from doing so by Tomé Cecial, who by now has cast off his disguise as squire of the 'Knight of the Mirrors'.

Sansón's answer, untranslatable in English, makes fun of the housekeeper's nitwitted bleat by playing with two alternative senses of *salirse*, which besides 'go away', means 'spill or leak' and 'talk nonsense'.

A characteristic feature of double-meaning in *Don Quixote*, inherent in its citational irony, is the way in which Cervantes insinuates it almost unnoticed in passages that at first appear solemnly respectful. Often, the sting is in the tail. Examples include the nicely dissimulated insult to Avellaneda in one of the clauses of Don Quixote's testament (see above, p. 121). Another is the cliché 'nunca vistas ni oídas', meaning unprecedented, but taken in a literal sense, never seen or heard; it yields a series of mischievous double-meanings inspired by a jest in the prologue to *Lazarillo de Tormes*: for example, 'Parecióme cosa imposible y fuera de toda buena costumbre que a tan buen caballero le hubiese faltado algún sabio que tomara a cargo el escrebir sus nunca vistas hazañas' (I, 9; p. 105) (It seemed to me impossible and against all good custom that so worthy a knight should have lacked a sage to undertake to record his unprecedented/unseen deeds).[13] The quietness of Cervantes's quiet irony is doubtless what led Italian translators to 'correct' the malicious 'tan entera como la madre que la había parido' (as intact as the mother who bore her) so as to make it conform to its original source in Ariosto, who says of Angelica in *Orlando furioso* Canto I, stanza 55: 'e che'l fior virginal così avea salvo, / come se lo portò del materno alvo' (whose virginal flower was as intact as when she bore it from her mother's womb).[14] Even the normal form of the Spanish idiom – 'tan entera como la había parido su madre' (as intact as when her mother bore her) – though lacking the ribaldry of Cervantes's deformation, is inherently vulgar. The ribald version occurs in the first paragraph of I, 9 in order to cast doubt on the virginity of errant-damsels; and Don Quixote, I presume ingenuously, repeats it in referring to Dulcinea's chastity (I, 26; p. 291). The abbreviated form 'como la madre que la parió' (as the mother who bore her) was a traditional, vulgar way of expressing emphasis or surprise, without reference to motherhood, birth or virginity. This is how the Duchess uses it, slyly imitating Sancho's style, in her dialogue with him in II, 33, p. 909, in order subtly to deny Dulcinea's

---

[13] Cf., among other examples, the chapter-heading of I, 20: 'de la jamás vista ni oída aventura que con más poco peligro fue acabada de famoso caballero en el mundo ...' (of the never seen nor heard adventure accomplished with least peril by the most famous knight in the world).

[14] I owe this information to Aldo Ruffinatto, who included it in his lecture 'Cervantes en Italia, Italia en Cervantes', delivered at the tenth congress of the Asociación Internacional de Cervantistas (Rome, September 2001). The first Brussels edition of *DQ* (1607) makes the same misguided amendment to the hero's version of the solecism, quoted in the text.

enchantment, and Sancho repeats it in his letter to his wife in II, 36, p. 931, to emphasise how disenchanted she will be after his self-administered lashes.

In similar vein to 'tan entera como la madre que la parió' is the dissimulated ribaldry at the end of Sansón Carrasco's profession of support for Don Quixote's projected third sally: 'yo encargaría mucho mi conciencia si no intimase y persuadiese a este caballero que no tenga más tiempo encogida y detenida la fuerza de su valeroso brazo y la bondad de su ánimo valentísimo, porque defrauda con su tardanza el derecho de los tuertos, el amparo de los huérfanos, la honra de las doncellas, el favor de las viudas y el arrimo de las casadas' (II, 7; p. 683) (I would gravely burden my conscience if I failed to urge and persuade this knight to put his valiant arm and dauntless courage to work at once, because by his delay he deprives those who have been wronged of justice, orphans of protection, damsels of their honour, widows of succour and married women of their prop and stay).

Much to Cervantes's taste, and aligned with the tendency that we have been discussing, are double-meanings, which by an auxiliary inflexion that accords with the literal logic of the original word or image give it an unexpected twist. They are integral to his habit of playing with commonplace idioms. Thus, the deranging effect upon the hero's wits of addictive reading of chivalry books elicits this: 'se le pasaban las noches leyendo de claro en claro, y los días de turbio en turbio' (I, 1; p. 39) (he spent his nights reading without a break – literally, from clear patch to clear patch –and his days going from greater to greater befuddlement/obscurity). Another pun of this type is: 'Y dad gracias a Dios, Sancho, que ya que os santiguaron con un palo, que no os hicieron el *per signum crucis* con un alfanje' (II, 28; p. 862) (And give thanks to God, Sancho, that in bestowing on you their blessing with cudgels, they didn't make the sign of the cross on your face with a scimitar). *Santiguar*, to bless, and in the reflexive, to cross oneself, was colloquially used in expressions meaning to thrash somebody, and a *per signum crucis* had the idiomatic sense of a face-slash. A large cluster of jokes reactivate, with comically bathetic effect, the dead metaphors in colloquial expressions based on parts of the body: the many which involve *mano* (hand) or *pie* (foot),[15] *coserse la boca* (sew up one's mouth, keep quiet), *morderse la lengua* (bite one's tongue, i.e. keep quiet), tener grabado en el corazón (to have engraven

---

[15] Such as 'una mano de ...' (a quantity of, literally 'a hand of'), 'mano a mano' (hand in hand), 'de mano en mano' (from hand to hand), 'estar en pie' (stand), 'dar del pie' (kick aside, i.e. reject), 'tomar en la mano' (undertake, in the context of a journey), 'andarle bien/mal ...' (to go – turn out – well/badly for somebody), not to mention sundry variants on *andante*.

on one's heart), *descoserse* (unstitch oneself, i.e. unburden oneself of something), *desbuchar* (disgorge, i.e. unburden oneself), *desjarretar* (hamstring).
Cervantes's habitual foolery with such expressions is an aspect of his amused
attitude towards trite colloquialisms in general, and is well illustrated by the
densely ingenious play with a series of them, including *comerse las manos
tras* (literally, 'to eat one's hands after'; figuratively, to enjoy hugely), in the
verses of the enchantress Urganda la Desconocida (Urganda the Unknown),
addressed to the book *Don Quixote* in the preliminaries to Part I (p. 21).
They do not merely mix metaphors but simultaneously put them through the
mangle:

> Mas si el pan no se te cue-,
> Por ir a manos de idio-,
> Verás de mano a bo-
> Aun no dar una en el cla-,
> Si bien se comen las ma-
> Por mostrar que son curio-.

> But if you're impatient [literally, if your bread can't cook fast enough] to
> end up in the hands of fools, not once will you see them hitting the nail
> on the head [literally, not once will you see their hands hit the nail on the
> head on the way to their mouths],[16] however much they fancy [literally, eat
> their hands after] showing how clever they are.

The same kind of trick yields humorous versions of the continued metaphors of courtly style (b) in passages where Cervantes appropriates imagery
reminiscent of that mode and perverts it for comic effect. Thus, taking the
commonplace symbol of the gardens of Aranjuez as epitome of summer
bloom and fragrance, he plays between the literal and metaphorical sense of
fuentes – fountains, but also, suppurations – and of the idiom 'echar en la
calle' (literally, to throw in the street; figuratively, to make public) in order
to poke fun at the Duchess's fury with Doña Rodríguez for having revealed
the intimate secret of the suppurations in her legs by which, according to
the doctors, the evil humours are drained from her body: 'cuando oyó la
duquesa que Rodríguez había echado en la calle el Aranjuez de sus fuentes,
no lo pudo sufrir' (II, 50; p. 1035) (when the Duchess heard that Rodríguez
had revealed the secret of the gardens of Aranjuez of her fountains/suppura-
tions, she could not endure it).[17] Sancho's intention conscientiously to apply

---

[16] This alludes to the proverb 'de manos a boca se pierde la sopa', meaning the soup is
often lost between hand and mouth.

[17] The same joke occurs in the farce *El rufián viudo* (The Widowed Pimp), in *Comedias*

his master's precepts of government is expressed by: 'pensaba guardarlos y salir a buen parto de la preñez de su gobierno' (II, 43; p. 973) (he intended to keep them and arrive at a good delivery of the pregnancy of his governorship), which plays on the customary, dignified metaphor for bringing a project to fruition: 'llegar a buen puerto', to arrive at safe haven.[18] An ingeniously elaborate example is provided by Don Quixote's rejection of Sansón Carrasco's offer to serve him as a squire. It plays with the allusion to the Biblical strong man implicit in Sansón's name: 'pero no permita el cielo que por seguir mi gusto desjarrete y quiebre la coluna de las letras y el vaso de las ciencias, y tronque la palma eminente de las buenas y liberales artes' (II, 7; p. 683) (Heaven forbid that just to please me he should hamstring and break the column of learned letters and the vessel of the sciences, and cut down the lofty palm of the liberal arts).

This brings us to the subject of play on proper names, beginning with the titles of Don Quixote's library. Whereas the priest says of Gálvez de Montalvo's *Pastor de Fílida* (Phyllis's Shepherd): 'no es ése pastor ... sino muy discreto cortesano' (I, 6; p. 86) (this is no shepherd but a very discreet courtier), he condemns *El caballero de la cruz* (The Knight of the Cross) to the bonfire, with jocular allusion to the proverb 'tras la cruz está el diablo' (p. 79) (behind the cross lurks the devil). The similarity of the titles of *Palmerín de Inglaterra* (Palmerín of England) and *Palmerín de Oliva* (Palmerín of the Olive-Tree) leads the priest ingeniously to juxtapose them in his verdict, playing on the similarity of the name Palmerín to *palma*, palm-tree: 'Esa oliva se haga luego rajas y se queme, que aun no queden della las cenizas, y esa palma de Ingalaterra se guarde y se conserve como a cosa única y se haga para ello otra caja como la que halló Alejandro en los despojos de Dario' (pp. 81–2) (Let this olive-tree be shredded and burnt so that not even the ashes remain, and let this palm of England be kept as a thing of unique value, and let a chest be made for it like that which Alexander found among the spoils of Darius).

In general, puns on proper names in *Don Quixote* are intended to produce a wittily burlesque effect, which alludes to some characteristic of the person

---

y entremeses, ed. Schevill and Bonilla, vol. iv, p. 25. Cervantes also uses the image seriously, as in this passage of *El casamiento engañoso*: 'Mis camisas, cuellos y pañuelos eran un nuevo Aranjuez de flores, según olían, bañados en el agua de ángeles y de azahar que sobre ellos se derramaba' (*Novelas*, ed. García López, p. 528) (My shirts, collars and handkerchiefs were like Aranjuez in bloom, so sweetly did they smell, bathed in the perfume and orange-blossom showered on them).

[18] Don Quixote began his precepts in II, 42, p. 969, by offering to be the pilot 'que te encamine y saque a seguro puerto deste mar proceloso donde vas a engolfarte' (who will steer and bring you to safe heaven through the stormy sea in which you are about to set sail).

in question. An example of this is the name of the bogus doctor who, during Sancho's governorship, subjects the poor governor to the torments of Tantalus at meal times by citing medical aphorisms that prevent him from touching the appetising food laid before him. He introduces himself thus: 'Yo, señor gobernador, me llamo el doctor Pedro Recio de Agüero, y soy natural de un lugar llamado Tirteafuera, que está entre Caracuel y Almodóvar del Campo, a la mano derecha' (*DQ* II, 47; p. 1006) (My name, esteemed governor, is Doctor Pedro Recio de Agüero, and I come from a place called Tirteafuera, which is between Caracuel and Almodóvar del Campo, on the right-hand side). Literally, the doctor's name is Peter Harsh of Omen;[19] and 'tírate afuera' means 'get lost'; vulgarly, 'tirteahuera' was an expression that warded off bad luck or evil, as in 'get thee behind me' or 'touch wood'.[20] Since Tirteafuera, like Caracuel and Almodóvar del Campo, was a real place, the word, by its punning similarity to 'tírate afuera' or 'tirteahuera', implies the desire to banish the evil of ill-omened doctors. This is made plain by Sancho's reply: 'Pues, señor doctor Pedro Recio de Mal Agüero, natural de Tirteafuera ... quíteseme delante' (Well then, Doctor Peter Harsh of Bad Omen, from the village of Get Lost ... get lost). This might be considered a comic inversion of the combination of pun and double-meaning in Cervantes's verses to St Teresa, cited above (a).

The practice of baptising characters with comically symbolic names is pursued throughout *Don Quixote*. Though this was already an established convention in fiction and the theatre, there is an added reason for its prevalence in Cervantes's novel: the parody of chivalry books. Moreover, it is linked to the send-up of the medieval practice, still perpetuated by the Renaissance, of discovering occult significance in etymologies.[21] We have already considered the names of Don Quixote, Dulcinea, Sancho Panza, Rocinante (see above, pp. 31–32, 97). As for Cide Hamete Benengeli, though various explanations of the name's origin have been proposed, the most plausible is its relation to the Arabic for 'aubergine', *berenjena* in Spanish; it is confirmed by Sancho's mispronunciation of Benengeli as *berenjena* when he hears the name for the first time (II, 2; p. 645). Though the continuation of Sancho's

---

[19] 'Recio' has the primary sense of 'strong'; but here the subsidiary senses of 'harsh', 'intolerable' are doubtless intended.

[20] Correas, *Vocabulario de refranes*, 479b.

[21] So the hermit, searching for a name that will be consonant with Amadís's grief and manly beauty, calls him Beltenebros, beautiful darkness (*Amadís de Gaula*, Chap. 48, ed. Buendía, p. 527). On the tradition of deciphering the etymological symbolism of names, which stretches from the Middle Ages to the Baroque, see Curtius (1953: appendix xiv), and, with reference to *DQ*, Spitzer (1955: 163–79).

remark would suggest that the notorious partiality of Moors for aubergines put the solecism in his head, there is another reason for the association, since the natives of Toledo (Benengeli's home town) were known as *berenjeneros*, auberginers. The etymologies of the names of Countess Trifaldi (II, 38), the wooden horse Clavileño (II, 40) and the hideous Clara Perlerina (II, 47) are all helpfully unpicked for us upon the first reference to them in the story.[22] The captains in the imaginary armies described by Don Quixote prior to his battle with the sheep (I, 18), like the personages dreamed up by Dorotea in the burlesque role of Princess Micomicona (I, 29; p. 336) have, generally, high-sounding names with absurdly degraded associations. Micomicona, can be construed as leg-pulling supermonkey,[23] the giant Pandafilando de la Fosca Vista as thieving cardsharp of the frowning gaze,[24] Brandabarbarán de Boliche as bearded sword-waving savage of the gambling-den,[25] Alfeñiquén del Algarbe as wimpish fop of the Portuguese Algarve,[26] Laurcalco señor de la Puente de Plata as Laurcalco (possibly, Fame-Shunning Lord) of the Silver Bridge – the silver bridge being a proverbially easy escape route for one's enemies, sparing one the need to confront them. A similar caricaturist effect is achieved in a simpler way by the numerous deformations of names, due either to the speaker's malice or ignorance. So the name of the sage enchanter Fristón, who is supposed to have spirited away the hero's library, is corrupted by the niece and housekeeper into Muñatón (bawd or pander with knowledge of witchcraft) and Fritón (fry-up) (I, 7; p. 96); the goat-herd Pedro turns the Biblical Sara, of legendary longevity, into *sarna*, itch (I, 12; p. 131); Sancho corrupts Fierabrás, the giant with the magic balsam, into feo Blas, ugly Blas (I, 15; p. 161); Dorotea, acting the role of Princess Micomicona turns Quijote into Azote or Jigote, whip or cold roast meat hash (I, 30; p. 348), etcetera.

(ii) Devices of Intensification

In general, the Golden Age's sense of humour delights in extremes: the more degraded, grotesque, irrational the object of mirth, the funnier, provided that it satisfies the requirement of wit. The recipe for maximum risibility is formulated as follows by the age's most intelligent theorist of comedy,

22 For Trifaldi's name, see below, p. 218.

23 *Mico* means monkey; *dar mico* is to deceive; *micona* is a feminine augmentative.

24 *Panda* is a fraudulent play in a card game; *filar* is to bamboozle verbally; *fosco* is dark or wild, frowning.

25 *Brando* is Italian for sword; *blandir* means brandish; *barba* means beard and *bárbaro* savage; *boliche* is a gambling-den-cum-brothel.

26 *Alfeñique* means sugar-paste.

Alonso López Pinciano: 'el primor mayor en mayor fealdad' (the greatest exquisiteness combined with greatest ugliness),[27] with ugliness to be understood in the Aristotelian sense of any kind of disfigurement or indignity. What I call intensifying devices are those that serve to highlight this quality for comic effect.

They comprise: (i) graphic energy; (ii) amplification of circumstances; (iii) comparisons, metaphors, fanciful exaggerations, and they are all affected by Cervantes's fundamental principles of composition, which to some extent moderate the extremism implicit in his theme. Apart from those mentioned already, they include the avoidance of scatology and the discreet dissimulation of ribaldry, in conformity with his norm of *propiedad*, propriety.

The point can be illustrated by the comic scenes of cudgelling, fisticuffs, and other mayhem in the novel. If we compare them with equivalent scenes in contemporary Spanish literature, we note that Cervantes either tones down or suppresses degradation of a crude and elementary kind, and applies intensifying rhetorical devices in moderation. The only resort to scatological comedy in *Don Quixote* – the description of how the terrified Sancho contrives to relieve himself without letting go of Rocinante's saddle (I, 20; pp. 215–16) – is notable for Cervantes's euphemistic description of the complicated operation, which manages never to mention its purpose in plain language. In the scene where Don Quixote is discovered slashing the wine-skins (I, 35; pp. 415–16) under the illusion that he is doing battle with the giant who has usurped Princess Micomicona's kingdom, the details that create an impression of grotesque impropriety – his long, hairy, filthy legs, scantily covered by his shirt-tails, which, we are coyly told, were six fingers' breadth shorter behind than in front; his state of somnambulism, unaffected by his frenzied sword-strokes; the innkeeper's red, greasy sleeping-cap on his head; the blanket wrapped round one arm; the uncontrolled rage that all this provokes in the innkeeper when he sees the spillage of his livelihood – are narrated plainly and graphically, without jocular asides or comparisons; and their ridiculous effect depends on an incongruity peculiar to *Don Quixote*: the contrast between sordid reality and heroic illusion. Though the spectacle is highly indecorous, Cervantes maintains a certain primness in narrating it, reflected in the attitude of Dorotea, Velázquez-like observer in the open doorway, who takes one look at her scantily clad champion and looks no more. The plainness of the style of the passage, also its strong visual impact, rely on the way in which comedy is derived from significant circumstances rather

---

[27] *Philosophia antigua poetica*, ed. Carballo Picazo, vol. iii, p. 42.

than from jocular embroidery: these include the implicit contrast between Don Quixote's aspect and that of an armed knight. Also, they derive from Cervantes's wish plausibly to explain an astonishing prodigy: the fact that the *hidalgo*, even though fast asleep, believes he is doing battle with a giant. His purpose throughout this novel is to mediate unreason in comprehensible terms to rational readers.

The style of the fencing-match between the expert and the amateur merits more particular attention, since it exemplifies all the rhetorical intensifiers mentioned above, as well as the tendency to moderate their potential excess (II, 19; pp. 788–9):

> Las cuchilladas, estocadas, altibajos, reveses y mandobles que tiraba Corchuelo eran sin número, más espesas que hígado y más menudas que granizo.[28] Arremetía como un león irritado; pero salíale al encuentro un tapaboca de la zapatilla de la espada del licenciado, que en mitad de su furia le detenía, y se la hacía besar como si fuera reliquia, aunque no con tanta devoción como las reliquias deben y suelen besarse. Finalmente, el licenciado le contó a estocadas todos los botones de una media sotanilla que traía vestida, haciéndole tiras los faldamentos, como colas de pulpo; derribóle el sombrero dos veces, y cansóle de manera, que de despecho, cólera y rabia asió la espada por la empuñadura, y arrojóla por el aire con tanta fuerza, que uno de los labradores asistentes, que era escribano, que fue por ella, dio después por testimonio que la alongó de sí casi tres cuartos de legua; el cual testimonio sirve y ha servido para que se conozca y vea con toda verdad cómo la fuerza es vencida del arte.

> The cuts, thrusts, down-strokes, backhanders and two-handers that Corchuelo delivered were innumerable, thicker than a haystack and as torrential as hail. He charged like an angry lion, but was stopped by the button of the licentiate's foil against his mouth, forcing him to kiss it like a holy relic, though with less devotion. Finally, his adversary's sword-thrusts made a precise tally of all the buttons of a half-cassock that he wore, tearing its tails to strips like octopus's tentacles; his hat was knocked off twice, and and he was left so worn out that in a fit of resentment, fury and rage he took the sword by the pummel and hurled it so far, that one of the peasants standing by, a scribe, who went to fetch it, testified later that he threw it three-quarters of a league: testimony that stands to this day as clinching proof how brute force is conquered by art.

Ángel Rosenblat, in his study of the language of *Don Quixote* (1971: 167), was surely right to emphasise the clarity and normality of Cervantes's imagery in general, that is, its avoidance of far-fetched bizarreness; this applies to all

---

[28] 'Más espesas que hígado' means literally thicker than liver. On the popularity of the comparison, see Rodríguez Marín's edn of *DQ* (1947), vol. v, p. 98.

the images used in this passage. While Cervantes bases the description on amplification of circumstances, beginning with the enumeration in line one, he avoids the congestion of incongruous analogies and witty allusions found in some contemporary comic texts, such as *La pícara Justina*. Nonetheless, like other writers of the age, he resorts to comparisons drawn from carnival revelry, animal rampages, children's games, storms, battles and other such disorder in order to emphasise the anarchy of scenes of farce. He typifies his age, again, in highlighting the loser's ineptitude in battle by comic violation of decency of body and dress, without, however, habitually resorting to the horseplay in which the picaresque novelists delight: nudity, shit, whipping, pelting with refuse. Cervantes is also typical in seasoning jocularity with the spice of irreverence, as he does in the analogy drawn from the veneration of relics, yet in so doing, he avoids the sacrilegious connotations tapped by Quevedo.[29] A similar respect for moderation is observable in the fact that rarely in *Don Quixote* does he resort to two very popular species of comparison: first, the *apodo*, the dehumanising characterisation of a person's aspect or mannerisms that consists in likening him or her, as bizarrely as possible, to an animal, a vegetable, an artefact, and secondly, the impossible exaggeration based on double-meaning, whose sheer impossibility marks the extremity of the thing described.[30] One of the few instances of the use of *apodos* in *Don Quixote* occurs during the description of Sancho's plight during the feigned attack on the 'island', where he is compared in the space of a few lines to a turtle, a side of bacon and an upturned boat (quoted below, p. 224). The only example of the other kind of jest occurs in the initial description of Rocinante: 'Fue luego a ver a su rocín, y aunque tenía más cuartos que un real, y más tachas que el caballo de Gonela, que *tantum pellis et ossa fuit*, le pareció que ni el Bucéfalo de Alejandro ni Babieca el del Cid con él se igualaban' (I, 1; p. 42) (He then went to inspect his nag, and though it had more hoof-mange than an athlete's foot,[31] and more defects that Gonella's horse, which was all skin and bone, he thought that neither Alexander's Bucephalus nor the Cid's Babieca were a match for it).

To be sure, Cervantes does not spurn far-fetched comparisons and fantastic exaggerations. The one that concludes the description of the fencing-bout typi-

---

[29] For instance, in the description of the drunken orgy during Pablos's visit to his uncle's lodgings (*El Buscón* II, 4).

[30] On their frequency in *El Buscón*, see Chevalier (1992: 136, and, in general, Chapters 9 and 10).

[31] The double-meaning involved in *cuartos/real* is untranslatable. The first word means both hoof-mange and coins of very small worth; a *real* was a coin worth 34 *maravedís*, the *maravedí* being, like the penny, the basic small unit of currency.

fies his penchant for quirky extravagance; it is in the same vein as Sancho's
assertion that Aldonza Lorenzo's voice was so loud that once it carried half-
a-league from the belfry to the fallow fields where some farm-hands of her
father were working (I, 25; p. 283), the *hidalgo*'s comparison of the outsize
beads of Montesinos's rosary to ostrich-eggs (II, 23; p. 819), the narrator's
eulogy of the quality of Trifaldín's woollen cape, such that were it frizzled,
each curl would be the size of a chick-pea grown on the fields of Martos (II,
38; pp. 938–9). I conclude with this example, which effectively illustrates
Cervantes's tendency to subordinate comic embroidery to relevance (II, 13;
p. 732):

> Se la puso en las manos a Sancho, el cual, empinándola, puesta a la boca,
> estuvo mirando las estrellas un cuarto de hora, y en acabando de beber
> dejó caer la cabeza a un lado, y dando un gran suspiro dijo: '¡Oh hideputa,
> bellaco, y cómo es católico!'

> The other squire put the wine-skin in Sancho's hands, who tilting it upwards,
> and applying it to his mouth, stayed there gazing at the stars for a quarter
> of an hour, and when he had finished, wagged his head, gave a deep sigh
> and said: 'Oh son of a bitch, wicked, how good it is!'

The jocular exaggeration of the time the swig lasted is incidental to the
essential point of the passage: first, Sancho's familiar addiction to wine, and
second, the comic inversion by which, after having previously protested at his
colleague's use of the exclamation 'hideputa', son of a bitch (literally, whore),
to ponder admiringly the strength of Sancho's daughter, he now commits the
same alleged impropriety in respect of the draught just consumed. That is,
witty hyperbole is subservient to comedy of character and situation.

(iii) Devices of Attenuation

Attenuation is the opposite of intensification, and is integral to Cervantes's quiet irony. Understatement is a major aspect of it; another is an urbane
elegance which, just as it tends to veil coarseness by euphemism and periph-
rasis, prefers discreet allusion to heavy-handed insistence, curbs explicit
commentary on the action, and postpones the explanation of mysteries in
order to enhance their tantalising drama.

Cervantes's treatment of the theme of Rocinante's decrepitude, culminating
in the tourney between the Knight of the Wood (alias Sansón Carrasco) and
Don Quixote (II, 14) is a superb example of all this. The initial portraits of
Rocinante's ricketiness and lack of agility (I, 1; p. 42, and I, 9; p. 109) are
followed by a series of playful, elegant variations on the theme: a reference to
an unwonted sexual impulse, which highlights his normal lack of machismo

(I, 15; p. 160); double-edged eulogies of his fidelity and docility, implying his lack of mobility (I, 18; p. 196; I, 43; p. 508); mentions of the occasions when he breaks into a trot or shows other surprising signs of nimbleness (I, 19; p. 202), which remind us how unusual they are. Now, from the moment when Don Quixote overhears the conversation between the Knight of the Wood (or the Mirrors) and his squire until near the end of the adventure – that is, for most of three chapters (II, 12–14) – Cervantes is silent about the identities and purposes of the two mysterious strangers, supposedly a knight-errant and his squire. Dialogue predominates; and the narrator's interventions, while occasionally revealing sly amusement at the proceedings, are either limited to factual descriptions of what happens, or else, in accord with the citational manner, are adapted tongue-in-cheek to Don Quixote's language and view-point. By the time the climax of the adventure is reached – that is, the joust – the reader has already deduced that the unknown knight is a sly joker who is playing cat-and-mouse with the hero, though does not yet know precisely who he is or what he is up to. Discovery of this coincides with the realisation that the cat has fallen into the mouse-trap owing to two ridiculous circumstances: the uselessness of the strange knight's horse and Sancho's cowardice.

Cervantes narrates the joust with evident delight because it involves a number of his favourite situational ironies: tables turned or hoist with own petard; arrogant confidence defeated by common nature; standing on the evidence yet failing to see it; concatenation and snowballing; ridiculous inversion of the normal and proper state of affairs. The humour of the narrative discourse springs directly from these ironies and serves to highlight them; they consist mainly in laconic incidental comments, which by their auxiliary function and understated or euphemistic style disguise their deflating purpose.

While the Knight of the Mirrors takes the amount of the field required for his charge (II, 14; p. 743), Sancho, terrified by the other squire's grotesquely large and warty nose, which is now visible thanks to the light of dawn, begs his master to help him up into a cork-oak so that, he alleges, he can get a better view of the fight. Don Quixote, though well aware of Sancho's true motive, humanely obliges, despite the request's scant compatibility with the code of chivalry. The Knight of the Mirrors begins his charge while this operation is still under way, and this is how Cervantes describes it, showing an exquisite sense of timing:

> y creyendo [el de los Espejos] que lo mismo habría hecho don Quijote, *sin esperar son de trompeta ni otra señal que los avisase*, volvió las riendas a su caballo – *que no era más ligero ni de mejor parecer que Rocinante* – y

a todo su correr, *que era un mediano trote*, iba a encontrar a su enemigo; pero viéndole ocupado en la subida de Sancho, detuvo las riendas y paróse en la mitad de la carrera, *de lo que el caballo quedó agradecidísimo, a causa que ya no podía mover*.

And assuming that Don Quixote must have done the same, without waiting for a trumpet-blast or any other signal to the two contenders, he wheeled his horse, which was no nimbler or better-looking than Rocinante, and making it go at full tilt, which is to say at an average kind of trot, he charged at his adversary, but seeing him occupied in helping Sancho to climb the tree, turned the reins and checked in mid-career, for which the horse was deeply grateful, since it could budge no more.

Jocular enhancement is provided by the expressions in italics: 'sin esperar son de trompeta ...' echoes a line from Ariosto's *Orlando furioso*, and evokes the heroic scenario of a tourney while reminding us how far we are from it here; 'que no era más ligero ni de mejor parecer que Rocinante' is a euphemism for 'was a walking skeleton'; the incidental, matter-of-fact interjection 'at an average kind of trot' wrecks the effect of 'at full tilt'; 'for which the horse was deeply grateful ...' produces a sudden, deflating switch from the rider's viewpoint to his mount's, making us see the sudden halt from the perspective of the gasping, worn-out animal.

The narrative continues:

Don Quijote, que le pareció que ya su enemigo venía volando, arrimó reciamente las espuelas a *las trasijadas ijadas de Rocinante, y le hizo aguijar de manera*, que cuenta la historia que *esta sola vez se conoció haber corrido algo; porque todas las demás siempre fueron trotes declarados*, y *con esta no vista furia* llegó donde el de los Espejos *estaba hincando a su caballo las espuelas hasta los botones, sin que le pudiese mover un solo dedo* del lugar donde había hecho estanco en su carrera. *En esta buena sazón y coyuntura* halló don Quijote a su contrario embarazado con su caballo y ocupado con su lanza, *que nunca, o no acertó, o no tuvo lugar de ponerla en ristre*. Don Quijote, *que no miraba en estos inconvenientes, a salvamano y sin peligro alguno* encontró al de los Espejos, *con tanta fuerza, que mal de su grado le hizo venir al suelo por las ancas del caballo, dando tal caída, que, sin mover pie ni mano, dio señales de que estaba muerto.*

Don Quixote, who assumed that his foe was already flying towards him, dug his spurs deep into Rocinante's hollow flanks to such effect that the history relates that this is the only time when he actually achieved a sort of gallop, because all his other attempts at this had been no more than brisk trots, and with this unprecedented fury bore down upon the Knight of the Mirrors, who was desperately digging in his spurs without, however, making the beast move an inch from the spot where it had stalled in mid-career. It was at this happy juncture that Don Quixote came upon his adversary, who was still struggling with his horse while trying to keep hold of his lance, which he never managed or never had the chance to tilt at his foe. Don Quixote, unconcerned by such niceties, and without any kind of hindrance or risk to himself, met the Knight of the Mirrors with such force, that he drove him backwards over the horse's rump crashing to the ground, where unable to move hand or foot, he lay as though dead.

The description is a masterpiece of irony of events, being designed to highlight the delightfully unexpected yet logical outcome. I merely draw attention to those examples of verbal humour that have not already been covered by previous comments: the elegant assonance of 'trasijadas ijadas de Rocinante'; the tongue-in-cheek irony of 'con esta no vista furia' and 'en esta buena sazón y coyuntura'; the brilliant understatement of 'que no miraba en estos inconvenientes', which treats the stranger's defenceless state as a minor snag, when in fact Don Quixote's disregard for it constitutes a flagrant infraction of the code of chivalry;[32] the splendid citational irony of the last two and a half lines, which echo the stirring language used in chivalry books to describe the conclusive victory of one knight over another in a joust.

Don Quixote unlaces his enemy's helmet, and is astonished to behold the following:

> ¿Quién podrá decir lo que vio, sin causar admiración, maravilla y espanto a los que lo oyeren? Vio, dice la historia, el rostro mesmo, la misma figura, el mesmo aspecto, la misma fisonomía, la mesma efigie, la perspetiva mesma del bachiller Sansón Carrasco.

> And he beheld ... but who may say what he beheld without causing astonishment, wonder and shock to the listeners? He beheld, relates the history, the very face, the very countenance, the very aspect, the very physiognomy, the very effigy, the very semblance of bachelor Sansón Carrasco.

Cervantes does *not* say: 'and he beheld Sansón Carrasco'. The intensifying effect of those repeated 'mismos' is deceptive: what we have here is not intensification but a form of attenuation: to be precise, the ironic mimicry of Don Quixote's thought-processes without comment on them. What seems extraordinary to him is not that the knight just defeated by him should turn out to be Sansón, which is what any sensible person would assume, but that, thanks

---

[32] The precept is explicit in the *Doctrinal de caballeros*: 'que si cayere la lanza a algún caballero en yendo por la carrera ante de los golpes, que el otro caballero que le alze la lanza e non le dé, ca non sería caballería ferir al que non lleva lanza' (if a knight should drop his lance during the charge preceding the encounter, his adversary should raise his own lance and refrain from striking him, for it would be contrary to the code of chivalry to attack a defenceless foe). Cited in Clemencín's edn of *DQ*, vol. iv, p. 255.

to magic, he should look so uncannily like Sansón, and that is what all those *mismos* imply. This is the amazing prodigy that he summons Sancho to witness; and his squire's first, credulous reaction echoes his master's inference and his astonishment, to such an extent that he suggests that Don Quixote should run through the prostrate foe with his sword just in case he should prove to be a hostile enchanter. The *hidalgo* is only prevented from murdering his young friend by the hasty advent of the other squire, now without his false nose, who calls loudly on Don Quixote to desist. Divested of his disguise, the strange squire proves to be – or rather, to look exactly like – Sancho's kinsman Tomé Cecial, who straight away identifies himself as Tomé Cecial and reconfirms Sansón's identity, adding that their presence in that spot is the result of a wily stratagem that has badly backfired. Were Sancho a person of average common sense, he would be satisfied with this explanation; however, Sancho is a nitwit endowed with merely sporadic lucidity, so, torn between his master's assertions and Tomé's, he no longer knows whom to believe. Don Quixote, of course, continues unshaken in the assumption that his defeated foe's resemblance to Sansón Carrasco is a magical hallucination, and, having extracted from him the confession that Dulcinea is superior in beauty to his own lady, and a promise to go to El Toboso to pay homage to her, he rides off exulting in his victory.

Cervantes's attitude, as narrator, to this extraordinary outcome is typical of his quiet irony. He does not tell us that Don Quixote's interpretation is crazy, and that Sancho shares his gullibility, nor does he convey this by any kind of sarcastic wink at the reader. He merely implies it by his citational manner. To be sure, towards the end of Chapter 14, for the sake of clarity, he abandons this poker-faced reticence. He plainly calls the belief of master and squire an error, noting that Don Quixote's words had the effect of making Sancho doubt the evidence of his own eyes. Moreover, he devotes the greater part of Chapter 15 to explaining who precisely were the Knight of the Mirrors and his squire, and what was their purpose in coming in quest of Don Quixote. Cervantes's irony may be quiet, and it is also teasing and tantalising insofar as it tends to defer explanations, but it is never deliberately mystificatory; sooner or later, he offers full and detailed explanations for potentially confusing mysteries, of which there are several in the novel (cf. Part II, Chapters 27, 50, 62, 65, 70). This policy is consistent with his already noted respect for truth, enshrined in the phrase 'así era la verdad' or its variants. The prevalent modern view of him as a deeply enigmatic author, forever hidden behind the masks of his narrators and characters, would have puzzled and pained him, since one of features of *Don Quixote* in which he obviously takes pride is its transparent clarity, associated with its universal popularity (II, 3; pp. 652–3).

However, there is a difference between factual explanation and judgements on the action and characters; while Cervantes never witholds the first, he seldom imposes the second on us. In this respect, his attitude is very different from that of Avellaneda, who, in his own version, guides the reader's interpretation with schoolmasterly pedantry.[33] By contrast, the reader gets used to inferring Cervantes's opinion from hints and nuances. We are not told, for example, that Sansón Carrasco has behaved like a presumptuous fool in this affair. But the reader infers it from various clues: among them, the connotations of a jest previously cited (see above, page 134). The joke ironically alludes to the licentiate's arrogant confidence about achieving his ends, and by the punning insistence on his university degree suggests the bad use that he made of his intelligence. Typically, Cervantes's attitude to the outcome is merrily impartial. If, in that joke, he plays with proverbs at Sansón's expense, he has similar fun with Don Quixote's confidence that his defeated adversary will pay homage to Dulcinea, commenting: 'pero uno pensaba don Quijote y otro el de los Espejos' (II, 15; p. 747) (but he thought one thing and the Knight of the Mirrors another). Here Cervantes humorously modifies the proverb 'uno piensa el bayo y otro el que lo ensilla' (the bay horse thinks one thing and the groom who saddles him thinks another). In this way he associates Don Quixote with the horse, taunting him as a beast.

The key to Cervantes's impartiality lies in a passage that immediately precedes the joust between the two knights and sets the scene for it (II, 14; pp. 740–1). It begins with a precious, opulent dawn-description on which Cervantes lavishes lyrical imagery associated with this topic, both mocking and savouring it, before focusing on the objects and persons revealed by the light of day: the grotesque nose of the unknown squire, the infantile panic that this inspires in Sancho, the dashing aspect of the Knight of the Mirrors, which Don Quixote notes without fear. Here, unlike what happens in pastoral or epic, an exquisitely beautiful dawn bathes the human drama in an ironic light, eloquently emphasising its bizarreness and absurdity. Yet Cervantes notes it without contempt. On the contrary, the characteristic ambivalence that he shows by this blend of lyrical, heroic and burlesque tones, and by the contemplative gaze that non-committally embraces such heterogeneous

---

[33] I refer to comments like the following 'Volvió el soldado a mirar a Sancho, y como le vio con las barbas espesas, cara de bobo, y rellanado en su jumento, pensando que era algún labrador zafio de las aldeas vecinas … le dijo: "¿Quién le mete al muy villano en echar su cucharada donde no le va ni le viene?"' (Chapter 14; ed. Riquer, vol. ii, p. 31) (The soldier turned to look at Sancho, and when he saw him slouched on his ass, with his thick beard and idiot's face, taking him for some coarse peasant from a nearby village, he said to him: 'What's this bumpkin doing sticking his spoon in what doesn't concern him?').

objects, implies a richly nuanced conception of the comic that includes a recognition of its artistic dignity and the refusal to treat the characters as mere butts of laughter. As the luscious dawn-description suggests, this distinctive posture – unique in the Spanish Golden Age – is conditioned, directly or indirectly, by Cervantes's mind-set as author of romantic and heroic fiction, which contributes to his mock-gravity, his elegant urbanity, and his ludic and benign conception of the action of *Don Quixote* as a kind of comically skewed epic, full of remarkable, absurd trifles.

Commonplaces and Colloquialisms

These expressions are an important feature of the novel's style, including the discourse of the two heroes, and are often lost in translation. Awareness of them affects not only the appreciation of Don Quixote's humour but also, more generally, that of Cervantes's attitude to his characters.

In 1971, the Venezuelan critic Ángel Rosenblat published a useful book on the language of *Don Quixote* (1971), which brought together and classified, under headings like 'antitheses', 'comparisons', 'commonplaces', 'metaphors', 'repetition', abundant examples of these. His purpose was to define the distinctive character of Cervantes's style, and he maintained that Cervantes handles the common usage of the Spanish of his age in keeping with basic principles of clarity, discretion and naturalness, imposing a distinctive stamp on this material by ludic variations of its habitual form. So, in the second chapter of the novel, he refers to the swine-herd's pigs by the plain, indelicate 'puercos', adding 'que sin perdón así se llaman' (p. 49) (for without begging your pardon that's what they're called). Here he inverts the commonplace 'con perdón' (begging your pardon), which habitually qualified the mention of these animals. He begins Part II, Chapter 9, which describes Don Quixote's and Sancho's nocturnal search for Dulcinea's palace in El Toboso, with a facetious 'Media noche era por filo, poco más o menos' (It was the stroke of midnight, more or less), where the contradictory effect of the qualifier plays with a well-known ballad-line. One could cite scores of other examples, but there is no need, since we have already encountered plenty in considering Cervantes's habit of reviving the dead metaphors enshrined in commonplace idioms.

So, according to Rosenblat, this verbal foolery is what gives the language of Cervantes, identified with that of *Don Quixote*, its distinctive stamp. This argument involves some questionable assumptions: first, the belief that *Don Quixote* is fully representative of Cervantes's style; second, that the pervasive presence of colloquialisms and commonplaces in it is a habitual characteristic of that style; third, that playfulness marks Cervantes's divergence from the contemporary norm. Let us take these points in order. First, Cervantes's style varies in accord with the genre in which he writes: its air of sententious gravity in the tragic interpolation of *El curioso impertinente* (*DQ* I, 33–35) or in the epic *Persiles y Sigismunda* is different from the levity prevalent in most of *Don Quixote*, even though we can find constant characteristics running through these contrasted modes. Secondly, the massive presence of colloquialisms in *Don Quixote* is due to the comic purpose that governs it; we would look in vain for a similar proportion in *Persiles y Sigismunda*. Thirdly, Cervantes's habitual tinkering with them is not a practice peculiar to him; it is equally evident in the burlesque picaresque novel, *La pícara Justina*, which came out in the same year as *Don Quixote* Part I (1605), and which shares a number of other common features with its style and manner.[34] However, despite these similarities, the two novels differ fundamentally from each other, and this difference affects the ludic attitude that they both exhibit. So, when Rosenblat assumed that 'el juego' (play, playfulness), often linked by him with such qualifiers as 'humorístico', 'burlesco', 'cómico', 'parodia', is the factor that individualises Cervantine style, he begged the question what precisely is it that individualises Cervantes's playful humour, distinguishing it from the apparently quite similar attitude exhibited by the author of *La pícara Justina*, or indeed, by other Golden Age writers one could mention.

Before characterising the intention that governs the novel's colloquial clichés, it is first necessary to identify them, and for this purpose we can take as a preliminary guide Quevedo's satiric *Premática* (Government Edict) of 1600, which enumerates two hundred and seventy-six colloquialisms guilty of having 'corrupted good prose and exasperated us all'.[35] Of these expressions, seventy four can be found in *Don Quixote*, and about a quarter of them appear more than once. The great majority of them occur in comic contexts, either being treated as typical of the way in which plebeian or funny characters talk, or being attributed to discreet characters in jocular mood, including the narrator.

Quevedo's *Premática* is not the only indicator of Cervantes's resort to colloquialisms. Whenever some kind of commonplace is cited in his works – proverbial saying, set phrase, familiar image – it is typically signalled by 'como dicen' (as they say) or something similar. These interjections are attached to many colloquial expressions that are not on Quevedo's list; again, the great majority, about three-quarters by my reckoning, occur in *Don*

---

[34] See below, pp. 165–66, also Close (2000: 23–5, 77–80, 312–21).
[35] See the edition of the *Prosa festiva completa* by García-Valdés, pp. 147–57.

Quixote. Here is a brief sample. The narrator describes the nocturnal free-for-all at the inn with an allusion to a popular tale, rather like that of the giant beetroot, where more and more people get caught up in the same chain of circumstances: 'y así como suele decirse, "el gato al rato, el rato a la cuerda, la cuerda al palo", daba el arriero a Sancho, Sancho a la moza, la moza a él …' (I, 16; p. 175) (just like the saying 'the cat chased the rat, the rat chased the string, the string chased the stick', the mule-drover pummelled Sancho, he pummelled the wench, she pummelled him). Sancho, after his master's rout of the funeral cortège, proposes that they should escape possible retaliation by heading for the nearby *sierra*, where they can satisfy their hunger with the looted provisions. He cites a cynical proverb equivalent to 'life must go on': 'y, como dicen, váyase el muerto a la sepultura y el vivo a la hogaza' (I, 19; p. 207) (and, as they say, the dead to the grave and the living to their crust). Needless to say, many of these clichés are woven into the narrator's discourse or the dialogue of the characters without any such comment as 'como suele decirse'. The mere fact that they are subjected by Cervantes to comic modification is potentially a sign that he finds them trite, vulgar or, in some way, amusingly odd. In his habitual tendency to unpick popular expressions and reassemble them in idiosyncratic form one perceives a master of language whose familiarity with its every nook and cranny, coupled with his inventive facility, result in persistent ludic experimentation.

To the previous instances of the abundance of colloquialisms in *Don Quixote* must be added Sancho's proverbs, oaths and exclamations, and the habitually domestic and familiar register of his dialogues with his master, including a plethora of comparisons, metaphors and other tropes articulated by these two and other characters. There are two basic reasons for this proliferation: the requirement of plainness that is trenchantly formulated in the prologue to Part I (cited above, p. 68), and Cervantes's aim ironically to contrast the hero's idealising literary mania, reflected in his style, with a level of everyday, familiar language. That is, it is basically for the same reason as the omnipresence of things like donkeys, windmills and barbers' basins. In this respect, we can see Cervantes's frequent play with them as an aspect of one of his major novelistic innovations: his depiction of a prosaic and homely level of experience, very different from the delight shown by the risible vileness and degradation of his contemporaries.

To illustrate the previously made point about the kind of contexts in which colloquialisms occur, I take a sample of those mentioned in Quevedo's *Premática* that are also found in *Don Quixote*:

dares y tomares. 'porque no vamos a bodas, sino a rodear el mundo, y a tener *dares y tomares* con gigantes, con endriagos y vestiglos' [Sancho, in conversation with his wife; II, 5; p. 664; cf. the clause relating to Sancho in Don Quixote's testament, cited above, p. 122] (For we're not going to some wedding or other, but to roam the world and get into serious differences of opinion [literally, give and take] with giants, dragons and monsters).

por sí o por no. 'Soy de parecer, señor mío, que *por sí o por no*, vuesa merced hinque y meta la espada por la boca a éste que parece el bachiller Sansón Carrasco; quizá matará en él a alguno de sus enemigos encantadores' [Sancho's reaction when he sees the face of the defeated Knight of the Mirrors; II, 14; p. 744] (I'm of the opinion, sir, that just to be on the safe side [literally, either in case it's yes or no], you should stick your sword through the mouth of this person who looks like bachelor Sansón Carrasco; that way, maybe you'll get rid of one of those enemy enchanters).

vuesa merced me la haga. 'Mi señora Dulcinea del Toboso besa a vuestra merced las manos, y suplica a *vuestra merced se la haga* de hacerla saber cómo está' [a wench accompanying the enchanted Dulcinea to Don Quixote, II, 23; p. 827] (My lady Dulcinea del Toboso kisses your hand and begs you to do her the favour of telling her how you're doing).[36]

hombre de chapa. See Sancho's use of 'moza de chapa', cited above, p. 127.

las ollas de Egipto. 'A sólo Sancho se le escureció el alma, por verse imposibilitado de aguardar la espléndida comida y fiestas de Camacho, que duraron hasta la noche; y así, asenderado y triste siguió a su señor, que con la cuadrilla de Basilio iba, y así se dejó atrás *las ollas de Egipto*, aunque las llevaba en el alma' (II, 21; p. 808) (Only Sancho's soul was plunged in gloom, on realising he would be unable to stay for the splendid banquet and festivities provided by Camacho, which lasted till night; and so, sad and disconsolate, he followed his master, now attached to Basilio's party, leaving behind the fleshpots of Egypt even though they were engraved upon his soul).

desgarrarse; predicar en desierto. 'por mil señales iban coligiendo [la sobrina y el ama] que su tío y señor quería *desgarrarse* la vez tercera, y volver al ejercicio de su, para ellas, mal andante caballería: procuraban por todas las vías posibles apartarle de tan mal pensamiento, pero todo era *predicar en desierto* y majar en hierro frío' (II, 6; p. 671) (The housekeeper and niece could plainly see by scores of signs that their master and uncle was planning to do a runner once again, and take up his, in their view,

---

[36] What led Quevedo to include this seemingly anodyne expression in his list of censured clichés was doubtless the facile ellipsis involved in the substitution of *merced*, now invested with a new meaning (a favour), by the pronoun *la*.

erringly errant chivalry, and so tried everything possible to divert him from this crazy scheme, but all their efforts were like preaching to the deaf or striking when the iron is cold).

poner puertas al campo. 'Cuanto más, que desnudo nací, desnudo me hallo: ni pierdo ni gano; mas que lo fuesen, ¿qué me va a mí? Y muchos piensan que hay tocinos, y no hay estacas. Mas ¿quién puede *poner puertas al campo*? Cuanto más, que de Dios dijeron' [This idiom is part of Sancho's first outpouring of proverbs, in the context of the supposed amorous liaison between two minor characters in *Amadís de Gaula*; I, 25: p. 273] (Besides naked I came into this world, and naked I am now; I've neither lost nor won; and if they were lovers, what's that to me? Many go looking for sides of bacon and don't even find the poles to hang them on. Besides, what's the point of doors in an open field? What's more, they even spoke ill of God).

al reír del alba. 'Pues así es, Sancho, que Rocinante no puede moverse, yo soy contento de esperar a que *ría el alba*, aunque yo llore lo que ella tardare en venir' [Don Quixote on discovering his steed's immobility in the fulling-mills adventure; I, 20: p. 211] (Well in that case, Sancho, since Rocinante can't move, I'm content to wait till dawn smiles on us, even though I should weep until it comes). *Al reír del alba* was a cliché meaning daybreak.

coger las de Villadiego. 'Pero, dejando esto aparte, dígame vuestra merced qué haremos deste caballo rucio rodado, que parece asno pardo, que dejó aquí desamparado aquel Martino que vuestra merced derribó; que, según él puso los pies en polvorosa y *cogió las de Villadiego*, no lleva pergenio de volver por él jamás' [Sancho to his master on whether he may claim the ass of the owner of 'Mambrino's helmet'; I, 21; p. 227] (But that aside, sir, tell me what we're going to do with this dapple brown horse, which looks like a brownish ass, left behind by that thingummy Martino you defeated; for to judge by how he took off at a speed of knots [literally, put on Villadiego's shoes] he isn't ever likely to come back to reclaim it).

comerse las manos tras ello. 'Y paréceme a mí que en esto de los gobiernos todo es comenzar y podría ser que a quince días de gobernador *me comiese las manos tras* el oficio' [Sancho to the Duchess; II, 33; p. 908] (And it seems to me that when it comes to governorships it's just a matter of getting stuck in, and it could turn out that after a couple of weeks in the job I find myself licking my fingers with relish); 'Si una vez lo probáis, Sancho,' dijo el duque, '*comeros heis las manos tras* el gobierno, por ser dulcísima cosa mandar y ser obedecido' (II, 42; p. 968) ('Once you get a taste of the governorship,' the Duke said, 'I promise you you'll be licking your fingers, because nothing beats giving orders and being obeyed'). [See also the fragment of the burlesque verses of Urganda la Desconocida cited above, p. 137.]

This selection, though brief, is a fair indication of Sancho's prominent role, either as articulator of colloquialisms or as a kind of magnet who elicits them from other characters.

In view of that, the question arises whether Cervantes sees these expressions as typical of rustic speech in particular, since Sancho's rusticity of language and manners is often signalled in the course of the novel,[37] and furthermore, it was customary in the Spanish Golden Age to treat rusticity as the opposite of courtliness. However, such a view of the matter would be too restrictive. Just as Cervantes treats sound judgement, rather than courtly status, as the essential criterion of good usage, so he regards incorrect and slipshod speech as liable to come from anyone not equipped with the requisite discretion, though he assumes at the same time that such a person will probably be of plebeian origins. In *Don Quixote*, the colloquialisms that he makes fun of come not only from Sancho and his wife, but also from various characters who are presumably not of peasant background, like the niece, the housekeeper, the innkeeper Juan Palomeque and his family, Doña Rodríguez. Furthermore, the habit of stringing proverbs together in disorderly profusion, which becomes a principal feature of Sancho's language, is treated in Spanish Golden Age literature as typical of plebeian characters of urban, rather than rustic, origins. It is, for example, a common trait of delinquent characters in the *Celestina* tradition and the picaresque novel, whose natural sphere of activity is town not country. In Quevedo's satiric writings, it is associated with the *vulgo*, the vulgar of whatever social extraction, vacuous in thought and speech, and is a primary aspect of the colloquial clichés that he habitually mocks. Furthermore, in depicting Sancho's discourse, which is such a prominent feature of *Don Quixote* Part II, Cervantes, unlike Avellaneda, makes no effort to accentuate identifiably rustic features (cf. above, p. 97).[38] Cervantes, as he himself implies, deliberately avoids the coarseness typical of his rival's portrayal of the character.[39] He shows the same discretion in respect of other traits of Sancho that were traditionally considered rustic: gluttony, addiction to the bottle, simple-mindedness, association with asses.

So Sancho's interventions, instead of stamping dialogue in *Don Quixote* with a specifically rustic character, contribute strongly to its air of colloquial familiarity. How do we characterise Cervantes's attitude to this? Revealing

---

[37]   E.g. *DQ* II, 12; p. 720; cf. II, 19; p. 786.

[38]   Cf. Riquer's comments on Avellaneda's characterisation of Sancho in his introduction to the apocryphal version of *DQ*, i, p. xcii.

[39]   The reactions of those who contrast the authentic Sancho with the apocryphal one insist on this point: see Part II, Chapters 59 and 72, pp. 1112–13 and 1206.

clues are provided by the reactions shown towards Sancho by other characters, such as the way in which the Duke picks up the expression 'comerse las
manos tras' (see above), which at this stage of the novel is closely linked to
Sancho's anticipation of his governorship. The Duke cites it when addressing
Sancho and ironically mimicking his style, as is shown as his use of the
archaic future form 'comeros heis', rare in *Don Quixote* and associated by
Cervantes with rustic discourse.[40] The Duke's attitude is shared by his consort,
who delights in listening to Sancho talk, and provokes and encourages his
interventions. In so doing, she too deliberately mimics him, as she implies on
several occasions: for example, 'En fin, en fin, hablando a su modo, debajo
de mala capa suele haber buen bebedor'; (II, 33; p. 910) (so, as you would
put it, a ragged cape often hides a good drinker); 'daremos orden como vaya
presto a encajarse, como él dice, aquel gobierno' (p. 911) (we'll arrange for
you to stash away this governorship, as you would say); 'Dad el sí, hijo, desta
azotaina, y váyase el diablo para diablo, y el temor para mezquino; que un
buen corazón quebranta mala ventura, como vos bien sabéis' (II, 35; p. 927)
(Say yes to this whipping, son, and two fingers to the devil and to fear,[41] for
fortune favours the brave, as well you know). The amused fascination with
Sancho's style implied by such remarks was first shown by his master, in a
conversation in early Part II in which the squire attempted to renegotiate the
basis of his service with his master (cf. above, pp. 117–18). The chief source
of interest in it is Sancho's folksy style, in relation to which Don Quixote,
despite his indignation with his servant's request, reacts with indulgent and
appreciative amusement, quite different from the impatience with his servant's diffuseness that he tended to show in Part I (notably in I, 20, pp. 213–15,
221; cf. I, 25; p. 273). He makes fun of his solecisms, and, unusually tolerant
of his crab-like approach to his real purpose, applauds the string of proverbs
in which he sums up his wife's counsel: 'Teresa dice ... que ate bien mi dedo
con vuestra merced, y que hablen cartas y callen barbas, porque quien destaja
no baraja, pues más vale un toma que dos te daré. Y yo digo que el consejo
de la mujer es poco, y el que no le toma es loco' (II, 7; p. 680) (She says I
should nail you down to a firm agreement, actions speak louder than words,
you can't deal and shuffle at the same time, a bird in the hand is worth two
in the bush, and before you ignore a woman's advice, think twice). He even

---

[40] There are two examples of it in the retorts of the rustic wenches intercepted by master
and squire in II, 10, pp. 707–8.

[41] The Duchess euphemistically modifies the vulgar 'váyase el diablo para puto' (sod off
to the devil). I know no equivalent in modern English.

parodies Sancho's addiction to them, sarcastically rather than benignly, in rejecting his proposal for a new contract out of hand (p. 682).

Evidently, we have to do with another aspect of the citational manner, exhibited not by the narrator but by the characters (cf. above, pp. 56–57). The attitude of ironic amusement implicit in it extends, as it does in Quevedo's works, to various kinds of linguistic commonplace apart from those mentioned above: poetic hyperboles, corruptions of the liturgy and other examples of naïve popular devotion, underworld slang, the affectations of *dueñas*, verses of poetasters, the digressions and lapses of memory of the folksy storyteller. It is a satiric attitude common to Spanish men-of-letters around 1600: Juan Rufo, Alonso López Pinciano, Mateo Alemán, Gaspar Lucas Hidalgo, Quevedo, Francisco López de Úbeda.

What distinguishes Cervantes from the writers just mentioned is the sheer range of genres and registers liable to become targets of his satire, and also, the frequent indulgence that he shows towards many of them. In *Don Quixote*, virtually any type of language, literary or non-literary, which has become fossilised through familiarity is likely to become a target. The list extends from well-known lines of Garcilaso, Juan de Mena, Virgil and traditional ballads to formulae derived from legal, commercial and ecclesiastical jargon, embracing a host of other styles in between, including, of course, those typical of chivalry books. We have already noted the ambivalence of Cervantes's parodies of high-flown registers, like the Baroque luxuriance of Don Quixote's story of the Knight of the Lake, or the learned preciosity of the Golden Age speech. We observe a somewhat similar ambivalence in the mixture of fascination, hilarity, indulgence and astonishment with which other characters react to Sancho's discourse. The Duchess may mock him; yet her enthusiastic appreciation for his sallies, which includes amusement at their wit as well as at their incoherence and folksiness, suggests something more nuanced than mere mockery. She says, for instance: 'de que Sancho el bueno sea gracioso lo estimo yo en mucho, porque es señal que es discreto; que las gracias y los donaires, señor don Quijote, como vuesa merced bien sabe, no asientan sobre ingenios torpes' (II, 30; p. 879) (I find it very estimable that Sancho is funny, because it's a sign that he's smart; for as you well know, sir, jests and witticisms don't come from slow minds), and, lest we should dismiss this comment as mere sarcasm, her attitude is shared by those who appreciatively contrast Sancho with his apocryphal rival in Avellaneda's version.[42]

---

[42] Cf. II, 59; pp. 1112–13; II, 72; p. 1206.

The indulgence extends to Sancho's uneducated colloquialisms. Though I cannot subscribe to Rosenblat's thesis that Cervantes reveres the untutored language of the plebs (1971: 41, 44), it is true that he treats it with greater benevolence than Quevedo, who, in some other respects, reveals comparable attitudes to style and language. His divergence from Quevedo's character-istic contempt – shared by Avellaneda – is reflected in Don Quixote's inner thoughts on the general improvement of Sancho's style in Part II, capable, on occasions, of attaining courtly elegance, though always prone, given his igno-rance and simple-mindedness, to ridiculous lapses from grace. Don Quixote concludes that his real claims to memorable and elegant expression lie in quoting proverbs, whether or not pertinent to the occasion (II, 12; p. 720). This willingness to recognise aesthetic merit in colloquialism, even despite its diffuse inconsequentiality, is unusual in the context of that age, and it also reveals a rounded conception of Sancho's character, as showing, over and above its risibility, individuality and psychological evolution that merit sympathetic understanding.

Cervantes's tolerance is typical of his view of the action of *Don Quixote* in general, which he regards benignly as a sort of storm in a teacup, a combina-tion of the bizarre, the extraordinary and the trivial, the latter being defined by the key-term *menudencias*, trifles. Of course, were it no more than trivial, Cervantes would not have bothered to write his novel. What makes it consum-mately interesting is the astonishing cause of the storm and the disproportion between it and the teacup: that is, the extravagant oddity of the famous pair's delusions, the intensity with which they live them, and the childish credulity of their surrender to them. It is an unfailing source of astonishment, as well as mirth, to those around them. And here we come to the essential difference between the humour of Cervantes and that of contemporary picaresque novel-ists, exemplified by the author of *La pícara Justina*. Theirs tends to be mirth provoked by grotesquely degraded subject-matter, as though in accord with Hobbes's famous definition of laughter as 'sudden glory', implying a sense of superiority to other people's weaknesses or deformities.[43] Cervantes's two heroes, by contrast, arouse merriment of a more indulgent kind, since both are marked by likeability and well-meaning innocence, to which the hero adds head-in-clouds idealism, traits rather different from the victims of the *pícaro*'s or *pícara*'s duplicity, and even more from the duplicity itself. This is why Cervantes insists on the therapeutic and restorative power of laughter, and presents a world in which it momentarily dissolves social barriers, creates

---

[43] *Leviathan*, ed. Oakeshott, p. 36.

affable relations between sane and insane, and makes the latter objects of sympathy rather than contempt.

The Narrator's Personality

Here we come to the fundamental premise of *Don Quixote*'s narrative discourse: Cervantes's presentation of his story as a chronicle of the exploits of a contemporary Spanish hero, which, sending up the Renaissance ideal of history enshrined in Cicero's famous definition of it as 'testimony of ages, light of truth, life of memory, teacher of life, messenger of antiquity',[44] focuses relentlessly on events that are prosaic, footling and imaginary.[45] The jest combines two tendencies: ironic imitation of a historian's manner, which accords with the hero's premise that since it is the story of the doings of a knight-errant it must necessarily be 'grandiloquent, lofty, illustrious, magnificent and true' (II, 3; p. 646), and repeated mischievous pinpricks that deflate this pretence. They are intrinsic to the treatment of the absurdly contradictory figure of Cide Hamete Benengeli, the Moorish chronicler who, from Part I, Chapter 9 onwards, is supposedly Cervantes's main source. At once scrupulously truthful and yet member of a race of liars,[46] he belies his laudatory role as chronicler by ridiculously belittling his protagonist. This blend of incongruities is conveyed by the passage immediately preceding the Ciceronian definition, where Cervantes suggests that Benengeli reveals a Moor's typical enmity towards Spaniards by, as he puts it, falling short of the truth: 'for when he could and should extend himself in praise of so worthy a knight, it seems that he deliberately omits to do so, which is quite deplorable given that historians should be scrupulously objective and faithful to fact, so that neither fear nor self-interest, rancour or partiality, deflect them from the path of truth'. Of course, this show of righteous indignation is all a joke; the reader, unless very naïve, understands this disparagement of Benengeli's chronicle as implying that it is not a chronicle at all, but a work of fiction, whose purpose is not to extol glorious deeds, but to excite laughter at a mad aberration. The implications are made quite explicit in the preamble to Chapter 22, which begins: 'Cuenta Cide Hamete Benengeli, autor arábigo y manchego, en esta

---

[44] 'historia testis temporum, lux veritatis, vita memoriae, magistra vitae, nuntia vetustatis' (*De oratore* II, ix), roughly paraphrased in *DQ* I, 9; p. 110.

[45] There is extensive bibliography on the pretence of historiography adopted by Cervantes in *DQ*. E.C. Riley's treatment (1962), Chapter 6, section ii, is classic and still recommendable.

[46] Cf. 'siendo muy propio de los de aquella nación ser mentirosos' (*DQ* I, 9; p. 110) (since that race is congenitally mendacious).

gravísima, altisonante, mínima, dulce e imaginada historia, que …' (Cide Hamete Benengeli, Arabic and Manchegan author, relates in this momentous, high-sounding, trifling, pleasing and imaginary history, that …). The adjectives 'trifling, pleasing and imaginary', which contradict the implications of the two previous ones, leave no doubt as to what kind of 'history' we are reading.

Benengeli's treatment of his theme is repeatedly defined and evaluated by a standard of minuteness. Of the five passages in which he is mentioned in Part I, three associate his chronicle with the epithet 'mínimo', and elsewhere we find 'menudencias' (minutiae), 'semínimas' (minutiae), 'átomos' (atoms), 'zarandajas' (trifles).[47] The theme attains a kind of majestic zenith in the preamble to II, 40 (p. 949), which praises Benengeli 'for his punctiliousness in recounting its [the story's] minutiae, without leaving a single thing unclarified, however tiny. He reveals inner thoughts, sheds light on imaginings, clarifies doubts, resolves arguments, and finally, attends to the atoms of the most inquisitive curiosity.' The passage doubtless alludes to the dramatic revelation, towards the end of Chapter 39, of what lay behind the masks of Countess Trifaldi and her escort of *dueñas*: the bushy beards inflicted on them by the enchanter Malambruno.

The theme is implicit in Cervantes's superb account of how he came across the Moor's manuscript in a street of merchant shops in Toledo (*DQ* I, 9; pp. 107–10). Moved by his compulsive addiction to reading, which even extends to scraps of paper in the street, he casually picks up a folder written in Arabic, which a boy is selling to a silk-merchant, presumably for use as wrapping-paper. Unable to understand what it says, he asks a bilingual *morisco* to translate for him, and this individual bursts into laughter on reading the marginal note: 'Fame has it that among the women of La Mancha, none had as good a hand for salting pork as the said Dulcinea del Toboso, so often mentioned in this history.' His curiosity aroused, Cervantes asks for the title of the folder, and when he learns it, hardly able to conceal his excitement, he repairs with the translator to the cathedral cloister and engages him to translate the manuscript for a fee of a large measure each of raisins and wheat.

Now, it was traditional in chivalry books, and in other works of fiction too, to allege that the story is based on a manuscript written by a sage in

---

[47] See, for example, the function attributed to sage enchanters in chivalry books, and by extension to Benengeli, in I, 9, quoted above, p. 45. And in I, 16 (p. 171), the Moor is praised for not passing over the detailed description of the mule-drover's bedding, despite the vileness and insignificance of the subject-matter. See also I, 9, p. 110, and the chapter-heading of II, 24.

some ancient tongue and discovered in an exotic location: Armenian cave, enchanted house of Hercules, ruined hermitage or sepulchre. The venerable topic goes back to the so-called *Turpini Historia Karoli Magni et Rotholandi* (about 1150) (Turpin's History of Charlemagne and Roland), of anonymous authorship, though alleged to be by Charlemagne's warrior archbishop, Turpin, whose chronicle is frequently cited tongue-in-cheek by Ariosto in *Orlando furioso* (1516). Teofilo Folengo's macaronic chivalric poem *Le Maccheronee* (1521) spoofs this pretence by attributing the story to the wizard Merlin, and relates the circumstances of the discovery of Merlin's manuscript in an Armenian cave (ed. Luzio, appendix ii). The prologue to *Amadís de Gaula* makes a similar claim about the story to follow, albeit in serious vein. In the decade previous to the publication of *Don Quixote* Part I, the device acquired topicality thanks to the publication of *La historia verdadera del rey don Rodrigo* by Miguel de Luna (1592) (The True History of King Rodrigo) and the very popular *Guerras civiles de Granada* by Ginés Pérez de Hita (1595) (Civil Wars of Granada), both of which, though manifestly fabulous, purport to be authentic chronicles based on Arabic sources.[48] In his book Luna revives the legend of a Visigothic chest discovered by King Rodrigo in a tower in Toledo, the so-called 'casa de Hércules' (house of Hercules), containing prophecies about the invasion of Spain by the Arabs should the locked tower be violated; Rodrigo's seduction of Count Julián's daughter La Cava was traditionally supposed to be the cause of that invasion in the early 8th century A.D. Luna also had a hand in the fake 'libros plúmbeos', leaden tablets discovered in 1595 in an area just outside Granada now known as Sacromonte; they were engraved in Arabic script and purported to tell of the evangelisation of Arabs by St James and his disciples. The discovery caused a sensation in Spain; and its fraudulence was not definitively established for some years.

Such is the background to Cervantes's account of the discovery of Benengeli's manuscript in Part I, Chapter 9. He parodies his precedents by setting the event in prosaic, familiar circumstances, and adopting the enthusiastic tone of a bibliophile who recounts an extraordinary find with a wealth of anecdotal particulars. These, like the reference to Dulcinea's expertise in salting pork, the wrapping-paper, the payment in wheat and raisins, may fairly be described as comic *menudencias*.

There are many other contexts where Benengeli parades his attention to tiny detail, or occasionally, is censured for his omission of it: for example, the question whether master and squire slept under holm-oaks or cork-oaks

---

[48] See Chapter ix of Luna's book and *Guerras civiles de Granada*, Part I, Chapter xvii, in BAE 3, p. 585a. The 'libros plúmbeos' are discussed by Harvey (1974) and Case (2004).

(preamble to II, 60), whether Don Quixote washed himself in five or six pitch-erfuls of water (II, 18; p. 772), and whether the three wenches intercepted by him and Sancho outside El Toboso were mounted on *pollinos* or *pollinas* (male or female donkeys), or even more likely, *borricas*, another term for donkey (II, 10; p. 704). This sort of cavilling, which, in relation to the hero's surname, goes back to the first chapter of the novel, is a parody of the attitude of the scrupulous historian hesitating among the divergent versions of names, places, numbers and events offered to him by his sources.[49] In Benengeli's case, the sources are not just written, like that parchment in Gothic script mentioned at the end of Part I, supposedly discovered in a leaden chest in the ruins of a hermitage. Folklore and oral tradition are also invoked by vague phrases such as 'it is firmly held that' (II, 24; p. 829), 'according to the traditional belief preserved in the memories of La Mancha' (I, 52; p. 591) and even 'a tradition handed down from father to son holds that the author devoted particular chapters to this theme' (II, 12; p. 721; cf. II, 44; p. 979). In sum, if we were to take Cervantes's pretence about Benengeli seriously, we would be left in a state of utter confusion about the origin and evidential basis of what we read, compounded by the occasional reminders that the narrative discourse is attributable to three persons – Benengeli, the translator, and Cervantes as editor – of whom the last two have added their comments and alterations to the original. Moreover, as we can see from some of the foregoing examples, the original pretence that the story of Don Quixote's exploits is modern (I, 9; p. 106), even amazingly up-to-date (II, 3; p. 646), is amusingly contradicted by allusions to its antiquity.[50] It would of course be absurd to treat the impression of muddle and inconsistency as a fault on Cervantes's part, since it is all part of a deliberately intended joke.

It is scarcely surprising that Cervantes should systematically spoof the manner of a chronicler since this was partly imitated by Spanish epics of the Golden Age, which customarily flaunt their care for historical accuracy (Pierce, 1961); and that genre, being a near neighbour to chivalric romances, influences Cervantes's narrative manner almost as much as history. This applies particularly to the epic poet's personal interventions in his story. For example, the appeals for inspiration to the Muse that launch epics like *The Iliad* and *The Aeneid* are echoed at the beginning of the chapters concerning Sancho's governorship with a comically familiar invocation to Apollo, god of poetry: 'Oh perpetual discoverer of the Antipodes, torch of the world,

---

[49] See Close (2000: 134).

[50] Cf., apart from examples previously given in this paragraph, I, 52, p. 591, and II, 44, p. 985.

eye of the sky, sweet swayer of water canteens, Timbrio here, Phoebus there, now a bowman, now a doctor, father of poetry, inventor of music, you who always rises, and though it appears so, never sets! To you, I say, oh sun, with whose help man engenders man, grant me your aid' (II, 45; p. 991). The epic poet would frequently mark momentous events in the narrative by means of apostrophe to the characters or other rhetorical exclamations. Thus, Ariosto expresses outrage that Angelica should spurn so many noble admirers for the embraces of the Moor Medoro (*Orlando furioso*, Canto XIX, 31ff.), and Tasso is unable to contain his emotion at Tancredi's recognition of Clorinda (*Gerusalemme liberata* XII, 67). Cervantes parodies this practice with his rhetorically overblown eulogy to Don Quixote when on the point of telling what happened when the lion's cage was opened and he stood face to face with the beast: 'Oh doughty and ineffably valiant Don Quijote de la Mancha, shining example to other heroes, worthy successor to Don Manuel de León who was the glory of Spanish chivalry ...', and so on, inflating the balloon deliberately so as to enhance the anti-climax of the dénouement (II, 17; p. 765). The moralistic reflections on general themes that often appear at the beginnings of cantos in Renaissance epics, such as Ercilla's invective against avarice in *La Araucana*, Canto III, have their counterpart in Benengeli's reflections on the mutability of human affairs prior to the narration of the ending of Sancho's governorship (II, 53; p. 1061), and his double-edged lamentation about the cruelty of poverty, provoked by the laddering of the hero's stocking (II, 44; pp. 984–5), which, beginning on a seemingly compassionate note, turns into mischievous satire on the underhand subterfuges employed by destitute *hidalgos* to disguise their soiled and threadbare gear. The epic poet would frequently break off his narrative at the end of a canto, postponing the continuation until the next one; and a well-known example of this in Cervantes's novel, which parodies the break between cantos 14 and 15 of Ercilla's *La Araucana*, is the interruption of Don Quixote's battle with the Basque squire at its critical juncture by means of the lame announcement that the narrator's source of information has run out. Another model of Cervantes's narrative manner is the pastoral tradition, parodied by the lush dawn-description in II, 14 (p. 740; cf. also II, 20; p. 790), and by Benengeli's valediction to his quill at the end of Part II, echoing the shepherd's to his flute at the end of Virgil's eighth eclogue.

The personality of Benengeli, and the trinity constituted by him, the translator and Cervantes as editor or 'second author', are merely a mask for Cervantes as narrator of his novel. In certain quarters of Cervantine criticism it is fashionable to make hair-splitting distinctions among the different narrative

voices,[51] and to maintain that Cervantes, with the aim of distancing himself
from his story, seriously expects the reader to perceive them. However, the
distinction between the two principal ones – Benengeli's and Cervantes's – is
just as hazy as the previously mentioned aspects of the fictitious authorship,
and dissolves in numerous passages where the narrator makes comments in
the first person which, were this a translated history, would obviously be in
the third, and in any case, could not conceivably be attributed to a historian. It would be very odd, for example, if a historian began his narrative by
saying: 'In a village in La Mancha whose name I do not choose to recall',
and even odder to begin Part II, Chapter 45, by appealing to Apollo, the god
of *poetry* not history, to 'give me your aid'. Since the reference of that 'me'
is not specified, one is naturally inclined to associate it with Cervantes, as
narrator of his own story; and this applies even more strongly to the use of
the first-person pronoun in Part I, where Benengeli, after being introduced
with a fanfare in Chapter 9, is mentioned on only four subsequent occasions
(Chapters 15, 16, 22, end of 27), and on each of these merely in passing. The
inseparability of 'first' and 'second authors' is surely clinched by the ending
of the novel. Benengeli's refusal to name the hero's birthplace (II, 74), so that
the villages and towns of La Mancha may contend for the honour as did the
seven cities of Greece over Homer's, harks back to the novel's self-assertive
opening sentence (see above), with its marked Cervantine connotations. Also,
the Moor's valediction to his quill clearly echoes the claims of fatherhood and
copyright made by Cervantes himself in the two prologues to *Don Quixote*,
particularly the prologue to Part II, with its jibes at Avellaneda's unfitness
for the task.

   As we have seen, the references to Benengeli's chronicle imply a metadiscursive relationship of Cervantes to his own narrative – an acknowledgement,
for example, of its imaginary status and comical concern with minute particulars; and this is reflected in the effervescent, flippant and introverted nature of
its humour, which, in Part II, becomes tinged with authorial pride. This is the
underlying reason for the Moor's ascent to prominence in this Part, caused
by the recurrent allusions in it to the universal popularity of Part I, which,
for the characters, is not a story invented by Cervantes but the chronicle of
Cide Hamete Benengeli.

   The flippancy is revealed in Cervantes's predilection for clarifications,
which, like the previously mentioned quibble about the precise sex of the

[51] The most systematic is Parr's stimulating book (1988); cf. also, among other American critics, El Saffar (1975). See too the debate between Parr and Mancing in *Cervantes* 24
(2004).

mounts of the three wenches encountered outside El Toboso, flaunt their triviality. It is also shown by the chapter-headings of Part II. Whereas those of Part I maintain either a factual tone ('in which is related the amusing manner in which Don Quixote became an armed knight') or else an ironical one that mimics the hero's language ('which relates the heroic adventure and lucrative capture of Mambrino's helmet, with other events that befell our invincible hero'), those of Part II intersperse these two types with headings that frivolously nullify their conventionally informative function: 'in which are related a host of trifles as impertinent as they are necessary to the correct understanding of this great history' (II, 24); 'which treats of what will be learnt by the reader who reads it, or will be heard by the listener who hears it read' (II, 66); 'which treats of matters pertaining to this history and none other' (II, 53); 'which follows chapter sixty-nine, and contains matters essential to the elucidation of this history' (II, 70). Since these whimsical pirouettes reduce the traditional formulae to an empty shell, they are related to the diverse species of play with commonplaces studied in a previous section, and, like them, attest an overflowing jocularity that seeps into all the pores of the work.

It is a type of introverted humour that links *Don Quixote* to *La pícara Justina*, published, like Part I of Cervantes's novel, in 1605. The link between them, added to their almost simultaneous publication, seems in one respect an extraordinary coincidence. Lacking any precedent known to me, these two Spanish novels, independently of each other, poke systematic fun at the introductory and explanatory apparatus that serves to present a book to the reader and provide orientation in it, including such things as the prologue, preliminary verses, chapter-headings and marginal notes. In both cases, the parody, which extends to the content of the two works as well as their frame, is motivated by the didactic pretentiousness of literature of entertainment published around 1600. In *La pícara Justina*, the prime target is Alemán's *Guzmán de Alfarache*, while Cervantes, in *Don Quixote* at least, is probably aiming principally at Lope de Vega. The most striking example of this whimsy in *La pícara Justina* is the so-called 'Introducción general' (General Introduction), in which, with pen poised to begin her autobiography, the heroine is brought up short by a succession of fantastic objectors to her autobiographical project, personifications of her shame or others' envy: the hair stuck in her pen nib, the inkstain on her dress, the trademark on the paper. From these impediments Justina derives a firework-display of witty conceits, which define her personal attributes and prove her fitness to tell her story. Justina's dramatisation of the abortive inception of the act of writing anticipates Sterne's *Tristram Shandy*, and it turns attention not just on the heroine but her creator, since it is a burlesque of a literary prologue and of a rhetorical exordium. Furthermore, the 'Prólogo summario' or preliminary synopsis of the work enumerates its contents by means of a long list of the heroine's comical epithets, like 'the finicky scribe, the honourable syphilitic, the shop-worn girl of La Mancha, the swallower of taunts', and this acts as a burlesque table of contents, for the epithets are subsequently repeated as chapter-headings. At the beginning of each chapter, below the heading, are stanzas of verse that describe the contents in more detail, and on each occasion, a different metric form is adopted; here again, Justina parodies previous Spanish works,[52] achieving a burlesque effect by the comic nature of her subject-matter and her preference for eccentric verse-endings.

The most obvious examples of such fun and games in *Don Quixote*, apart from the chapter-headings, are the prologue to Part I and its preliminary verses. The prologue's theme might be summed up as: 'how I stopped worrying about the need to write this prologue'; and Cervantes begins it by drawing a picture of himself in a dithering quandary, pen behind ear, cheek on hand, elbow on desk, not knowing how to proceed until rescued by his flippant friend and counsellor. We have already noted what kind of remedies this friend proposes (above, p. 67).

One of the most interesting and influential aspects of Cervantes's nonchalantly playful manner consists in the way in which he foregrounds within the story the assumptions about its fictional nature traditionally masked by the author from the reader so as not to interfere with the 'willing suspension of disbelief'.[53] These concern things like the artifical conventions and devices of fiction, the novelist's technical procedures and problems, the reader's responses to what he or she reads. So, in Part II, Chapter 2 (p. 645), Sancho expresses astonishment that the author of the chronicle could have discovered what he and his master said to each other in private conversations: a mystery readily explained, in his master's view, by the agency of enchantment. Here Cervantes draws implicit attention to the contradiction between the pretence that this is a chronicle and the omniscience habitually assumed by fictional narrators. At the beginning of the next chapter, Don Quixote is inwardly amazed by the speed of publication of Benengeli's chronicle (p. 646), in print even before the blood of the enemies slain by him has had time to dry on his

---

52 Initial verse summaries can be found in *Los problemas* (Problems) of the doctor Francisco de Villalobos, a didactic work published in 1543, and *El patrañuelo* (The Little Story-Book) by Juan de Timoneda (1569), which is a story collection; the virtuoso diversity of metric forms parodies the poetic treatises of the age, such as Sánchez de Lima's *El arte poética* (1580) (Art of Poetry), which offers a similar array for purposes of illustration.

53 This subject was studied in a seminal article by Wayne Booth (1952).

sword. Here Cervantes signals the contradiction between lived time for the characters – according to the fiction, a scant month since the hero returned home at the end of the second sally – and real, historical time outside the fiction: the period of years necessary for Part I of the novel to be written, printed, published, and to attain national and international fame. Three of the most influential novelists of the eighteenth century, Marivaux, Fielding and Sterne, precisely because of their critical and parodic stance towards the traditional forms of romance, deliberately subvert its scaffolding of tacit conventions, and all regard Cervantes as a primary model. It is instructive to contrast his practice in *Don Quixote* with what they subsequently make of it, since this illuminates what he was trying to do.

Henry Fielding's *Joseph Andrews* (1742), whose subtitle reads 'written in imitation of the manner of Cervantes, author of *Don Quixote*', and his masterpiece, *Tom Jones* (1749), apart from imitating the flippant irony of Cervantes's chapter-headings, systematically extend his practice of beginning chapters, or high points in the narrative, with burlesques of the grand style: descriptions of dawn, night, springtime, brawls and battles (e.g. *JA* Book I, Chapter 8, and III, 6; *TJ* Book IV, Chapter 2; IV, 8; XI, 9); apostrophes to the characters, the Muse, and personified abstractions (*JA* I, 7; III, 6; *TJ* IV, 2); elaborate comparisons reminiscent of Virgil (*JA* IV, 14; *TJ* II, 4; V, 11; VI, 9). As in *Don Quixote*, parody of epic and romance conventions implies a metadiscursive awareness of the kind of story intended to supplant them. Moreover, in both works, particularly the second, Fielding cultivates an ironically free-and-easy, bantering rapport with the reader, which includes reflections on the story, disparagement of other writers, mock-attacks on certain kinds of reader and occasional self-mockery, though always with the implication that he is a writer of remarkable genius and originality (e.g. *TJ* XII, 2).

Though this highly sophisticated manner goes far beyond anything to be found in *Don Quixote*, it nonetheless often takes its cue from Cervantes, as is shown by the following passage (*TJ* XII, 3):

> We would bestow some pains here in minutely describing all the mad pranks which Jones played on this occasion, could we be well assured that the reader would take the same pains in perusing them; but as we are apprehensive that after all the labour which we should employ in painting this scene, the said reader would be very apt to skip it entirely over, we have saved ourself that trouble. To say the truth, we have, from this reason alone, often done great violence to the luxuriance of our genius, and have left many excellent descriptions out of our work, which would otherwise have been in it.

Here Fielding is thinking specifically of the flippantly worded preamble to *Don Quixote* II, 44 (see above, pp. 65–66), where Cervantes, through Benengeli, explains the omission of long, detachable interpolations like *El curioso impertinente* from Part II as due to his suspicion that the reader will skip them, and craves the reader's praise for having kept his inventive genius on a tight rein, just as Fielding does in the above-quoted passage.

The preamble to *Don Quixote* II, 44 is linked to an earlier passage in which, in the course of a general conversation about the reception of Part I, Sansón Carrasco reports the critical reactions of readers to the inclusion of *El curioso impertinente*, provoking Don Quixote's indignant reaction to the news that extraneous material has been added to the story of his exploits (II, 3; pp. 652–3). He vilifies the Moorish chronicler by comparing him to the slapdash painter Orbaneja, who would reply to questions about what he was painting with 'Whatever comes out', and subsequently complains that the record of his sighs, tears, noble intentions and armed exploits would have been quite enough by itself to fill a tome greater than the works of the prolific El Tostado without any need for supplementary tales. Don Quixote's inno-cent vanity and proneness to exaggeration are typical of him, and his protest serves as an amusingly overstated version of those critical reactions, which, just because of this, enhances the effect of Sansón's subsquent, reasoned appeals for indulgence.

We perceive in these exchanges, on a secondary level of implication, a dialogue between the author and his readers; and in the novels of Cervantes's eighteenth-century imitators, the dialogue becomes explicit. It serves various purposes, from knockabout whimsy in Marivaux's *Pharsamon ou les folies romanesques* (1737), to rhetorical manipulation in Fielding, to an integral aspect of the comic refusal of the narrator of *Tristram Shandy* (1759) to control his endlessly proliferating subject-matter.

In *Pharsamon*, later entitled *Le Don Quichotte moderne*, it is part of a systematic parody of romance conventions. Thus, in a scene that mocks the touching recognition-scenes typical of such fiction, the narrator abruptly breaks off his reflexions on the tumultuous inner feelings of his hero and heroine, with this intervention:[54]

> 'Oh do hurry up, get on with it,' says the critic, 'you left your lovers in a daze, pale as death, and there you are writing a treatise on the cause and quantity of their emotions, which shows a fine sense of priorities at this point. What has become of them?' My critic is right, my characters are in too pitiful a state to be abandoned.

---

[54] *Oeuvres de Marivaux*, vol. xi, pp. 259–60.

This is similar to Don Quixote's complaint that his tears and sighs should have commanded his chronicler's sole attention, with the difference that the reaction is not embodied in the idiosyncracies of a fictional character within the story, as happens in Cervantes's novel, but is articulated in an imaginary parenthesis to it, as the protest of an imaginary reader addressed to the author/narrator.

Herein lies the essential difference between interventions such as those of Marivaux, which confront the writer in the act of writing his novel with the reader in the act of reading it, and their anticipations in *Don Quixote*. These are characteristic of Part II, since here, references to the published first Part and to the reader's reactions to it become a dominant theme, implicit in the many encounters between readers of Benengeli's chronicle and its two heroes. However, these references are always part of the pretence that the book is a chronicle, that the narrator who presents it to the reader is its editor, and that the heroes, at the time when the record of what happened in Part I appeared in print, were still living, active and capable of meeting its readers and commenting on what they are told about the nature of the chronicle. Even these readers, despite showing an intelligent grasp of what kind of a story Part I is, show no awareness that it is a *story*. Thus, in Part II, whatever inferences we may make about whose voice speaks through Benengeli's mask, and about the narrative's pretence of being a history, that mask and that pretence are more or less consistently kept in place.

The same conclusion arises from how Cervantes anticipates one of the major themes in Sterne's *Tristram Shandy*: the difference between lived time for author or reader, and time as represented in the narrative. It arises because Tristram's autobiography, though entitled *The Life and Opinions of Tristram Shandy*, largely focuses on events prior to and immediately following his own birth, and, continually deflected by digressions, interpolations and overspills, never gets round to delivering the promise of the title. At one point Tristram proposes this paradox to the reader: 'I am this month one whole year older than I was this time twelve-month: and having got, as you perceive, almost into the middle of my fourth volume – and no farther than to my first day's life – 'tis demonstrative that I have three hundred and sixty-four days more life to write just now, than when I first set out' (p. 286). Normally, the written record of a life, be it fictional or real, shapes, selects and compresses it, without attempting literally to account for every moment of it. Tristram's paradox takes for granted that it should, thus focusing attention on the diffuseness of normal human experience as compared with its written representation, and more particularly, on the artificial conventionality with which that experience is usually depicted in fiction, where, typically, the hero's pre-history, birth and infancy are dispatched in just a few lines. At the same time, he draws attention to the relation between time as really lived by the writer and the way that he represents it in his story. For example, the letter from Sancho Panza to his wife, in *Don Quixote* II, 36, is dated 20 July 1614. Was that literally the date when Cervantes wrote this chapter? Likewise, is Tristram's above-quoted assertion that he is one year older than when he started to be understood as applying to Sterne, the author of *Tristram Shandy*? We are left to wonder.

There is another, much earlier allusion in *Don Quixote* Part II to the stage reached by Cervantes in the composition of his manuscript, and it sheds light on the relative naïvety of his handling of it, despite his playful irony, as compared with Sterne's. In Part II, Chapter 4 (p. 658), Don Quixote asks Sansón Carrasco whether the author – that is, Benengeli – promises a second part of the published chronicle, and Sansón replies: 'Yes, he does … but says that he hasn't yet found it nor knows the person who has it; and so, we don't know if it will come out or not', adding as a further reason for uncertainty the division of opinion among readers about whether a second part would be desirable. The conversation continues thus:

> 'And what is the author's opinion?'
> 'That as soon as he finds the history, which he is looking for with extraordinary diligence, he will publish it, moved more by the prospect of financial reward than any kind of praise.'

This grotesquely disparaging account of the Moor's, and by implication, his creator's motives, is typical of Cervantes's self-mocking humour. Further-more, read between the lines, Sansón's answer, which presumably reflects Cervantes's state of mind in the midst of drafting this early chapter of Part II, including his awareness of the expectations and opinions of his readers, conveys this kind of imaginary message to them: 'Yes there will be one, but give me time to write the next seventy chapters.' However, this is not how things are explicitly represented. Sansón suggests that the publication of Part II is dependent on whatever time and effort it takes for Benengeli to discover the unknown owner of the written record, and this in turn depends, as Sancho's subsequent intervention makes plain, on the embarkation by the two heroes on a new round of adventures.

In other words, whereas Sterne, by means of Tristram's paradox, deliber-ately draws attention to the relation between art and life, Cervantes consist-ently pretends that there is no difference between them, proceeding as if Don Quixote, Sancho and the other fictional characters were autonomous, independent of the creative imagination that produced them, and that the truth of Benengeli's chronicle could be confirmed by meeting the two heroes in the flesh.

Truth implies excellence, for a reason made plain by this passage (II, 7; p. 684):

> Admirado quedó el bachiller de oír el término y modo de hablar de Sancho Panza, que, puesto que había leído la primera historia de su señor, nunca creyó que era tan gracioso como allí le pintan; pero oyéndole decir ahora 'testamento y codicilo que no se pueda revolcar' en lugar de 'testamento y codicilo que no se pueda revocar', creyó todo lo que dél había leído y confirmólo por uno de los más solenes mentecatos de nuestros siglos.

> Sansón was left astonished by Sancho Panza's way of expressing himself, for, though he had read the first part of the history of Don Quixote, he never supposed that Sancho could be as funny as he is depicted there; but on hearing him say 'testament and codicil which one cannot revolt', instead of 'testament and codicil which one cannot revoke', he believed all that he had read and decided that he was one of the prize nitwits of our age.

The premise of this passage is a variation on the maxim that direct witness offers more reliable evidence than reading; for Sansón and all subsequent readers of Benengeli's chronicle depicted in Part II, including those who have also read Avellaneda's version, it offers proof not only of fact but of quality. Or rather, in this proof, fact and quality are treated as indistinguishable. The reader of the apocryphal sequel featured in Part II, Chapter 59, on over-hearing Don Quixote's indignant rejection of the suggestion that he no longer loves Dulcinea, followed by Sancho's identification of his master, passes into the adjoining room from which the voice has come, and flings his arms round the hero's neck, exclaiming: 'Ni vuestra presencia puede desmentir vuestro nombre, ni vuestro nombre puede no acreditar vuestra presencia: sin duda vos, señor, sois el verdadero don Quijote de la Mancha, norte y lucero de la andante caballería, a despecho y pesar del que ha querido usurpar vuestro nombre y aniquilar vuestras hazañas, como lo ha hecho el autor deste libro que aquí os entrego' (pp. 111–12) (Neither can your presence belie your name, nor can your name belie your presence; without doubt, sir, you are the true Don Quijote de la Mancha, pole and morning star of knight-errantry, despite the individual who has tried to usurp your name and annihilate your deeds, namely, the author of this book that I now hand to you). What prompts this instant identification? Not Don Quixote's presence alone, obviously, but rather, the consistency of his behaviour now with the way in which it was represented by Benengeli in Part I. Meeting him in flesh-and-blood confirms him to be the uniquely original character depicted in the Moor's chronicle. Obviously the proof furnished by such empirical verification would have no validity in real life, where the fact that somebody no longer loves somebody else does not prove that he or she is an imposter. An immigration official would not be impressed by this criterion of identity, and would want to check the individual's passport. Implicitly, the proof only has validity of an artistic kind, within the realm of fiction, where consistency of characterisation is a criterion of merit.

There are two reasons why Cervantes chooses to conduct his metafictional dialogue with his readership in this way. First, the theme of Part I's reception, as embodied in Part II, revolves essentially around the popularity of the two heroes with contemporary readers and the extraordinary attraction of their personalities, in which Cervantes invests fierce authorial pride. This is the implication of the claim by Benengeli's quill at the end of the novel: 'Para mí sola nació don Quijote, y yo para él; él supo obrar y yo escribir, solos los dos somos para en uno' (II, 74; p. 1223) (For me alone was Don Quixote born, and I for him; he knew how to act, and I how to write; we alone belong to each other). Hence, in the handling of this theme, the focus falls primarily on the two heroes, and on the reactions of delight and fascination shown by readers in their presence, reflected in their contrivance of occasions, such as the sequence of events in the Duke's palace, which will incite them to manifest their familiar traits. Secondly, Cervantes's whole narrative strategy is alien to the self-promotion of the narrator undertaken by Fielding and Sterne. In general, he prefers to subordinate narrative to dialogue, to delegate it to his fictional characters, to present events from the viewpoint of witnesses who observe them unfold at first-hand – tactics all designed to create an effect of immediacy and of directly lived experience. This tendency to self-effacement, which includes curtailment of authorial comment on the narrative, is born of the conviction that 'the excellence of fiction is in direct proportion to its approximation to truth or the semblance of it, and, as for history, the truer the better' (end of II, 62; p. 1146). The metafictional games played by Cervantes's eighteenth-century imitators result from a sophisticated readiness to incorporate in the story, as an integral element, the open recognition of its nature as literary artefact; Cervantes's practice in *Don Quixote*, while often foreshadowing those games, is based on the premise that art needs to be disguised as life.

6

The Adventures and Episodes of
Don Quixote Part II

The Introductory Chapters

The first seven chapters of *Don Quixote* Part II are devoted primarily to two things: first, the discussion between Don Quixote, Sancho and Sansón Carrasco about the reception of Benengeli's chronicle – that is, Part I – and second, the crystallisation of the resolve of the two heroes to embark on a new sally, together with the reactions of their intimate circle to this news. The chapters are a splendid example of the major innovation brought by Cervantes to the genre of the novel: the comic depiction of traits of character displayed in colloquial style and a context of homely familiarity. Like the overture to an opera, they introduce a major theme to be developed in the rest of the work, and two new emphases that distinguish this Part from its precursor. The theme results from the characters' awareness of the publication of a chronicle of Don Quixote's and Sancho's adventures; and this introduces a new reflexivity into the novel on various levels. The new emphases fall on the Don's lucidity and on Sancho's comic interventions, which will not only be treated as counterpoint to his master's, but will also frequently occupy the reader's principal or exclusive attention in chapters devoted specifically to them.

We are offered a succession of intimate conversations, mostly set in the *hidalgo*'s home. The first, marking the modified focus on his character, takes place in his bedroom following a visit by the priest and barber, who, encouraged though not convinced by the niece's and housekeeper's reports of his recovery of sanity, go to his house to put them to the test. They find him in bed, wearing a green dressing-gown and red bonnet, with a dried-up, mummi-fied aspect, which would suggest, despite his judicious and elegant contributions to the ensuing discussion on politics, that nothing has really changed. This is because, from the beginning of the novel, Cervantes's conception of his madness reflects his age's assumptions about the physical determinants of the human psyche: its dependence on the specific mix of the four 'qualities' (heat, cold, humidity, dryness) and the four 'humours' (choler, phlegm, blood, melancholy), which, together with the individual's physical constitution, are conditioned by the influence of the planets, diet, climate, age and sex.[1] In Don Quixote's case, we may take it that the 'adustion' or burning up of either the melancholic or choleric humour, together with his gaunt, emaciated frame and principled abstemiousness, contribute to the extravagantly capricious fantasies to which Cervantes refers in the prologue to Part I. Just as these flare up under the stimulus of an adventure, combining with beatings and hardships to bring him to a state of delirious exhaustion at the end of the second sally, so their absence, reinforced by a month's rest, result in a mental condition deceptively like complete sanity. However, the patient's desiccated features tell another story, and the two investigators are not deceived for long.

In depicting the conversation between the three friends, Cervantes plausibly imbues it with an atmosphere of relaxed, bantering informality, while capturing at the same time the outward signs of the priest's and barber's ulterior motives, which are reflected in ironic innuendo and their oblique approach to what really concerns them. The conversation is partly satiric in its focus. In the early seventeenth century, a generation after the defeat of the Turkish navy at Lepanto, there was constant apprehension in Spain about a renewed threat from that quarter; and the priest raises the topic as bait to draw out Don Quixote's lurking mania. He duly obliges, announcing, after tantalising delays, his hairbrained proposal for dealing with the Turkish menace: the enlistment of the knights-errant currently roaming Spain – a mere half-dozen would suffice – as a defensive coast-guard. His proposal is treated by the barber as equivalent to the memoranda of political reform – *arbitrios* – that were frequently submitted to the king in these years of incipient decline (p. 627). Though some of these prescriptions were intelligent and far-sighted, Cervantes, like many of his contemporaries, regards the *arbitristas* as crackpots, portraying one of them, towards the end of *El coloquio de los perros*, as an inmate of the Hospital de la Resurrección in Valladolid.

At this point, the barber tells his anecdote about the lunatic of the madhouse of Seville who gave such a convincing impression of sanity in his pleas for release to the Archbishop that a chaplain was dispatched to investigate the case. Despite the asylum rector's warnings, the chaplain finds the madman completely sane and orders his discharge; at the last moment, the patient lets slip the fatal remark that proves the rector right. The story – doubtless a source

---

[1] On this, see Redondo (1998: 121–46), with extensive bibliography.

of Cervantes's conception of his hero's character – is an exact *mise-en-abîme* of the dialogue of which it forms part; and its point is the ambiguous nature of a madness capable of deceiving even an intelligent observer into thinking that the subject is sane. This idea will determine the portrayal of the hero in many subsequent chapters, notably those based on his encounter with Don Diego de Miranda (II, 16–18).

The major new theme is ushered in by Sansón Carrasco in Chapter 3. His introduction into the story is related to two motives, of which the first is less evident than the second. Having recently returned from Salamanca University armed with his B.A. – that is, from the realm of public affairs beyond the parochial world of Don Quixote's village – he is implicitly qualified to bring news of a contemporary, historical event that is external to that world: the publication of *Don Quixote* Part I in 1605 and its achievement of widespread fame. Cervantes treats it as external in the sense that he carefully avoids inclusion of the book and its author, or even Benengeli and his chronicle – their metaphoric equivalents within the fiction – among the things and persons encountered by the two heroes in Part II. Of course, several characters have read the chronicle. We are even given to understand in Chapter 4 that Sansón Carrasco is somehow privy to the chronicler's intentions. But neither the Moor nor his product – unlike Avellaneda's book – is ever allowed on stage, doubtless because Cervantes sensed that this would raise difficult questions of credibility and consistency. Sansón's emergence is also motivated by considerations of decorum: Cervantes's need to find an appropriate substitute for the priest as perpetrator of the burlesque hoaxes designed to bring Don Quixote home. He fits that requirement since he is characterised from the start as conforming to the type of the mischievous, prank-playing student: quick-witted, of sallow complexion, large mouth and snub nose, 'all signs of devilry and partiality for witticisms and practical jokes' (*DQ* II, 3; p. 647).

Despite this advance billing, he proves to be a surprisingly tactful mediator of news about Benengeli's chronicle to the hero, while allowing the reader to perceive ironic implications in the euphemistic language that he uses. At the beginning of Chapter 3, after Don Quixote has already learnt from Sancho that the book is by a Moor and that Sansón can inform him about it, he is gnawed by apprehension about the author's fitness for the task, since no good can be expected from his ethnic origins. So he soon asks Sansón whether his chivalric virtues have received just recognition, and is fulsomely reassured by him (II, 3; p. 648), though the reassurances need to be taken in an ironic sense by the reader. Thus, the praise of the hero's platonic love for Dulcinea can be construed as meaning that it is non-existent; the reference to his fortitude in adversity evokes the beatings he has suffered, and so on. Sansón's discreetly leg-pulling role combines with that of spokesman for the author; hence, the tripartite discussion serves as an authorial prologue incorporated within the fiction, in a way consistent with other metafictional comments by Cervantes on his own work. Thus, Sansón's flippantly grandiloquent greeting to Don Quixote is followed in the next breath, with an evident undercurrent of authorial pride, by congratulations to Benengeli and redoubled congratulations to 'the curious person who took the trouble to get the story translated out of Arabic into romance Castillian', that is, Cervantes himself. Pride is evident too in Sansón's hyperbolic account of the book's international impact: hyperbolic, that is, by what was foreseeable in 1615, though from a modern perspective, his conjecture that there will eventually be no language into which the book will not have been translated seems near the literal truth. One perceives it again in Sansón's categoric rejection of Don Quixote's suggestion that the work must be an incomprehensible mess, which is prompted by the news that readers have criticised the interpolation of *El curioso impertinente* 'not as being bad or badly written, but for being out of place' (p. 652). On the contrary, Sansón tells him, the book is transparently clear, universally understood, enjoyed and appreciated, so much so that whenever people see a bony nag, they cry 'There goes Rocinante'. Implicitly, this is a claim by Cervantes to have abundantly fulfilled the objectives proposed by his friend in the prologue to Part I (see above, p. 68), and it is completed by Don Quixote's subsequent remarks about the wit and intelligence required to write a humorous book (II, 3; p. 653), which make clear what kind of enjoyment it has afforded. The remarks are the more striking for being out of character, since the hero is not supposed to know that his chronicle corresponds to that description.

For their part, Don Quixote and Sancho react to Sansón's information in a manner broadly consistent with their familiar traits. So, when their friend informs them that some readers would have preferred less insistence on the beatings suffered by the hero, the knight characteristically argues in favour of suppression, learnedly citing Aristotle's principle of the universal truth of poetry: 'Doubtless Aeneas wasn't as pious as Virgil depicts him, nor Ulysses as prudent as he is made out to be by Homer' (p. 649). Sancho, in his usual role of harping bluntly on the facts, remarks that the truth of the history is in question. Sansón supports this, refuting Don Quixote's plea by citing the complementary part of Aristotle's argument, namely: 'the poet can relate or sing things not as they were, but as they should have been, and the historian must tell them not as they should have been, but just as they were' (pp. 649–50). The amusingly pedantic echoes of a theme of contemporary poetics serves to highlight the novel's nature as a pretended history relentless focussed on trifles.

Cervantes also uses the discussion to take account of two major objections raised against Part I. These are: the already mentioned inclusion of *El curioso impertinente*, and the omission of the passages relating to the theft and recovery of Sancho's ass. Regarding the latter, Cervantes delegates the responsibility for explaining the author's oversight or printer's error to Sancho, who, while he gives an amusing account of what should have been included, is unable, for obvious reasons, to explain why it was omitted (II, 4; pp. 656–7). Cervantes's way of turning questions relating to the consistency of composition of his own story into puzzles for the characters within it is typical of the carefree levity with which he handles it in general. The principal example of it is his treatment of the story of the Cave of Montesinos (see below, pp. 199–200).

The other new emphasis in the second Part, apart from the hero's increased lucidity, is the promotion of Sancho. It is exemplified by the conversation between Sancho and his wife Teresa in Chapter 5, in which she pours cold water on his ambitions of social advancement for himself, her and their daughter Mari-Sancha. The contrast between his illusory aspirations and her robust common sense repeats on a lower level the typical exchanges between him and his master, and this is also reflected in the style. Sancho's attempts at courtly elegance, exemplified by his elaborate opening paradox about being sad to be so happy, and later, by aphorism, metaphor and witty references, show the influence of Don Quixote upon him. Though they are combined with lapses to a colloquial register (cf. II, 12; p. 720), they elicit repeated comments by Cervantes on the implausibility of his language. Clearly, he feels that he has gone too far in attributing elevation of style to Sancho, yet it is a sign of the greater stylistic range that will accompany the squire's prominence in this Part.

By contrast, Teresa comes back at her husband with a typically Sancho-panzine repertoire of proverbs, solecisms, picturesque epithets and rustic analogies. In various respects, her character and language are a compendium of traits transmitted from him to her. For example, her opposition to his dizzy dreams of governing an island, marrying off their daughter Mari-Sancha to a count, and turning her, Teresa, into a fine lady echo the earthy wisdom about contentment with one's lot that was articulated by Sancho himself just one chapter before (II, 4; pp. 660–1). Yet the transmission is not just a one-way process, since her influence will be plainly visible in his performance as governor many chapters later. To his proposals for Mari-Sancha she retorts (pp. 665–6):

> Eso no, Sancho ... casadla con su igual, que es lo más acertado; que si de
> los zuecos la sacáis a chapines, y de saya parda de catorceno a verdugado
> y saboyanas de seda, y de una Marica y un tú, a una doña tal y señoría,
> no se ha de hallar la mochacha, y a cada paso ha de caer en mil faltas,
> descubriendo la hilaza de su tela basta y grosera.

> Not that, Sancho ... marry her with her kind; that's the best. If you take
> her out of clogs and put her in lady's high-heeled shoes, and out of plain
> brown frocks into farthingales and silk slit skirts and from Marykins and
> thou to Doña So-and-So and My Lady, the girl won't know where she is
> and will put her foot in it at every turn, showing the true stitching of her
> coarse cloth.

This repeats, with a new variation, Don Quixote's premonitions of how
Sancho's shaggy beard would give him away if dressed in ducal ermine (I,
21; p. 234), and looks forward to Sancho's own analogy, at the moment of
abdication from the governorship, for choosing his former lot rather than
remaining in his prestigious office: 'y volvámonos a andar con pie llano,
que si no le adornaren zapatos picados de cordobán, no le faltarán alpargatas
toscas de cuerda' (II, 53, p. 1066) (let's return to walking on flat ground, for
if my feet aren't adorned with nicely worked Cordoba leather, they won't
lack plain hemp sandals). And when Teresa dismisses his visions of her being
titled Doña and sitting in the best pews in church, in defiance of the gossip
of the local gentlewomen, with: 'Siempre, hermano, fui amiga de igualdad,
y no puedo ver entonos sin fundamentos. *Teresa* me pusieron en el bautismo,
nombre mondo y escueto, sin añadiduras ni cortapisas, ni arrequives de *dones*
ni *donas*' (p. 667) (I was always one for equality, brother, and can't stand
people putting on airs. They called me Teresa at baptism, a plain unvarnished
name, without additions, frills or trimmings of *dones* or *donas*), she repeats
one of her husband's characteristic solecisms – the pairing of the non-existent
masculine *ínsulo* with feminine *ínsula* (I, 26; p. 297; and cf. the housekeeper,
II, 2; p. 640) – and anticipates precisely what he will say when referred to
as 'el señor don Sancho Panza' on taking up his office as governor: 'Sancho
Panza me llaman a secas, y Sancho se llamó mi padre, y Sancho mi agüelo,
y todos fueron Panzas, sin añadiduras de dones y donas' (II, 45; p. 992) (I'm
called plain Sancho Panza, and my father was called Sancho, and so was my
grandfather, and all of them were Panzas, without the addition of *dones* or
donas).

Structure of Part II. Convergence of Adventures and Episodes

Part II is a more coherently planned book than Part I, which evolved by a series of ad hoc additions and modifications. The heroes embark on their wanderings with a fixed destination in view – the jousts of Zaragoza – which was anticipated in the last chapter of Part I, and is re-confirmed in Part II, Chapter 4 (p. 659), with further allusions to it in Chapters 18, 27 and 57. If it changes from Zaragoza to Barcelona in Chapter 59, this is in order to give the lie to Avellaneda's sequel. Cervantes's idealised conception of the Catalan city, repeatedly expressed, makes it, for him, a worthy substitute.[2] The consequences of the enchantment of Dulcinea, engineered by Sancho at the beginning of the third sally, provide a continuous theme sustained until the very end. Another constant theme, imbued with celebratory reference to the first Part's popular success, is the recognition of the two heroes by other characters as the famous subjects of Benengeli's chronicle. Though established in Chapters 3, 4 and 7, it does not significantly reappear again until Chapter 30, when they run into the Duke and Duchess; from that point, it fairly comes into its own, being basic to their reception in the Duke's country-estate (II, 30–57 and 69–70) and in Barcelona (II, 61–65), including the whole series of pranks that are played on them in those two places.

From Chapter 59, Cervantes ingeniously adapts this theme to deal with Avellaneda, ridiculing his book, in a way consistent with his metafictional comments on his own novel, from within the premises of his story.[3] So, the readers of that sequel who meet the authentic Don Quixote at an inn in Part II, Chapter 59, instantly recognise him as such on hearing him confirm that he still loves Dulcinea (see above, p. 171). Implicitly, as we have seen, authenticity and superior quality are treated as equivalent. For those two readers, the crudeness and coarseness of the apocryphal Sancho, compared with the comicality and wit of Benengeli's, proves which of the two is genuine. Subsequently, in Chapter 72, the two heroes, at another inn, meet Don Álvaro Tarfe, the principal aristocratic patron of Avellaneda's pair, counterpart to the Duke

---

[2] See *DQ* II, 72; p. 1207. Cf. *Las dos doncellas*, in *Novelas*, ed. García López, p. 465, and *Persiles* III, 12, ed. Schevill and Bonilla, vol. ii, p. 131.

[3] It has traditionally been supposed that he became acquainted with the apocryphal version on reaching this point in the composition of his own second Part. However, that assumption has been contested with some insistence in recent years by various scholars who have argued on the strength of various similarities between the two works that Cervantes drafted or revised several chapters previous to Chapter 59 after reading his rival's book or the manuscript. This leaves open the question at what stage of composition he read it. See Romero Muñoz (1990: 98–100) for a review of the various hypotheses; also, Chapter 2, n. 6.

in Cervantes's story. They get him to vouch before a scribe that they are not
the same persons as those whom he has hitherto known by the same names,
leaving us to wonder whether Don Álvaro is victim of a hallucination or has
been put upon by impostors of flesh and blood. Obviously, behind these playfully amusing 'proofs' of ID lies Cervantes's fierce authorial pride of copyright, and conviction that his two characters are infinitely more successful
than his rival's.

Despite the differences between Part II and Part I, basic features of the
latter are retained: the imitation of the form of a knight-errant's wanderings in search of adventure; the outward-and-return loop of the journey; the
sequence of a long series of encounters on the open road followed by another
series of adventures in a castle, a real one this time, not imaginary. The
adjustment of the two heroes' itinerary to the coordinates of time and space is
even more haphazard than in Part I, with their arrival in Barcelona on 24 June
(Chapter 61) occurring one month before Sancho's letter to his wife, dated 20
July (Chapter 36), despite coming later in the sequence of events. Similarly,
their presence in Barcelona on midsummer's day in Chapter 61 presupposes
a sudden jump forward in time, since they were still heading for the feast of
St George in Zaragoza, traditionally held on 23 April, at the beginning of
Chapter 59. An even mightier leap forward in space is required to transport
them in the space of just five chapters and no more than two or three days
from the Cave of Montesinos, in the south of La Mancha (Chapter 23), to
the banks of the river Ebro, hundreds of kilometres to the north (Chapters 27
and 29). Cervantes was clearly not troubled by the considerations of realistic
consistency that alarmed his neo-classical critics.[4]

Part II transpires in holiday mood in a season that oscillates imprecisely
between springtime and summer. This is a green world largely removed from
urban bustle; it teems with entertainers, people in costume or disguise, adven-
turers, social outcasts. These types are different from those encountered in
Part I: more exotic than obscure wayfarers like those merchants of Toledo (I,
4) and generally more in touch with public, historical reality than characters
like Grisóstomo and Marcela (I, 12–14), who seem to step out of the pages
of sentimental romance. The greater topical reference is largely explained by
the invasion of the hero's world by Benengeli's readership. Whereas in Part
I Don Quixote's adventures never occupied more than individual chapters,
now they are often spread over two or more, and the sequences of talk and
incident tend to be framed within an itinerary from A to B or something like

---

4 See the introduction to Clemencín's edn of *DQ* (1833), pp. xxix–xxx.

the 'country-house weekend'. His fame secured by Benengeli's chronicle, the hero is now less single-minded about his chivalric mission, and resembles a tourist on a leisurely excursion, showing a compulsive interest in novelty, the curiouser the better. He makes a special pilgrimage to the Cave of Montesinos to witness for himself the marvels recounted of it by folklore (Chapter 18; p. 780). He cannot wait to hear the story of the man driving a mule laden with lances and halberds (Chapter 24; pp. 831–2), and his impatience is such that, when he gets to the inn, and finds him in the stable feeding his mule, he assists in this menial operation in order to hasten the telling of it (beginning of Chapter 25).

By contrast with Part I, where the hero projected his fantasies on the external world, the incidents of Part II tend to reverse this process, either because casual wayside encounters spontaneously satisfy his thirst for the unusual, or else because other characters practise burlesque hoaxes in chivalric style on him. With these changes his madness sheds much of its active, aggressive character, and largely consists in credulity about the deceptions practised on him by others. Before, it flared up under any propitious stimulus, and even some most unpropitious ones; now he tends to see things as they are. Since his imaginative transformation of inns into castles was the original indicator of its vigour, it is significant that on three occasions in Part II,[5] he simply recognises them as inns. On the last occasion, Cervantes comments that after his defeat at Barcelona, he discoursed more rationally on all subjects than before. From this we may infer that his previous failures to see inns as castles were a consequence of the cumulatively chastening effect of defeats in general. The hero's increased lucidity has consequences for his attitude to himself, to Sancho and to others. We often see him in introspective and reflective mood. Henceforth, those whom he meets will be just as impressed by the wisdom of his opinions on education, poetry, honour, fame, sainthood, marriage, the rights of war, and government, as they continue to be astonished and amused by his chivalric delusions. He becomes more affable, courteous and peaceable; and they tend to treat him with friendliness, hospitality, courtesy and occasional respect, rather different from the amused or pitying condescension shown in Part I.

His encounter with the company of actors, at an early stage of the new sally (*DQ* II, 11), marks these changes clearly.[6] He and Sancho are confronted

---

[5] II, 24, p. 835; II, 59, pp. 1108–9; II, 71, p. 1202.

[6] See Stefano Arata's introductory comments on this chapter in vol. 2 of Rico's edn (2004). In this volume, the reader will find introductions by specialists in Cervantes, with up-to-date

182 ANTHONY CLOSE

by a mule-drawn cart occupied by a motley collection of fantastic figures: an ugly devil holds the reins; inside the waggon are Death with a human face instead of the usual grinning skull, an angel with large gaudy wings, an emperor wearing a gold crown, Cupid with eyes unbandaged and equipped with bow, quiver and arrows, an armed knight with a plumed hat on his head, instead of helmet and visor. With its bizarrely supernatural air, this sight is in some ways reminiscent of the meeting with the funeral cortège in I, 19, save that it takes place in broad daylight. As on the previous occasion, Don Quixote confronts the apparition and challenges the driver to say who he and his companions are and where they are going. This individual amiably replies that they are actors in the company of Angulo el Malo, who have performed that morning, which is the eighth of Corpus Christi, the sacramental allegory *Las cortes de la muerte* (The Courts of Death) in a village that lies behind them, and are due to perform it again in the village that can be seen ahead. For that reason, they have not changed out of their stage-costumes. To that Don Quixote replies: 'Por la fe de caballero andante ... que así como vi este carro imaginé que alguna grande aventura se me ofrecía, y ahora digo que es menester tocar las apariencias con la mano para dar lugar al desengaño' (II, 11; p. 714) (On my honour as a knight-errant, I swear that when I saw this cart I imagined some great adventure was imminent, but now I say one must set hand to appearances so as not to be deceived by them). He wishes the company god speed, and, courteously offering his services, confesses his love of the theatre since boyhood.

Cervantes does not tell us that this new and remarkable awareness of the need to look before leaping is based on the hero's painful recollection of the occasions in Part I when he failed to do so. He does not need to. The striking resemblance of the encounter to previous ones, together with Don Quixote's unexpected departure from previous behaviour, makes the point implicitly. Moreover, the title of the play, identical to that of an extant *auto* by Lope de Vega, which is an updated version of the medieval theme of the Dance of Death, endows the dispelling of false illusions with a religious dimension, suggesting the correlation, basic to *Don Quixote*, between factual and moral truth, seeing straight and acting well. Balancing the two sides of that equation is the end-goal of the hero's psychological evolution in Part II. There is

bibliography, to every chapter of *DQ*, including the episodes discussed in this section. See in particular, Carrasco Urgoiti's on the encounter between Sancho and Ricote (II, 54), Redondo's on Camacho's wedding (II, 19–21), Riquer's on the meeting of DQ and Roque Guinart (II, 60), Ignacio Arellano's on Maese Pedro's puppet-show and the episode of the braying aldermen (II, 25–27), Egido's on the Cave of Montesinos (II, 23–24), Canavaggio's on the Duke's palace adventures (II, 30–32), Chevalier on part of Sancho's governorship (II, 45, 47, 49).

another sense in which the meeting with the players is typical of this Part: it offers a historically faithful, informal glimpse into a typical and picturesque scene of rural life. It was customary for theatre companies during the Corpus Christi festival to take their sacramental plays to country villages after staging them in the towns. The troupe of Angulo el Malo was one of the most famous in Spain. Some of the actors in the cart have evidently removed part of their costume in order to travel at ease; so we see them as they might appear behind the scenes, rather than on stage.

However, the meeting, so far uneventful, has a comic codicil which threatens to revive the Don's combativeness with its habitually farcical consequences. The clown of the company, dressed in the motley worn by fools who preceded the carts in Corpus Christi processions, prances before Rocinante, thumping the ground with three cow's bladders attached to a stick. This causes the nag to stampede and pitch his rider off. Sancho dismounts to help his master, but is dismayed to see the fellow ride off with his beloved ass. He reports this to Don Quixote, who vows to recover it in terms that seem a self-conscious parody of the extravagant bombast that he employed in Part I: for example, 'Pues yo le cobraré … si bien se encerrase con él en los más hondos y oscuros calabozos del infierno' (II, 11; p. 716) (Well, I shall bring it back even if he [the 'devil' who took it] should hide in the darkest and deepest dungeons of hell). This threat, and others in the same vein, is more playful than irate since Don Quixote knows perfectly well that the clown is not really a devil but an actor; also, it soon becomes superfluous when the joyrider dismounts and the ass returns to its master. Nonetheless, having remounted Rocinante, Don Quixote speaks of seeking revenge and, in two minds about whether to charge at the actors, who prepare to receive him with a hail of stones, he is deterred by a clinching argument from Sancho in favour of non-aggression: though his adversaries look like kings, princes and emperors, there is not a real knight-errant among them. Since equality of status between foes was a precondition of combat that he himself laid down in Part I (Chapter 15, p. 162), he gratefully accepts this face-saving device for getting off the hook. The chapter ends on a note of conciliatory and amicable serenity between him and his squire.

Suggesting that they should let these phantasms be and seek more authentic adventures, Don Quixote raises in the reader's mind what type of incident this is. Is it an adventure or an episode? Unlike what happens in Part I, the hero's initial illusions are quickly dispelled, and confrontation with reality does not so much serve to mock *them* as to focus on *it*, as is shown by the beginning of Chapter 12, where Don Quixote's partly ludic indignation with the players gives way to his warm praise of their profession and of its social utility, and his pious commonplaces on the theme 'All the world's a stage'. So it is in many subsequent encounters in Part II. In them, adventure often does not present itself in the semblance of a story, whether imagined by Don Quixote or really experienced and narrated by some other character, but in that of acquaintance with interesting strangers, who inform the heroes about their style of life, opinions and personal history. In this respect, Cervantes takes a leaf out of the third book of *Persiles y Sigismunda*, and also of his satiric *novelas*, to which several of these episodes are related. For instance, Don Quixote's praise of the acting profession following the meeting with the players, which runs counter to contemporary diatribes against it on grounds of immorality, echoes a passage in *El licenciado Vidriera*;[7] and there are indulgently humorous scenes featuring playwrights or actors in both *Persiles* and *El coloquio de los perros*.[8]

This brings us to the vexed question how to distinguish between the episodes of Part II and its main theme (cf. above, pp. 65–66). In Part I, the problem scarcely arose, since Don Quixote was largely excluded from them, and the focus of attention fell on matters more serious than his chivalric mania. However, in Part II, discrimination is much more difficult and the either/or dichotomy typical of Part I becomes blurred.

The difficulty is well illustrated by the magnificent scene that greets the two heroes' eyes when, on the beach of Barcelona at daybreak on midsummer's day, they see the sea for the first time (*DQ* II, 61; pp. 1130–1). White dawn shows its face at the balconies of the orient. Galleys with pennants fluttering in the breeze perform manoeuvres on the placid water to the accompaniment of fifes, clarions and trumpets. Cannon salutes from the city walls are answered by naval artillery. Riders in gay livery on handsome steeds sally from the city and show off their horsemanship. Cervantes summarises: 'The gay aspect of the sea, the jocund earth, the clear air, only smudged by the artillery-smoke, seemed to infuse sudden joy into all men.' This mood of universal rejoicing is recurrent in Part II (cf. Chapters 14, 20, 36). It is as if nature joined with the Spanish navy and the city of Barcelona to render tribute to Don Quixote.

That, at least, is how he sees it, and not without cause. A group of horsemen breaks off from the rest, gallops towards the two astonished heroes amid whoops and Moorish war-cries, and one of them welcomes Don Quixote to the city in floridly burlesque style, identifying him as the authentic subject of

---

7 *Novelas*, ed. García López, pp. 292–3.

8 *Persiles* Book III, Chapter 2, ed. Schevill and Bonilla, vol. ii, pp. 18–20, and *Novelas*, pp. 611–15.

Benengeli's chronicle, not the impostor featured in the apocryphal continuation (p. 1131). Then the horsemen form an escort and conduct master and squire into the town to the accompaniment of fifes and tambourines, as though they were princes making a ceremonial entry. We are told in the next chapter that Don Quixote assumed that these public festivities were being staged just for his sake; and the style of his reception thereafter helps to confirm that impression. I refer particularly to his ceremonial visit to a Spanish war-galley, where he and Sancho are welcomed aboard with a burlesque pomp similar to the honours accorded to royalty (Chapter 63; see p. 214).

However, Don Quixote is mistaken in his belief that Barcelona is rolling out the red carpet for him personally. As any contemporary reader would have guessed, the festivities described in Chapter 61 were those customarily held on midsummer's day. Don Antonio Moreno, who will be the hero's host in Barcelona, takes advantage of the coincidence in order to welcome him in the style that he expects (II, 62; p. 1133). So, Don Quixote's entry into Barcelona has two aspects, illusory and real. For him it is another high point of his chivalric career, comparable to his grandly ceremonious reception in the Duke's castle (Chapters 30–31) and confirmation of his fame as a knight-errant. For the reader, until the moment of Don Antonio's burlesque welcome, it is the lavish description of the picturesque pageantry of a public feast-day in a great city: in effect, an ornamental digression. The scene, alien to the either/or nature of the first Part, is typical of the diversified focus of the second. Also, its epic grandeur, tinged with humour by being addressed to the ingenuous eyes of Quixote and Sancho, exemplifies the novel's equipoise between romance and comedy.

Cervantes's decision to make episodes arise, as he puts it in II, 44 (p. 980), 'from the very events that the truth proposes' – that is, from incidents which directly affect the two heroes – has consequences that are radical and far-reaching. At a stroke, Don Quixote, and to some extent, Sancho, take over the role of rational commentators formerly exercised by *discreto* characters like the priest. Consequently Cervantes is forced to carry to its limits the coordinative method by which he formerly linked episodes to the main theme. Instead of falling outside the sphere of comedy occupied by Don Quixote and Sancho, they now merge with it, harmonised with their perspective. The two former figures of fun, excluded from grave matters as classical decorum required, become the discreet fools of Part II, centres of all they survey: centres, that is, in their capacity as observers and commentators, not as protagonists. Thus, when Don Quixote suggests to Don Antonio Moreno that he, as a knight-errant, rather than the Spanish renegade, is best qualified to rescue Don Gregorio from Algiers, the suggestion is humoured but ignored (II, 64; p. 1157).

The hybridisation of styles, modes and themes resulting from these changes brings about a revolutionary expansion of the range of a comic novel, whose repercussions only become perceptible in the eighteenth century: it is a medley where novelesque motifs fuse with documentary ones, picturesque scenes of rural life with the pastimes of an aristocrat's country estate and the pageantry and bustle of a big city, moral satire with politics and religion, all designed to provoke the reflection of the two heroes and elicit their familiar mannerisms. In accord with this dual, unifying perspective, Cervantes skilfully varies the tone and matter of his episodes and also makes the strangers featured in them shed the scales of stereotype and reveal themselves with a marvellous blend of humour and naturalness. Also, he generally ensures that they present themselves in either a Quixotic or Sanchopanzine aspect, as the following examples illustrate.

The encounter with the Catalan outlaw Roque Guinart, who really existed and was a legend in his own lifetime, is tense and dramatic (II, 60). Previous chapters have alluded to contemporary history, but now, embodied in the person of Guinart, it is represented on stage. Brigandage, a residue of historic feuds between warring clans, aggravated by agrarian decline and other factors, was an endemic affliction in Cataluña in that age, which the government was powerless to check. The two heroes become aware of being in a region of brigands when, near Barcelona, they find themselves in a wood and see corpses hanging from the trees, the result of the summary executions to which outlaws were liable. Soon they are surrounded by a band of armed men, and are in the process of being stripped of their possessions when Roque himself intervenes, telling his followers to desist and return the stolen property, thus living up to the idealised image of his magnanimity that is reflected in the contemporary theatre. Later, they are given evidence of his brutal authority over his men, when one of them dares to question his leniency towards a party of captured travellers, including a well-heeled noble lady, and is murdered on the spot. Like other characters in Part II, Roque is delighted to meet the celebrated subjects of Benengeli's chronicle, and confides to Don Quixote that his own style of life might be considered a kind of knight-errantry (p. 1125). More specifically, it illustrates the practical consequences of the characteristically Quixotic impulse to 'vengar agravios' (to avenge offences): an abyss of disquiet, fear and violence. The point has just previously been made by the sudden appearance of the dashingly attired Claudia Jerónima, who pours out, with hectic brevity, the tragic story of how she has just shot her own lover in a fit of jealousy. It is the story of a love-affair between young people of warring clans; Claudia begs Roque, out of friendship for her father, to protect him from reprisals and smuggle her across the border to France. They both catch up with the mortally wounded Don Vicente, who just has time before expiring to tell his mistress that she acted on a false rumour.

Several chapters before (II, 25; pp. 836–9), the theme of avenging offences has been illustrated in an altogether different key by the story of the braying aldermen, who made perfect asses of themselves by revelling in their virtuoso capacity to imitate an ass's bray. The story, told with superb comic polish by a man from their village, has a Sanchopanzine flavour by virtue of its asinine theme and folkloric associations. The ending speaks of sinister conse-quences: war between the 'braying' village and those who have insultingly dubbed it with this attribute. In the sequel (II, 27; pp. 857–62), Don Quixote sights a squadron of armed men from the top of a hill, and identifies them by their banner, which depicts a small donkey in the act of braying and carries the defiant device: 'No rebuznaron en balde / el uno y el otro alcalde' (the two mayors didn't bray in vain).[9] Don Quixote descends the hill, fearlessly approaches the small army, and, gathering the armed men around him, delivers them an affable and learned lecture on the conditions of the just war in order to dissuade them from their purpose. His familiar expertise on the military code is here tuned in a lucid key. Rustic comedy is thus elevated to a reflec-tive level, before collapsing in undignified farce when Sancho endorses his master's speech with an inopportune imitation of an ass's bray, bringing down the predictable consequences on himself. The encounter is in obvious respects a transposition of incidents in Part I, including the hero's rash harangue to the liberated galley-slaves, and the prelude to the battle with the sheep, in which he rides to the top of a hill, and from there describes in detail the imaginary armies in battle-array, together with their captains, armour and devices.

Just prior to this episode (Chapter 24; p. 833), the two heroes meet a page-boy singing a popular song: 'A la guerra me lleva / mi necesidad; / si tuviera dineros / no fuera en verdad' (Poverty is taking me to join the army; if I had any money, I wouldn't be going, to tell the truth). His whole demeanour suggests carefree nonchalance; he wears his shirt-tails out and a sword over his shoulder, from which hangs a bundle containing his breeches. He reveals that he travels thus because of the heat and to save wearing out his clothes, and that he has left the court in disillusionment, having had the bad luck to serve

---

[9] Since Gonzalo Correas in his proverb-collection *Vocabulario de refranes* (1627) includes the proverb 'Rebuznaron en balde el uno y el otro alcalde', one infers that the story is based on a popular folk-tale to which the proverb refers. Rodríguez Marín, in vol. 10, appendix xxx of his edn of *DQ* gives numerous examples of the mocking epithets applied to the natives of Spanish towns and villages, implying rivalry between them like that depicted in Cervantes's episode.

impoverished social climbers with scarcely enough money to starch a shirt collar. In the household of a grandee, by contrast, he could have expected a handsome bonus on departure, or the gift of a military commission. We might note in passing that his benign view of the generosity of great noblemen is not shared by contemporary satirists (Close, 2000: 219). The knight commends his honourable motive in a homily that echoes his praise of the military vocation in the Arms and Letters speech. Clearly this episode is juxtaposed with the one immediately following for thematic reasons: a praiseworthy motive for taking up arms is contrasted with the frivolity of the villagers' quest for revenge. Also, it partly resembles an episode in *Persiles* III, 10, where two penniless students from Salamanca, begging for alms by pretending to be ex-captives from Algiers, are exposed as frauds by an officious village mayor – an ignorant rustic – and sentenced summarily to a hundred lashes and a spell in the galleys. One of the students spiritedly argues against the disproportionate severity of the sentence, revealing that their motive for the fraud was the honourable one of defraying their expenses for the journey to join a regiment destined for the war in Flanders. His eloquence is such that the mayor, an ex-captive himself, swings to the other extreme, not only revoking the sentence, but taking the lads home to make them more proficient in their lie. The episode is typical of Cervantes's amusement at rustic foolishness, aversion to gratuitous judicial severity and nonchalant readiness to turn a blind eye to the letter of the law. What links it to the episode in *Don Quixote* is his nostalgic idealisation of the soldier's life, reflected in the sympathetic portrayal of the youths who embrace it. Cervantes, aged 23, in Italy, and possibly on the run from the Spanish law, once found himself in the shoes of those students and that ex-page.

As the foregoing examples indicate, the episodes of Part II tend to be treated loosely as mirror-images of the two heroes' experience and personalities, and throw light on the central, perennial dilemmas posed by Don Quixote's behaviour: head or heart? discretion or valour? heroic adventurousness or stay-at-home conformism? Most of these conflicts are ethical. In only one case is the problem political, and, in a way that is typical of Cervantes, it highlights the injury done to innocent individuals by actions designed to do good on a larger scale.

In Chapter 54, Sancho runs into Ricote, an exiled *morisco* from his native village and a former neighbour. In part, Ricote's revelations are a prelude to his later reunion with his daughter Ana Félix, and to her romantic story of Don Gregorio's love for her and of the vicissitudes which took him into exile with her to Algiers, then brought her back to Spain on a Turkish brigantine as its captain, disguised as a man (Chapter 63). The ship is pursued and captured by a Spanish war-galley off Barcelona; and she tells her story with a noose around her neck; it culminates in Ricote's dramatic recognition of his daughter and the remission of the death-sentence. Yet Ricote's narrative is no mere preamble to his daughter's but an episode in its own right, whose extensive treatment, from an exile's viewpoint, of the still burning political question of the mass expulsion of the *morisco* community gives it a focus of interest quite distinct from romantic considerations. The comic circumstances in which it is told, and their satiric implications, contrast starkly with the sinister context of the daughter's tale.

Returning from his ill-starred tenure of office in Barataria, Sancho finds himself accosted by half-a-dozen German pilgrims who, as was their custom, form a line and beg for alms by chanting in chorus. One of them suddenly steps forward and embraces him, identifying himself, in fluent Spanish, as Ricote, who, like the rest of the *morisco* population, was victim of its mass expulsion from Spain between 1609 and 1614. He confides to Sancho that he is returning illegally disguised as a pilgrim in order to recover his buried treasure, and that the wanderings of his companions from shrine to shrine are motivated less by devotion than by the lure of the alms, food and wine that they scrounge from the villages through which they pass. The ugly old woman encountered by the protagonists of *Persiles y Sigismunda* in Book III, Chapter 6, is by implication one of this kind, even though she denounces the malpractice. Ricote's German friends give proof of their epicureanism by heading for a nearby grove, casting aside cloaks and staffs, and spreading on the ground an extraordinary array of appetizers and six hefty wine-skins, with which they proceed to make a merry and boozy picnic.

While they sleep off the effects, Ricote tells Sancho the moving story of how the edict of expulsion has affected him and his family, ripping them from their home and homeland, turning them into unwanted refugees, and separating him from his wife and daughter. Cervantes, who, in the *El colo-quio de los perros* and *Persiles y Sigismunda* III, 11, writes about the expulsion from a viewpoint which faithfully echoes the vehement social prejudice against the *moriscos* as disaffected heretics, quite lacking in civic and patriotic spirit, presents a more nuanced and compassionate view of the question here, though in making Ricote obsequiously and implausibly praise the edict as a well-merited punishment, he is careful not to stray from the government line. One perceives in this the struggle between his humane compassion for exiles uprooted from the Spanish homeland, a fate that he had suffered himself, and acquiescence in the majority belief that the expulsion was necessary. The change in his attitude relative to the *Persiles* and, more especially, to the *novela*, is probably explained by the fact that when he wrote the chapter of *Don Quixote*, some time in 1614, he had become aware of the mass misery that it had caused.[10]

The antithesis between head and heart, the call of home and the discovery of new horizons, is posed in a very different way by the encounter between Don Quixote and Don Diego de Miranda (DQ II, 16–18).[11] Cervantes seems to imply the hero's sense of affinity with this stranger, as he did in the confrontation between Don Quixote and Cardenio (end of I, 23; p. 260; cf. I, 24; pp. 260–1). On that occasion he marked it by bestowing mock-chivalric epithets on Cardenio; here, he suggests it in similar fashion by calling Don Diego 'the Knight of the Green Cloak'. He suggests it too by insisting on the intense curiosity with which each regards the other. Don Diego's astonishment at the *hidalgo*'s extraordinary aspect – lanky figure, emaciated yellow face, makeshift armour, bony nag – is matched by the very favourable impression made on Don Quixote by the stranger's dignified elegance, which is described with a painter's attention to detail. He is mounted on a handsome dapple mare, wears a fine green cloak with tawny velvet trimmings and matching accessories: hunting-cap, Moorish scimitar hanging from a gold and green shoulder-belt, riding-boots, curiously worked spurs. He is about fifty, with angular features, a scant sprinkling of white hair, and a face at once grave and cheerful. In some ways, the description corresponds to Cervantes's self-portrait in the prologue to the *Novelas ejemplares*. The significance of the contrast between Don Diego and Don Quixote, is that one is an ideal, upmarket version of what the other might have been had his mind not been turned by chivalry books.

Irony is implied by Don Diego's amazed reaction to his companion's self-introduction, which consists in a synopsis of his career of knight-errantry and proud allusion to the publication and diffusion of Benengeli's chronicle. However, this attitude is soon overlaid by keen curiosity, which will mark his and his son's relation to Don Quixote over the next three chapters: the attempt to resolve the question whether he is mad or sane, and if mad, where to draw the dividing-line between one and the other. That is, there is a relative shift of

---

10   The dogs' colloquy was probably written before the expulsion edict, in or about 1606, and refers darkly to plans for a final solution to the *morisco* problem, implying that they have not yet crystallised. See *Novelas*, ed. García López, pp. 609–11. The chapter in *Persiles* (ed. Schevill and Bonilla, vol. ii, pp. 114–21) was almost certainly written sometime after 1609, when they had already been put into effect, even though the reference to it is cast in the form of a prophecy. Like the chapter in *DQ*, it alludes to the harsh reception encountered by the *moriscos* in North Africa.

11   There have been many divergent interpretations of this episode. Fundamentally, I agree with Redondo's (1998: 265–89).

emphasis, typical of Part II, from the absurdity of Quixotic delusions and of the genre that inspires them to the extraordinariness of his mental condition and its ambiguous oscillation between madness and lucidity.

In this psychological enquiry, the balance tilts first one way then the other. When the topic of children arises, Don Diego confesses anxiety about his son, who spends his time at Salamanca University composing and discussing poetry instead of devoting himself to the study of theology or law. In reply, the *hidalgo* delivers an eloquent homily on the nobility of poetry and the upbringing of children, drawing on familiar topics of Renaissance poetics and pedagogy, and recommends the father to treat his son's literary pursuits with greater tolerance (Chapter 16; pp. 756–9). Don Diego is suitably impressed. However, the balance soon tilts the other way. They meet a cart bearing a pair of lions as a gift from the governor of Oran to the king, and the *hidalgo*, in a display of crazy bravado, treats the beasts as foes sent personally against him by hostile enchanters (end of Chapter 16 and beginning of 17). He asks for his helmet, which Sancho has just happened to use as a shopping-bag for curds purchased from some shepherds, and when, after clapping it on his head, white matter starts oozing down his face, believes that his brains must have addled. This confirms Don Diego's worst suspicions about his sanity. Then the *hidalgo* orders the lion-keeper to open the cages so that battle may commence. The build-up to the confrontation is a superb example of Cervantes's handling of dramatic suspense prior to ironic anti-climax. The sensible pleas and remonstrations by Don Diego, the lion-keeper, and Sancho; Don Quixote's supercilious response to them; the undignified haste with which the non-combatants get as far from the scene as possible; Benengeli's over-blown panegyric to the *hidalgo*'s valour just before the fateful confrontation – all serve to inflate the balloon. When the cage door is opened and the challenger stands face to face with his foe, it crumples absurdly. The king of beasts yawns, licks its face like a fireside tabby, turns its hind quarters to the challenger, and lies down again. Cervantes's phrase about the generous lion's courteous disdain for puerile bravado shows whom he regards as the true hero of this affair.

In the mood of self-congratulation following his 'victory', Don Quixote addresses a lengthy reply to Don Diego's previous admonition that rashness is not courage but foolhardiness, which the *hidalgo*, in the heat of preparation for combat, insolently rebuffed by telling Don Diego to mind his own tame decoy partridge and bold ferret, and leave heroic exploits to those whose business it is to perform them (II, 17; p. 763). His speech returns to the contrast that he drew in Part II, Chapter 1 between the pampered, ornamental life of the courtier and the heroic vocation of a knight-errant, battling in

wild and lonely places against all kinds of monsters and enemies in quest of
fame. Starting from the Aristotelian premise that valour consists in the mean
between rashness and cowardice, he argues that it is better, in the context
of that vocation, to err on the side of excess. It is another of Don Quixote's
virtuoso set-pieces, in which glimmerings of sense are blended with nonsense
in disconcertingly elegant style. Don Diego's courteously ironic rejoinder to
this sophistry is a clear indication of Cervantes's thinking, which is decidedly
against treating heroics as a necessary concomitant to heroism, and insistently
distinguishes between excess and mean, the principle and the circumstances
of application. He devotes an entire play, the comedy *El gallardo español*
(The Gallant Spaniard), to making that very point. The balance will swing yet
again during Don Quixote's stay at Don Diego's house (Chapter 18), and the
investigation of his mental condition is undertaken by the son, Don Lorenzo,
who arrives at the conclusion that Don Quixote's is an intermittent madness,
full of lucid intervals.

So, the focus of these three chapters is trained firmly on the hero, in Cervantes's terms, on 'la verdad de la historia'. Yet how he is appraised gains much
of its significance from the perspective of the chief appraiser, Don Diego,
whose way of life is an ideal embodiment of the virtue of cultivating one's
garden that is enjoined on the hero from the beginning of the novel to the end.
In reply to Don Quixote's self-portrait in Chapter 16, Don Diego supplies his
own. He is a rich gentleman farmer, who spends his life among his family,
friends and neighbours; he hunts in a modest way, presides over a clean,
quiet, well-regulated household, enjoys giving hospitality, and has a library of
some six dozen books. He shuns malicious gossip, vainglory and hypocrisy,
shares his goods with the poor, and is a devotee of the Virgin. The same ideal
of virtuous contentment in rural seclusion, away from the careworn turmoil
and glamour of the court, runs insistently through the writings of Cervantes's
contemporaries,[12] and Cervantes himself gives idealised expressions to it in
his portrayal of the self-exiled Renato and Eusebia (*Persiles* II, 19) and the
sage Soldino (*Persiles* III, 18). Hence, Don Quixote's casuistical rebuttal of
Don Diego's charge of foolhardiness is wide of the mark; for Cervantes, the
latter's way of life is quite opposed to the courtier's. Those critics who treat
the Knight of the Green Cloak as some kind of sanctimonious prig overlook
the twinkle in his eye, his urbane irony towards Don Quixote, and the fact
that, though considering his guest mad, he entertains him at his home for

---

[12] Including, notably, Bishop Antonio de Guevara's *Menosprecio de corte y alabanza de
aldea* (1539) (Contempt for Court and Praise of Country). See Rallo's introduction to her
edition of it (1982), pp. 62–82.

three days, treating him throughout with humane courtesy. How many of the critics, one wonders, would do as much?

My last example, which again turns on the opposition of head and heart, illustrates by itself the heterogeneity of the episodic material of Part II. It is the pastoral interlude of Camacho's wedding, similar in its triangular conflict to that of Daranio and Quiteria in Book III of *La Galatea*. The macabre fake suicide by which the penniless lover Basilio manages to filch the bride from under the bridegroom's nose is reminiscent of an incident in Folengo's macaronic poem *Baldus*.[13] The episode is comparable in structure to that of Marcela and Grisóstomo in Part I, in that Don Quixote and Sancho first learn of the affair from a character who is going to the wedding and conducts them there, then witness the crisis and resolution at first hand. In this case their informant is the senior of a couple of sociable students accompanied by two peasants. Whereas in the earlier episode attention was concentrated on Grisóstomo's unreciprocated passion and the question of Marcela's responsibility for his death, in this case, thanks to the perspective of Don Quixote and Sancho, it is far more diversified.

The student who relates the story to them strikes a superlative note appropriate both to pastoral and myth: Camacho is the richest farmer in the region; Quiteria the most beautiful woman yet seen by man; Basilio, a consummate fencer, athlete, guitarist, singer; his and Quiteria's love evokes that of Pyramus and Thisbe. The conflict of interests that is provoked by the bride's father's decision to prefer the rich suitor to the poor one is a reminder of the cause of the separation of Sireno and Diana in Montemayor's *La Diana*, and also of the crisis that looms for Galatea and Elicio at the end of Cervantes's *La Galatea*. The morbid melancholy in which Basilio is cast by the decision is another reminder of the pastoral genre. Yet the conflict of love versus pecuniary interest and filial obedience is no mere literary topic; it has real reference to contemporary life: a familiar theme of comedies about the hearbreaks and dilemmas provoked by the imposition of parental authority on the choice of spouse, like Tirso de Molina's *Marta la piadosa* (Pious Martha) or Lope de Vega's *Sembrar en buena tierra* (Sowing in Fertile Ground). And Sancho's cynical solidarity with the haves against the have-nots in Chapter 20 echoes a recurrent satirical theme of an age that feared that money trumped everything, not just love, but even the powerful talisman of noble pedigree.

---

[13] On this see Close (2000: 147, note), also Redondo's note on *DQ* II, 20 in vol. ii of Rico's edn (2004). Redondo sees in the trick the influence of a folkloric tale perpetuated by Spanish chap-books.

It is summed up by Quevedo's refrain: 'Poderoso caballero / es don Dinero' (A powerful gentleman is Sir Money).

The rights and wrongs of this decision are discussed by Don Quixote and Sancho on the way to the wedding, with the former taking the role of prudent marriage counsellor that was discharged by Lotario in I, 33 (pp. 381–8) and the priest in I, 36 (p. 431), and inclining to a conservative viewpoint, while the latter intervenes with folksy proverbs in favour of young love and like marrying like and about the volatility of woman and fortune. However, these positions are not static. When the crisis comes, Don Quixote reacts with romantic impetuousness in support of the lovers, but after it is resolved, leans back towards prudent conformism, warning Basilio with wise maxims about the dangers of being the impecunious husband of a beautiful wife. Sancho, initially sympathetic to the lovers, is all for Camacho once he sniffs the preparations for the wedding banquet.

The episodic material in these chapters is not confined to the ethics of the love triangle. Don Quixote's pedantic scolding of Sancho for his diffuse proverbs leads to the question of the criteria of good linguistic usage, on which one of the student guides, the graduate, pronounces a judgement that reflects the nub of Cervantes's thinking on the subject (see above, p. 128). Then, a jibe from the other student about the graduate's abject Finals' result, caused by his passion for fencing, provokes an argument, leading to an impromptu fencing-bout, about whether fencing is or is not a geometrical science. The description of the scoffer's furiously ineffective swipes and lunges, and of the effortless ease with which the expert picks him off and reduces him to dishevelled exhaustion, is a comic masterpiece (see p. 142). Finally, Corchuelo flings away his foil in exasperation, embraces his friend and admits his error. With typical mock-scrupulousness, Cervantes relates that one of the accompanying peasants, a scribe, measured the distance of the throw and pronounced it to be three-quarters of a league, 'testimony which serves to make irrefutably plain art's superiority over brute force'. The comment, like Sancho's above-cited proverbs, anticipates the episode's dénouement.

So far the themes raised and the focus of attention on them have been benignly satiric. Yet, from the end of Chapter 19, the description of the preparations for the wedding and the accompanying festivities, including the provisions and cooking of the Gargantuan banquet, takes us into the mode of lyricism and picturesque folklore, with echoes of the pastoral wedding in Góngora's first *Soledad*, and of the descriptions of masques and dances in contemporary *relaciones* (written records of public festivals). Throughout Chapter 20, which is devoted to these scenes, we witness them alternately from the viewpoint of Don Quixote and Sancho. The gluttonous squire's interest is fixed on the sixty cooks at work, the roasting bullock spitted on an elm trunk, the infinite game and birds hanging from the trees, the innumerable wine-skins, the stacked ramparts of bread and cheeses, while Don Quixote's attention is focused on the sword dance, the peasants riding gaily bedecked mares, the allegorical masque danced by two quadrilles of nymphs who represent the factions of Love and Interest and mime the siege of the Castle of Modesty. The dénouement of the masque, in which Interest throws a purse full of coins at the castle's walls and knocks them down, leaving the maiden defenceless, elicits a pertinent comment by Don Quixote on the author's satiric wit.

The Cave of Montesinos adventure (*DQ* II, 23)

This adventure is central to Dulcinea's enchantment, which constitutes the main thematic axis of Part II. No other chapter in *Don Quixote* has attracted such a diversity of speculative interpretation as this one: the standpoints include the metaphysical, Freudian, mystic, autobiographical and Jungian–archetypal.[14] The reason for this is partly the intertextual suggestiveness of Don Quixote's story about his experience in the cave, with its links to prophetic dreams, visionary allegory and descents into the underworld, which traditionally convey a portentous significance. The intertextuality is also reflected in its nature as burlesque. It is, in the first place, a parody of chivalry books, resembling the type of incident that Don Quixote invents for the canon of Toledo's benefit in Part I, Chapter 50, to persuade him of the delights to be had from reading them. In it, the brave knight, challenged by a mysterious voice to attempt this adventure, plunges into a lake of seething pitch full of serpents to find himself in an idyllic fairyland, and, after being lavishly entertained in a gorgeous palace by beauteous maidens, learns from one of them that she is being held captive there in enchanted state. What happens next, we never know, since the story breaks off at that point. In devising the adventure in the cave, Cervantes was doubtless thinking, among other chivalric precedents,[15] of Chapter 99 of *Sergas de Esplandián* (Deeds of Esplandián), where the author falls into a deep well, and has a vision similar to Don Quixote's in various particulars. At the same time, his account of his experience is a burlesque of the ballad-tradition and Ovid's *Metamorphoses*,

---

[14] Some of the bibliographical references are given in Chapter 4, n. 13. The full panoply is surveyed by Aurora Egido in her notes on *DQ* II, 22–23 in vol. ii of Rico's edn (2004).

[15] See Clemencín's edn of *DQ* (1833), vol. iv, p. 429.

interweaving with these strands folkloric legends about the cave and the immediately surrounding region.

The possibilities of interpretation are multiplied still further by the fact that nowhere else in the novel is the unexplained arbitrariness of the hero's motivation more apparent. The predominant reading of it, deriving from Salvador de Madariaga (1948), is psychoanalytic, treating his oddly degraded vision of the chivalric world as a subconscious revelation of the self-doubt and disillusionment provoked in him by the enchantment of Dulcinea (see p. 107). However, this runs into the difficulty that Don Quixote's first reaction on emerging from this underworld is regret at being torn from a rapturously blissful vision, an attitude not easily reconciled with the repressed melancholy ascribed to him by the critics.

The visit to the cave is anticipated by his reference, near the end of his stay with Don Diego de Miranda (II, 18; p. 780), to the wonders popularly ascribed to it, including the mysterious origin of the seven lagoons of Ruidera. Here he alludes to folkloric legends that associated a ruined castle near the cave with Montesinos – a character featured in old Spanish ballads – and also linked the cave to those lagoons and to the partly subterranean river Guadiana, which was believed to flow through it. He is conducted there, after the dramatic dénouement of Camacho's wedding festivities, by Basilio's cousin, a comically pedantic scholar who is preparing a burlesque of Ovid's *Metamorphoses*, designed to explain the supernatural geneses of some notable, and notably mundane, Spanish landmarks. This project anticipates some aspects of Don Quixote's story. Once he arrives at the cavern's mouth and hacks away the brush blocking access to the interior, Sancho and the cousin lower him down by rope, and after half-an-hour haul him out again fast asleep. Once awakened, he gives his companions the following account of what happened to him.

After descending some way into the cave, he stopped in a kind of recess and fell asleep, then waking up, found himself in a wondrously beautiful meadow, and saw before him a splendid castle made of crystal. A venerable ancient with a long white beard came out to meet him, clad in an antiquated purple gown worn by people in mourning, a green scholar's sash, a black Milanese hat, and carrying a rosary with beads the size of middling ostrich eggs. He introduced himself as Montesinos, and, from this point on, treated Don Quixote with fulsome courtesy as a famous knight-errant whose arrival at the cave had been eagerly awaited by its enchanted inmates.

Any contemporary reader of *Don Quixote* would have been familiar with the pair of old ballads in which one of Charlemagne's knights, Durandarte, as he lies dying on the field of Roncesvalles, asks his cousin Montesinos to cut out his heart after he is dead and take it to his mistress Belerma. The ballads are notable for their pathetic and declamatory style, their gruesomeness and their curious punctiliousness about the small dagger used for the autopsy and the grave-digging. These features invite parody; and Cervantes was not the only writer who rose to the challenge. Another was the poet Góngora, in an aggressively demeaning sequel picturing Belerma's mourning. Cervantes's humour is gentler, evoking a wonderland like that of Lewis Carroll's Alice, characterised by a bizarre blend of surrealistic fantasy and prosaic banality. Its inhabitants, quite impervious to this oddity, behave with a mix of ingenuous matter-of-factness, solemnity and grief. Thus, if Montesinos's tearful compassion for the plight of his enchanted companions is consonant with his tragic and heroic background, his scholarly and sanctimonious get-up, tasteless particularity about how he performed the autopsy and pickled the excised organ, and amusing indelicacy about Belerma's biological functions reduce these associations to comic bathos. Throughout Don Quixote's story, a deflatingly factual or questioning note is juxtaposed with supernatural prodigy; and it is facetiously articulated by Sancho's sceptical comments on it, which become increasingly impertinent and derogatory as it unfolds.

Having invited Don Quixote to see the marvels of the castle, Montesinos leads him to a room where the corpse of Durandarte lies stretched on a marble sepulchre, mysteriously declaiming, with loud groans, the ballad-lines in which he makes his lugubrious last request. On hearing them, Montesinos informs his cousin in detail how he executed his dying wishes, going on to relate, in a pedestrian style that anticipates Teresa Panza's letter to her husband with the latest village and family news (II, 52; pp. 1059–60), that the enchanter Merlin has brought him and his mistress, kindred and friends to the cave in enchanted form, where they have remained immortal for the last five hundred years. He particularly mentions Durandarte's squire 'Guadiana' and Belerma's *dueña* 'Ruidera', together with her seven daughters and two nieces, metamorphosed by Merlin out of compassion for their grief into the subterranean river and the lagoons bearing those names. None of these personages are featured in the ballads; they are conjured up by Cervantes, or derived from popular lore, in order to parody Ovid's *Metamorphoses*, which relate the mythic transformations by which particular pools, trees and rivers of Ancient Greece came into being. When Montesinos presents Don Quixote to Durandarte as the possible agent of their deliverance from enchantment, the corpse surrealistically replies with a colloquial catchphrase expressive of shoulder-shrugging resignation: 'Y cuando así no sea ... paciencia y barajar' (p. 822) (and should that not be so, patience and shuffle the cards). This flattening and banal rejoinder and the lapse into colloquialism are typical of the chapter's humour.

After witnessing a ceremony of lamentation for the deceased Durandarte performed by a procession of white-turbaned damsels, in which the haggard figure of Belerma brings up the rear with the mummified heart in a linen cloth, Don Quixote sees a prodigy that is the culmination of all the previous ones: three peasant girls hopping and leaping like goats over delightful fields – the very same ones that he and Sancho saw outside El Toboso (pp. 825–6). Clearly the athletic leap with which 'Dulcinea' remounted her donkey in that encounter, vaulting onto its back from behind, has etched itself indelibly on Don Quixote's imagination, since he will refer to it on a later occasion. Montesinos informs him that they are three noble ladies recently brought to this place in enchanted form, and that he should not be surprised at their appearance, since many other legendary heroines, including Queen Guine-vere and her *dueña* Quintañona, celebrated by the ballad-tradition, are held in the cave in strange and diverse shapes (p. 826). Thus, Don Quixote receives answers to questions that have been nagging him since the incident outside El Toboso: whether his mistress was physically transformed by the spell, or whether it only affected his eyesight, what has become of her and how she is to be disenchanted. The reassuring news is that, though Dulcinea has been magically metamorphosed, she is in excellent company, since a host of heroes and heroines share her fate, and he is the destined agent of her deliverance.

Though, when he tries to speak to Dulcinea, she flees from him, emulating Dido's abrupt flight from Aeneas in the underworld, one of her companions approaches him and humbly asks him, on her mistress's behalf, for a loan of six *reales* on the pledge of a cotton petticoat. After expressing astonish-ment to Montesinos that even enchanted persons should suffer poverty, and being reassured that this predicament is universal and spares nobody, the knight apologises for not having more than four *reales* on him, and asks the emissary to convey to his mistress that he vows not to rest until he has disenchanted her. Taking the money, the lass performs, instead of a curtsey, a caper which lifts her two measuring rods into the air, thus proving to be a worthy companion to the vaulting Dulcinea (pp. 827–8). So Don Quixote's story ends, provoking a final display of derision from Sancho at this evidence of his madness.

In one respect, its motivation is clear: by means of it, the hero clarifies the disturbing mystery of Dulcinea's fate, and at the same time, persuades himself, as he has done on previous occasions (e.g. I, 15; p. 164), that the undignified mishaps inflicted upon him are the common lot of famous knights-errant. That, for him, is the point of the story. However, in another two respects, it is, or seems, more problematic. Critics have often remarked upon the apparently anomalous nature of its degraded and absurd features: the rosary with beads the size of ostrich eggs; the heart pickled in salt; Belerma's huge turban; Dulcinea's companion's extraordinary caper. Riley writes: 'These ridiculous details puncture the fabric of his chivalric vision ... They do not *fit*' (1986: 142). He goes on to resolve the anomaly with a psychoanalytic explanation: 'It is as if his unconscious mind which engendered them were mocking him with their incongruity.' This line of interpretation presupposes that Cervantes's conception of his hero's character is primarily determined by considerations of naturalness and consistency, rather than by his function in the system of burlesque by which the Dulcinea theme is governed. As we have seen, that system rests on recurrent grotesque contrasts between high and low, in which, up to this point in the novel, Don Quixote's imagination has supplied the first element, and Sancho the second. However, down there in the cave, Sancho is missing; and Don Quixote's fantasy has free rein. By a type of arbitrary transference of functions of which the Dulcinea theme offers numerous examples, Don Quixote discharges the role previously performed by Sancho, and turns the cave into a fit place for the Sanchopanzine Dulcinea to dwell in. Thus, he incorporates in his vision the uncouth, hopping, malodorous wenches previously presented to him by his squire, envisaging this henceforth as Dulcinea's enchanted state.

However, it is not exactly true to say that the debased features of Don Quixote's story represent a deviation from his previous behaviour. From the beginning he has ingenuously accepted that his chivalric world includes anomalously prosaic things, reconciling them to it by enchantment, as he does in the story of the cave or, very often, not questioning them at all. For example, his incongruously clerical portrait of Montesinos is consonant with his habit of giving familiar, idiosyncratic sketches of his literary idols: like that of bandy-legged, swarthy, red-bearded Roland (II, 1; p. 637). His and Montesinos's comic candour about the physical functions of enchanted persons repeats the tone and substance of the conversation that he had with Sancho when he was being transported home in an ox-cart (I, 48; p. 559). And it was he who drafted the commercially worded promissory note authorising his niece to make over three donkey foals to Sancho (I, 25; p. 287); it is not so extraordinary, then, that he should imagine Dulcinea's companion requesting a loan of petty cash on the pledge of a cotton petticoat.

In another respect, the problematic nature of his motivation is insoluble, and this concerns the story's sheer unlikelihood, for which Cervantes has no satisfactory explanation, pronouncing it as apocryphal in the chapter-heading of II, 23, and noting its deviation from the novel's habitual verisimilitude in the preamble to II, 24. With typical nonchalance, he passes the buck to his characters, including chronicler Benengeli, who begins Chapter 24 by dismissing the only two possibilities deemed available: either that the story is based on fact, or that Don Quixote invented it. Eventually the Moor lamely severs the Gordian knot by assuring us of the hero's death-bed recantation of it (p. 829). Benengeli's puzzlement is transmitted to Don Quixote, who consults oracles – Maese Pedro's monkey (II, 25; pp. 844–5), Don Antonio Moreno's enchanted head (II, 62; p. 1140) – to verify whether the experience in the cave was real or a dream. The fact that both oracles are fraudulent does nothing to inspire a sense of the seriousness of the problem. It is significant that neither the characters nor Cervantes seriously consider, let alone treat as self-evident, the idea that most critics and editors propose as the obvious explanation: that Don Quixote's story is based on a dream or hallucination. This is probably because dreams in Cervantes's works take the form of visions – things seen – rather than of lengthy dialogues in which characters interact with each other.

Two comparable cases prove the point. The first is the description by Periandro, the hero of *Persiles*, of a beautiful island paradise in which, among fruit-laden trees, crystal brooks, lush flowers and meadows, he saw two allegorical processions, one representing Sensuality and the other Chastity.[16] At first he gives to understand that this was a real experience, but lamely concludes his story by confessing that it was a dream. Apart from two brief, lapidary pronouncements by allegorical figures in the procession, there is no dialogue; essentially, this is, literally, a vision. The other relevant example, different from the one just cited, is the status of the dialogue between two dogs supposedly overheard by ensign Campuzano in *El coloquio de los perros* as he lies feverishly on his bed sweating off the effects of pox. Though his condition might seem positively to invite the suggestion that the dialogue is a dream or hallucination, the only possibilities that are seriously entertained in the discussion about its nature are either that he heard what he heard or that he invented it. Campuzano, like Don Quixote at the beginning of his story, maintains that he was in full possession of his faculties, but his critical reader, Peralta, dismisses this as nonsense and takes for granted that the *novela* is an invention.[17] If Campuzano gives ground somewhat, conceding that the story might be *sueño* rather than *verdad*, the word *sueño* is used in the weak sense of fantasy as opposed to truth, and in any case, seems a concession designed to get Peralta to read the manuscript. What Campuzano relates in his manuscript, unlike Periandro's dream, is pure dialogue; hence the different explanation given for it.

16 *Persiles y Sigismunda*, Book II, Chapter 15, ed. Schevill and Bonilla, vol. i, pp. 273–8.
17 *Novelas*, ed. García López, pp. 535–7; cf. p. 623.

The three narrators mentioned above, Don Quixote, Periandro and Campuzano, conform to a character-type who holds a certain fascination for Cervantes: the tall-story-teller, emblematic of his own impulse to fantasise. The impulse always ends by being reined in by critical common sense, but not before it has had some freedom to roam. The same tension is observable in his presentation of those three narrators. All relate incredible events as though they really witnessed them, and all are confronted by critical listeners who pour cold douches of scepticism on their stories. This helps to explain the attraction of Don Quixote's story of the cave for Cervantes: its combination of exuberant inventiveness and idiosyncratic daftness, which succeeds in bringing together folklore, the ballad-tradition, Ovid and the familiar geography of La Mancha in order to provide a new twist to the ongoing saga of Dulcinea's enchantment. He finds the surrender to free-wheeling fantasy irresistible, at once enchanting and absurd. With such a story, coming from such a character, who cares about credibility?

Master Peter's Puppet-Show (*DQ* II, 25–26)

Maese Pedro's puppet-show, and Don Quixote's violent intervention in it, are one of the most suggestive incidents in the novel. In his *Meditaciones del Quijote* (1914) (Meditations on *Don Quixote*), the philosopher Ortega y Gasset interpreted it as a symbol both of the reader's imaginative response to the reading of novels and of the constant challenge to transcend reality's constraints by which human life is confronted.[18] More specifically, George Haley (1965) treated it as an allegorical dramatisation of the interplay between the narrator, the story he creates, and its reader, hence as a microcosm of *Don Quixote* in the process of its composition and consumption. Whether Cervantes would have perceived quite such far-reaching implications in an adventure intended primarily for comic effect is doubtful; however, it certainly carries metafictional implications, including a light-hearted extension of the censure of the dramatic school of Lope de Vega in *Don Quixote* I, 48.

The episode (*DQ* II, 25–26) is interleaved between the first and second instalments of the affair of the two braying aldermen. After the first instalment is finished, Maese Pedro, dressed in chamoix leather and wearing a green patch over one side of his face, appears at the inn door asking for accommodation. The leather outfit was typically worn by low, disreputable characters, and the green patch suggests that this individual has something to hide. The

---

[18] In *Obras completas* (1961), vol. i, pp. 380–1.

innkeeper enthusiastically greets him, explaining to Don Quixote that this is a famous puppeteer who tours the region, exhibiting his puppet-theatre and giving proof of the extraordinary abilities of his soothsaying monkey, for each of whose answers to the questions put to it Maese Pedro charges two *reales*. With that income he has become rich, is excellent company, lives like a lord, talks enough for six and drinks enough for a dozen.

The image that is painted of this ambulant charlatan, who will later turn out to be none other than Ginés de Pasamonte, the most villainous of the liberated galley-slaves, responsible for the artful theft of Sancho's ass and now on the run from the law, is mysterious, colourful and considerably more genial than the vituperative references to this social type in the *Coloquio de los perros* and *El licenciado Vidriera*, though it coincides in substance with them. There is a passage in the dogs' colloquy where Berganza inveighs against puppeteers, peddlars and sellers of ballads, branding them as useless social parasites, 'sponges of wine and weevils of bread', whose ill-gotten gains are spent in taverns fuelling their bouts of drunkenness.[19] Maese Pedro's way of making a living, his criminal past and addiction to the bottle clearly align him with this class. The difference in tone between the portrayal in *Don Quixote* and the passages in the two *novelas* is explained by the difference in genre. The two *novelas* are moral/social satires, notably severe in their condemnation of delinquents, misfits and outcasts. *Don Quixote* is a comic novel, which presents Maese Pedro as an entertaining and intriguing personality, creating suspense about his identity and his, or his monkey's, mysterious clairvoyance. What is hidden by that green patch? What explains his or his monkey's instant identification of Don Quixote and Sancho without prior introduction? As in the case of other mysteries in *Don Quixote*, Cervantes delays clarification in order to arouse suspense and enhance the effect of surprise when we discover, after Maese Pedro's hurried, early morning departure from the inn, that the encounter with him was, though the two heroes never realised, a reunion with one of their principal tormentors in Part I. It is one of several surprising reunions in the second Part, and, like those with the disguised Sansón Carrasco (II, 12–15 and 64–65), leaves the heroes innocently unaware of its significance.

Though the portrayal of Maese Pedro differs in tone from the passage in the *Coloquio*, it does not lack a satiric dimension, which centres on the personage as an exploiter of popular credulity, whose fraudulent practices, like the oracular utterances of Don Antonio Moreno's enchanted head (*DQ*

---

[19] *Novelas*, ed. García López, p. 586, and for the passage in *El licenciado Vidriera*, pp. 291–2.

II, 62), are capable of misleading the vulgar. This is made clear by Don Quixote's suspicion, communicated to Sancho, that Maese Pedro must have made
a Faustian pact with Satan, since the monkey's clairvoyance, like the devil's,
is limited to past and present (II, 25; p. 843). The portrayal of this charlatan
thus links up with the recurrent satire of types of popular superstition in *Don
Quixote*. One of them, denounced by Don Quixote in the same passage, is the
practice of amateur astrology, as distinct from supposedly scientific astrology,
in whose validity, like other educated men of his age, Cervantes believed.
The other is the belief in omens (*DQ* II, 58; p. 1098; cf. II, 73; p. 1211).
Cervantes's debunking attitude towards such notions is generally reflected in
his ridicule of Don Quixote's belief in enchantment.

The main point of the encounter with Maese Pedro is the exhibition of his
puppet-theatre, which like the Cave of Montesinos story, furthers the burlesque
of chivalric ballads: in this case, the group-telling of Don Gaiferos's rescue
of his wife Melisendra from her captivity in the Moorish town of Sansueña,
traditionally identified with Zaragoza. Puppets were a popular form of entertainment in the Spanish Golden Age. The ambulant Italian showman would
carry his box called *mundinovi* from place to place, and for a few coins would
exhibit a marionette show usually based on Bible stories and accompanied by
a ballad narrative sung in a mixture of Spanish and Italian. The more elaborate theatres, like Maese Pedro's, were operated by the showman from within,
either by hand or mechanically, while an assistant armed with a pointer recited
the accompanying narrative. Puppets were a recurrent literary theme, particularly in the theatre (Varey, 1957: 189ff.). The most famous example is Cervantes's farce, *El retablo de las maravillas*, where the showmen purport to bring
to life sensational Old Testament stories like Samson destroying the temple
and the dance of the daughter of Herodias. None of the later treatments of the
subject matches Cervantes's indulgent attentiveness to the circumstances of
live performance: above all, to the style of the commentary and the intimate
rapport between performers and spectators, causing what happens on stage
both to reflect and excite their reactions. The show's air of being a slice of
country life casually served up, an exciting novelty that breaks the monotony
of evening at a wayside inn, is one of its many charms.

For the reader, its comic effect, and also its marvellous air of naturalness, result from the accompanying narrative of Maese Pedro's apprentice,
which combines a showman's histrionic tone with colloquial familiarity, and
incongruously adapts the heroic matter of the Carolingian ballads to the
folksy medium of representation (II, 26; pp. 846–50). He solemnly treats the
subject-matter as both prodigious and historical, interjects explanatory asides
for the audience's benefit, sporadically quotes familiar ballad lines, including,

with amusing topicality, a well-known couplet from one of Quevedo's *jácaras* (ballads of thieves' slang). Pointer in hand, he continually draws attention to the expressions, gestures and movements of the marionettes with injunctions to see and look, in a way that implies their exaggerated animation as in a child's cartoon strip. Notable examples of this are the touches added to the ballad story for theatrical effect: Melisendra's disgust when a lascivious Moor creeps up behind her and plants a smacking kiss on her lips, for which he is summarily sentenced to a public whipping, as though the action were set in a contemporary Spanish town; her undignified plight when her petticoat catches on the iron balcony railing and she is left dangling in mid-air, unable to reach her husband waiting below.

The critical interruptions of the boy's commentary by Don Quixote and Maese Pedro contribute to the bathos, reminding us at the same time of the informal intimacy of the performance, and of the dynamics of the interrelationship of the principal characters involved. This applies in particular to Don Quixote's pedantic protest at the anachronistic mention of alarm-bells ringing in Sansueña, which Maese Pedro cynically defends on the grounds that in contemporary theatres one routinely sees plays happily run their course despite being stuffed with anomalies. Here Cervantes indulges in another dig at the dramatic school of Lope de Vega, though the effect is milder than the hard-hitting censure in *DQ* I, 48, not just because of the comic impudence of Maese Pedro's justification but also because of the hint of self-mockery in Cervantes's jibe. Don Quixote's application of an Aristotelian sledgehammer to an art-form 'never heard of by Aristotle, nor mentioned by St Basil, nor grasped by Cicero' (prologue to *Don Quixote* Part I) makes us retrospectively see the priest's invective against the contemporary theatre as tarred with the same pedantic brush. Yet inopportune as Don Quixote's quibbles are here, they are obviously valid as a general principle of narrative, and the same goes for the other critical comments on the apprentice's performance, concerning irrelevance and affectation. By repeatedly measuring it against ideal norms, Cervantes implicitly makes it stand for prose narrative in general, just as Maese Pedro's self-defence casts him in the role of unscrupulous actor-manager and his show as a symbol of shoddy theatre.

The culmination of Don Quixote's critical interruptions, and in a way, his tribute to the vividness of the apprentice's narrative, is his violent intervention in the show in order to defend the fleeing lovers from the pursuing posse of Moors.[20] Here he confuses theatrical illusion with reality, and the fact that

---

20 This is primary evidence for those who argue (see n. 3 above) that Cervantes drafted or systematically modified his own text to take account of Avellaneda's well before the composi-

theatre is performed, and romances like *Amadís* are not, offers him a novel way of perpetrating his error. What follows is a scene of high comedy, burlesque demolition effected in the most literal way possible: the description of Don Quixote furiously raining sword-blows on the pasteboard Moorish army; the resulting scene of ruin; the haggling over the cost of repairs to the disfigured pasteboard heroes and heroines. The haggling follows Don Quixote's recognition of his error, which marks a further stage in his habitual recourse to the excuse of enchantment and his ongoing disillusionment. Though he assumes as usual that his persecutors put things in their true shapes before him, then capriciously change them into false ones, the conclusion that he draws is new: that the illusion that he suffered was the belief that the pasteboard Melisendra, Don Gaiferos, King Marsilio and Charlemagne were real persons. In Part I, he would have affirmed precisely the reverse. Yet, as always in the novel, the step forward towards sanity is soon followed by half a step back. Mid-way through the bargaining over Melisendra's missing nose he imagines her and her husband safe in France rejoicing in their escape and accuses Maese Pedro of extorting money from him under false pretences.

The Adventures in the Duke's Country Estate. Basic Premises. The Dulcinea Theme Revisited

Of the long series of chapters devoted to the heroes' stay in the Duke's country estate (II, 30–57, with a brief return visit in 69–70), the first three are a detailed fulfilment of part of Don Quixote's ideal sketch of how a knight-errant's career should typically unfold, improvised for Sancho's benefit in I, 21 (pp. 229–32) in order to explain the circumstances in which he and Sancho may expect their respective rewards. In this rose-tinted scenario, the imaginary knight, preceded by his fame, arrives at a royal court, is publicly acclaimed by the king's knights, embraced on the palace steps by the king himself, then led to a room where he is disarmed and robed in scarlet; he falls in love with the *infanta* at first sight and she with him, and so on and so forth, until he marries the *infanta* and inherits the kingdom, thus being in a position to ennoble the faithful squire and marry him off to the *infanta*'s damsel. 'And what of Dulcinea?' asked a great nineteenth-century editor of *Don Quixote*

tion of *DQ* II, 59. In Chapter 27 of the rival version, Don Quixote sees the rehearsal of a play by Lope de Vega, *El testimonio vengado* (The Libel Avenged), in which a queen is accused of adultery by her son. Incensed by the absence of a champion to defend her, he interrupts the performance by challenging the actor playing the part of the accuser to a duel, provoking general hilarity. Beyond a general similarity between this scene and Maese Pedro's puppet-show, I perceive no specific connections between them.

in a footnote to this story.[21] 'And what of Señora Panza?' we might also ask, with regard to Sancho's enthusiastic approval of the prospect dangled before him. The circumstances of Don Quixote's reception by the Duke and Duchess in Chapters 30–32 inclusive correspond pretty specifically to what befalls the imaginary 'Knight of the Sun' on his arrival at the royal palace. The correspondence becomes less precise thereafter, yet does not altogether break down: thus, Sancho gets his governorship, and the enamoured *infanta*'s role is performed from Chapter 48 onwards by Altisidora, one of the Duchess's damsels, whose feigned advances, contrary to the script outlined in I, 21, are chastely resisted by the hero out of loyalty to Dulcinea. The effect is comic, rather than exemplary, because of his ingenuous vanity in supposing himself irresistibly attractive to a swarm of love-lorn noble damsels.

The way in which the supposedly urbane Duke and his consort make fun of the two heroes by playing up to their cherished illusions has proved gratingly offensive to modern readers, who too hastily assume that Cervantes is on their side.[22] In part, he does indeed consider the behaviour of these aristocrats reprehensibly frivolous, the more so in view of their honourable status. By contrast, the practical jokes played on Quixote and Sancho by servants or other menials, less bound by considerations of decorum, elicit little adverse comment from him in the novel. Towards the very end of the series of hoaxes executed beneath the Duke's general supervision, though never directly by him, Benengeli condemns him and his wife as being as virtually as mad as their two victims for so persistently making fun of them (II, 70; p. 1193). A very similar opinion is voiced by the Duke's chaplain in the form of direct reprimands to him at the beginning of the series of pranks (II, 31–32; pp. 888, 891), by Tomé Cecial about the ridiculous backfiring of Sansón Carrasco's scheme to bring the third sally to an abrupt end (II, 15; p. 748), and by an anonymous Castillian bystander about the conduct towards Don Quixote of Don Antonio Moreno, the *hidalgo*'s host in Barcelona (II, 62; pp. 1136–7).

The sheer recurrence of this kind of censure shows that Cervantes considers it a likely reaction among some of his readers. However, this does not mean that he unreservedly endorses it. In all these cases, save the final judgement on the Duke and Duchess, the strictures are either contested or qualified by the surrounding context; and that judgement itself must be weighed against

---

21 See Clemencín's edn (1833), vol. ii, p. 185.

22 For bibliography, see Canavaggio's coverage of these chapters (n. 6 above). The conception of the Duke's palace as a cruel purgatory goes back to Schelling (Close, 1978: 36) and is perpetuated by Unamuno. See his comments on *DQ* II, 31 in *Vida de don Quijote y Sancho*. For more recent examples, Murillo (1988: 177ff.), Sullivan (1996), Márquez Villanueva (2006).

the numerous previous passages in which Cervantes comments on the wit and artistry of the burlesque hoaxes performed by the Duke's servants and the pleasure they afford to the spectators (see, e.g., II, 44; pp. 980–1). The contrast between the eulogies and the censures reflects a characteristic split in Cervantes's conception of his story (see above, p. 95); he rejoices in the deed but, in the end, tut-tuts disapprovingly at the doer. In Barcelona, soon after their departure from the Duke's estate, the two heroes are entertained in the house of Don Antonio Moreno, who proceeds to play jokes on them no less cruel – from a modern viewpoint – than the series just ended, since, in pretending to parade him before the admiring citizenry, he and his friends turn Don Quixote, unbeknown to him, into an object of public ridicule. Yet Cervantes explicitly commends this character, on introducing him to us in Chapter 62, as a 'caballero rico y discreto y amigo de holgarse a lo honesto y afable, porque no son burlas las que duelen, ni hay pasatiempos que valgan si son con daño de tercero' (p. 1132) (a rich, intelligent nobleman, who enjoyed decent and civilised amusements, for jokes aren't worth the name if they're harmful, nor are pastimes worthwhile if they injure third parties').[23] Probably this characterisation implies censure on the Duke and Duchess for having carried the joke too far. Yet at the same time it conveys emphatic endorsement of the validity in principle of such amusements. Cervantes would scarcely have commended the *burlas* (practical jokes) in advance as being so witty and true to chivalric style that they are 'the best adventures that this great history contains' (II, 34; p. 912), nor would he have devoted so much space to them, had he considered them a protracted sick joke and their authors as somewhat unhinged (see, e.g., Riley, 1986: 131).

Though we prefer to imagine otherwise, Cervantes was a man of his time, and in the society in which he lived it was considered acceptable fun to play practical jokes on persons marked by risible conceit, foolishness or other qualifying traits –pranks quite as humiliating, from our viewpoint, as those played on his two heroes.[24] Buffoons in particular, who frequented not just the courts of the Spanish monarchy but also the households of aristocrats, were regarded as fair game; and in the Duke's palace, Don Quixote and Sancho implicitly have that status, or something quite like it.[25] By the standards of that age, they are treated with relative humanity.

---

[23] On the chapters devoted to DQ's stay in Barcelona, see Joly (1991) and Redondo (2001).

[24] On the premises and practices relating to *burlas* Joly's book (1982) is seminal. See Redondo (1998: 191–203 and 453–73) and Iffland (1999: 439–70) on the carnivalesque origins and nature of the *burlas* in the Duke's palace.

[25] In Avellaneda's continuation of *Don Quixote* Part I, Sancho ends up as a buffoon in the

In effect, the *burlas* serve to bring the action of the novel firmly back onto the rails of chivalric parody, after it has pursued a somewhat meandering course in that respect from the beginning of Part II. Unlike other characters who have previously met the two heroes in this Part, the Duke and Duchess are solely interested in them as figures of fun,[26] and this does much to explain the unattractive image that they present to the modern reader. Nonetheless, Cervantes's choice of them as original movers and general supervisors of the *burlas* is intended to function as a guarantee that these will not overstep the boundaries of good taste. The distinction between their care not to offend the heroes openly and their servants' occasional horseplay is one sign of this; another is the emphatic contrast between them and their killjoy chaplain, introduced in II, 31 (p. 884) with a witheringly sarcastic string of 'Destos que ...' (one of those who ...), strikingly different from the benign or non-committal attitude that Cervantes habitually shows towards his created characters. These typecast him as a sanctimonious, narrow-minded cleric ignorant of the urbane behaviour appropriate to eminent aristocrats. He is set up as an embodiment of the severely moralistic opinion voiced by those of Cervantes's contemporaries who brand *Don Quixote*, the book, as idle frivolity.[27] We are told that he would scold the Duke and his consort for reading and enjoying it; and his aversion to it, as soon as he identifies Quixote and Sancho as its principal subjects, is disapprovingly extended to them, since their presence provides the noble readers with pretexts for extending their pleasure by more active means. His disapproval is expressed in an insulting tirade against Don Quixote, whom he treats as a deranged nitwit, wasting time in pursuit of chimerical adventures that would be better occupied in looking after his home and family (end of II, 31). The *hidalgo*'s just and measured censure of the timing and manner of this reproof, and his eloquently expressed if chimerical claims for the nobility of his profession highlight his adversary's

household of a nobleman. Luis Zapata, a former courtier, comments at the end of the sixteenth century: 'It is only right that buffoons, who make a practice of playing jokes on others, should themselves be subjected to them' (1859: 134).

26 We are told in passing that when the Duke and his wife read the manuscript in which Don Quixote wrote down his counsels of government to Sancho, they were astonished by his combination of madness and intelligent lucidity; however, in practice, their attention is almost exclusively given to the former at the expense of the latter (II, 44; p. 980).

27 Juan Valladares de Valdelomar refers to 'las ridículas y disparatadas fisgas de Don Quijote de la Mancha, que mayor la deja en las almas de los que lo leen, con el perdimiento de tiempo' (the ridiculous and absurd parody of Don Quijote de la Mancha, which leaves a bigger *mancha* (stain) on the souls who read it, by wasting their time). Cited in Herrero-García (1930: 345–55). The best-known example, though not unambiguous, occurs in Gracián's allegory of man's journey through life, *El Criticón* (1651–7), discussed below, pp. 228–29.

intemperate lack of charity and reinforce Cervantes's previous disparagement of his narrow-mindedness (beginning of II, 32). The Duke then mischie-
vously adds fuel to the flames of the busybody's fury by awarding Sancho
his promised island.

We learn that he and his wife are knowledgeable and appreciative readers
both of Benengeli's chronicle – that is, Part I – and of chivalry books, and
intend to fulfil to the letter Don Quixote's expectations about how a knight-
errant should be treated (II, 30; p. 877). So, with regard to outward appearances, they behave towards him with elaborate courtesy, carefully concealing
their leg-pulling motives and instructing their servants to do the same (II, 31;
p. 883); moreover, they show concern for his and Sancho's physical welfare,
and reward them both with a well-stuffed purse on their departure (II, 57).
There is a difference between the Duke's attitude and his wife's, since she,
by her teasing of Sancho and other ways, makes little attempt to maintain
his outward air of *gravitas*. For example, the caterwauling that interrupts
Don Quixote's nocturnal serenade is her idea (II, 46; p. 1000), though the
Duke approves it. No doubt Cervantes assumed that frivolity would be more
plausible as coming from her, a woman, than from him, a grandee. However,
in general, it is their servants, exceeding or disobeying their brief, who are
responsible for the pranks of a robustly farcical kind, such as the lathering
and shaving of Don Quixote's beard after the meal, and the attempt to inflict
the same treatment on Sancho with dirty washing-up water (II, 32; pp. 893–
4, 901–3).[28] Certainly, the ducal pair are capable of pettiness beneath their
station: the Duchess, by her farcical fury with her *dueña*'s indiscreet revelations to Don Quixote at the end of Chapter 48 (p. 1022; cf. p. 1035), and the
Duke, by his high-handed and ungenerous treatment of his servants (II, 48;
p. 1021; II, 66; p. 1172); but this just reveals them as averagely imperfect
human beings, not monsters of inhumanity.

Don Quixote, for his part, is so impressed by the courtesy and flattery
shown to him by these grandees that 'aquel fue el primer día que de todo en
todo conoció y creyó ser caballero andante verdadero, y no fantástico, vién-
dose tratar del mesmo modo que él había leído se trataban los tales caballeros
en los pasados siglos' (II, 31; p. 880) (That was the first day when he fully
and truly believed he was a real knight-errant, not a fantastic one, seeing

---

[28] Cervantes must surely have heard of an incident reported by Luis Zapata in the late
sixteenth century (1859: 114–15). Gentlemen of the count of Benavente's household play
precisely this practical joke on a Portuguese emissary whom they considered unworthy of the
ceremonious treatment bestowed on him. The count reacts in much the same way as the Duke
and Duchess do towards their servants; he laughs privately at the joke, but is furious with the
perpetrators, whom he chastises.

himself treated in the same way as knights-errant of past centuries had been). His vanity, and to a lesser extent Sancho's, is hugely tickled; he reciprocates the courtesy with extravagant obsequiousness, absurdly overdoes the honorific forms of address to his hosts and makes unavailing efforts to prevent Sancho, by his impertinence, from making him lose face. In this subversive role, Sancho is covertly aided and abetted by the Duchess (II, 30, 31, 33, 34), partly because of her delight in his interventions – strings of proverbs, ingenuous folly, plebeian tactlessness and indignity – and partly because of her enjoyment of Don Quixote's discomfiture.

The Dulcinea theme is central to Chapters 32, 33 and 35, which lay the basis for the burlesque comedy of her disenchantment, to be played out intermittently after the pair's departure from the Duke's estate. Chapter 32 is mainly taken up by Don Quixote's defence of his conception of his lady in reply to the ducal pair's needling questions about her physical appearance, her status and her very existence, an interrogation rather similar to the one to which he was subjected by the ironic Vivaldo on the way to Grisóstomo's funeral (I, 13; pp. 136–43), with two major differences. The first is that his hosts have read Part I, and are well aware of what was said about her there, particularly what the hero candidly revealed to Sancho in I, 25. They can thus put insinuating questions to him that probe the contradiction between his ideal image of her and the base reality. The second difference is that much water has flowed beneath the bridge since mid-Part I, including two major developments of which the interrogators are unaware: the hoax practised by Sancho on his master outside El Toboso, and the *hidalgo*'s vision of her in the Cave of Montesinos. Though he mentions, and laments, the malign way in which enchanters have persecuted him by transforming her into a country wench, thus interfering both with Sancho's perception of her during his embassy (I, 31) and his own encounter with her at the beginning of the third sally (II, 10), he knows nothing of Sancho's lies and trickery, and says nothing about his descent into the cave. These facts will be fully revealed to the Duchess by Sancho in the following chapter (II, 33) when he is closeted with her and her attendants during the siesta hour, disclosures that will rebound directly upon him (see above, p. 108).

Since Don Quixote, during the interrogation, reveals little that the reader does not already know about his attitude towards Dulcinea, what is its significance? The answer lies in the new perspective that it offers on his attitude towards her, both because of the noble status of the interrogators and his own air of living autonomy. This perspective includes two contrasted viewpoints. From the hero's, his interrogators are just the kind of audience he needs to impress, equivalent to the royal hosts of the 'Knight of the Sun' in the story that he improvised in I, 21; in this respect they are unlike ignorant, unthreatening Sancho, up to this point his principal confidant about his lady. Seen from our perspective, these are two *aficionados* of Cervantes's book who are confronted in the flesh by its celebrated subject, and are able to hear from his own lips his crazily sophistical justification of what is, for him, the most embarrassing aspect of his mania. It is as though a personality previously shown in two dimensions were now seen in three.

His answers to their questions repeat in substance what he said to Vivaldo in I, 13 and confessed to Sancho in I, 25 (pp. 282–5), though they phrase it more euphemistically and evasively, and augment it with his notions about being persecuted by enchanters. One answer in particular is often misunderstood. The Duchess, quoting back to him almost verbatim his words to Sancho, puts to him that Dulcinea is a pure invention, decked out in his fantasy with all the perfections appropriate to a heroine. To this he replies (II, 32; p. 897):

> En eso hay mucho que decir … Dios sabe si hay Dulcinea o no en el mundo, o si es fantástica o no es fantástica; y estas no son de las cosas cuya averiguación se ha de llevar hasta el cabo. Ni yo engendré ni parí a mi señora, puesto que la contemplo como conviene que sea una dama que contenga en sí las partes que puedan hacerla famosa en todas las del mundo,[29] como son hermosa sin tacha, grave sin soberbia, amorosa con honestidad, agradecida por cortés, cortés por bien criada, y, finalmente, alta por linaje, a causa que sobre la buena sangre resplandece y campea la hermosura con más grados de perfeción que en las hermosas humildemente nacidas.

> There is much to be said about that … God knows the truth about Dulcinea's existence, and whether she is a mere fantasy or not; and these aren't matters whose verification should be pursued to the very end. I neither engendered nor conceived my lady in my mind, though I contemplate her as befits one who has the attributes to merit world-wide fame, namely, beautiful without blemish, proud but not arrogant, loving yet modest, grateful because courteous, courteous because well-bred, and lastly, of high lineage, since beauty is more perfect and resplendent in a woman of noble blood than in one humbly born.

'Dios sabe si … o no' (God knows whether … or not) is *not* a confession of agnosticism, but a strong affirmation of the positive alternative of the two that are mentioned; it is used in exactly that sense at the end of I, 31 (p. 367).

---

[29] 'Puesto que' in Cervantes's works does not mean 'since', as in modern Spanish, but 'although'.

To interpret it as an expression of doubt makes no sense in the light of Don Quixote's subsequent vehement assertion that he has not invented his lady, nor of the Duchess's later pretence (p. 898) of having been convinced that Dulcinea is a living person. Essentially, what he now says to the Duchess repeats his original admission to Sancho that the flesh-and-blood Dulcinea was the peasant wench Aldonza Lorenzo, with the accompanying claim that her low birth was no impediment to his choice of her, since beauty and virtue, not rank, are the prime motives of love.[30] He also told Sancho that the invention of her rank was of no consequence 'since nobody is going to investigate it in order to confer on her the habit of a military order', an idea repeated in variant form in the above-quoted passage. The *hidalgo* rounds off this dinner-table discussion with an affectionately perceptive diagnosis of the blend of simplicity and shrewdness in his servant's character, hence of his aptitude for the governorship (p. 900). In the context of the teasing to which the hero has been subjected, including Sancho's mockery (II, 31; pp. 885–57), these remarks testify to his innocent generosity of spirit.

The *tête-à-tête* between the Duchess and Sancho in the following chapter (II, 33) is notable not only for the disclosures already mentioned, but also for the way in which it exemplifies the increasing depth and self-consciousness that his character acquires in Part II, and in another respect, for the mixture of amusement and fascination with which the Duchess, and by implication, contemporary readers, react to his personality and style.[31] Since the second aspect has already been discussed (pp. 156–58), I concentrate on the first. When Sancho confesses to the Duchess his belief that his master is quite mad, and tells her how he pulled the wool over his eyes about Dulcinea outside El Toboso, she puts it to him that his confession disqualifies him from the governorship. For how can someone knowingly follow and serve a madman without being even madder? Sancho's reply repeats the substance of what he said to his neighbour Tomé Cecial, disguised as the squire of the Knight of the Wood, who, in their nocturnal dialogue before the joust between their two masters on the following dawn, made veiled insinuations to him about the advisability of quitting his master and returning home. There, Sancho spoke touchingly of his affection for Don Quixote because of his well-intentioned lack of malice and trusting innocence, such that 'a child could make him believe it was night in the middle of day' (II, 13; p. 731), and declared that because of that, he could not bring himself to leave him, whatever follies he might commit.

---

30 See the discussion of this passage above, pp. 101–02.
31 For an alternative reading of this scene, see Canavaggio (1994).

Now, he repeats the previous affirmation of fidelity on grounds of principle as well as of affection. The declaration is nobly eloquent, all the more for its simplicity (II, 33; p. 906):

> Pero esta fue mi suerte y esta mi malandanza: no puedo más, seguirle tengo; somos de un mismo lugar, he comido su pan, quiérole bien, es agradecido, diome sus pollinos, y sobre todo, yo soy fiel, y así, es imposible que nos pueda apartar otro suceso que el de la pala y azadón.

> But this was my lot and my misfortune; I cannot do otherwise; I'm bound to him; we come from the same village, I've eaten his bread, I'm fond of him, he's grateful to me, he gave me his donkey foals,[32] and above all, I'm faithful, and so, nothing can separate us save the gravedigger's shovel.

How many forbearing husbands or wives, tied through affection and loyalty to their very imperfect spouses, have felt and said the same as Sancho, though rarely in words so worthy of being engraved in gold? His reply to the Duchess does not stop at that. Picking up her point about whether he is unfit to be a governor, he replies with a moral maturity that echoes what he previously said in conversation with Don Quixote and Sansón Carrasco (II, 4; p. 660). On both occasions he comes out with a string of proverbs that express two general themes: if I don't get one, it's not the end of the world, since I can still find contentment as plain Sancho Panza, and, power corrupts, so I might be better off without one. He will repeat these ideas again at the end of his master's counsels of government to him, eliciting warm praise for his discretion (II, 43; pp. 978–9). Clearly, by depicting from the beginning of Part II a more prudent, morally mature Sancho than the self-seeking simpleton of Part I,[33] Cervantes anticipates the astonishing sagacity that he will display in the governorship.

Three Major Hoaxes: the Disenchantment of Dulcinea; Countess Trifaldi's Petition; Sancho's Governorship

Several of the practical jokes to which the two heroes are subjected from Chapter 34 onwards – in particular, the encounter with Merlin and Dulcinea (II, 34–35), the ceremonial welcome to Don Quixote and Sancho by the citizens of Barcelona (II, 61–64), and the resuscitation of Altisidora (II, 69–70) – closely imitate the civic or palace festivities so popular in the Spain of that

---

[32] A reference to his master's gift of three donkey foals to him for undertaking the embassy to Dulcinea (I, 25; p. 287).

[33] See, e.g., I, 21: pp. 233–4; I, 29: p. 340; I, 50: p. 573.

age, in which its love of theatrical pageant was given free rein (Close, 1993). These included masques, tourneys, costumed processions, mock-battles, cavalcades and open-air plays with spectacular montage that were usually staged privately for a royal audience. It was natural for Cervantes to turn to them as a model, since soon after the publication of Part I, the figures of Don Quixote and Sancho were incorporated in festive processions, such as those which, in various Spanish towns in the period 1614–18, celebrated the beatification of St Teresa of Avila and the dogma of the Immaculate Conception.[34] Moreover, masques, tourneys and open-air plays were frequently based on chivalric themes, one of the favourites being the liberation of a damsel held captive in an enchanted castle. The festivities of which these spectacles formed part were usually designed to celebrate some notable event, like those just mentioned, or a royal entry into a town, and so are naturally adapted to the motives for the reception of Don Quixote in the Duke's palace and the city of Barcelona. These are, overtly, acclaim for a famous hero; implicitly, homage to him and Sancho as popular, mirth-provoking literary characters; and at a metafictional level, tribute to Cervantes's book.

The hoax featuring Merlin and Dulcinea, devised by the Duke's major-domo, also turns on the disenchantment of an enchanted maiden, i.e. Dulcinea, though its culmination, instead of liberating her, proposes the ridiculous penance imposed on Sancho as a condition for that to happen: 3300 lashes to be applied by himself to his own behind. Most of Chapter 35 is taken up by the diverting dialogue in which his vehement and indignant refusals to violate his own tender instinct for self-preservation are met, and finally overcome, by the implacable pressure put on him by the other parties: his master, the Duchess, the Duke, the enchanter Merlin, and Dulcinea, whose entreaty to him grotesquely contravenes all the norms of rhetoric, let alone virginal decorum, by its macabre and insulting tenor. Sancho's response to it is on a level with its indignity, since, in protesting at its vituperative tone, he suggests that bribery would have been a preferable alternative, and alleges that Dulcinea's pleas are all the more inopportune for coming so soon after the ripping of his green hunting costume: an accident during the boar-hunt that preceded the encounter with the enchanters' carts in the forest. The costume was a gift to him from the Duke and Duchess; and Sancho had the intention of selling it at the first opportunity.

The picturesque description of the hunt (II, 34; pp. 913–14), performed with the martial ardour and ritual pageantry proper to such aristocratic

---

[34] On this, see Rodríguez Marín (1911: 58–67).

pastimes, is conceived as an episode contrasting with the burlesque comedy of the ensuing confrontation with Merlin and other enchanters. Such scenes were a consecrated topic of epic and pastoral poetry; we find them in the *Aeneid* Book VII, Garcilaso's first and second eclogues and Góngora's first *Soledad* (Solitude). This one accords with the Duke's intention of giving his guest the impression of being treated with all the honours due to a famous knight-errant, since only princes and aristocrats could afford to keep a retinue of hunters, packs of hounds, and hawks, used for big game like deer and boar. It might seem, to those who vote for the Green Party in national elections, that in the post-hunt discussion about the merits of the sport, Sancho is to be understood as putting the more persuasive case (II, 34; pp. 915–16). In fact the arguments adduced by the Duke in favour of hunting: that it toughens the body, is a microcosm of warfare, and is exclusive to the nobility, had been standard topics in manuals of education of noblemen since the fifteenth century, and Sancho's arguments against, including the – to us – eminently reasonable objection to killing an animal that has done humans no harm, would have been seen as a symptom of his plebeian frivolity, motivated by the torn costume, that is, fear and covetousness. The alternative pastimes that he proposes to practise as governor, bowling and playing cards, would have been regarded as clinching confirmation of his unworthiness.

After the hunt, evening falls, and the forest is lit up by a fearsome *spectacle de son et de lumière*, so colossal that the whole forest seems ablaze; this sight is accompanied by Moorish ululations, a horrendous creaking as of the wheels of ox-carts, the sound of cornets and trumpets, the din of cavalry, artillery, and what seem to be several battles (II, 34; pp. 918–20). While Don Quixote and Sancho respectively react with fear and amazement to this prodigy, the contemporary reader, though not told of its cause by Cervantes, would have been inclined to interpret it as artificially contrived. For example, among the festivities staged to celebrate the visit of Philip III to the castle of Denia in 1599, there were several mock-battles such as the one described in this chapter, including a practical joke very similar to the one played on governor Sancho in Chapter 53; it consisted in putting the whole castle on a war footing to repel the supposed invasion by a Muslim armada. In contemporary reports of such war-games it was customary to extol, as Cervantes does, the convincing splendour of the incendiary and martial effects.[35] These are a prelude to a supernatural procession that now passes before the two heroes: a succession of ox-drawn carts draped in black with torches attached

---

[35] See Close (1993: 75), where numerous references are given.

to the oxen's horns, each driven by ugly devils and bearing a legendary enchanter. In the last cart, which is heralded by sweet music, pulled by a team of mules draped in white, and accompanied by musicians and penitents in white tunics, there is a raised throne on which are seated Dulcinea, in the guise of a beauteous maiden in a silvery spangled dress, and the enchanter Merlin, personified as Death, who intones the verses stipulating the conditions for Dulcinea's disenchantment (II, 35; pp. 920–3). The montage of this procession, notwithstanding its burlesque purpose, is impressively lavish, and corresponds to the kind of fabulous, allegorical spectacle typical of contemporary civic festivities, which imitated the style of Roman triumphs. The *relación* (official record) of those held in Valladolid to celebrate the birth of the future Philip IV on Good Friday, 1605 records the participation of an elaborately ornate cart like the one just described, allegorically representing the city and the mood of public rejoicing.[36] It has been attributed to Cervantes himself; whether or not he wrote it, he would almost certainly have witnessed the events that it describes, since he was living in the city at that time.

Another model for the *burlas* is the contemporary theatre, in which burlesque hoaxes, taken seriously by the ingenuous dupes, hence relished all the more by the audience, were commonplace. The *burla* featuring the Countess Trifaldi (II, 36–41), culminating in the ride on the wooden horse Clavileño, conforms partly to this type. Its obvious precursor in *Don Quixote* is Dorotea's pretence of being the Princess Micomicona, with the barber acting as her squire, disguised with a huge red beard consisting of the ox-tail borrowed from the innkeeper (I, 26 and 29–30). That hoax is basically similar to several in the contemporary *comedia*, including Act I of Cervantes's own comedy *La entretenida*,[37] where the deceiver, to achieve his purpose, usually marriage, assumes a false identity and tells the lady or her family a cock-and-bull story about being a wealthy, well-connected foreigner or *indiano* (native of the Latin American colonies) just arrived from a faraway land.[38] In the charade enacted by Dorotea and the barber, typical theatrical gags are repeated. His beard falls off and a hasty cover-up is needed; 'Micomicona' begins by forgetting her own name, then drops another clanger, claiming to have disembarked at the inland town of Osuna; her name, and others that she

---

[36] It is described and edited by Marín Cepeda (2005).

[37] See *Comedias y entremeses*, ed. Schevill and Bonilla, vol. iv, pp. 34–9.

[38] Other examples can be found in Lope de Vega's *El testigo contra sí* (The Witness Against Himself) and *El perro del hortelano* (The Dog in a Manger), and Tirso de Molina's *La villana de Vallecas* (The Country Girl from Vallecas).

cites, are deliberately absurd. The tale told by Trifaldi and her squire features beards even more prominently, these being frequent accessories of burlesque figures in public processions, as sign of a grotesque sex-change (Redondo, 1998: 425–6). This hoax is the longest and most elaborate of the series staged in the Duke's estate (II, 36–41 inclusive), and is emphatically commended for its wit (II, 36; p. 929).

It begins with the description of the entry of the squire Trifaldín – a masterpiece of burlesque funereal pomp – and his announcement of the arrival of his mistress, the Countess Trifaldi (II, 36). The description of Trifaldín is designed to suggest that this will be the quintessence of the solemnly doleful missions undertaken by afflicted *dueñas* in chivalry books. There are three such adventures in the fourth book of *Amadís de Gaula* (1508), fountainhead of Spanish chivalric romances. Everything about Trifaldín is extreme in size and quality: his gigantic stature, horrendously long white beard, pitch-black gown in which he is 'bemantled' rather than clad, and the sonorously booming voice in which he craves an audience with the famous knight-errant Don Quixote on behalf of his mistress, just arrived from the Oriental kingdom of Candaya. Unaware of the irony, the *hidalgo* triumphantly takes this request for aid by a distressed *dueña* as clinching refutation of the Duke's chaplain's derogatory opinion of the chivalric profession (end of Chapter 36).

It is necessary at this point to make a distinction between, on the one hand, the *dueña* and *escudero* (squire) as portrayed in chivalric literature, and, on the other, the *dueña de servicio* and *escudero* of real life, both familiar members of the staff of noble households of Cervantes's time. Ironic play between the pathetic or heroic associations attaching to the former pair, and the mundane ones relating to the latter, is basic to the comedy of the entire *burla*, and is actively embodied by the amusing altercations between Doña Rodríguez and Sancho, who comment on it as it unfolds. In chivalry books, the *dueña* is a noble matron, not necessarily a lady-in-waiting, who comes to the hero in great tribulation to seek his aid in righting a wrong that has been done to her, while the *escudero* is the knight's page, of noble birth, who after proving his mettle, can expect to be dubbed a knight himself. In real life, however, the terms signified something different.

The *dueña de servicio* (chaperone, lady-in-waiting) was a type mercilessly caricatured in the literature of that age, not least by Cervantes, as a middle-aged widow, clad in black gown and white coif, unattractive, sanctimonious, gossipy, malicious, meddlesome and immoral. The last attribute derived from her common reputation as a go-between. Rodríguez, one of Cervantes's finest minor creations, has the typical functions of her office: to boss the inferior servants and lend authority to her mistress by attending her on the *estrado* (the living-room dais designated for women's use) and elsewhere in the house. She has most of the stereotyped traits of her kind save the last, since she is basically honourable. She will come to the hero's bedroom in great distress in Chapter 48, in order to plead with him to restore her disgraced daughter's honour by getting the seducer to marry her, by force if necessary. In so doing she conforms to the *dueña* of chivalry books, revealing herself to be a prize nitwit, since she is the only one of the Duke's servants to take Don Quixote seriously. The traits that she reveals in that nocturnal interview – ingenuousness, grievance about her lack of status in the Duke's household, incredible pretensions of nobility, complex about her frumpish unattractiveness – are already evident in her exchanges with Sancho in I, 31, 33 and 37.

In real life, the *escudero* or squire was a sort of male version of the *dueña de servicio*, an aged retainer, honourable but poor, whose job was to accompany his mistress in the streets when she was out of the house. A white beard was the stereotyped sign of his venerability.[39] Of course, Sancho is not a real *escudero*, but supposedly an equivalent to the literary one. However, Sancho is a servant of plebeian status, hence can behave as though he were an *escudero* in his relation to Doña Rodríguez, especially in view of the traditional enmity between *escuderos* and *dueñas de servicio*, noted by Rodríguez in II, 37. From the moment when Sancho, soon after arrival at the Duke's estate, impertinently asks her to stable his ass (II, 31; p. 881), and gets a flea in his ear in reply, he loses no opportunity to make insulting and malicious comments to or about her. Though Trifaldín and his mistress, the Countess Trifaldi, are ostensibly the squire and *dueña* as portrayed in chivalry books, their function and character mark them, and particularly Trifaldi, as amusingly similar to their real-life counterparts.

The entry of Countess Trifaldi in Chapter 38 is marked by two splendid passages of verbal foolery (pp. 939–40). The first is the narrator's flippantly laborious and pedantic etymology of her name, 'Three-Skirted', derived from the three-pronged train of her skirt, each prong of which forms an acute angle held at its tip by a page. Cervantes/Benengeli illuminatingly adds that it was the custom in her country for its rulers to take names from the things in which the country most abounded: in that case, *lobos* (wolves), for which reason her proper name was *la condesa Lobuna*. Had Candaya teemed with *zorros* (foxes), she would naturally have been called *la condesa Zorruna*. However, proud of the geometrical novelty of her skirt, she went for Trifaldi. The explanation continues the mock-pedantic quibbling over the precise form of names

---

39 Cf. *La gitanilla*, in *Novelas*, ed. García López, p. 45; *Don Quijote* II, 48, p. 1019.

that began in the first chapter, and is a send-up of the cult of symbolically significant names given to characters in chivalry books. The other passage to which I referred is Trifaldi's plea for benevolent attention, where a rash of superlatives in 'ísimo', contaminate nouns and names – e.g. don Quijote de la Manchísima – and in Sancho's reply, not only do this in spades, but even corrupt the archaic form of the second-person plural subjunctive: *quisieridísimis* instead of *quisiéredes*.

The Duke's majordomo plays Trifaldi, and the centrepiece of the performance is the story of her and Princess Antonomasia's disgrace (II, 38–39; pp. 942–9). No previous burlesque tale in the novel matches this one in resources of style, plot and character; in effect, it is a full-blown parody of a *novela*, comparable, except for its tongue-in-cheek motive, with Doña Rodríguez's ingenuous story in II, 48. Though its fabulous setting and the ludicrous transformations inflicted on Trifaldi and the lovers by the cruel enchanter Malambruno mimic the enchantments of chivalric romances, the ill-fated love-affair that she relates is a comic mirror-image of those in which Cervantine heroines tend to find themselves involved. Thus, the clandestine affair of the *infanta* Antonomasia (*antonomasia*: a person's common epithet, and by extension, analogy), for whose virtue Trifaldi was supposedly responsible, is reminiscent of *El celoso extremeño*, particularly in respect of the roles of Clavijo and Trifaldi. Antonomasia, obviously, is of royal blood, and her seducer, Don Clavijo (*clavija*: wooden peg, here, with phallic connotations), is a gentleman of no great standing in the court. Clavijo, by virtue of his talents as a poet, dancer and maker of bird-cages, reminds us of Loaysa, the good-for-nothing, guitar-playing charmer of that *novela*, who gains access to the naïve wife of the jealous old husband by promising to sleep with her chaperone, while Trifaldi reminds us strongly of the lewd, hypocritical *dueña* Marialonso, including her taste for Spanish pop songs and dances, the jollier and more wanton the better.

The narratives of Cervantes's romantic heroines make a strong pitch at our pity; when Dorotea finishes hers, her male audience melts in sympathy and compassion (see the beginning of *DQ* I, 29). Trifaldi's story ostensibly has the same purpose, sustaining a passionate tone of self-pity and self-recrimination, yet ruins the effect by shameless disclosures and lapses into vulgarity: an incongruity similar to the anachronistic conjunction of a fabulous setting with the popular folklore of Cervantes's Spain. Like the narrator of *El curioso impertinente*, she conveys the idea of yielding to seduction by the allegory of surrendering a castle (cf. I, 34; p. 396), yet whereas in the *novela* this imagery is fittingly accompanied by sententious, sorrowful disapproval, its decorous purpose is short-circuited in Trifaldi's story by the scandalous revelation that Clavijo's charms would have been of no avail 'para rendir la fortaleza de *mi niña*, si el *ladrón desuellacaras* no usara del remedio de rendirme a mí primero' (p. 943) (to overthrow the fortress of my girl's virtue, had the thieving scoundrel not got round the difficulty by laying me low first). The italicised expressions are typical of the sudden lurches into low familiarity. Like Dorotea and umpteen *comedia* heroines who extract a solemn promise of marriage from their seducers before yielding to them (*DQ* I, 28; pp. 325–56), Trifaldi derives self-justification from having obtained a similar vow from Don Clavijo on Antonomasia's behalf before letting him have his way with her 'for, though a sinner, I wouldn't allow him to come as far as the soles of her shoes except as her husband. No, indeed! Marriage comes before anything else in any affair of this kind that I have a hand in' (p. 945). The implication that she is a practised go-between imbues this claim with a jolly cynicism. Trifaldi's narrative closes with a grandiose, self-pitying peroration, which echoes the well-worn topics of funeral lamentation and imprecations against cruel fortune, applying them ludicrously to what, before that point, has been mysteriously concealed behind her and her companions' face-masks. Putting them aside, they reveal that Malambruno's fiendish master-stroke has consisted in inflicting on their faces an excrescence of multi-coloured hair, humiliating trans-sexual equivalent to the squire's trademark beard. At the same time, he has transformed Antonomasia into a bronze monkey and Clavijo into the statue of a crocodile of unknown metal.[40]

In accordance with the tradition of chivalric masques, the story's resolution sets the enchanted victims free from their spells. Don Quixote learns from Trifaldi that when she finds her predestined champion – whoever it may be – a magic flying horse, controlled by a wooden peg in its forehead, will be provided to take him the 3227 leagues to the kingdom of Candaya, there to perform the necessary deed. The horse is identified as the one on which Pierres of Provence abducted the fair Maguelone, mentioned by Don Quixote himself in I, 49, and is eventually brought into the garden of the palace by four savages (beginning of Chapter 41). During the flight, our attention is fixed on the comically innocent reactions of the two heroes, sitting blindfold on the immobile wooden horse, to the sensation of supposedly flying through the upper regions of the air, while servants with bellows and lighted tapers contribute the required illusory effects. It is a practical joke much to the taste of the Spanish Baroque, with its delight in elaborate stage machinery. The montage was especially spectacular in palace plays on chivalric themes,

---

[40] Cf. the enchantments in chivalry books mentioned in Clemencín's edn of *DQ*, vols iv, p. 429, and v, p. 289.

like *El caballero del sol* (1617) (Knight of the Sun) and *La gloria de Niquea* (Niquea's Glory) (1622): the performances included allegorical figures descending on clouds, storms with thunder and lightning, fire-breathing giants, characters mounted on flying dragons. Before and after the flight, the focus falls primarily on Sancho: first, on his dismay when he discovers that his participation in the airborne continental journey is unavoidable; second, on the lies that he tells about what he saw in the heavens when he suppos-edly lifted his blindfold. His master's reaction to them is reminiscent of the scepticism expressed by Benengeli and Sancho about the story of the Cave of Montesinos, and the implications of his Parthian shot to Sancho at the end of Chapter 41 are devastating: 'Since you want to be believed about what you saw in the sky, I want you to believe me about what I saw in the cave of Montesinos. I say no more.' By offering to exchange his acquiescence in Sancho's transparent fibs for Sancho's acquiescence in that story, he puts both on the same footing. This would imply that the whole edifice of his love for Dulcinea is a fake. Typically, Cervantes does not say whether we should draw that inference or not.

Sancho's governorship does not take place on an island, as he ingenu-ously believes even after he has left it (II, 54; pp. 1074–5), but in a walled town called Barataria within the Duke's feudal domains. During his brief tenure of office he remains innocently unaware that he is merely a puppet governor manipulated by his underlings, the Duke's servants, and that the cases submitted to him are mostly either contrived tests or practical jokes. His tormentor-in-chief is the *opera bufa* figure of Dr Pedro Recio Tirteafuera, related not just to the pedants and doctors of the comic stage but also to the miserly tutors of the picaresque novel, armed with pious sophisms about the benefits of a starvation diet to body and soul. Aristocrats and princes in that age often had fun with buffoons by pretending to honour them as dignitaries; and the Duke's appointment of Sancho to a governorship conforms to this practice. Velázquez's series of paintings of palace fools and jesters offers examples of this; it includes one in the guise of Don Juan de Austria, victor of Lepanto. Avellaneda, in describing the tourney in Zaragoza in which Don Quixote takes part, alludes to the normality of letting fools participate as though they were competitors on a par with the other knights.[41] Luis Zapata, in his *Miscelánea*, relates a practical joke that was played by Duke Cosme de Medici of Florence on a merry doctor. It consisted in inviting him to sit on a

---

[41] See *Don Quijote de la Mancha*, ed. Riquer, Chapter 11, vol. i, p. 207.

throne beneath a brocade canopy, which was suddenly hoisted aloft by ropes, exposing the victim to a pelting with fruit. The treatment of Sancho in Barataria not only corresponds to customs like these, but also to the burlesque enthronements and tribunals that were a regular feature of Carnival merry-making.[42]

The reason why Sancho's achievement of his seemingly impossible ambition brings this theme to a perfect and astonishing culmination is because his performance, contrary to the expectations aroused by the above-mentioned precedents, belies everyone's expectations that he will make a ridiculous hash of the job. This is frankly acknowledged by the Duke's majordomo, chief impresario of the hoax (II, 49; p. 1025). Despite the ingenuousness of his previous ambitions, and the fantasies about feathering his own nest that accompanied them in Part I, he shows inspired acumen in solving the tests of judicial sagacity brought before him and robust good sense in other respects, leaving Barataria with empty pockets and a zealous schedule of reforms behind him. Cervantes has a typically Spanish suspicion of the corruption and Byzantine intricacy of the law and of public administration. His ideal of the good ruler is reflected in Sancho's straight-from-the-hip, no-nonsense, equitable settlement of cases and his zealous stamping out of vagabondage and racketeering.[43] This is an anti-Machiavellian, simplistic and conservative ideal, which treats integrity as the ruler's cardinal virtue, and reflects the age's concept of kingship as a pastoral, Christ-like tutelage.[44] Don Quixote's precepts of government (II, 42–43), with their ethical and non-political bias, rooted in a long tradition of 'mirrors of princes' going back to the Middle Ages, express it clearly.

Had Cervantes made Sancho, as governor, conform to predictable stereotype, the result would have been equivalent to the nitwitted mayors of his and his epoch's comic theatre. One of his farces, *La elección de los alcaldes de Daganzo*, which, as the title indicates, is about the election for the office of mayor in a small village, gives a clue as to why he did not go down this path. The first three candidates are as frivolous in their pretensions as the Sancho of Part I. The fourth is made of worthier stuff; honest, well-intentioned and conscious of his place in the social hierarchy. He chides an insubordinate sacristan with this forelock-tugging sentiment, repeated by Cervantes on

---

[42] Redondo (1998: 453–73, especially 461, 463). This chapter of his book, and a previous one (191–203), are relevant to Sancho's governorship in general.

[43] See Chapter 3, n. 49.

[44] Cf. McKendrick (2000: 152–4). The ideal is summed up in the title of Quevedo's political treatise *Política de Dios* (1626) (God's Politics), designed for the instruction of ministers.

other occasions: 'Dexa a los que gobiernan, que ellos saben / lo que han de hacer mejor que no nosotros; / si fueren malos, ruega por su enmienda; / si buenos, porque Dios no nos los quite' (Leave those in authority over us alone, for they know their obligations better than we do; if they are bad, pray for their reform; if good, for their preservation).[45] Sancho exhibits similar virtues on a grander scale. His supreme act of wisdom, despite all the good things that he has done prior to it, consists in abdicating: that is, knowing his place.

So, Cervantes took the subject of government too seriously to treat Sancho's tenure of office in a merely frivolous way. The seriousness is reflected in his sporadic, unexpected displays of moral maturity when the subject is broached in Part II (II, 4, 33, 42–43), and in the authority, gravity and worldly wisdom that he miraculously assumes in taking up office and to some extent relinquishes with it. Yet the novel's light tone, Sancho's inherent comicality, and, above all, Cervantes's ingrained sense of the inevitability of the established order and reticence about political matters inevitably channel the expression of his ideals of government in a form that blends seriousness with farce, fantasy and legend, and avoids the direct critique of contemporary institutions.

The factors adduced half-jokingly by Cervantes to explain the prodigious transformation of naïve, impertinent, ignorant, jocose Sancho into a paragon of judicial wisdom hardly suffice to explain it. They are: the stimulus of office, his master's precepts, divine inspiration, Sancho's innate potential.[46] However, in a character so much larger than life, in whom arbitrary reversals of behaviour are normal, the inverisimilitude scarcely matters. Cervantes implies by his manner of presentation that the transformation belongs to the realm of fantasy. The cases brought for the governor's adjudication include traditional riddles and riddling jests (II, 45 and 47), a marriage-suit that is mainly a pretext for the burlesque portrait of the hideous bride-to-be (II, 47), the romantic story of a teenage escapade (II, 49) – hardly ones that might exercise a governor in real life. The two which most nearly merit the name – the judgement of the gold coins concealed in the staff and of the false accusation of rape (II, 45) – are derived from devotional literature; both cast Sancho in a role defined by the medieval exemplum tradition: the wise judge who by his acumen saves an innocent man from being wronged by a clever fraud.

---

[45] *Comedias y entremeses*, ed. Schevill and Bonilla, vol. iv, p. 56. For references to other passages where Cervantes expresses this attitude, Close (2000: 30).

[46] See *DQ* II, 45: p. 996; II, 49: p. 1023; II, 51: p. 1047.

Yet despite the episode's unreality, the governor's conduct maintains a realistic consistency with the Sancho we know, and this is illustrated by his reaction to the mock-assault on the 'island' (II, 53), designed by the perpetrators to hasten his departure. They succeed, yet the manner of his leaving makes a dignified contrast with their provocation of it, and gives depth and ambivalence to the comedy. Cervantes's description of how the alarm is sounded in the town at dead of night with bells, shouting, trumpets and drums builds up an impressive atmosphere of crisis and is meant to provoke wonderment. The mood changes to hilarity with the description of how the governor, strapped in his monstrous carapace of armour, is trampled underfoot. The relish with which Cervantes switches his vivid and degrading analogies suggests that he shares the merrymakers' glee, and his allusion to Sancho's terror underline the joke's efficacy (II, 53; p. 1063):

> Quedó como galápago, encerrado y cubierto con sus conchas, o como medio tocino metido entre dos artesas, o bien así como barca que da al través en la arena; y no por verle caído aquella gente burladora le tuvieron compasión alguna, antes, apagando las antorchas, tornaron a reforzar las voces y a reiterar el '¡arma!' con tan gran priesa, pasando por encima del pobre Sancho, dándole infinitas cuchilladas sobre los paveses, que si él no se recogiera y encogiera metienda la cabeza entre los paveses, lo pasara muy mal el pobre gobernador.

> There he was a like a turtle enclosed and covered by its shell, or like a half side of ham pressed between two tubs, or just like a boat keeled over on the sand; and not a scap of pity did the sight of his fallen body cause those merry persons. Rather, extinguishing their torches, they renewed their cries more loudly, urgently reiterating 'To arms!' and trampling on poor Sancho's body, with numberless stabs upon those shields, so much so that if he had not huddled and tucked his head between them it would have gone badly for the poor governor.

The pity implied by the last part of the passage accords with Cervantes's attitude to the sequel, which, without forsaking humour, does justice to the gravity of Sancho's decision to quit. The burlesque euphoria of the pranksters' acclaim for his valour contrasts with his dignified rejection of it: 'Enemies I've conquered? Pull the other one! I'm not interested in sharing out spoils, just in asking some friend, if I have one, to give me a drop of wine, because I'm parched, and wipe off this sweat, because I'm dripping' (p. 1064). The description of his subsequent actions, reflecting his inward resolve, have a sober and factual simplicity. This, together with the awed curiosity of the bystanders, enhances their significance: 'They wiped him, brought him the wine, undid his shields and he sat on his bed and fainted from the fear, the shock, and the fatigue … He asked what time it was, and they answered that it was already dawn. He fell silent and, saying no more, began to dress, buried in silence, with everybody looking at him and wondering what was the purpose of his dressing so fast.' Then he goes to the stable, embraces and kisses his ass, and tearfully addresses to him – symbol of the homely things that he forsook to become governor – the preamble of his abdication speech.

The speech itself is an impressive expression of pent-up disillusionment and mature resolve (p. 1065):

> Abrid camino, señores míos, y dejadme volver a mi antigua libertad: dejadme que vaya a buscar la vida pasada, para que me resucite de esta muerte presente. Yo no nací para ser gobernador ni para defender ínsulas ni ciudades de los enemigos que quisieren acometerlas. Mejor se me entiende a mí de arar y cavar, podar y ensarmentar las viñas, que de dar leyes ni de defender provincias ni reinos.

> Make way, sirs, and let me return to my former liberty; let me return to my former life so that I may be resurrected from this present death. I wasn't born to be governor, nor to defend islands or cities from their attackers. I know more about ploughing and digging, pruning vines and trussing them, than about making laws or defending provinces and kingdoms.

Don Quixote too, on leaving the Duke's palace (II, 58; p. 1094), will contrast with heartfelt relief the prospect of enjoying a crust of bread in freedom with the servitude of being indebted for *haute cuisine* to a lordly patron. For Cervantes, the recovery of liberty was an experience fraught with personal significance. Yet Sancho's speech, though it turns on the time-honoured, literary topics of Country versus Court, is humorously in character. He employs analogies, proverbs and a down-to-earth register bristling with peasant stubbornness and no-nonsense directness, reminiscent of Teresa's style (see pp. 177–78): e.g. 'Más quiero hartarme de gazpachos que estar sujeto a un médico impertinente que me mate de hambre' (p. 1064) (I'd rather stuff myself with gazpacho than be subject to an impertinent doctor who starves me to death),[47] and this superb punch line: 'Cada oveja con su pareja, y nadie tienda más la pierna de cuanto fuere larga la sábana, y déjenme pasar, que se me hace tarde' (p. 1066) (Each sheep with its mate, and don't stick your leg out further than the sheet allows, and let me pass, for it's getting late). It is Sancho's finest hour.

---

[47] The term *gazpacho* refers here to a hot rustic soup made with bread and meat, not to the modern blend of tomatoes and other vegetables, served cold.

The memorability of the episode of the governorship arises, among other factors, from Cervantes's knack of seamless and unobtrusive 'quotation'. The traditional precedents of Sancho's wisdom, apart from ones already mentioned, include the traditional mystique about the inspired insights granted to the fool, legendary examples of peasants such as the Visigothic king Wamba who acquit themselves well as rulers, the wise rustics of Lope de Vega's theatre who prefer their simple lot to the cares of court. Implicit in the episode as a whole is a complex of critical or reformist ideas about justice, government, and the requisites of honour and social advancement.[48] Implicit is the keyword here. The zeal, integrity and competence shown by Sancho, an ignorant peasant, point an accusing finger at notoriously corrupt rulers on various levels in contemporary Spain, from governors of small feudal domains like Barataria to the king's ministers. One cannot tell which of these is intended since Cervantes doesn't say. The universality of the episode's symbolism is due precisely to his refusal to tie it to a specific time and place.

---

[48] On the concept of Utopia in Cervantes with reference to the governorship see Maravall (1976: 216–28) and Scaramuzza Vidoni (1998: 82–90).

7

Don Quixote and the Modern Novel

The Classical Age

In the Introduction to this book, I drew attention to the profound repercussions of *Don Quixote* on modern culture, in spheres ranging from classical music to strip cartoons and from highbrow literature to commercial marketing (Riley, 1988; Canavaggio, 2005). As one might expect, the most important area in which one perceives this influence is the modern novel. Cervantes's masterpiece contributed significantly to the birth of the genre in the first half of the eighteenth century, and ever since then, has been a model for general theories of it as well as an inspiration to novelists. In this final chapter I want to examine the historical evolution of this process, paying particular attention to its theoretical aspect; and for this purpose, it is necessary to take some account of the changes in the interpretation and appreciation of *Don Quixote* and the advances in scholarly investigation of it, since they are linked to both creation and theory.

From a modern perspective, the prevailing conception of *Don Quixote* in seventeenth-century Spain appears depressingly simplistic and limited. The same is true, at least until the last forty years of the century, in contemporary France and England, where, thanks to the translations by Shelton, Oudin and Rosset, which appeared in the decade 1610–20, Cervantes's novel was well known.[1] In the case of Spain, which may stand as an example for the two near neighbours, the innumerable references to it in literature and life reduce the main characters and the action to impressionistic stereotypes: Don Quixote the self-appointed champion of damsels-in-distress and avenger of other people's wrongs, the worshipper of a sublimely idealised Dulcinea mouthing quaint chivalric archaisms, accompanied by greedy, lazy, cowardly, money-grubbing Sancho. Inseparably associated with this pair are their two mounts: spindly Rocinante, and Sancho's docile, beloved donkey (Herrero-García,

---

[1] On *DQ*'s fortunes in France and England, apart from Canavaggio (2005), see Bardon (1931), Knowles (1941), Wilson (1948), Paulson (1998).

1930: 353–420). However, we need to bear in mind that these impressions consist of droll remarks made by characters in plays, representations of the two heroes in festival processions, satiric caricatures in lampoons. They are far from being considered literary criticism. In fact, we seldom find that kind of criticism of outstanding Spanish literature of the age, other than in contexts that oblige the commentators to give close attention to it: such as eulogistic prefaces, exegeses of poems, translations, or which discuss it for linguistic or educational reasons. It is in places such as these, and also in the indispensable *Agudeza y arte de ingenio* (1648) (The Art of Wit) by Baltasar Gracián, who quotes literary examples abundantly to illustrate his theory of wit, that we find judgements, though often not very far developed, on the acknowledged Spanish classics: Garcilaso, Góngora, Quevedo, Alemán, *La Celestina*, Lope de Vega, Calderón. It would have occurred to few Spaniards to include the author of *Don Quixote* in that list.

This is because they regarded Cervantes, in that capacity, as a superior kind of P.G. Wodehouse: immensely funny, enjoyable and popular, creator of legendary characters, a master story-teller, urbane, edifying, admirably inventive, but perhaps a little lightweight. *Don Quixote* didn't quite have what it takes to raise a comic work to classic status: moral substance, wit (in the seventeenth-century sense), gravity mixed with mirth. These were the reasons for the high estimation accorded to Alemán's *Guzmán de Alfarache* and Fernando de Rojas's *La Celestina*, comparable to *Don Quixote* by virtue of being popular comic works in prose.[2] The brilliant comicality of Cervantes's parody of chivalry books, evident to all readers since all were thoroughly familiar with the genre, seems to have blinded them to the latent seriousness and profundity of his story; and his own insistence in the prologue to Part I on its risibility and avoidance of didactic pretensions scarcely helped them to think otherwise. However, attitudes towards *Don Quixote* are characterised by a certain ambivalence. It is typified by Baltasar Gracián, who, in his caustic, bleak and wittily sententious allegory of man's pilgrimage through life, *El Criticón* (1651–7), Part II, Crisi i, forbids the reading of *Don Quixote* to the man of mature judgement, along with other emblems of youthful frivolity, such as being French, favouring green costume, wearing lockets with the lady's image, playing the guitar. However, in the same work, Gracián continually and quietly adapts situations from that source, and in many ways models his two pilgrims, the impulsive Andrenio and the judicious Critilo, on

---

    [2] See, for example, Gracián's discussion of these two works in discourse 56 of his *Agudeza*.

Cervantes's pair (Close, 2004a). Gracián the moralist denies transcendence to *Don Quixote*; Gracián the creative writer contradicts him.

In general, then, Spaniards of the Baroque period tend to focus on what are, for us, the most obvious and least interesting aspects of *Don Quixote*, privileging in the process the comically abrasive first Part over its more subtle and nuanced sequel. The primary example is Avellaneda's apocryphal continuation. It treats Don Quixote's adventures as unmitigatedly ridiculous, and obliterates all the nuances that give depth and complexity to Cervantes's novel, such as the continuous transitions from comedy to romance, the blending of madness with lucidity, the psychological finesse of the portrayal of the two heroes and its occasional pathos. This is illustrated by Avellaneda's version of Sancho, which mechanically repeats and coarsely accentuates the model's traits, making laborious allusions to farting and shit, uttering rustic oaths or garbled imprecations to the saints, and so on. For more sensitive interpretations of *Don Quixote* by seventeenth-century Spaniards, we must turn to its indirect recreations in the theatre of Tirso de Molina and Calderón, both warm admirers of it, or, despite his disparaging comments on its shallow frivolity, to Gracián's *El Criticón*.

Before leaving the Spanish seventeenth century, we need to ask one question about it. Why, despite *Don Quixote*'s immense popularity, was there no more than one direct imitation of it in this period: that is, Avellaneda's? I mean, works of prose-fiction that apply Cervantes's method of parody either to chivalric romances or to some other form of escapist romance, like pastoral novels.[3] This, to us, puzzling absence is perpetuated in some ways in eighteenth-century Spain, even though it produced a number of continuations or imitations of *Don Quixote*. These tend to harness its example to the characteristic objective of that century's prose-narrative: the didactic satire of social abuses, rather than the parody of other novels. Also, they are deficient in narrative interest and insufferably moralising.[4] The most meritorious

---

[3] Neither Tirso de Molina's comedy *La fingida Arcadia* (1621) (Feigned Arcadia) nor Salas Barbadillo's satiric novel *El caballero puntual* (1614, 1619) (The Proper Gentleman) are direct imitations in this sense, though both are significantly influenced by *Don Quixote*. In Tirso's play the satire of pastoral fiction is benign, since the heroine's obsessive enthusiasm for imitating Lope de Vega's pastoral romance *Arcadia* is presented partly as a quirkish – though not ridiculous – idiosyncrasy, and partly as a trick to keep her unwanted suitors at bay. In Salas Barbadillo's novel, the protagonist's mad urge to pose as a member of Madrid high society, though modelled on Don Quixote's mania, is intended as a satire on social climbers, not on a literary genre.

[4] An example is Ribero y Larrea's *Don Pelayo Infanzón de la Vega, Quijote de la Cantabria* (1792). On *DQ* in eighteenth-century Spain, see Aguilar Piñal (1983) and Barrero Pérez (1986).

works of prose narrative, like Torres Villarroel's autobiography (1743), either
do not imitate Cervantes, or else, like father José de Isla's *Fray Gerundio
de Campazas* (1758), which ridicules the extravagances of pulpit oratory,
only do so in part. The artistic poverty of the imitations is largely owing to
the persistence in Spain of the conception of Don Quixote, the character, as
an extravagant maniac, instead of the more nuanced perspective, balanced
between sympathy and irony, that we find in the attitudes of Fielding, Sterne,
Wieland, Goethe, Jane Austen towards characters cast in a Quixotic mould.

Two possible answers to the question posed above occur to me. The first is
that in seventeenth-century Spain the pastoral romances that continued to be
written never attained the influence of Honoré d'Urfé's monumental *L'Astrée*,
published in several Parts from 1607 to 1628, nor was there any precise equivalent to the sentimental historical novels of Mademoiselle de Scudéry (e.g.
Le grand Cyrus, 1649–53) and La Calprenède (e.g. *Cassandre*, 1642–60),
which, like *L'Astrée*, and equally interminable, were all the rage in contemporary France and gave fictional form to the sentiments and conventions of the
précieux movement. Another answer is that in the Spanish Baroque, the space
that might have been occupied by imitations of *Don Quixote* was already
taken by the picaresque novel, which, even though implicitly an antithesis
to the heroic or sentimental mode, is an autonomous genre that does not
explicitly set itself up as a parody of another one, as *Don Quixote* does. In
seventeenth-century France, the tradition of comic novels initiated by Charles
Sorel's *Le berger extravagant* (1627–8) (The Extravagant Shepherd), about a
character unhinged by reading d'Urfé's romance, is from the beginning, and
quite consciously, in the line of *Don Quixote*, insofar as it always maintains
a self-consciously ironic relation to the predominant heroic and sentimental
modes of fiction. The tradition of 'anti-romans' – a term coined by Sorel
– includes Scarron's *Le roman comique* (1651–57), followed in the eighteenth century by Marivaux's *Pharsamon ou les folies romanesques* (see above,
p. 168) and Diderot's *Jacques le fataliste* (1770–5).[5] In the latter, Diderot
parodies the conventions of romance within the frame of a dialogue between
Jacques and his master on the theme of the servant's fatalistic determinism.
It is a knockabout parody, not just of traditional fiction but of any philosophic
system that aspires to certainty.

It is in 1669, in France, when the tide begins to turn against the reading of
Don Quixote as nothing more than a hilarious burlesque of chivalry books.

---

[5] On this, see Martínez García (2006).

That year marks the publication of the learned and influential *Lettre-traité sur l'origine des romans* (Letter on the Origin of Novels), by Pierre-Daniel Huet, bishop of Avranches. This lengthy treatise, soon translated into English, defines the term *roman*, offers a brief Aristotelian theory of the genre, and traces its history from early Antiquity until Huet's own times, when, thanks to works like *L'Astrée* or *Le grand Cyrus*, it was in its pomp. We need to bear in mind that Huet has a restricted conception of the term *roman*, which does not have the scope it would acquire from about 1800 onwards. For him it means, specifically, a long fictional prose-narrative of a romantic, senti-mental kind, like those just mentioned; in one form or another – Byzantine, chivalric, pastoral – it had predominated in Europe since Antiquity. In other words, he understands it as a particular kind of romance, and so, does not treat *Don Quixote* as a *roman*, but as a satire on the chivalric species of it. Moreover, he considers it a satire of exceptional quality, calling it 'une si fine et judicieuse critique' (so fine and judicious a critique) of chivalry books and bestowing on Cervantes the compliment 'l'un des plus beaux esprits que l'Espagne ait produits' (Huet, 1971: 121–2) (one of the finest talents Spain has produced). This is the first such judgement to be published in a work of weighty academic authority, and its significance for Cervantes does not end there. Huet maintains, just as Cervantes did through the canon of Toledo's discourse on chivalry books in *Don Quixote* Part I, Chapters 47–48, that *le roman*, always provided that it obeys the classical rules, may be consi-dered one of the canonical poetic genres, a kind of epic, even though written in prose. This upgrading of one form of prose-fiction can quite easily be extended to another on the same neo-classical grounds, and so Huet's trea-tise paves the way for *Don Quixote*'s elevation to the classical canon in the eighteenth century.

The treatise implicitly poses a problem: how does one designate a work like *Don Quixote*, and – a directly related question – to what genre does it belong? Huet got round the problem (p. 99) by classifying *Don Quixote*, together with novels like Scarron's, as *romans comiques* – a makeshift label in which one term implicitly negates the other. In seventeenth- and eighteenth-century Spain the lack of a suitable word was aggravated by the variability and imprecision of the equivalents to *roman*. The principal one was *historia*, which could alternate with *fábula*, *romance* and even *novela* (Haidt, 2003: 32–3). Predominantly, as in England, this last term referred to a short story, being synonymous with French *nouvelle* and German *novelle*.[6] So, throughout

---

[6] Dr Johnson in his dictionary (1755, 1765), defines it as 'a small tale, generally of love'.

Europe till the end of the eighteenth century we have a Pirandellian situation
in which *Don Quixote* wanders confusedly in search of a generic label to
describe it, while the handiest available labels remain stuck to genres destined
to pass out of fashion and be replaced by works like *Don Quixote*.

Huet's admiration for Cervantes's novel was not universally shared
by Frenchmen in the Classical age. In a letter of 1662, Jean Chapelain, a
learned Hispanist and translator of *Guzmán de Alfarache*, finds it amusing
but insubstantial, and in something like the spirit of Baltasar Gracián, sniffily
puts it on a par with works of light entertainment like *Lazarillo de Tormes*,
pastoral romances and popular jest-books (Bardon, 1931: vol. i, p. 270).
Pierre Perrault, brother of Charles, the collector of fairy-tales, writes a long,
nitpicking critique of *Don Quixote* (1679), accusing it of contravening verisimilitude and propriety, and, by its mixture of jest and earnest, of pedantry
and inconsistency of tone (Bardon, 1931: vol. i, pp. 304–17). So, the neo-
classical values by which, from this point on, it would gradually be raised to
the summit of the literary canon could also be used as a cudgel with which to
belabour it. However, these dissenting voices gave ground before a growing,
widely shared perception of qualities of refinement, civility, discretion and
moral wisdom in Cervantes, which, outside Spain, is insistently expressed in
opinions from now on. An example just as authoritative as Huet's judgement
is the discussion of Cervantes as a satirist by the Jesuit René Rapin in his
*Refléxions sur la poétique d'Aristote et sur les ouvrages de poètes anciens
et modernes* (Reflexions on Aristotle's Poetics and on the Works of Ancient
and Modern Poets), published in 1674. Esteeming 'délicatesse', tact, to be the
highest merit in a satirist, personified among the Ancients by the poet Horace,
he finds only two modern writers who meet the requirement (pp. 228–9), one
being Cervantes and the other the author of the *Satire Ménippée* (Menippean
Satire), a pamphlet satirising the Catholic League, published in 1594. He
compares these two favourably with Rabelais, whom he considers, despite his
wit, so coarse and buffoonish as to be quite unsuited to the decency of the
present times. Let us remember that Rapin writes at the zenith of the Classical age, when 'le bon goût' (good taste), 'les bienséances' (propriety) and
'la raison' (reason) were paramount norms, not just preached by theorists like
Boileau, but actively embodied by leading writers like Racine. This explains
the much higher valuation that is placed on Cervantine 'délicatesse' by Rapin
than by the Spanish Baroque half a century before.

It is not that Cervantes's compatriots failed to notice it: the lengthy *aprobación* in the preliminaries to *Don Quixote* Part II by the licentiate Márquez
Torres is a dithyramb to Cervantes as a sort of Christian Horace, who artfully
tempers reproof with mildness and geniality, and sets a shining example to

others 'así por su decoro y decencia como por la suavidad y blandura de sus discursos' (both for his decorum and decency and for the smoothness and blandness of his style). The snag was, as may be inferred from Márquez Torres's very text, that these virtues were more preached than practised in Golden Age Spain. We need look no further than the leading satirist of the reigns of Philips III and IV, Francisco de Quevedo, whose satiric *Sueños* employ a rhetoric designed to shock as well as to ridicule: coarseness, obscenity, vituperation, grotesque caricature and caustic wit. In those times, the Spanish reading-public expected from its satirists – not just Quevedo, but Alemán, Góngora, Suárez de Figueroa, not to mention the slanderous Conde de Villamediana –a stronger and more biting brew than bland 'delicatesse'.

Another sign of the shift in values towards the end of the seventeenth century is that where *Don Quixote*'s first Spanish readers rejoiced in the ridiculous extravagances of the hero's behaviour, discerning Frenchmen and Englishmen, without failing to be amused by them, now appreciate the way in which Cervantes tempers their abnormality. An example of this is the judgement on him by his warmest French admirer, the satirist Saint-Évremond, who, in a private letter written in 1671, says that *Don Quixote* stands out from all the other books that he's ever read because 'il n'y en a point à mon avis qui puisse contribuer davantage à nous former un bon goût sur toutes choses. J'admire comme dans la bouche du plus grand fou de la terre, Cervantès a trouvé le moyen de se faire connaître l'homme le plus entendu' (there is no other book in my opinion that can contribute more to teaching us good taste in all things. I admire the art with which Cervantes has managed to convey the impression of being the wisest of men through the utterances of the maddest person on earth).[7] So, what impresses him particularly is not the hero's madness, but the way in which it blends with wisdom, an effect linked directly to consummate good taste. We hear a rather similar opinion from the English philosopher, John Locke, in his *An Essay Concerning Human Understanding* (1690): 'Of all the books of fiction I know there is none that equals Cervantes's *History of Don Quixote* in usefulness, pleasantry, and a constant decorum. And indeed no writings can be pleasant, which have not nature at the bottom, and are not drawn after her copy.'[8] This appreciation of the quality that Cervantes himself most insists on in *Don Quixote*, verisimilitude or truth to life, is now considered a mark of excellence in the characters of its two heroes, and a reason for seeing them as universal representatives of anyone's experience. Peter Motteux, a French Huguenot exiled in England,

---

[7] Cited in Bardon (1931), vol. i, p. 298.
[8] Cited in Cherchi (1977: 21).

who wrote in English, published a translation of Cervantes's novel in 1700, and the preface begins: 'Every man has something of Don Quixote in his Humour, some darling Dulcinea of his thoughts that sets him very often upon mad Adventures. What Quixotes does not every Age produce in Politicks and Religion?', and develops this idea at some length, applying it to Sancho too, whom he somewhat unkindly considers an embodiment of 'the mean, slavish and ungenerous spirit of the Vulgar in all countries and Ages: a crouching Fear, an awkward Lying, sordid Avarice, sneaking Pity, a natural inclination to Knavery and a superstitious Devotion'. Thereafter, the notion of the universality of Cervantes's pair of heroes becomes one of the commonplaces of eighteenth-century criticism.

It goes together with a broadening of the target of Cervantine satire, now deemed more momentous than a mere literary genre; and both these tendencies are a consequence of a weakening perception of *Don Quixote*'s connection with chivalry books,[9] in proportion as these become less and less familiar. Father Rapin, in his previously mentioned treatise, reports an anecdote supposedly originating from a Spaniard to the effect that Cervantes, motivated by resentment at being shabbily treated by the Duke of Lerma, intended *Don Quixote* as a satire on the Spanish nation, and more specifically, on the Spanish nobility's cult of chivalry. This story spread to England, via Louis Moréri's widely known *Le grand dictionnaire historique* (1674), and in Sir William Temple's *An Essay on Ancient and Modern Learning* (1690), turns into the notion that Cervantes so effectively ridiculed the Spanish devotion to honour that he sapped his nation's fighting spirit and caused its decadence (Cherchi, 1977: 21–2). This too becomes an endlessly repeated cliché, culminating in Lord Byron's famous lament that Cervantes 'smil'd Spain's chivalry away',[10] and it is reinforced by an equally famous jibe about Spain's cultural mediocrity uttered by a character in letter 78 of Montesquieu's *Lettres persanes* (1720): 'le seul de leur livres qui soit bon est celui qui a fait voir le ridicule de tous les autres' (their only good book is the one that has shown how ridiculous all the others are).[11] The link thus established between *Don Quixote* and Spanish decadence has profound and long-lasting repercussions in Spain, where, about the mid-eighteenth century, Cervantes's novel

---

[9] This is evident in Charles Jarvis's prologue to his translation (1742), which identifies the target of Cervantes's satire with the social practices implanted by chivalry – tourneys, duelling, and so on – rather than with a literary genre. In those years, unfamiliarity with chivalry books was even common in Spain, to judge by the comment on their rarity by the learned Benedictine Martín Sarmiento. See Cherchi (1977: 114–15).

[10] *Don Juan*, Canto xiii, st. 9.

[11] Cited in Canavaggio (2005: 93).

becomes a seminal text in the confrontation between conservatives and libe-
rals over Spain's past and future destiny. On the one hand, the traditionalists
defend the Spanish Golden Age and disparage Cervantes as 'the assassin and
executioner of Spain's honour', who has rendered Spain, together with its
glorious military past and the values that inspired them, ridiculous in the eyes
of foreigners. On the other hand, the reformers imbued with Enlightenment
values rightly point out that Cervantes attacked the fantastic extravagances
of one particular literary genre, not Spanish chivalry or Spanish literature
in general, and that his novel, by virtue of the classical purity of its style,
the universality of its characters, and its moral utility, is widely and rightly
acclaimed as the outstanding achievement of Spanish literature.[12]

This was the view of Gregorio Mayans y Siscar, the Spanish Royal
librarian, in his 'Vida de Cervantes', which is the introduction to the de
luxe, beautifully produced edition of *Don Quixote*, in Spanish, published in
London in 1737, and commissioned by the wealthy patron Lord Carteret,
as a presentation volume to adorn the shelves of Queen Caroline's grotto in
Richmond Park. Despite its title, this essay, which was specially solicited for
this volume, is much more than a biography of Cervantes; it is a systematic
and substantial analysis of his works, especially his masterpiece, the first
such study to be written and, in my view, one of the greatest. It starts from
the premise that the Spanish Baroque was so reluctant to admit: that *Don
Quixote*, together with Cervantes's other works in prose, are literary classics, fully compliant with classical norms. To prove this point, and assign
it to one of the canonical genres, the Valencian humanist takes a leaf out
of Huet's book, and also Cervantes's (cf. *DQ* I, 47; p. 550), by positing on
legitimate Aristotelian grounds that a long fictional narrative, despite being
in prose, may be considered a form of epic, provided that it fulfils the other
requirements: verisimilitude, unity of action, mixing of pleasure and profit,
and so on. So, Mayans decides that *Don Quixote* is a counterpart to Homer's
Iliad, though he makes due allowance for its comic and popular nature, by
adding that Cervantes has boldly crossed the epic genre with others normally
deemed remote from it: comedy, satire and farce.[13]

This is Mayans's central contention about *Don Quixote*, and thanks to the
international diffusion of his essay, translated into English in 1738 and into
French in 1740, it was picked up by Henry Fielding, whose *History of Joseph
Andrews* (1742) launches the English comic novel. Fielding reveals by the

---

[12] Cherchi (1977: 94–104, 124–7).
[13] Mayans, *Vida*, sections 158, 159, 165.

subtitle that *Joseph Andrews* is 'written in the manner of Cervantes, author of Don Quixote', and in the preface, echoing Mayans, defines it generically as 'a comic epic poem in prose', expounding its principles, as the Valencian did, by reference to neo-classical poetics, and drawing also on the English aesthetic tradition for his ideas about comedy, burlesque and characterisation.[14] Now, both in theory and in practice, Fielding conceives *Joseph Andrews*, and subsequently his masterpiece *Tom Jones* (1749), as types of 'anti-romance' in the Cervantine tradition. Just as *Don Quixote* is a parody of chivalry books, so *Joseph Andrews*, in initial conception at least, is a parody of Richardson's popular romance *Pamela*, and in *Tom Jones*, though the indebtedness to Cervantes and *Don Quixote* is less overt, Fielding repeatedly elaborates his conception of it as a kind of comic history and epic in prose, distinct from romance and other serious genres.[15] His collaborator in the task of founding the English comic novel, Tobias Smollett, in the preface to *Roderick Random* (1748), endorses this conception and acclaims Cervantes's historic role in ridiculing the extravagant implausibilities of romance and 'converting [it] to purposes far more useful and entertaining, by making it assume the sock and point out the follies of ordinary life' (ed. Boucé, p. xxxiv). 'The sock' was the footwear worn by actors in Classical Antiquity when they represented comedies.

As the quoted words imply, these two writers perpetuate the Cervantine heritage in the further sense that the new form of fiction that they bring into being does not so much aim to demolish romance, as radically reconstruct it: conserving features like the love-interest, the twists of fortune, the use of episodes, the conflict of good and evil, while rejecting its inverisimilitude, placing ordinary characters at its centre and setting the action in a satirically observed contemporary world (Pardo García, 2005). In Fielding, this goes together with the playful parody of romance conventions, and in both writers, with the creation of characters reminiscent of Don Quixote, who exhibit an extravagant mania or hobby-horse in a generally estimable personality. From now on, the conception of the novel as a kind of anti-romance will be reflected in the motivations of characters like Arabella of Charlotte Lennox's *The Female Quixote* (1752) and Catherine Morland of Jane Austen's *Northanger Abbey* (1818), both compulsive readers of escapist

---

[14] Ed. Goldberg, pp. 3–8. The English translation of Mayans's essay was published by J.R. Tonson in London, 1738. Like the original essay, it is divided in numbered sections.

[15] He does this in the preambles to the Books in which *Tom Jones* is divided. See, e.g., the first chapter of Books IV, V and IX respectively.

fiction. The form in which Fielding and Smollett cast those ingredients is miscellaneous, drawing on the examples of history, biography, travel-writing, satiric sketches, letters and memoirs (Ardila, 2001). Fielding's contribution to the genesis of the modern novel is particularly important; and while his creation goes far beyond the neo-classical ideas derived from Mayans, and before him, from Huet, their triangulation of epic, romance and comedy has an important influence on his theoretical conception of it.

As we have seen, *Don Quixote*'s impact on the practice of the major eighteenth-century novelists in English is made possible by the enhanced valuation of it from about 1660 onwards. This is stimulated in England by the publication of a brilliant imitation of *Don Quixote*, Samuel Butler's *Hudibras* (from 1663), a Royalist satire on the hypocrisy of Puritanism, and secondly, by the restoration of the monarchy and the consequent return of the Cavaliers from France, where, until that point, Cervantes's novel had been more popular than across the Channel. The awakened interest brought new translations and imitations, and important new aesthetic theories of laughter, comedy and burlesque based on *Don Quixote* in the writings of Shaftesbury, William Congreve, Sir William Temple and Addison (Paulson, 1998).

I have concentrated on England, because it is there where the foundations of the modern novel were laid. The next decisive step would be taken in Germany, with the publication of Goethe's *Wilhelm Meister* in 1794. Though Goethe makes no explicit reference to Cervantes other than to his *Novelas ejemplares*, his major novel is indebted to Wieland's *Die abenteur des Don Sylvio von Rosalva* (1764) (The Adventures of Don Sylvio von Rosalva) where the influence of *Don Quixote* is strong and explicit. This is a charmingly humorous story about an impressionable youth brought up by an eccentric aunt in a dilapidated castle in a remote province of Spain, who reads fairy stories voraciously, confuses fiction with reality, and falls in love with a young woman depicted on a medallion that he finds fallen in the grass. He sets off in search of her accompanied by his loyal, Sanchopanzine servant Pedrillo, believing her transformed into a butterfly; eventually he finds Doña Felicia, who falls in love with him and gradually weans him from his illusions. In *Wilhelm Meister*, the conflict of illusion and reality takes the form of the erosion of the young bourgeois hero's ideal of the theatre as an instrument of social and moral cultivation, and its modification into a project of useful self-fulfilment as a surgeon. Founding text of the German *Zeitroman* (the novel as mirror of the contemporary age), *Wilhelm Meister* reflects the basic principles of Goethe's philosophy of life. While its wide, realistic panorama of eighteenth-century German society takes the novel's depiction of contemporary manners to a new level, it still conserves many of the characteristic

features of the genre in its early stages of development: including the string
of episodic encounters with new characters on a type of picaresque journey.

The London 1738 edition of *Don Quixote* was the first one which, by
virtue of the quality of its print and production, the elegance of the engra-
vings by John Vanderbank, and Mayans's substantial introduction, accorded
Cervantes's novel the honours of a classic text, and this manifest proof of
the esteem in which it was held abroad prompted Spanish scholars to revalue
it and try to go one better than England. This reaction of national pride was
accompanied, in the second half of the eighteenth century, by a blossoming
of the kind of serious scholarship anticipated by Mayans's essay, beginning
with curiosity about Cervantes's life and admiration for his heroism and other
virtues, which were enhanced in the eyes of his admirers by the misfortunes and apparent lack of recognition that he suffered. In the period 1750
to 1770, a number of important documents relating to his biography were
discovered: including the parish register of his baptism, which proved that
he was born in Alcalá de Henares. In 1780 the Real Academia Española
brought out a splendidly produced edition in four volumes, textually sounder
than any of its predecessors, with carefully supervised illustrations; it was
accompanied by two important introductory essays on *Don Quixote* and the
life of Cervantes by Vicente de los Ríos. It marks a progressive consolidation
of the neo-classical age's scholarly investigation of the text and its author,
most of which, with one important exception, comes from Spain. The exception is the richly annotated edition in five volumes by John Bowle, vicar of
Idmiston in the county of Hampshire, published in Salisbury in 1781. The
scholarly excellence of the notes, based on some twenty years of devoted
research into *Don Quixote*'s background in medieval and Renaissance literature, is the more admirable and astonishing for the fact that Bowle was
armed only with self-taught Spanish and never set foot in Spain. Other landmarks are the biographies by Juan Antonio Pellicer and Martín de Navarrete,
which appeared respectively in editions published in 1797–8 and 1819, and
the 1833–9 edition of *Don Quixote* by Diego Clemencín, whose erudite notes
elucidate Cervantes's parodic allusions to chivalric literature.

Romanticism and the Nineteenth Century

So, by the end of the eighteenth century, *Don Quixote* is definitively
enthroned as a classic. But what kind of classic? Satire? Parody? Comic epic
in prose? The Age of Enlightenment did not come up with a satisfactory solution to these questions, until, around 1800, the German Romantics settled them
once and for all by taking Cervantes's novel, together with Goethe's *Wilhelm*

Meister, as paradigm of the genre they considered their own: the novel, and as a key text in their reconstruction of aesthetics and literary history.[16] With this, they put an end to the Pirandellian comedy in which *Quixote* criticism had been involved throughout the eighteenth century. The notion that *Don Quixote* is the first modern novel is theirs, though, as we have seen, its seeds were sown some time before. Turning neo-classicism's conception of its satirically burlesque nature upside down, they discovered exquisite serious-ness in it, a blend of lyricism and humour, the transcendental symbolism of the conflict between idealism and reality, and an attitude at once ironic and admiring towards the hero and towards medieval chivalry. Where Englishmen had praised the mock-gravity of Cervantes's irony for its effectiveness as an instrument of parody and satire, the Romantics found in it a new pathos and sophistication, seeing it as the means by which the artist mocks his own most cherished illusions and playfully draws attention to the scaffolding of his own work. F.W.J. Schelling, in his lectures on the philosophy of art (1802–5), considers Don Quixote and Sancho as great symbolic myths, representative of all humanity, and compares the first Part of Cervantes's novel, because of its polemical character, to the *Iliad*, and the second, because of society's mystificatory treatment of the hero, to the *Odyssey*. In making this kind of analogy, eighteenth-century critics like Mayans y Siscar and Vicente de los Ríos chiefly had in mind the work's long narrative form; Schelling, more ambitiously, intends it to convey the idea of its ethos and universality too. August-Wilhelm Schlegel (1812) emphasised the way in which *Don Quixote* glowingly portrays the customs and sensibility of the Spain of its age, and, Herder (1772), precursor of the Romantics, considered it a kind of national epic, which expresses the Gothic–Arab spirit of its people. In the two or three decades after 1800, the ideas of the German Romantics, in simplified form, would become commonplaces of literary criticism, transmitted to the rest of Europe by mediators such as Mme de Staël, Bouterwek and Simonde de Sismondi. However, thanks to the prevailing influence of neo-classicism, they did not become definitively established in Spain until about 1860.

In the remainder of the nineteenth century, the advances in the theory of the novel, such as they are, centre on the genre's commitment to social realism. Honoré de Balzac, in the preface to his *Comédie humaine* (1842), paves the way by claiming to offer a comprehensive inventory of the manners of contemporary France, analogous to the study of the animal kingdom by naturalists like Saint-Hilaire and Cuvier. The novel, appropriating the methods

---

[16] On this, Close (1978), Chapter 2.

of scientific empiricism, thus acquires pretensions of social anthropology and claims for itself the dignity of history. With one major exception, there are no significant new developments that concern *Don Quixote*, considered as the genre's foundational text, until the second decade of the twentieth century. The exception is the philosopher Georg Wilhelm Friedrich Hegel, whose ideas are developed in Part II, subsection iii of his *Aesthetics* (1832). For Hegel, the novel emerges at the stage of dissolution of so-called Romantic art and the spirit of chivalry enshrined by it, perpetuating that spirit in a form that sheds the medieval epic's predilection for chance and wilful individualism, and reduces the knight's heroic striving to the subjective dreams of love and social conquest of the novel's protagonist. These are destined to be defeated by the established order of modern society, which ends by enlisting him in its philistine ranks as husband of his previously adored angel, father of a nume-rous brood and harassed man of affairs, a scene characterised as 'marital caterwauling'. Despite this decidedly sarcastic view of the genre's bourgeois and popular nature, Hegel sees Don Quixote, the original novelistic hero, as a noble character, who inspires sympathy by the grandeur of his ideal. His ideas have an important influence on the major twentieth-century treatises of the novel, particularly those of Ortega and Lukács.

The interpretation of *Don Quixote* in the rest of the century consists largely in the consolidation of the Romantic view of it; and the innovations mainly come from Spain and have a nationalist bias. One of them is dedicated to the rebuttal of the historic suggestion, highly unflattering to what was now deemed the national classic, that Cervantes satirised Spanish chivalry and sapped its spirit. Inaugurated by the ballad-anthologist Agustín Durán in 1828–32, and culminating in essays by the medievalist Menéndez Pidal (1920, 1948), it took inspiration from Romanticism's idealisation of medieval chivalry and of the Spanish ballad-tradition considered as distillation of the people's collective soul, arguing that Cervantes had no quarrel with that tradi-tion, which he venerated, but with a degenerate type of chivalric literature imported from north Europe. In demolishing the second, he respected the nobility of the first. Since this approach is not significantly reflected in either the theory or practice of the novel, I shall say no more about it.

However, such is not the case with the so-called 'philosophical' interpre-tation of *Don Quixote*, inaugurated by Nicolás Díaz de Benjumea, whose articles in the Madrid review *La América* in 1859 establish the Romantic conception of Cervantes's novel in Spain. The 'philosophic' method aimed to bring to light the profound sense of the text hidden beneath the literal surface, which had been the sole concern of neo-classical scholars like Clemencín, preoccupied with sources and questions of style. Benjumea started from the premise that *Don Quixote* is a novel with a prophetic social message, presaging the liberal and humanitarian ideals of the modern era, and furthermore, that it is a clever allegory bristling with esoteric allusions to events, personalities and institutions in Cervantes's Spain. So, for example, the hero personifies Cervantes himself; the Golden Age speech proclaims the ideals of liberty, equality and fraternity; Dulcinea symbolises Free Thought. While this esotericism aroused heated controversy, another aspect of Benjumea's philosophic method was widely accepted. It lay in the supposition that the profound significance of *Don Quixote* was determined by the circumstances of Cervantes's life, the trajectory of Spanish history during it, and the enduring traits of the Spanish race. Since, for Spanish critics of that period, there is a direct correlation between these three items, with the first reflecting the second, which it turn is the moment when the third definitively crystallised, it is possible to read *Don Quixote* as a key to Spanish history, a diagnosis of the causes of its decadence and a recipe for its cure. These historicist notions about the relationship between *Don Quixote* and racial character will be systematically developed by the Spanish writers of the so-called generation of 1898 – Unamuno, 'Azorín', Ganivet, and others – in essays, treatises, novels, poems that turn obsessively about the subject of Spanish decadence.[17]

Whereas the eighteenth-century novels of evidently *Quixotic* derivation came mainly from England, France and Germany, and moreover, were predominantly comic, the range in the nineteenth century extends to Russia, North America, Spain and beyond, and acquires a much more grandiose, sombre and occasionally tragic character. One of the few exceptions – two others are Mark Twain's *Tom Sawyer* and *The Adventures of Huckleberry Finn* – is Dickens's *The Pickwick Papers* (1836–7), which, with its genially ironic style, its gallery of Hogarthian characters, its form as the memoirs of a random series of encounters and adventures in the course of a journey, its pairing of the innocently idealistic Mr Pickwick with his street-wise, jocular servant Sam, harks back to the light-hearted creations of Fielding, Sterne and Smollett. The change of predominant mood does not affect the indebtedness to Cervantes. His admirers include many of the century's greatest novelists: apart from Jane Austen, Charles Dickens and Mark Twain, they are Stendhal, Balzac, Flaubert, Herman Melville, George Eliot, Dostoyevski, Henry James, Leopoldo Alas, and Galdós. In Flaubert's *Mme Bovary* (1856–7), for example, the reminders of *Don Quixote* include the falsifying influence of the clichés of romantic literature on Emma's thirst for emotional fulfil-

---

[17] On Spanish interpretations of *DQ* in the nineteenth and early twentieth centuries, Close (1978), Chapters 3, 4 and 5.

ment, the similarity of the community of the drab Norman town of Yonville
– priest, apothecary, doctor, store-keeper, tax-collector – to its equivalent in
that anonymous place in La Mancha, the ironic juxtaposition of Rodolphe's
wooing of Emma with the pompous oratory at the agricultural fair, reminiscent of the brutal contrast between the knight of La Mancha's stilted speech
on the Golden Age and its coarse, rustic circumstances. Like *Mme Bovary*,
the century's great novels play over and over again a theme of unmistakably
Quixotic origin: an epic story of a character fired with illusions that collide
with the disillusioning facts of social life and end in some kind of awakening.
The epic scale appealed to the nineteenth century's thirst for grand metaphysical, historical and moral designs; the opposition of illusion and reality
proved a subtle instrument for analysing the complexities of moral experience;
and the location of passion and heroism on an ironically observed social stage
satisfied the aim of writers like Balzac, Zola and Galdós to study and dissect
the social fabric in its broad sweep and minute detail. It also chimed with a
characteristic tension in the mentality of the age, between, on the one hand,
the heritage of Romanticism, with its idealisation of grand passion, flights of
the imagination, the fantastic, myth, mysticism, primitivism, childhood, and
on the other, the cult of positivism, sociology and science.

The above-mentioned theme not only echoes Romanticism's attitude
towards Quixotic subjectivity, ironic and identificatory at once, but also the
grandiose symbolism that it attributed to Cervantes's masterpiece. So, in
Herman Melville's *Moby Dick* (1853), the oceanic wanderings of the *Pequod*,
captained by the monomaniac Captain Ahab and crewed by a sordid gang of
savages and outcasts, become a symbol of the common man's capacity to
scale heights of heroism and idealism. In Chapter 26 of the novel, they elicit
from Ishmael, the narrator, a Whitmanesque hymn to the Spirit of Equality
and God of Democracy. In Dostoyevski's *The Idiot* (1868), the protagonist,
Prince Myshkin, is a blend of Don Quixote, Mr Pickwick and Christ, and is
comparable to the idea of Cervantes's hero as the archetypal man of faith
that is proposed by his contemporary Turgenyev in his essay *Hamlet and
Don Quixote* (1860), translated into several languages. The symbolism of
Galdós's novels, while echoing the Romantic notion of the conflict between
Ideal and Real, has a historical and nationalistic bias. Though, in respect of
quality, no just comparison can be made between such an outstanding novelist
and a second-rate critic like Benjumea, nonetheless, the latter's 'philosophic'
reading of *Don Quixote* has its equivalent in Galdós's *episodios nacionales*
(national episodes) and *novelas contemporáneas* (contemporary novels).
Following the path of the French realists, he aspired to create a complete
representation of the Spain of his age, exhaustively detailed, encompassing

all levels of society and bearing implicitly the marks of its previous history. It was informed by a conception of the Spanish character, derived from his constant meditation on *Don Quixote*, which has a profound and lasting influence on his novels. Galdós saw that character as subject to unstable oscillation between exalted idealism and degraded materialism, the basic cause, in his opinion, of Spain's decadence (Benítez, 1990: 39–40). Hence the carefully documented realism of his novels is always subordinate to an idea of how the individual destinies of the personages, motivated in many cases by Quixotic illusions, symbolically reflect that of the nation.

Thus, the slide into moral corruption of Isidora Rufete, heroine of *La desheredada* (1881) (The Disinherited Lady), who arrives in Madrid in April 1872 with the dream of inheriting the title and fortune of the Marquess of Aransis, and ends up three years later, all illusions lost, as a common prostitute, mirrors the political disorientation of Spain after the assassination of General Prim, leader of the Republican revolution of 1868. In *La de Bringas* (1884) (Mrs Bringas), whose action is set in the royal palace in the latter stages of the reign of Isabel II, the blindness of the prosaic, penny-pinching functionary Don Francisco Bringas, and the snobbery and extravagance of his wife Rosalía, reflect the pretentiousness, ostentation and materialism of that regime, and the ruin of the Bringas family coincides with the corruption and fall of the monarchy to which its destiny is tied. The town of Orbajosa, which is the setting of *Doña Perfecta* (1876), is a symbol of all Spain, and the novel's action involves a Hegelian conflict between Culture and Nature, the forces of scientific progress and those of primitive reaction, which are nourished by Doña Perfecta's religious fanaticism and the materialistic peasantry. All the town's inhabitants are species of Quixote since all compensate for the empty tedium of their lives by fabricating fantasies about themselves and their honourable status.

Despite the continuing importance of *Don Quixote* as a source of inspiration for creative novelists, it is largely neglected, with the already noted exception of Hegel, in the century's theories of the novel. These are mainly supplied by the novelists, through their reflections on their own or other writers' works in prologues, letters and other contexts. Particularly noteworthy are 'The Art of Fiction' (1888) and the prefaces of Henry James, where, branching off the main road of contemporary realism, he expounds his conception of the novel as a species of window from which the reader can observe, wonder-struck, the interesting objects to be seen through and beyond it. This window is the consciousness of the character to whom authorial viewpoint is delegated. By this means, James broaches a theme that will occupy theorists and literary critics until well into the second half of the twentieth century.

Though James evidently knows *Don Quixote*, since he has given us an authentically Quixotic heroine in *A Portrait of a Lady* (1881), he does not take it into account in his theoretical reflections; and the omission is repeated in the Anglo-Saxon tradition of theory and criticism of Jamesian derivation, beginning with Percy Lubbock's *The Craft of Fiction* (1921), and continuing in the counter-movement initiated by Wayne Booth's *The Rhetoric of Fiction*, 1961.[18] Against Lubbock's central thesis, which is that the novelist's task is to 'show' not to 'tell' his story, Booth argues that narration is a rhetorical act, rather than a vivid dramatisation; and his argument complements the line followed by the leading narratologists, for whom narration constitutes a complex of signs, a semiotic system, designed to elicit a determinate kind of response from the reader. I refer here to Vladimir Propp, Tzvetan Todorov, Julia Kristeva, Roland Barthes, Gérard Genette, Mieke Bal, Umberto Eco, who, with the sole exceptions of Cesare Segre (1974) and Genette in *Palimpsestes*, which is a theory of parody, likewise omit *Don Quixote* from their reflections on narrative.

Given its generally acknowledged foundational status within the genre of the novel, how does one account for this omission? Part of the answer is that some of the theorists are engaged in elucidating the structural principles of a particular species of narrative, like the Russian fairy tale in Propp's case. Another part is that where the object of study is prose-fiction in general, the end can just as well be attained by the quantity of examples adduced, or by their general representativeness, as by their quality. To analyse a mouse's anatomy, any mouse will do; it need not be the Adam or Eve of the species. So Barthes, in *S/Z* (1970), to illustrate the mechanisms of the novel in its classic period, chooses an obscure short story by Balzac, *Sarrazine*, while Kristeva, in *Le texte du roman* (1970), traces the origins of the genre's structure to an even obscurer French fifteenth-century novel by Antoine de La Sales, entitled *Jehan le Saintré*. The question arises, then, which theories of the novel put *Don Quixote* in the foreground? The answer is: those that reflect on the novel's historical origins and its function as a medium of expression of the modern mind.

[18] On this, see Hale (1998). Given that Booth knows *DQ* well, the scarcity of references to it in his book is somewhat surprising; only one passage discusses it in any detail (1961: 212). He takes most of his examples from later novelists, such as Fielding, Sterne, Austen, James, Faulkner, Joyce.

Modernism and Postmodernism

The principal ones corresponding to that description came out between 1914 and 1941, and comprise Ortega y Gasset's *Meditaciones del Quijote*, published in 1914, György Lukács's *Die Theorie des Romans*, 1920 (The Theory of the Novel), and four essays by Mikhail Bakhtin written in the 1930s and early 1940s, which deal with the chronotope of the novel and its dialogic nature. Bakhtin had previously discussed the last item in *Problems of Dostoyevsky's Poetics*, whose original Russian version was published in 1929. All these studies achieved wide diffusion, although the translations of Bakhtin did not begin to circulate in the West until the end of the decade 1960–70. Significant contributions to the theory of the novel, and to *Don Quixote*'s role in its development, are also made by well-known books or essays by Auerbach, Spitzer, Trilling, Levin, Marthe Robert and René Girard, which, by contrast with the treatises by Ortega and Lukács, approach the subject from the angle of comparative literature rather than from philosophic premises derived from German Romanticism and Hegel.

Both Ortega's *Meditaciones* and Lukács's *Theory* start from the Hegelian premise that the epic expresses the world-view of Antiquity by painting a heroic picture of the past in which there was harmony and communication between the divine and human spheres. When that primitive faith in the reality of a transcendent world was eroded, *Don Quixote*, and with it the modern novel, emerged. For both philosophers, this genre residually perpetuates the themes of epic, and aspires to the same totalising form and vision, though it takes an ironic view of the protagonist's striving to bridge the gap between ideal and real. While Ortega depicts this aspiration in heroic colours, seeing it as the creative principle of all human culture, Lukács finds that, in the modern epoch's disintegrated world, art is doomed to sing its tragic failure, taking refuge in a superior sense of irony. Though, after his conversion to communism, Lukács would retract the ideas expounded in *Theory*, his conception of the novel's protagonist as a spiritually rootless character, wandering in search of transcendental ideals in a world abandoned by the gods, has important later repercussions: for example, in René Girard's *Mensonge romantique et vérité romanesque* (1961), in Marthe Robert's detailed comparison of *Don Quixote* with Kafka's *The Castle* in *L'ancien et le nouveau* (1963), and in the pages on *Don Quixote* in Michel Foucault's *Les mots et les choses* (Part I, Chapter 3, section i).[19] The Hungarian thinker's reorientation after 1920 confirms what

---

[19] Though Foucault does not take *DQ* as symbolic of the modern mentality, but of the collapse of the Renaissance episteme with the corrosion of faith in the divinely established link

was previously said about the kinds of theory that foreground *Don Quixote*. What is at issue in *Theory* is precisely the genesis of the novel and its function as vehicle of the modern mind. After embracing communism, Lukács shifts his attention to the crisis of bourgeois capitalism that dates from the end of the eighteenth century, and, turning aside from Cervantes, draws his examples from a series of novelists from Goethe to Thomas Mann.

In contrast to nineteenth-century positivism, Ortega's neo-Kantian philosophic system presupposes that the human mind does not passively reflect reality, like a mirror or a camera, but imposes a conceptual structure upon it. These structures, whose sum represents the complex of human culture, are transitory and need to be recreated by each civilisation, each generation, each individual. The task is as necessary to human beings as breathing oxygen or drinking water. However, unlike these biological functions, it must be undertaken freely, since Ortega, together with twentieth-century Existentialism, takes for granted that man is free to live his life authentically or not. Herein lies the significance of Don Quixote's encounter with the windmills of Criptana, and later, his illusion about Master Peter's puppet-show. In both cases, his behaviour symbolises for Ortega the restructuring activity of mind before matter, together with the wilful self-affirmation in which existential heroism consists.[20] Moreover, Ortega perceives in the latter adventure a metafictional dimension, since, in it, Cervantes builds a bridge between our own experience as readers and Don Quixote's fictional world, by sympathetically representing, in his reaction to the theatre, the process by which any reader of fiction escapes from reality's orbit into that of the imagination.

For Ortega, then, *Don Quixote* enshrines a lesson of cultural renewal, epistemological relativism and existential self-creation, delighting in novelistic illusion at the same time as he ironically undercuts it and puts it *en abîme*. These ideas have profound repercussions on Américo Castro's *El pensamiento de Cervantes* (1925),[21] and as mediated by this seminal work, on later twentieth-century Cervantine criticism. It is necessary to explain briefly what Castro was reacting against in that book, and what were the new paths that he marked out.

In a way, his book is an extension of Benjumea's 'philosophical' method, while taking it to a far more sophisticated level, and shedding its crude esote-

---

between words and things, his mad disorientation is reminiscent of the spiritual rootlessness of the novelistic hero as conceived by Lukács.

[20] I summarise sections 9 and 12 of the 'Meditación primera' (First Meditation), in *Obras completas*, vol. i, pp. 380–1, 385.

[21] On this, see Close (1978, Chapter 6, and 1995: 312–15).

ricism and anachronistic attribution of a republican, anti-clerical ideology to Cervantes. The profundity that Castro reads between the lines of Cervantes's works consists of the imprint in them of enlightened, innovative Renaissance thought and, in particular, of the individual mind-set that guides his assimilation of it. Castro perceives this as a profoundly ambiguous, self-critical cast of mind, attracted to transcendent ideals such as neo-platonic love or the myth of the Golden Age, yet also ironically sceptical towards them. Hence Cervantes's habit of subjecting any question to an open, unresolved dialectic of antithetical views and his presentation of a fictional world fragmented in multiple perspectives, in which none has priority over others and each individual version of the truth is valid. The anti-dogmatic humanism and relativism thus attributed to Cervantes are quite alien to the reactionary ideology of the Spanish Golden Age, including Counter-Reformation Catholicism. They represent a radical departure from the image of his thought that prevailed in the period 1875–1925 and was propounded by the great literary historian Menéndez Pelayo, according to whom he was an inspired, uncritical, intuitive writer, marvellously original by virtue of his portrayal of human nature, not because of his ideas.

Castro's book would have a delayed impact on Cervantine criticism, the delay being explained by the interruptions of the Spanish Civil War and the Second World War and by the conservatism of Spanish culture of the period 1940–60. Its influence, and that of Castro's later writings on Cervantes, did not attain full strength until the 1960s and 1970s. It is explicable by a combination of factors: his treatment of Cervantes's thought as an individual system, interesting in its own right, and displayed across the whole range of his writings; the signalling of self-evidently important aspects of the Renaissance background to it, like neo-Aristotelian poetics and the Erasmian tradition. Also, Castro presented a much more attractive picture of Cervantes than the traditional one, anticipating the liberal, relativist, humanist outlook of twentieth-century intellectuals.

Furthermore – and this is the factor most immediately relevant to our present purpose – this picture was fully in accord with the revolution within the genre of the novel that was being undertaken in the period 1910–30 by Proust, Joyce, Unamuno, Virginia Woolf, Kafka and Faulkner, and with the theoretical reflections arising from it, formulated in the same period by Unamuno, Woolf, Viktor Shklovski, Ortega y Gasset, and retrospectively, by Erich Auerbach, Natalie Sarraute, José María Castellet.[22] This vanguard of

---

[22] Though the editions cited in the Bibliography are in several cases more recent, the original dates of the works to which I refer are: Unamuno (1914); Woolf (1919 and 1924);

novelists rejects the project of realism undertaken by its precursors in the
previous century: that of making an objective and exhaustive inventory of
contemporary society, with an empirical method akin to sociology and the
natural sciences.[23] The new world discovered by them is deliberately fragmented in multiple perspectives, or presented as an enigma that permits
divergent interpretations, or assimilated to the subjective flow of individual
consciousness. For the new generation, there are no innocent eyes or ears,
nor impartial testimonies: reality is the point of convergence of innumerable
points of view. Consequently, the narrator opts for self-effacement, adopting
a non-judgemental complicity with the impressions and perceptions of the
characters: a method described by Erich Auerbach in his fine analysis of
a passage from Virginia Woolf's *To the Lighthouse*, a novel published in
1927. Alternatively, reality is presented as a Kafkaesque maze in which the
quest for truth or justice keeps losing itself in blind alleys: a theme whose
implications for *Don Quixote* and Kafka's *The Castle* are fully explored by
Marthe Robert (1963). Starting from the rejection of fiction's traditional
premises, the novelists of this generation subject their own to ironic scrutiny
as well, by including within the fictional world a writer engaged in writing
a novel very like the one that we read. This is what happens in Unamuno's
Niebla and Gide's *Les faux monnayeurs* (The Counterfeiters), subsequently
becoming a trite device of twentieth-century fiction, which is inevitably
echoed by Cervantine critics in their observations on the metafictionality of
Don Quixote. Renouncing omniscience within the created world, the novelist refuses to be arbiter of its truth. So, the text offers itself enigmatically
to alternative readings; avoiding definitive closure, it invites the reader to
supply his or her own resolution; instead of the grand, tragic dramas logically unfolded by Zola or Hardy, it chooses banal, inconsequential subjects,
like that of Joyce's *Ulysses*, whose development imitates life's unstructured
flow. These developments have been defined by Natalie Sarraute, José-María
Castellet and Claude-Edmond Magny, and they too have become well-worn
themes of modern Cervantine criticism.

Just as the combined influence of Ortega's *Meditaciones* and Castro's
Pensamiento de Cervantes is partly due to their coincidence with the semi-

---

Shklovski (1925); Ortega (1925); Auerbach (1946); Sarraute (1950); Castellet (1956). For
Unamuno's scattered comments in his novel *Niebla*, see the edition by Zubizarreta, pp. 73–84,
178–81, 230–3. Auerbach's analysis of a passage from Virginia Woolf's *To the Lighthouse* is
in the chapter 'The Brown Stocking' in *Mimesis* (1953), pp. 525–53. In referring to Ortega, I
have in mind his essays on the 'de-humanisation' of modern art and on the avant-garde novel,
which came out in 1925, rather than his *Meditaciones del Quijote*.

[23] On the new trends in the novel, see Albérès (1962) and Magny (1950).

nally influential literary fashions of the 1920s y 1930s, so the impact of Bakhtinian theory on literary, including Cervantine, criticism of the last thirty or forty years can be attributed to its convergence with the aesthetics of postmodernism.[24] Like Ortega and Lukács, Bakhtin believes that the transition from the epic to the novel is synchronised with the replacement of Antiquity's world-view by modernity's, though he differs from them in maintaining that embryonic forms of the novel already existed in Antiquity and the Middle Ages.[25] He refers to Socratic dialogues, Menippean satire, and the diverse species of medieval burlesque, which, by means of parody, mocked the noble genres such as epic, lyric and tragedy. These genres defended the established order and took for granted the equivalence of grandiose language, heroic action and enduring ethical/religious values. Like Barthes in *Mythologies* (1957), Bakhtin maintains that the air of unquestionable naturalness that the poet attributes to this equivalence is a deception designed to camouflage the real function of his utterance, that of being the means of diffusion of the ideology of the dominant classes. To the univocal character of the serious genres, the novel and its precursors rebelliously oppose a polyphony of voices and discourses without preeminence among them; against racial and linguistic uniformity, they pit ethnic and dialectal difference; instead of the transparent unity of signifier and signified, they offer their problematic divorce. The 'monologic' voice of the epic bard is replaced by voices that mingle together and interfere with each other in dialogic tension, with the result that each one resonates with the echo of others. Naturally, these themes had a powerful echo in Western culture from the end of the 1960s onwards, since they coincided with various -isms simultaneously: deconstructionism, feminism, postcolonialism. The coincidence is not accidental, but results from the fact that the theories of Bakhtin formulated from 1929 to 1965 and the poststructuralist movements that emerge in Paris around 1968 share a common departure point. They are implicitly inspired by a Utopian yearning for liberation from two types of ideological tyranny: Russian communism in one case, Western capitalism in the other.

According to Bakhtin, at the beginning of the nineteenth century, the diverse novelesque precursors coalesce and are transformed into a new genre, the novel, whose distinctive trait is the predominance of the heteroglot or polisemic tendency, previously subordinate to the opposite one. Among the

---

[24] Its influence on Cervantine criticism is reviewed by Montero Reguera (1997: 68–74, 151–6).

[25] In what follows I summarise the essays 'Epic and Novel', 'From the Pre-History of Novelistic Discourse' and 'Discourse in the Novel' in Bakhtin (1981).

precursors, Rabelais's *Gargantua* and Cervantes's *Don Quixote*, above all the former, mark decisive stages in the evolution towards that result. In *Rabelais and his World*, which came after the studies on dialogue in the novel but is nonetheless complementary to them,[26] Bakhtin sees the work of Rabelais as the culmination of the burlesque, subversive spirit of Carnival, with its world-upside-down revelry, celebration of unihibitedly sensual appetites, cultivation of the language of the street, the tavern and the market-place – all designed to mock the established political and religious order.

The postmodernist connotations of Baktin's theories are manifest in its affinities with the reflections on the so-called postmodernist novel of critics and theorists like Margaret Rose, Linda Hutcheon and Christine Brooke-Rose.[27] These are echoed by the major novelists active since about 1960. In contrast with their predecessors of the 1920–30 period, who questioned the pretensions of nineteenth-century realism by turning individual subjectivity into the arbiter of reality, these writers break with tradition even more radically, by blurring the boundaries between fiction and history, and calling in question authorised language, ideological dogmatism and cultural monocentrism. In this endeavour, *Don Quixote* tends to be treated as an exemplary model. In novels like Carlos Fuentes's *Terra Nostra*, García Márquez's *Cien años de soledad* (One Hundred Years of Solitude), Salman Rushdie's *Midnight's Children* and *Satanic Verses*, Umberto Eco's *The Name of the Rose* and *Foucault's Pendulum*, Milan Kundera's *The Unbearable Lightness of Being*, Juan Goytisolo's *La reivindicación del Conde Don Julián* (Apology for Count Julian), fiction presents itself as the ironic double of history – palimpsest history, to quote Christine Brooke-Rose's term (1992) – suggesting by this means how hazy is the distinction between the two, and, by the grotesque parody of the reassuring official versions of a nation's past, insinuating that these are just another story.[28] According to Kundera (1988: 6), the historic destiny of the novel since the publication of *Don Quixote* has been to focus on an area of reality ignored by science, the nature of human existence, and to highlight its essential relativity and ambiguity in the face of the constant attempts by religion and ideology to constrain it in a dogmatic straitjacket: 'As God slowly departed from his seat whence he had directed the universe and its order of values, distinguished good from evil, and endowed each thing

---

[26] The original Russian version was published in 1965.

[27] For example, Bakhtin is a basic model for Rose's postmodernist theory of parody.

[28] On the Quixotic roots of the ironic interplay between the magic world of romance and the actual history of Latin America in García Márquez's *Cien años de soledad*, see Williamson (1994).

with meaning, Don Quixote set forth from his house into a world he could no longer recognise. In the absence of the Supreme Judge, the world suddenly appeared in its fearsome ambiguity; the single divine Truth decomposed into myriad relative truths parceled out by men.' For Carlos Fuentes, the novel's challenge to ideology begins with the questioning of reading, which then widens its focus to acquire universal application.[29] Cervantes set that particular ball rolling in *Don Quixote*, and novelists of later centuries have followed his example.

The challenge to ideological dogmatism is accompanied by the undermining of racial and cultural hegemony, an attitude eloquently espoused by Salman Rushdie –another *aficionado* of Cervantes – in an article published in the British daily *The Independent* following the *fatwa* pronounced against him by the *ayatollah* Khomeini. He says of his own work: 'It is written from the very experience of uprooting, disjuncture and metamorphosis ... that is the migrant condition, and from which, I believe, can be derived a metaphor for all humanity. ... [It] celebrates hybridity, impurity, intermingling, the transformation that comes of new and unexpected combinations of human beings, cultures, ideas, politics, movies, songs. It rejoices in mongrelisation and fears the absolutism of the Pure.'[30] Fuentes endorses this view of the novel, considering Bakhtin to be its principal champion. I cite remarks by the Mexican novelist that refer to the *fatwa* against Rushdie: 'Mikhail Bakhtin was probably the greatest theorist of the novel of this century [i.e. the twentieth] ... I have thought a great deal about Bakhtin these days in connection with my friend Salman Rushdie. His work perfectly fits Bakhtin's definition of our age as one of competition amongst languages. The novel is the privileged arena where languages in conflict can meet, bringing together, in tension and dialogue, not just opposed individuals, but whole civilisations, widely separated historical epochs, different social groups and other emerging manifestations of human life' (1993: 158). It would be easy to multiply examples of modern *Quixote* criticism where similar opinions are expressed: we find abundant examples in recent books by Diana de Armas Wilson and Carroll Johnson, both published in the year 2000.

In conclusion, in successive epochs since about 1740, the theory and criticism of *Don Quixote* have interpreted it in the light of the ideology and aesthetic values prevailing at the time of interpretation, including the trends

---

[29] This is the thesis of *Cervantes o la crítica de la lectura* (1976) (Cervantes or the Critique of Reading). Fuentes articulates the same conception of the genre in a later book, *Geografía de la novela* (1993) (Geography of the Novel).

[30] *The Independent*, London, 4 February 1990.

ANTHONY CLOSE

set by contemporary novels. It is therefore unsurprising that the history of its reception presents a chaotic kaleidoscope, in which the predominant views of it before 1800 are increasingly contradicted by those that become fashionable later. For the Spanish Baroque, *Don Quixote* was a merry burlesque of chivalry without transcendent significance; for the Enlightenment, it became a universal symbol, and the hero's story, among other things, signified the victory of enlightened reason over obscurantism; for the nineteenth century, his quest embodied the tragic conflict of the Ideal and the Real; the twentieth century read into it a lesson in epistemological relativism; the postmodernist age took it as signifying the deconstruction of establishment ideology, history, monocentrism. What, we ask in bewilderment, gives this now very old book, product of an age very remote from the modern one, its amazing power of self-renewal? We have to do with creative chaos, obviously: a sign of the book's vitality and of its power to elicit radically new readings.

One reason for the mystery, which doubtless affects most literary classics in one way or another, is the reader's urge in any age to see in it a reflection of his or her own experience; without some such sense of its living relevance, it would be an arid museum-piece. *Don Quixote* satisfies that urge in all sorts of ways, chiefly, as Dr Johnson noted in the mid-eighteenth century, by the lifelikeness, suggestiveness and memorable absurdity of its two heroes. Another reason lies in favourable spins of the roulette-wheel in the casino of literary history. For example, it was fortunate for Cervantes that French and English neo-classicism would set so high a valuation on precisely the qualities that he espoused, swimming somewhat against the prevailing aesthetic current of the Spanish Baroque: good taste, urbane irony, decorum, exemplariness, naturalness of style and, not least, the Aristotelian principles upheld in *Don Quixote* Part I, Chapters 47–48. While it is idle to speculate on what might have happened had the historic evolution of taste and values taken a different turn, it obviously could have done. A further set of reasons, as the foregoing pages have shown, lies in *Don Quixote*'s uncanny adaptibility to the intellectual and artistic fashions of succeeding epochs. Thus, it provided a convincingly apt model of the anti-romance for the eighteenth century, lent itself equally well to nineteenth-century's characteristic pitting of subjective illusion against the brutal facts of social life, and has persuaded many intelligent readers of the twentieth and early twenty-first centuries to see in it a mirror of their own intellectual relativism. This chameleonic suppleness is explained, I think, as much by the nature of the book itself, as by extrinsic cultural factors like those mentioned above. I refer above all to its inherent ambiguity: the hybrid mingling of anti-romance with romance; the light, ironic treatment of the conventional wisdom of its own epoch, relayed via a sporadically lucid madman; the larger-than-life indeterminacy of its two heroes, whose motivations often escape normal classification; the densely concentrated and smoothly disguised allusions to previous literature, which leave the reader constantly wondering what precisely, or what and how much more, is being alluded to. This is what provoked Ortega's anguished rhetorical questions in his *Meditaciones*: '¿Se burla Cervantes? Y ¿de qué se burla? Y ¿qué cosa es burlarse?' (Is he joking? And what is he joking about? And what is it to joke about something?).[31] Though yet more explanations could doubtless be offered for *Don Quixote*'s Phoenix-like capacity to rise with renewed life from the ashes of outmoded interpretations or recreations, the mystery ultimately resists our efforts to resolve it.

---

[31] 'Meditación preliminar', in *Obras completas*, vol. i, p. 360.

A GUIDE TO FURTHER READING

The bibliography relating to *Don Quixote* (henceforth *DQ*, with the Q being understood as Quijote with a *j* in Spanish) is dauntingly vast, and the following guide is selective; it is designed for the needs and interests of the readers envisaged in this book, omitting items likely to be primarily of interest to specialists.

Francisco Rico's two-volume edition of *DQ* (Barcelona: Crítica, 1998, re-edited and revised in 2004) has superseded all other easily accessible editions. The text of *DQ*, with introductory essays and notes on usage, is in volume one; the complementary second volume contains concise introductions to each chapter, together with reading-lists; notes on matters other than usage; various informative appendices, and a comprehensive bibliography. Rico's convincingly innovative departure from the previous slavish respect for the *princeps* is expounded in his essay on the history of the text in the preliminaries of vol. 1, and more fully in his *El texto del Q* (Barcelona: Destino, 2005). There is a much handier, condensed version of this edition in one volume (Madrid: Punto de Lectura, 2007).

With regard to recent translations I find John Rutherford's version in Penguin Classics (2000) more consistently reliable in its rendering of nuances and registers than that by Edith Grossman (New York: HarperCollins, 2003). However, the British flavour of Rutherford's translation of idioms may cause perplexity among American readers.

On the life of Cervantes (henceforth C), Jean Canavaggio's *Cervantès* (Paris: Mazarine, 1986), translated into Spanish as *C. En busca del perfil perdido* (Madrid: Espasa Calpe, 1992), is acknowledged as the most authoritative treatment to date. Also worth consulting are 'Hacia la nueva biografía de Miguel de C', 'C en primera persona' and 'La dimensión autobiográfica del *Viaje del Parnaso*' in the collection of Canavaggio's essays *C, entre vida y creación* (Alcalá de Henares: CEC, 2000). María Antonia Garcés's *C in Algiers: A Captive's Tale* (Nashville: Vanderbilt University Press, 2002), is a readable, informative account of life in Algiers in the period of C's captivity there, and traces the imprint of that experience, which Garcés assumes to have been harrowingly traumatic, on the various fictional recreations of it in C's writings.

Two classic general introductions to C's life and works, with particular reference to *DQ*, are Martín de Riquer's *Para leer a C* (Barcelona: Acantilado, 2003) – clear, factual, methodical, continually re-edited in revised versions with different titles since 1960 – and E.C. Riley's *DQ* (London: Allen & Unwin, 1986). Another helpful guide to *DQ* is Emilio Martínez Mata's *Cervantes comenta el Q* (Madrid: Cátedra, 2008), which offers a clear, well-balanced exposition of Cervantes's own comments on his masterpiece. Useful introductions of a different kind are provided by collections of essays and articles. *DQ: A Case-Book*, ed. Roberto González Echevarría (Oxford: Oxford University Press, 2005), contains old, but still influential pieces by Menéndez Pidal, Auerbach, Spitzer, Riley, etc.; *Discursos explícitos e implícitos en el Q*, ed. Christoph Strosetzki (Pamplona: Eunsa, 2006), has interesting contributions by German *cervantistas* on the ideological background; *Lecciones cervantinas*, ed. Aurora Egido (Zaragoza: Cazar, 1985), includes 'La prosa del *Q*' by Fernando Lázaro Carreter, and *Los rostros de DQ*, also edited by Aurora Egido (Zaragoza: Ibercaja, 2004), includes essays on DQ's personality by Augustín Redondo, Guillermo Serés, and others. Also well worth looking at are some of the less recent anthologies: *C*, ed. Lowry Nelson (Englewood Cliffs, NJ: Prentice Hall, 1969); *Suma Cervantina*, ed. J.B. Avalle-Arce and E.C. Riley (London: Tamesis, 1973); *El Q de C*, ed. George Haley (Madrid: Taurus, 1980); *Critical Essays on C*, ed. Ruth El Saffar (Boston: G.K Hall, 1986).

For most readers, the information supplied by Martín de Riquer in sections i, iv and xiv of *Para leer a Cervantes* provides sufficient information about the cultural context of C's attack on chivalry books: that is, about their nature, popularity and the opposition to them by moralists. However, readers wishing to know more about the genre are referred to the publications of the Centro de Estudios Cervantinos in Alcalá de Henares which, apart from a number of re-edited chivalry books, include a general introduction to the genre by Emilio Sales Dasí, *La aventura caballeresca: epopeya y maravillas* (2004). The director of the Centro, José Manuel Lucía Megías, has edited an anthology of it: *Antología de libros de caballerías castellanos* (Alcalá de Henares: CEC, 2001). The two chivalry books esteemed most by Cervantes, *Amadís de Gaula* and *Tirant lo Blanc* (Tirante el Blanco in Spanish), can be read in Felicidad Buendía's edition of *Libros de caballerías españoles* (Madrid: Aguilar, 1960). Sylvia Roubaud-Bénichou's *Le roman de chevalerie en Espagne: entre Arthur et Don Quichotte* (Paris: Champion, 2000) is an impressive *thèse d'état*, which traces it from its French origins, through its intersection with history in the Spanish Middle Ages, to its maturity in the sixteenth century.

In recent years, there has been a renewal of interest in the perennial enigma of Avellaneda's identity; it has been investigated by Martín de Riquer in *Cervantes, Pasamonte y Avellaneda* (Barcelona: Sirmio, 1988), and by several others more recently. The various rival proposals, all more or less plausible but – for the detached observer – equally inconclusive, have the effect of cancelling each other out. Luis Gómez Canseco's well-received edition of Alonso Fernández de Avellaneda, *DQ* (Madrid: Biblioteca Nueva, 2000) supplements Martín de Riquer's somewhat older, though sound and scholarly one (Madrid: Espasa Calpe, 1972).

The two weighty tomes entitled *El siglo del 'Q' (1580–1680)*, edited by José María Jover (Madrid: Espasa Calpe, 1982, 1986), which constitute volume XXVI of the series *Historia de España*, offer a wide coverage of the history, society and culture of the Spanish Golden Age. For a study centred specifically on the historical background, John Elliott's *Imperial Spain: 1469–1716* (London: Arnold, 1963) is still recommendable. Shorter general surveys include: Pierre Vilar, 'El tiempo del *Q*', a classic essay originally published in 1956 and reproduced in translation in George Haley's *El Q de Cervantes* (see above), pp. 17–29; Agustín Redondo, 'El *Q* histórico-social', in Anthony Close and other authors, *C* (Alcalá de Henares: Centro de Estudios Cervantinos, 1995), pp. 256–93; Barry Ife, 'The Historical and Social Context', in the *Cambridge Companion to C*, ed. Anthony Cascardi (Cambridge: Cambridge University Press, 2002), pp. 11–31. Javier Salazar Rincón's *El mundo social del Q* (Madrid: Gredos, 1986) is a methodical study of the social world depicted in C's novel. More general in its focus is James Casey, *Early Modern Spain: A Social History* (London/New York: Routledge, 1999). Chapter 7 of my *C and the Comic Mind of his Age* (Oxford: Oxford University Press, 2000), deals with the various kinds of discipline and control that writers of that age had to contend with. Agustín Redondo's *Otra manera de leer el Q* (Madrid: Castalia, 1997), using a method that fuses Bakhtinian concepts of Carnival with Goldmann's socio-historic perspective, brings massive erudition to bear on individual chapters and characters of *DQ*, and though occasionally liable to over-subtlety, often achieves impressive results. So-called cultural studies, by definition, look at C's novel in a socio-historic dimension. Worth mentioning in this category are two stimulating but debatable contributions by American scholars: *C, the Novel and the New World*, by Diana de Armas Wilson (Oxford: Oxford University Press, 2000), and *C and the Material World*, by Carroll Johnson (Urbana: University of Illinois Press, 2000). De Armas Wilson projects a vision of the novel as a polyglot, multi-cultural, anti-authoritarian genre, launched by *DQ*, and suggests that the discovery of the New World was the intellectual trigger for it; the postmodernist tendency of this interpretation is somewhat similar to the line taken by the Mexican novelist, Carlos Fuentes, in his *C o la crítica de la lectura* (México: Joaquín Mortiz, 1976). Carroll Johnson, drawing on the socio-historic studies of Américo Castro, José Antonio Maravall and Ferdnand Braudel, proposes a view of C's *novelas* and *DQ* as works with a subversive subtext, angrily critical of the patriarchal, feudal socio-economic circumstances of Golden Age Spain. Alban Forcione, in a trenchantly critical review article ('Quixotic Materialism: An Economic Reprocessing of C's Imagined Worlds', *Hispanic Review* 71 (2003), pp. 493–506), highlights the inconsistency between Johnson's aim to recontextualise Cervantes's works historically and his frequent comparisons of Golden Age Spain to present-day North America.

Study of the intellectual and ideological context of *DQ* used to be dominated until quite recently by three things: first, the continuing influence of Américo Castro's *El pensamiento de C* (Madrid: Hernando, 1925; re-edited by J. Rodríguez-Puértolas in 1972), which, reacting against the conservative image of Cervantine thought painted by Menéndez Pelayo, characterised it as secular, relativist, sceptical and in tune with the most innovative tendencies of Renaissance humanism; second, the assumption, originating with Castro, that it was deeply sympathetic to Erasmus's critique of the materialism and hypocrisy of the Roman church, and his project of a radical overhaul of Christian ethics that would return to its original sources and combine them with enlightened Stoic morality; third, the controversial thesis espoused by Castro in his post-Civil War writings, especially *Hacia C* (Madrid: Taurus, 1957) and *C y los casticismos españoles* (Madrid: Alianza, 1966), that C was of *converso* Jewish origins and that his fiction exhibits the characteristic mind-set that Castro attributes to that socially marginalised group. Tendencies one and two in particular were taken up, developed, and modified by scholars sympathetic to Castro's ideas: Marcel Bataillon in the chapter on 'El erasmismo de C', which concludes his monumental *Erasmo y España* (México: FCE, 1950); F. Márquez Villanueva, *Fuentes literarias cervantinas* (Madrid: Gredos, 1973) and *Personajes y temas del 'Q'* (Madrid: Taurus, 1975); Alban Forcione, *C and the Humanist Vision* (Princeton: Princeton University Press, 1982) and *C and the Mystery of Lawlessness* (Princeton: Princeton University Press, 1984); Antonio Vilanova, *Erasmo y C* (Barcelona: Lumen, 1989). The two books by Forcione, though centred on the *novelas*, have obvious relevance to *Don Quixote*. Recently, however, perhaps owing to the difficulty of pinning down C's alleged Erasmian affiliations in a period when most of Erasmus's writings were banned, attention has turned elsewhere. See, for example, the previously mentioned essays in *Discursos explícitos e implícitos en el Q*, ed. Christoph Strosetzki, or Stephen Hutchinson's *Economía ética en C* (Alcalá de Henares: CEC, 2001), which imaginatively considers C's ethics through the economic imagery in which the ideas are expressed. Hans-Jorg Neuschäfer's *La ética del Q: función de las novelas intercaladas* (Madrid: Gredos, 1999) argues that the interpolations function as a serious ethical counterpoint to the comedy of *DQ*'s main theme. Interest in C's Utopianism or anti-Utopianism, originally stimulated by José Antonio Maravall's *Utopía y contrautopía en el Q* (Santiago de Compostela: Pico Sacro, 1976), continues in Mariarosa Scaramuzza Vidoni's *Deseo, imaginación, utopía en C* (Rome: Bulzoni, 1989) and Myriam Yvonne Jehensen and Peter N. Dunn, *The Utopian Nexus in DQ* (Vanderbilt: Vanderbilt University Press, 2006). I have given a brief introduction to C's thought in 'C: Pensamiento, Personalidad, Cultura', which is one of the introductory essays in Rico's edition of *DQ*.

Ruth El Saffar, in *Beyond Fiction: the Recovery of the Feminine in the Novels of C* (Berkeley: University of California Press, 1984), and Diana de Armas Wilson, in the book already mentioned and also in *Allegories of Love: C's Persiles and Sigismunda* (Princeton: Princeton University Press, 1991), interpret Cervantine ideology from a feminist angle, though 'ideology' doubtless needs to be understood in terms of the subconscious rather than explicit thought. This also applies to the contributors to *Quixotic Desire: Psychoanalytic Perspectives on C*, ed. Ruth El Saffar and Diana de Armas Wilson (Ithaca: Cornell University Press, 1993), many of whom follow a similar feminist line. See also Anne Cruz's survey of the treatment of psyche and gender in Cervantes in *The Cambridge Companion to Cervantes*, pp. 186–205. In general, studies of *DQ* from some kind of postmodernist angle (e.g. poststructuralist, post-colonialist, Lacanian) are, except for Bakhtinian theory, much more strongly represented in the USA than in Europe, and find a natural home in the American journal *C*.

A less controversial and divisive kind of theory than some of the works just mentioned above is narratology. One of the first to apply it to *DQ* was Carlo Segre, with his essay 'Costruzioni rettilinee e costruzioni a spirale nel *Don Chisciotte*', in *Le strutture el il tempo* (Turin: Einaudi, 1974). Others who have followed this track include, James Parr, DQ: *An Anatomy of Subversive Discourse* (Newark: Juan de la Cuesta, 1988), where Gérard Genette's influence is combined with Bakhtin's; José María Paz Gago, *Semiótica del Q* (Amsterdam: Rodopi, 1995); Ruth Fine, *Una lectura semiótico-narratológica del Q* (Madrid: Iberoamericana, 2006). A common concern of the narratologists is the making of subtle distinctions among the narrative voices or levels of *DQ*. This question, with its implications for C's relationship to the Moorish chronicler Cide Hamete Benengeli, has particularly exercised *cervantistas* in the English-speaking world, including those outside the narratological circle. See E.C. Riley's *C's Theory of the Novel* (Oxford: Clarendon, 1962), Chapter 6, section ii ('The Fictitious Authorship Device'); George Haley, 'The Narrator in *DQ*: Maese Pedro's Puppet-Show', *Modern Language Notes* 80 (1965), pp. 145–65; Bruce Wardropper, '*DQ*: Story or History?', *Modern Philology* 63 (1965), pp. 1–11; Ruth El Saffar, 'The Function of the Fictional Narrator in *DQ*', *Modern Language Notes* 83 (1968), pp. 64–77; Santiago Fernández Mosquera, 'Los autores ficticios del *Q*', *Anales Cervantinos* 24 (1986), pp. 56–63. For other references, see José Montero Reguera's *El Q y la crítica contemporánea* (Alcalá de Henares: CEC, 1995), pp. 156–63.

The study of Cervantes's literary theory continues to be strongly influenced by E.C. Riley's seminal *C's Theory of the Novel* whose ideas were later incorporated and supplemented in the essay 'Teoría literaria', included in *Suma Cervantina* (1973), ed. Avalle-Arce and Riley, pp. 293–322. An important later development of the ideas expounded in *C's Theory of the Novel* was Riley's application of the novel/romance distinction to C's fiction both in the essay just mentioned and in 'C: a Question of Genre', in *Medieval and Renaissance Studies on Spain and Portugal in Honour of P.E. Russell* (Oxford: Society for the Study of Medieval Languages and Literature, 1981), pp. 69–85. This is reproduced in the collection of Riley's articles, in Spanish translation, entitled *La rara invención* (Barcelona: Crítica, 2001). Alban Forcione's *C, Aristotle and the* Persiles (Princeton: Princeton University Press, 1970), is complementary to Riley's *C's Theory of the Novel*, since it looks at C's *Persiles* and his attitude to chivalry books from the perspective of Renaissance literary theory. The theoretical ideas studied by Riley and Forcione centre on Cervantine romance, rather than the comic fiction. I aimed to fill that gap in my *C and the Comic Mind of his Age* (2000), already mentioned above.

The question of C's attitude to the picaresque is associated with his theory of the novel. Traditionally, and I think misleadingly, it has been treated as starkly opposed, a view that originates with Américo Castro, who in his *El pensamiento de Cervantes* (1925), contrasts C's nobly inclusive realism with the malign, farcical humour of the picaresque genre (see J. Rodríguez-Puértolas's re-edition of Castro's book, Barcelona: Noguer, 1972, pp. 231–2). This idea was influentially developed by Carlos Blanco Aguinaga, 'C y la picaresca: notas sobre dos tipos de realismo', *Nueva Revista de Filología Hispánica* 11 (1957), pp. 313–42, and repeated by several critics after him. E.C. Riley surveys the various critical views and takes an interestingly novel line towards them in his essay 'Sepa que yo soy Ginés de Pasamonte', in *La rara invención*, pp. 51–71 (especially 59–62). See also my *C and the Comic Mind of his Age*, pp. 37–41.

Ever since a ground-breaking article by Geoffrey Stagg, 'Revision in *DQ*,

Part I', in *Hispanic Studies in Honour of I. González Llubera*, ed. F. Pierce (Oxford: Dolphin, 1959), pp. 347–66, Cervantine scholars have shown keen interest in the process of composition of *DQ* Part I, and the successive stages of its reordering and revision. This includes the question whether in its primitive state the novel was originally a brief *novela*. The contributions include Chapter 3 of L.A. Murillo's *The Golden Dial: Temporal Configuration in* DQ (Oxford: Dolphin, 1975), which is also an illuminating study of the handling of time in the novel; Roberto Flores, 'C at Work. The Writing of *DQ*, Part I', *Journal of Hispanic Philology* 3 (1979), pp. 135–60, and José Manuel Martín Morán, *El Q en ciernes. Los descuidos de C y las fases de elaboración textual* (Turin: Edizioni dell'Orso, 1990). The essay by Ellen M. Anderson and Gonzalo Pontón Gijón, 'La composición del *Q*', in the preliminaries to Rico's edition of *DQ* (1998, 2004), contains an overview and synthesis of the whole debate. This is linked to the question of *DQ*'s genesis, which goes back to a lecture by Ramón Menéndez Pidal ('Un aspecto en la elaboración del *Q*') on the influence on *DQ*'s early chapters of the anonymous *Entremés de los romances*. The lecture was published in book form in 1924, and reprinted in various places (e.g. with other essays by Menéndez Pidal in an Austral edition entitled *De C y Lope de Vega*). His arguments were contested by later scholars, and the history of the debate is summarised by Geoffrey Stagg ('*DQ* and the *Entremés de los romances*', *C* 22 (2002), pp. 129–50). The case is reconsidered with fresh arguments in support of the *Entremés*'s influence by Antonio Rey Hazas, *El nacimiento del Q* (Guanajuato: Museo Iconográfico del *Q*, 2006). Another aspect of the novel's composition is the relation of episodes to the main theme, a subject treated by Ana Baquero Escudero, 'Las novelas sueltas, pegadas y pegadizas en el *Q*', *C y su mundo II*, eds Kurt Reichenberger y Darío Fernández-Morera (Kassel/Barcelona: Reichenberger, 2005, pp. 23–51, by Stanislav Zimic, *Los cuentos y las novelas del Q* (second edition, Madrid: Iberoamericana, 2003), and by me, *C and the Comic Mind of his Age*, pp. 128–42.

The influence of the theories of Mikhail Bakhtin on Cervantine criticism has led in the last thirty years to a spate of studies on the their two primary aspects: the carnivalesque and the dialogic, including an article by Walter Reed on the relative scarcity of references to *DQ* in the Russian theorist's writings: 'The Problem of C in Bakhtin's Poetics', *C* 7 (1987), p. 30. The many articles published by Augustin Redondo on *DQ* since the late 1970s, collected in his book *Otra manera de leer el Q,* centre on the first aspect, as does James Iffland's comparative study of the *DQ*s of Cervantes and of Avellaneda, *De fiestas y aguafiestas: risa, locura e ideología en C y Avellaneda* (Madrid: Iberoamericana, 1999). Notable among the treatments of the second, dialogic aspect is Lázaro Carreter's previously mentioned 'La prosa del *Q*' (2004). Others in this category are discussed by Montero Reguera, in *El Q y la crítica contemporánea*, pp. 151–6.

The relation of *DQ* to folklore and popular traditions has been the speciality of traditional Spanish philology and French Hispanism. Menéndez Pidal's work on the relation of *DQ* to the *Entremés de los romances* and the ballad-tradition has already been mentioned. Sancho Panza's style, including his proverbs, have been discussed by Ángel Rosenblat, *La lengua del Q* (Madrid: Gredos, 1971) and in various articles by Monique Joly: e.g. 'Ainsi parlait Sancho Pança', *Les Langues Néolatines* 215 (1975), pp. 3–37. Augustin Redondo's *Otra manera de leer el Q* studies the intersection of popular and learned culture. There are important considerations on C's portrayal of character and its roots in popular jests in Maxime Chevalier, *Folklore y literatura: el cuento oral en el siglo de oro* (Barcelona: Crítica, 1978). Monique Joly's innovative *La bourle et son interprétation* (Lille: Université de Lille III, 1982) analyses the terminology and practices of popular jokes, taunts, hoaxes and their assimilation in picaresque literature and *DQ*. Michel Moner's *Cervantès conteur: écrits et paroles* (Madrid: Casa de Velázquez, 1989) studies the influence of oral narrative on C, and Maurice Molho, in *C: raíces folklóricas* (Madrid: Gredos, 1976), traces the folkloric antecedents of Sancho Panza.

Lastly, the reception of *DQ* by posterity has been assiduously investigated over the last thirty years. A notable recent contribution is Jean Canavaggio's *Don Quichotte, du livre au mythe* (Paris: Fayard, 2005), which traces the process of the conversion of DQ from literary character into myth: that is, from C's text into the myriad recreations made of it through the centuries by engravers, painters, novelists, dramatists, composers, film-directors. Since literary criticism is involved in that process, Canavaggio looks at that too. Canavaggio's title is reminiscent of E.C. Riley's entertaining and instructive '*DQ*: From Text to Icon', originally published in a special number of *C* (1988), pp. 103–16, and reproduced in the previously mentioned collection of his essays, *La rara invención*, pp. 169–82. My own *The Romantic Approach to DQ* (Cambridge: Cambridge University Press, 1978) studies the after-effects of the revaluation of *DQ* by the German Romantics on subsequent criticism of it. This book was later supplemented by my 'La crítica del *Q* desde 1925 hasta ahora' in Anthony Close and other authors, *C* (Alcalá de Henares: CEC, 1995), pp. 311–33. Johannes Hartau, DQ *in der Kunst* (Berlin: Mann, 1987) and José Manuel Lucía Megías, *Leer el Q en imágenes* (Madrid: Calambur, 2006) are two recommendable histories of the iconography of the novel. Lucía Megías's *Banco de imágenes del Q* (www.qbi2005.com) is a valuable online archive of images of *DQ*, and is brought up to date from month to month. Maurice Bardon, *Don Quichotte en France au XVIIe et au XVIIIe siècle* and J.J. Bertrand, *Cervantès et le romantisme allemand* (Paris: Alcan, 1914) are still indispensable. They have recently been supplemented by Ronald Paulson's DQ *in England* (Baltimore: Johns Hopkins, 1998), which looks at *DQ*'s influence on theories of laughter in eighteenth-century England. Worth looking at, though of uneven quality, are the essays in *Cervantes in the English Speaking World*, ed. Darío Fernández Moriera and Michael Hanke (Kassel: Reichenberger, 2005). There is a concise history of literary criticism of *DQ* from a Spanish viewpoint by José Montero Reguera, *El Q durante cuatro siglos* (Valladolid: Universidad de Valladolid, 2005). Montero Reguera's *El Q y la crítica contemporánea* contains in its bibliography references to all the significant studies on *DQ*'s reception in the period 1975–90.

BIBLIOGRAPHY

Preliminary Note. The following is a list of works referred to in the text, and is chosen with the needs of likely readers of this book in mind.

In the case of *Don Quixote*, I have used Rico's edition, referring to the original 1998 imprint for references to the text, and to the re-edition of 2004 for updated notes and bibliography. I have referred to García López's edition of the *Novelas ejemplares*, and to those of Schevill and Bonilla for Cervantes's other works.

A. Cervantes's Works

Don Quijote de la Mancha
Miguel de Cervantes, *Don Quijote de la Mancha*, translated … by several hands and published by Peter Motteux, 2 vols (London, 1706).
——. *The Life and Exploits of the Ingenious Gentleman Don Quixote de la Mancha*, trans. Charles Jarvis (London, 1742).
——. ed. Diego Clemencín, 6 vols (Madrid: 1833–9).
——. ed. F. Rodríguez Marín, 10 vols (Madrid: Atlas, 1947–9).
——. ed. Francisco Rico and Joaquín Forradellas, 2 vols (Barcelona: Crítica, 1998), together with the re-edition (Barcelona: Círculo de Lectores and Galaxia Gutenberg, 2004). The text of *DQ*, with introductory essays by Lázaro Carreter, Rico and others, is in vol. 1. Vol. 2 contains introductions to each chapter, notes, bibliography, etc.
——. translated by John Rutherford (Penguin Classics, 2000).
——. translated by Edith Grossman (HarperCollins, 2003).

——. *Comedias y entremeses*, ed. R. Schevill and A. Bonilla, 6 vols (Madrid: Gráficas Reunidas, 1915–22).
——. *Entremeses*, ed. Eugenio Asensio (Madrid: Castalia, 1970).
——. *La Galatea*, ed. R. Schevill and A. Bonilla, 2 vols (Madrid: Bernardo Rodríguez, 1914).
——. *Novelas ejemplares*, ed. Jorge García López (Barcelona: Crítica, 2001).

——. *Persiles y Sigismunda*, ed. R. Schevill and A. Bonilla, 2 vols (Madrid: Bernardo Rodríguez, 1914).

——. *Persiles y Sigismunda*, ed. Carlos Romero (Madrid: Cátedra, 1997).

——. *Viaje del Parnaso*, ed. R. Schevill and A. Bonilla (Madrid: Gráficas Reunidas, 1922).

B. Pre-1800 Works by Authors Other than Cervantes

Aesop, *Fábulas de Esopo*. Facsimile of the 1489 edition (Madrid: RAE, 1929).

Alemán, Mateo, *Guzmán de Alfarache*, ed. S. Gili Gaya, 5 vols (Madrid: Espasa Calpe, 1972).

Amadís de Gaula: see Rodríguez de Montalvo; also, *Libros de caballerías españoles*.

Anon., *Lazarillo de Tormes*, ed. J. Cejador y Frauca (Madrid: Espasa Calpe, 1969).

Ariosto, Ludovico, *Orlando furioso*, ed. Giuseppe Raniolo (Florence: Le Monnier, 1960).

Avellaneda: see Fernández de Avellaneda.

Bandello, Mateo, *Tutte le opere*, ed. Francesco Flora (Verona: Mondadori, 1952).

Boccaccio, Giovanni, *Il decamerone*, ed. Angelo Ottolini (Milan: Hoepli, 1960).

Capmany, Antonio de, *Teatro histórico-crítico de la eloquencia española*, 5 vols (Madrid, 1786–94).

Correas, Gonzalo, *Vocabulario de refranes* (Madrid: Revista de Archivos, Bibliotecas y Museos, 1924).

Ercilla, Alonso de, *La Araucana*, ed. Marcos Morínigo and Isaías Lerner, 2 vols (Madrid: Castalia, 1987).

Fábulas de Esopo, facsimile of the 1489 edn, ed. E. Cotarelo y Mori (Madrid: RAE, 1929).

Fernández de Avellaneda, Alonso, *Don Quijote de la Mancha*, ed. Martín de Riquer, 2 vols (Madrid: Espasa Calpe, 1972).

——. ed. Luis Gómez Canseco (Madrid: Biblioteca Nueva, 2000).

Fielding, Henry, *Joseph Andrews* and *Shamela*, ed. Homer Goldberg (New York: Norton, 1987).

——. *Tom Jones*, ed. John Bender (Oxford: Oxford University Press, 1998).

Folengo, Teofilo, *Le macharonee*, ed. A. Luzio (Bari: Laterza, 1927).

Góngora, Luis de, *Obras completas*, ed. Juan and Isabel Millé y Giménez (Madrid: Aguilar, 1956).

——. *Romances*, ed. Antonio Carreño (Madrid: Cátedra, 1982).

Gracián, Baltasar, *Agudeza y arte de ingenio*, 2 vols, ed. E. Correa Calderón (Madrid: Castalia, 1969).

——. *El Criticón*, ed. M. Romera-Navarro, 3 vols (Lancaster: University of Pennsylvania Press, 1938–40).

Guevara, Antonio de, *Menosprecio de corte y alabanza de aldea*, ed. Asunción Rallo (Madrid: Cátedra, 1984).

Hobbes, Thomas, *Leviathan*, ed. Michael Oakeshott (Oxford: Blackwell, 1946).

Huet, Pierre-Daniel, *Lettre-traité de … sur l'origine des romans*. Éditions du tricentenaire, 1669–1969 (Paris: A.-G. Nizet, 1971).

Libros de caballerías españoles, ed. Felicidad Buendía (Madrid: Aguilar, 1960).

López de Úbeda, Francisco, *La pícara Justina*, ed. A. Rey Hazas, 2 vols (Madrid: Nacional, 1977).

López Pinciano, Alonso, *Philosophia antigua poetica*, ed. A. Carballo Picazo, 3 vols (Madrid: Consejo Superior de Investigaciones Científicas, 1953).

Luna, Miguel de, *Historia verdadera del rey don Rodrigo* (Granada, 1592).

Marivaux, *Le Don Quichotte moderne*, in vol. xi of *Oeuvres complettes de M. de Marivaux*, 12 vols (Paris, 1781).

Mayáns y Siscar, Gregorio, *Vida de Miguel de Cervantes Saavedra*, ed. Antonio Mestre (Madrid: Espasa Calpe, 1972).

Pérez de Hita, Ginés, *Guerras civiles de Granada* (1595), in Biblioteca de Autores Españoles, vol. 3, pp. 513ff.

Quevedo, Francisco de, *Poesía completa*, ed. José Manuel Blecua (Barcelona: Planeta, 1978).

——. *Prosa festiva completa*, ed. Celsa Carmen García-Valdés (Madrid: Cátedra, 1993).

Rapin, René, *Reflexions sur la poétique d'Aristote et sur les ouvrages des poetes anciens & modernes* (Paris, 1674).

Rodríguez de Montalvo, Garci, *Amadís de Gaula*, in *Libros de caballerías españoles*, ed. Buendía.

Rojas, Fernando de, *La Celestina*, ed. Julio Cejador y Frauca, 2 vols (Madrid: Espasa Calpe, 1968).

Smollett, Tobias, *Roderick Random*, ed. Paul-Gabriel Boucé (Oxford: Oxford University Press, 1999).

Sterne, Laurence, *The Life and Opinions of Tristram Shandy*, ed. Christopher Ricks (Harmondsworth: Penguin Books, 1979).

Torres Naharro, Bartolomé, *Propalladia and Other Works of …*, ed. J.E.

Gillet, 4 vols (Bryn Mawr: Banta, 1943–61). Vol. iv edited by Otis Green (Philadelphia; Philadelphia University Press, 1961).

Zapata, Luis, *Miscelánea*, in Memorial Histórico Español, vol. XI, ed. Pascual de Gayangos (Madrid: Imprenta Nacional, 1859).

C. Post-1800 Theory and Criticism

Aguilar Piñal, F., 'Cervantes en el XVIII', *Anales Cervantinos* 21 (1983), pp. 153–63.

Albérès, R.M., *Histoire du roman moderne* (Paris: Albin Michel, 1962).

Allen, John J., *Don Quixote: Hero or Fool?* Parts I and II (Gainesville: University of Florida Press, 1969 and 1979).

Alonso, Dámaso, *Góngora y el* Polifemo (Madrid: Gredos, 1960).

Alter, Robert, *Partial Magic: The Novel as a Self-Conscious Genre* (Berkeley: University of California Press, 1975).

Ardila, John, 'Cervantes y la *Quixotic Fiction*: el hibridismo genérico', *Cervantes* 21 (2001), pp. 5–23.

Asensio, Eugenio, *Itinerario del entremés* (Madrid: Gredos, 1965).

Auerbach, Erich, 'The Enchanted Dulcinea' and 'The Brown Stocking', in *Mimesis. The Representation of Reality in Western Literature*, trans. Willard Trask (Princeton: Princeton University Press, 1953), pp. 334–58 and 525–53.

Avalle-Arce, J.B., *Don Quijote como forma de vida* (Valencia: Castalia, 1976).

——. *La novela pastoril española* (Madrid: Istmo, 1974).

——. (ed.), La Galatea *de Cervantes, cuatrocientos años después* (Newark: Juan de la Cuesta, 1985).

Avalle-Arce, J.B. and Riley, E.C. (eds.), *Suma Cervantina* (London: Tamesis, 1973).

Babb, Lawrence, *The Elizabethan Malady: A Study of Melancholia in English Literature from 1580 to 1642* (East Lansing: Michigan State University Press, 1951).

Bakhtin, Mikhail, *Rabelais and his World*, trans. Hélène Iswolsky (Cambridge, MA: MIT Press, 1968).

——. *The Dialogic Imagination. Four Essays by M.M. Bakhtin*, ed. Michael Holquist, trans. Caryl Emersen and Michael Holquist (Austin: University of Texas Press, 1981).

Baquero Escudero, Ana, 'Las novelas sueltas, pegadas y pegadizas en el *Q*', in *C y su mundo II*, eds Kurt Reichenberger and Darío Fernández-Morera (Kassel/Barcelona: Reichenberger, 2005), pp. 23–51.

Bardon, Maurice, Don Quichotte *en France au XVIIe et au XVIIIe siècle, 1605–1815*, 2 vols (Paris: Champion, 1931).

Barrero Pérez, Óscar, 'Los imitadores y continuadores del *Quijote* en la novela española del siglo XVIII', *Anales Cervantinos* 24 (1986), pp. 103–21.

Bataillon, Marcel, *Erasmo y España*, 2 vols (México: FCE, 1950).

Benítez, Rubén, *Cervantes en Galdós* (Murcia: Universidad de Murcia, 1990).

Bertrand, J.J., *Cervantès et le romantisme allemand* (Paris: Alcan, 1914).

Blanco Aguinaga, Carlos, 'C y la picaresca: notas sobre dos tipos de realismo', *Nueva Revista de Filología Hispánica* 11 (1957), pp. 313–42.

Booth, Wayne, 'The Self-Conscious Narrator in Comic Fiction before Tristram Shandy', *Publications of the Modern Language Society of America* 67 (1952), pp. 163–85.

——. *The Rhetoric of Fiction* (Chicago: University of Chicago, 1961).

Brooke-Rose, Christine, 'Palimpsest History', in *Interpretation and Over-Interpretation*, ed. Stefan Collini (Cambridge: Cambridge University Press, 1992), pp. 125–38.

The Cambridge Companion to Cervantes, ed. Anthony Cascardi (Cambridge: Cambridge University Press, 2002), pp. 11–31.

Canavaggio, Jean, *Cervantès dramaturge: un théâtre à naître* (Paris: Presses Universitaires de France, 1977).

——. *Cervantès* (Paris: Mazarine, 1986).

——. 'Las bufonadas palaciegas de Sancho Panza', in K. Reichenberger (ed.), *Cervantes: Estudios en la víspera de su centenario* (Kassel: Reichenberger, 1994), pp. 237–58.

——. *Cervantes: entre vida y creación* (Alcalá de Henares: Centro de Estudios Cervantinos, 2000).

——. Don Quichotte*: du livre au mythe* (Paris: Fayard, 2005).

Case, Thomas, 'Cide Hamete Benengeli y los libros plúmbeos', *Cervantes* 22 (2002), pp. 9–24.

Casey, James, *Early Modern Spain: A Social History* (London/New York: Routledge, 1999).

Castellet, José María, *La hora del lector* (Barcelona: Seix Barral, 1956).

Castro, Américo, *El pensamiento de Cervantes* (Madrid: Hernando, 1925), re-edited by J. Rodríguez-Puértolas (Barcelona: Noguer, 1972).

——. *Hacia Cervantes* (Madrid: Taurus, 1957).

——. *C y los casticismos españoles* (Madrid: Alianza, 1966).

Cherchi, Paolo, *Capitoli di critica cervantina* (Roma: Bulzoni, 1977).

Chevalier, Maxime, *Folklore y literatura: el cuento oral en el siglo de oro* (Barcelona: Crítica, 1978).

——. *Quevedo y su tiempo: la agudeza verbal* (Barcelona: Crítica, 1992).

Close, Anthony, *The Romantic Approach to* Don Quixote (Cambridge: Cambridge University Press, 1978).

——. 'Characterisation and Dialogue in Cervantes's *comedias en prosa*', *Modern Language Review* 76 (1981), pp. 330–56.

——. 'Ambivalencia del estilo elevado en Cervantes', in Avalle-Arce (ed.) (1985), pp. 91–102.

——. 'Constructive Testimony: Patronage and Recognition in *Don Quixote*', in Peter Evans (ed.), *Conflicts of Discourse: Spanish Literature in the Golden Age* (Manchester: Manchester University Press, 1990), pp. 69–91.

——. 'Seemly Pranks: The Palace Episodes of *Don Quixote* Part II', in Charles Davis and Paul Julian Smith (eds), *Art and Literature in Spain: 1600–1800. Studies in Honour of Nigel Glendinning* (London: Tamesis, 1993), pp. 69–87.

——. 'La crítica del *Quijote* desde 1925 hasta ahora', in Close and other authors, *Cervantes* (1995), pp. 311–33.

——. 'Cervantes: pensamiento, personalidad, cultura', in Rico's edn of *Don Quixote* (1998), pp. lxvii–lxxxvi.

——. *Cervantes and the Comic Mind of his Age* (Oxford: Oxford University Press, 2000).

——. '¿Cómo se debe remunerar a un escudero: a salario o a merced? La cuestión del realismo del *Quijote*', in Isabel Lozano Rinieblas and Juan Carlos Mercado (eds), *Silva: Studia philologica in honorem Isaías Lerner* (Madrid: Castalia, 2001), pp. 153–65.

——. 'La idea cervantina de la comedia', in *Theatralia* 5 (2003), pp. 331–49. See *Theatralia*.

——. 'Gracián lee a Cervantes: la trascendencia de lo intrascendente', in Aurora Egido and others (eds), *Baltasar Gracián IV Centenario (1601–2001). Actas del II Congreso Baltasar Gracián en sus Obras* (Zaragoza: Institución Fernando el Católico, 2004), pp. 179–98.

——. 'Los clichés coloquiales como aspecto del humor verbal del *Quijote*', in Carlos Romero (ed.), *Le mappe nascoste di Cervantes* (Venice: Santa Quaranta, 2004), pp. 25–39.

——. 'La construcción de los personajes de don Quijote y Sancho', in Emilio Martínez Mata (ed.), *Cervantes y el* Quijote. *Actas del Coloquio Internacional* (Oviedo, 29–30 de octubre de 2004) (Madrid: Arco, 2007), pp. 39–53.

——. and other authors, *Cervantes* (Alcalá de Henares: Centro de Estudios Cervantinos, 1995).

Curtius, Ernst, *European Literature and the Latin Middle Ages*, trans. Willard Trask (London: Routledge, 1953).

De Armas Wilson, Diana, *Cervantes, the Novel and the New World* (Oxford: Oxford University Press, 2000).

——. with Ruth El Saffar (eds), *Quixotic Desire: Psychoanalytic Perspectives on Cervantes* (Ithaca: Cornell University Press, 1993).

Domínguez Ortiz, Antonio, *La sociedad española en el siglo XVII*, 2 vols (Madrid: Consejo Superior de Investigaciones Científicas, 1964, 1970).

Dunn, Peter, *Spanish Picaresque Fiction: A New Literary History* (Ithaca, NY: Cornell University Press, 1993).

——. 'La Cueva de Montesinos por fuera y por dentro: estructura épica, fisonomía', *Modern Language Notes* 88 (1973), pp. 190–202.

——. with Myriam Yvonne Jehensen, *The Utopian Nexus in* DQ (Vanderbilt: Vanderbilt University Press, 2006).

Egido, Aurora, 'Cervantes y las puertas del sueño. Sobre la tradición erasmista del ultramundo en el episodio de la cueva de Montesinos', in *Studia in honorem Prof. M. de Riquer*, 4 vols (Barcelona: Quaderns Crema, 1986–91), vol. iii, pp. 305–41.

—— (ed.), *Lecciones cervantinas* (Zaragoza: Cazar, 1985).

—— (ed.), *Los rostros de Don Quijote* (Zaragoza: Ibercaja, 2004).

——. *Cervantes y Gracián frente a Heliodoro* (Zaragoza: Universidad de Zaragoza, 2005).

Elliott, John, *Imperial Spain: 1469–1716* (London: Arnold, 1963).

El Saffar, Ruth, 'The Function of the Fictional Narrator in *DQ*', *Modern Language Notes* 83 (1968), pp. 64–77.

——. *Novel to Romance: A Study of Cervantes's* Novelas ejemplares (Baltimore: Johns Hopkins University Press, 1974).

——. *Distance and Control in* Don Quixote (Chapel Hill, NC: North Carolina University Press, 1975).

——. *Beyond Fiction: the Recovery of the Feminine in the Novels of Cervantes* (Berkeley: University of California Press, 1984),

——. (ed.), *Critical Essays on Cervantes* (Boston: G.K. Hall, 1986).

Fernández-Morera, Darío, and Hanke, Michael (eds), *Cervantes in the English Speaking World* (Kassel: Reichenberger, 2005).

Fernández Mosquera, Santiago, 'Los autores ficticios del Q', *Anales Cervantinos* 24 (1986), pp. 56–63.

Fine, Ruth, *Una lectura semiótico-narratológica del* Quijote (Madrid: Iberoamericana, 2006).

Flores, Roberto, 'Cervantes at Work: The Writing of Don Quixote Part I', *Journal of Hispanic Philology* 3 (1979), pp. 135–50.

Forcione, Alban K., *Cervantes, Aristotle, and the* Persiles (Princeton: Princeton University Press, 1970).

——. *Cervantes's Christian Romance: A Study of* Persiles y Sigismunda (Princeton: Princeton University Press, 1972).

——. *Cervantes and the Humanist Vision: A Study of Four Exemplary Novels* (Princeton: Princeton University Press, 1982).

——. *Cervantes and the Mystery of Lawlessness: A Study of* El casamiento engañoso y El coloquio de los perros (Princeton: Princeton University Press, 1984).

——. 'Quixotic Materialism: An Economic Reprocessing of Cervantes's Imagined Worlds', *Hispanic Review* 71 (2003), pp. 493–506). A review of the book (2000) by Carroll Johnson.

Foucault, Michel, *The Order of Things* (London: Routledge, 1974). Translation of *Les mots et les choses* (1966).

Fuentes, Carlos, *Cervantes o la crítica de la lectura* (México: Joaquín Mortiz, 1976).

——. *Geografía de la novela* (México: Fondo de Cultura Económica, 1993).

Ganivet, Ángel, *Idearium español*, sixth edition (Madrid: Suárez, 1933).

Garcés, María Antonia, *Cervantes in Algiers: A Captive's Tale* (Nashville: Vanderbilt University Press, 2002).

Genette, Gérard, *Palimpsestes* (Paris: Gallimard, 1982).

Gies, David (ed.), *The Cambridge History of Spanish Literature* (Cambridge: Cambridge University Press, 2004).

Girard, René, *Deceit, Desire and the Novel*, trans. Y. Freccero (Baltimore and London: Johns Hopkins University Press, 1966). Translation of *Mensonge romantique et vérité romanesque* (1961).

González de Amezúa y Mayo, A., *La vida privada española en el protocolo notarial* (Madrid: Aldus, 1950).

González Echevarría, Roberto (ed.), *Cervantes' Don Quixote: a Casebook* (Oxford: Oxford University Press, 2005).

Guillén, Claudio, *Literature as System* (Princeton: Princeton University Press, 1971).

——. 'Luis Sánchez, Ginés de Pasamonte y los inventores del género picaresco', in *Homenaje a Antonio Rodríguez-Moñino*, 2 vols (Madrid: Castalia, 1966), vol. i, pp. 221–31.

Haidt, Rebecca, 'The Enlightenment and Fictional Form', in Harriet Turner and Adelaida López de Martínez (eds), *The Cambridge Companion to the Spanish Novel* (Cambridge: Cambridge University Press, 2003), pp. 31–46.

Hale, Dorothy, *Social Formalism. The Novel in Theory from Henry James to the Present* (Stanford: Stanford University Press, 1998).

Haley, George, 'The Narrator in *Don Quijote*: Maese Pedro's Puppet-Show', *Modern Language Notes* 80 (1965), pp. 146–65.

——. (ed.), El Quijote *de Cervantes* (Madrid: Taurus, 1980).

Hamilton, Bernice, *Political Thought in Sixteenth-Century Spain* (Oxford: Clarendon, 1963).

Hartau, Johannes, DQ *in der Kunst* (Berlin: Mann, 1987).

Hegel, K.W.F., *The Philosophy of Fine Art*, trans. F.B.B. Osmaston, 4 vols (New York: Hacker Books, 1975).

Hendrix, W.S., 'Sancho Panza and the Comic Types of the Sixteenth Century', in *Homenaje ofrecido a Menéndez Pidal*, 3 vols (Madrid: Hernando, 1925), vol. ii, pp. 485–94.

Herrero-García, Miguel, *Estimaciones literarias del siglo XVII* (Madrid: Voluntad, 1930).

Hughes, Gethin, 'The Cave of Montesinos: Don Quixote's Interpretation and Dulcinea's Disenchantment', *Bulletin of Hispanic Studies* 54 (1977), pp. 107–13.

Hutcheon, Linda, *Narcissistic Narrative – The Meta-Fictional Paradox* (New York/London: Methuen, 1980).

——. 'The New Novel. The Post-Modern Novel', in Michael McKeon (ed.), *Theory of the Novel: A Historical Approach* (Baltimore: Johns Hopkins University Press, 2000), pp. 834–50.

Hutchinson, Stephen, *Economía ética en Cervantes* (Alcalá de Henares: CEC, 2001).

Iffland, James, *De fiestas y aguafiestas: risa, locura e ideología en Cervantes y Avellaneda* (Madrid: Iberoamericana, 1999).

James, Henry, 'The Art of Fiction', in *The Future of the Novel. Essays on the Art of Fiction*, ed. Leon Edel (New York: Vintage, 1956).

——. *The Art of the Novel. Critical Prefaces*, ed. Richard Blackmur (London: Scribner, 1935).

Johnson, Carroll, *Madness and Lust. A Psychoanalytical Approach to* Don Quixote (Berkeley: University of California Press, 1983).

——. *Cervantes and the Material World* (Urbana: University of Illinois Press, 2000).

Joly, Monique, 'Ainsi parlait Sancho Pança', *Les Langues Néolatines* 215 (1975), pp. 3–37.

——. *La bourle et son interprétation* (Lille: Université de Lille III, 1982).

——. 'Las burlas de don Antonio. En torno a la estancia de don Quijote en Barcelona', *Actas del II Coloquio Internacional de la Asociación de Cervantistas* (Anthropos: Barcelona, 1991), pp. 71–81.

Jover, José María (ed.), *El siglo del 'Quijote' (1580–1680)*, 2 vols (Madrid: Espasa Calpe, 1982, 1986). The two vols represent tome XXVI of the *Historia de España*, founded by Ramón Menéndez Pidal, and directed by Jover.

Knowles, Edwin, 'Allusions to *Don Quixote* before 1660', *Philological Quarterly* 20 (1941), pp. 573–86.

Kundera, Milan, *The Art of the Novel* (London: Faber, 1988).

Laspéras, Jean-Michel, *La nouvelle en Espagne au siècle d'or* (Montpellier: Université de Montpellier, 1987).

Lázaro Carreter, Fernando, Lazarillo de Tormes *en la picaresca* (Barcelona: Ariel, 1972).

——. 'La prosa del Quijote', in *Lecciones cervantinas*, ed. Aurora Egido (Zaragoza: Cazar, 1985, pp. 115–29.

Levin, Harry, '*Don Quijote y Moby Dick*', *Realidad* 5 (Buenos Aires, September/October 1947), pp. 254–67.

——. 'The Example of Cervantes', in *Contexts of Criticism* (Cambridge, MA: Harvard University Press, 1957), pp. 79–96.

——. 'The Quixotic Principle: Cervantes and Other Novelists', in M.W. Bloomfield (ed.), *The Interpretation of Narrative* (Cambridge, MA: Harvard University Press, 1970), trans. as 'Cervantes, el quijotismo y la posteridad', in *Suma Cervantina,* ed. Avalle-Arce and Riley, pp. 277–96.

Lozano Renieblas, Isabel, *Cervantes y el mundo del* Persiles (Alcalá de Henares: Centro de Estudios Cervantinos, 1998).

Lucía Megías, José Manuel (ed.) *Antología de libros de caballerías castellanos* (Alcalá de Henares: CEC, 2001).

——. *Leer el* Quijote *en imágenes* (Madrid: Calambur, 2006).

Lukacs, Georg, *The Theory of the Novel*, trans. Anna Bostock (London: Merlin, 1971).

Madariaga, Salvador de, *Don Quixote: An Introductory Essay in Psychology* (London: Oxford University Press, 1948).

Magny, Claude-Edmonde, *Histoire du roman français depuis 1918* (Paris: Seuil, 1950).

Mancing, Howard, *The Chivalric World of* Don Quijote (Columbia: University of Missouri Press, 1982).

——. 'Response to "On Narration and Theory"', *Cervantes* 24 (2004), pp. 137–56. This is a response to the article by Parr in the same number of *Cervantes*.

Maravall, J.A., *Utopía y contrautopía en el* Quijote (Santiago de Compostela: Pico Sacro, 1976).

Marín Cepeda, Patricia, 'Valladolid, theatrum mundi', *Cervantes* 25 (2005), pp. 161–93.

Márquez Villanueva, F., *Fuentes literarias cervantinas* (Madrid: Gredos, 1973).

——. *Personajes y temas del 'Quijote'* (Madrid: Taurus, 1975).

——. 'Estratigrafía literaria de Don Quijote y los Duques. ¿Un menosprecio de corte?', *Actas del X Simposio Nacional de Actualización científica y didáctica de lengua española y literatura* (Sevilla: Asociación Andaluza de Profesores de Español, 2006), pp. 15–40.

Martín Jiménez, Alfonso, *El* Quijote *de Cervantes y el* Quijote *de Pasamonte: una imitación recíproca* (Alcalá de Henares: Centro de Estudios Cervantinos, 2001).

Martín Morán, José Manuel, *El* Quijote *en ciernes. Los descuidos de C y las fases de elaboración textual* (Turin: Edizioni dell'Orso, 1990).

Martínez García, Patricia, 'El *Quijote* y la tradición novelesca francesa en los siglos XVII y XVIII', *Edad de Oro* 25 (2006), pp. 409–35.

Martínez Mata, Emilio, *Cervantes comenta el* Quijote (Madrid: Cátedra, 2008).

McKendrick, Melveena, *Theatre in Spain: 1490–1700* (Cambridge: Cambridge University Press, 1989).

——. *Playing the King: Lope de Vega and the Limits of Conformity* (London: Tamesis, 2000).

Menéndez Pidal, Ramón, *Un aspecto en la elaboración del* Quijote, second edition (Madrid: Cuadernos Literarios, 1924).

Molho, Maurice, *Cervantes, raíces folklóricas* (Madrid: Gredos, 1976).

Moner, Michel, *Cervantès conteur: écrits et paroles* (Madrid: Casa de Velázquez, 1989).

Montero Reguera, José, '*La Galatea y El Persiles*', in Close and other authors (1995), pp. 157–66.

——. *El Quijote y la crítica contemporánea* (Alcalá de Henares: Centro de Estudios Cervantinos, 1997).

——. *El* Quijote *durante cuatro siglos* (Valladolid: Universidad de Valladolid, 2005).

Murillo, Luis Andrés, *The Golden Dial: Temporal Configuration in* Don Quijote (Oxford: Dolphin, 1975).

——. *A Critical Introduction to* Don Quixote (New York: Peter Lang, 1988).

Nalle, Sara, *God in La Mancha. Religious Reform and the People of Cuenca: 1500–1650* (Baltimore: Johns Hopkins University Press, 1992).

Nelson, Lowry (ed.), *Cervantes* (Englewood Cliffs, NJ: Prentice Hall, 1969).

Neuschäfer, Hans-Jorg, *La ética del* Quijote*: función de las novelas intercaladas* (Madrid: Gredos, 1999)

Ortega y Gasset, J., *Meditaciones del* Quijote, in *Obras completas*, 6 vols, fifth edition (Madrid: Revista de Occidente, 1961), vol. i, pp. 311–400.

———. *Deshumanización del arte. Ideas sobre la novela* (Madrid: Revista de Occidente, 1925).

Pardo García, Pedro Javier, 'Tobias Smollett's *Humphry Clinker* and the Cervantine Tradition in Eighteenth-Century English Fiction', in Fernández-Morera and Hanke (eds) (2005), pp. 81–106.

Parker, A.A., *The Philosophy of Love in Spanish Literature* (Edinburgh: Edinburgh University Press, 1984).

Parr, James, *An Anatomy of Subversive Discourse* (Newark: Juan de la Cuesta, 1988).

———. 'On Narration and Theory', *Cervantes* 24 (2004), pp. 119–35.

Paz Gago, José María, *Semiótica del* Quijote (Amsterdam: Rodopi, 1995).

Paulson, Ronald, Don Quixote *in England. The Aesthetics of Laughter* (Baltimore: Johns Hopkins University Press, 1998).

Percas de Ponseti, Helena, *Cervantes y su concepto del arte*, 2 vols (Madrid: Gredos, 1975).

Pierce, Frank, *La poesía épica del Siglo de Oro* (Madrid: Gredos, 1961).

Redondo, Augustín, 'Acercamiento al *Quijote* desde una perspectiva histórico-social', in Close and other authors (1995), pp. 257–93.

———. *Otra manera de leer el* Quijote (Madrid: Castalia, 1998).

———. 'El episodio barcelonés de don Quijote y Sancho frente a don Antonio Moreno (II, 61–62)', *Volver a Cervantes. Actas del IV Congreso Internacional de la Asociación de Cervantistas*, ed. A. Bernat Vistarini (Palma de Mallorca: Universitat de les Illes Balears, 2001), pp. 499–513.

Reed, Walter, 'The Problem of Cervantes in Bakhtin's Poetics', *Cervantes* 7 (1987), pp. 29–37.

Rey Hazas, Antonio, *El nacimiento del* Quijote. *Edición y estudio del* Entremés *de los romances* (Guanajuato: Museo Iconográfico del Quijote, 2006).

Rico, Francisco, 'El título de *Don Quijote*', *Bulletin of Spanish Studies* 81 (2004), pp. 541–51.

———. *El texto del Q* (Barcelona: Destino, 2005).

Riley, Edward C., *Cervantes's Theory of the Novel* (Oxford: Clarendon, 1962).

——. 'Teoría literaria', in *Suma Cervantina*, ed. J.B. Avalle-Arce and E.C. Riley, pp. 293–322.

——. 'Cervantes: a Question of Genre', in *Medieval and Renaissance Studies on Spain and Portugal in Honour of P.E. Russell* (Oxford: Society for the Study of Medieval Languages and Literature, 1981), pp. 69–85.

——. 'Metamorphosis, Myth and Dream in the Cave of Montesinos', in R.B. Tate (ed.), *Essays on Narrative Fiction in the Iberian Peninsula in Honour of Frank Pierce* (Valencia: Dolphin, 1982), pp. 105–19.

——. *Don Quixote* (London: Allen & Unwin, 1986).

——. 'Don Quixote: From Text to Icon', *Cervantes*, special issue (Winter 1988), pp. 103–15.

——. *La rara invención* (Barcelona: Crítica, 2001). A collection of Riley's essays on Cervantes, translated by Mari Carmen Llerena.

Riquer, Martín de, *Cervantes, Pasamonte y Avellaneda* (Barcelona: Sirmio, 1988).

——. *Para leer a Cervantes* (Barcelona: Acantilado, 2003).

Robert, Marthe, *The Old and the New. From Don Quixote to Kafka* (Berkeley: University of California Press, 1977). Translation of *L'ancien et le nouveau* (1963).

Roca Mussons, María, 'Don Quijote y el Capitano', *Theatralia* 5 (2003), pp. 415–29. See *Theatralia*.

Rodríguez Marín, Francisco, *El* Quijote *y don Quijote en América* (Madrid: Sucesores de Hernando, 1911).

Romero Muñoz, Carlos, 'Nueva lectura del Retablo de Maese Pedro', *Actas del I Coloquio Internacional de Cervantistas* (Barcelona: Anthropos, 1990), pp. 95–130.

Rose, Margaret, *Parody: Ancient, Modern and Post-Modern* (Cambridge: Cambridge University Press, 1995).

Rosenblat, Ángel, *La lengua del* Quijote (Madrid: Gredos, 1971).

Roubaud-Bénichou, Sylvia, *Le roman de chevalerie en Espagne: entre Arthur et Don Quichotte* (Paris: Champion, 2000).

Rueda, Lope de, *Pasos*, ed. José Luis Canet Vallés (Madrid: Castalia, 1992).

Salazar Rincón, Javier, *El mundo social del* Quijote (Madrid: Gredos, 1986).

Sales Dasí, Emilio, *La aventura caballeresca: epopeya y maravillas* (Alcalá de Henares: CEC, 2004).

Sarraute, Natalie, *L'ère du soupçon: essais sur le roman* (Paris: Gallimard, 1950).

Scaramuzza Vidoni, Mariarosa, *Deseo, imaginación, utopía en Cervantes* (Roma: Bulzoni, 1998).

Segre, Carlo, 'Costruzioni rettilinee e costruzioni a spirale nel *Don Chisciotte*', in *Le strutture el il tempo* (Turin: Einaudi, 1974).

Shklovski, Viktor, *Teoria della prosa* (Turin: Einaudi, 1976).

Smith, Paul Jordan, *Bibliographia Burtoniana* (Palo Alto, CA: Stanford University Press, 1931).

Solé-Leris, Amadeu, *The Spanish Pastoral Novel* (Boston: Twayne, 1980).

Spitzer, Leo, 'Perspectivismo lingüístico en el *Quijote*', in *Lingüística e historia literaria* (Madrid: Gredos, 1955), pp. 161–225; English version, 'Linguistic Perspectivism in the *Don Quijote*', in *Linguistics and Literary History* (Princeton: Princeton University Press, 1948), pp. 41–85.

Stagg, Geoffrey, 'Revision in *Don Quixote* Part I', in Frank Pierce (ed.), *Studies in Honour of I. González Llubera* (Oxford: Dolphin, 1959), pp. 347–66.

——. '*Illo tempore*: Don Quixote's Discourse on the Golden Age and its Antecedents', in La Galatea *de Cervantes* ..., ed. Avalle-Arce (1985), pp. 71–90.

——. '*Don Quijote* and the *Entremés de los romances*: A Retrospective', *Cervantes* 22 (2002), pp. 129–50

Strosetzki, Christoph (ed.), *Discursos explícitos e implícitos en el* Quijote (Pamplona: Eunsa, 2006),

Sullivan, Henry, *Grotesque Purgatory. A Study of Cervantes's Don Quixote Part II* (Philadelphia: Pennsylvania State University Press, 1996).

Theatralia 5, ed. Jesús Maestro and María Grazia Profeti (Pontevedra: Mirabel Editorial, 2003).

Torrente Ballester, G., *El Quijote como juego* (Madrid: Guadarrama, 1975).

Trilling, Lionel, 'Manners, Morals and the Novel', in *The Liberal Imagination* (London: Mercury, 1961), pp. 205–22.

Unamuno, Miguel de, *Vida de Don Quijote y Sancho*, Austral edition.

——. *Niebla*, ed. Armando F. Zubizarreta (Madrid: Castalia, 1995).

Urbina, Eduardo, *El sin par Sancho Panza: parodia y creación* (Barcelona: Anthropos, 1991).

Valera, Juan, 'Sobre el *Quijote* y sobre las diferentes maneras de comentarle y juzgarle', discurso leído ante la Real Academia Española ... el 25 de septiembre de 1864, *Obras escogidas, XIV: Ensayos (Segunda Parte)* (Madrid: Biblioteca Nueva, 1928), pp. 9–74.

Varey, John, Varey, *Historia de los títeres en España* (Madrid, Revista de Occidente, 1957).

Vilanova, Antonio, *Erasmo y Cervantes* (Barcelona: Lumen, 1989).

Wardropper, Bruce, '*Don Quixote*: Story or History?', *Modern Philology* 63 (1965), pp. 1–11.

Williamson, Edwin, 'The Quixotic Roots of Magic Realism', in *Cervantes and the Modernists: The Question of Influence* (London: Tamesis, 1994), pp. 103–20.

Wilson, Edward, 'Cervantes and English Literature of the XVIIth Century', *Bulletin Hispanique* 50 (1948), pp. 27–52.

Wonham, Henry, 'Mark Twain: The American Cervantes', in *Cervantes in the English Speaking World*, ed. Fernández-Morera and Hanke (2005), pp. 159–68.

Woolf, Virginia, 'Modern Fiction', in *The Common Reader* (New York: Harcourt, 1953), pp. 150–8.

——. 'Mr Bennett and Mrs Brown', in *The Captain's Deathbed and Other Essays* (New York: Harcourt, 1950), pp. 94–119.

Zimic, Stanislav, *El teatro de Cervantes* (Madrid: Castalia, 1992).

——. *Los cuentos y las novelas del* Quijote (Madrid: Iberoamericana, 2003).

INDEX

Addison, Joseph 237
Aesop 6, 51, 86
Alberti, Rafael 8
Alemán, Mateo, *Guzmán de Alfarache* 14, 16, 23, 25, 47, 48, 62, 63, 68, 81, 82, 88, 126, 157, 165, 228, 233. See also Martí.
Allen, J.J. 110
Alonso, Dámaso 27
Alter, Robert 124
Amadís de Gaula 2, 31, 34, 41, 42, 48, 56, 59, 67, 74, 83, 97, 98, 139, 154, 161, 205, 217
amante liberal, El 55, 87n
Anderson, Ellen 38
Angulo el Malo 183
Apuleius, *The Golden Ass* 62
Arata, Stefano 181
arbitristas 174
Archbishop of Toledo (Cervantes's patron) 12
archetype, archetypal. See *Don Quixote*.
Arellano, Ignacio 182
Ariosto, Ludovico, *Orlando furioso* 26, 56, 62, 74, 89, 98, 109, 135, 146, 161
Aristotle 56, 62, 123, 141, 176, 192, 204, 231, 235. See also Classical rules.
Asensio, Eugenio 20, 80
Auerbach, Erich 247, 248
Austen, Jane 230, 236, 241
autores (actor-managers) 9, 204. For fictitious authors, see *Don Quixote*.
autos sacramentales 26, 182
Avalle-Arce, J.B. 2, 15, 100
Avellaneda 11, 68n, 70, 97, 110, 121, 135, 149, 155, 164, 171, 175, 179, 185, 204n, 221, 229
Azorín (José Martínez Ruiz) 241

Babb, Lawrence 98

Bakhtin, Mikhail 19, 36, 245, 249–50, 251
Bal, Mieke 244
Balbuena, Bernardo de 62
ballads. See romances, romancero.
Balzac, Honoré de 239, 241, 242
Bandello, Matteo 49, 74, 77
baños de Argel, Los 8
Barcelona 15, 28, 109, 119, 120, 179, 180, 181, 184, 185, 189, 207, 213
Barthes, Roland 244, 249
Belianís de Grecia 41
Benengeli, Cide Hamete 42, 43, 44–45, 65, 66, 139–40, 159–64, 166, 168, 170, 171, 173, 175, 179, 180, 185, 190, 199–200, 206, 209, 218, 221
Benjumea. See Díaz de Benjumea.
Bible 67, 68, 108, 113, 203
Blecua, J.M. 24
Boccaccio, Giovanni, *Decameron* 16, 17, 37, 48
Boiardo, Matteo 98
Boileau, Nicolas 232
Booth, Wayne 166, 244
Bouterwek, Friedrich 239
Bowle, John 238
braying aldermen 187, 201
Brooke-Rose, Christine 250
buffoons 207–08, 221
burlesque. See parody.
Burton, Robert 98
Butler, Samuel 237
Byron, Lord George Gordon 234

Calderón de la Barca, Pedro 4, 26, 27, 97, 121, 228, 229
Camacho's wedding 193–95, 196
Canavaggio, Jean 3, 7, 11, 20, 182
Capmany, Antonio 124, 125
captive's tale 7, 8, 52, 58, 65, 75–76, 78, 83, 128

30; lucid intervals 63, 68–69, 70, 75–76, 83, 113, 173, 181, 187, 191, 208n; motivation, traits, evolution of madness 30–33, 35, 83, 90–123, 173–74, 176, 181, 182, 185, 190–92, 199; nobility 100, 239, 240; relation to Sancho 90–94, 110–12, 113–23, 183, 194, 212, 213, and to others 91, 173–75, 181, 186, 190–93, 210–11; style 35, 55–56, 59–60, 99, 111, 112; testament 46, 114–16, 121–23

Other aspects: ambiguity 88, 252; archetypal quality, universality 5, 87–88, 91, 123, 226, 234, 235, 239; Benengeli's chronicle in Part II 4, 169, 170, 171–72, 175–76, 179, 180, 184–85, 186, 209, 210, 214; burlas, hoaxes 2, 48, 64, 109, 175, 179, in Duke's palace, 206–26; censure of burlas 206, 208, of chivalry books 9, 10, 28, 37, 41, 45–46, 53, 78, 120, 235, of Lope's school 9, 28, 78, 204; classic status 235, 238, 240; colloquialisms 91, 97, 99, 111, 122, 125, 137, 150–59, 173, 177; comic tone or ethos 1, 21, 79, 87, 124, 150, 158, 176, 223; common nature 45–46, 49, 51, 99, 145; composition 9, 36, 38–39, 43, 95, 96, 120, 126, 170, 179; devices of attenuation 144–50; devices of intensification 140–44; differences between the two Parts 173–78, 179–81, 190–91; eclecticism 48, 55, 56, 88, 89, 96–99, 195, 226, 253; episodes and interpolations 10, 42, 63–64, 65–66, 70–71, 73–79, 125, 177, 183, 184–95; festivities 4, 185, 194, 214; fictitious authors, 44–45, 66; generic classification 33, 231–32, 235, 236, 238–39; historic editions 235, 238; hybrid nature 49, 88, 186, 252; irony 33, 56–57, 59, 61, 91, 92, 93, 101, 107–08, 124, 144–50, 159, 167, 175, 192, 239; menudencias, trifles 150, 158, 159, 160–62, 177; metafictionality 124, 164, 166–72, 176, 177, 179, 201, 204, 246; moral lessons, ideology, outlook 14, 50–51, 88, 182, 186, 188, 192, 235, 247, 252; names and etymologies 31, 44, 45, 97, 120, 138–40, 190, 218–19;

narrator's viewpoint or techniques 36, 44, 45, 49, 51, 56–61, 85, 86, 88, 93, 124, 127, 145–50, 158, 159–72, 201, 202; parody of chivalry books 2, 30–35, 39, 53, 55–56, 59–61, 88, 99, 139, 161, 195, 203, 208, 228, 234, 238, and of other genres, 53, 55–56, 116, 124, 128, 149, 157, 162–63, 165–66, 167, 195, 203; as picture of national life 28–29; precepts of government 85, 87, 208n, 213, 222; as primitive novela 39–40; prologues and preliminaries 7, 8, 9, 12, 67–68, 88, 165–66, 204, 232; reception by contemporaries 4, 11, 12, 168, 173, 175, 176, 208, 227–29, and by posterity 1, 3–5, 227–53; relevance to main theme 65–66, 126, 144, 192, 204; repetition and variation 43–45, 69, 101–08, 127; as satire 10, 12, 16, 33, 39, 51, 56, 66, 67, 72, 73, 79, 88, 115, 157, 163, 186, 202, 203, 231, 234, 238, 239, 240; setting in time and space 28, 37, 170, 180; sources in folklore or literature 5, 30, 46–49, 51, 52, 55, 56, 90–91, 96–99, 195, 223, 225, 226; and Spain's decadence 234–35, 240, 241; structure 36–39, 43, 64, 71, 180; superstition 203; as symbol of history, race or human condition 239, 241, 242, 243, 250–51; theory of prose epic 10, 41, 56, 235; translations 54, 125, 150, 227, 234; as "true history" 44, 45, 64–66, 126, 148, 159–62, 164, 176; verisimilitude or realism 10, 15–16, 19, 35, 46–47, 49–51, 65, 68, 95, 106, 199, 233, against functionalism 100, 106, 113–23; verse tributes 67; wit and verbal humour 53–54, 123–59

See also Avellaneda, ballads, Benengeli, Cervantes, chivalry books, Dulcinea, enchanters, inns, pastoral romances, Sancho, and references to protagonists of specific episodes.

Dorotea. See Cardenio.

dos doncellas, Las 18, 179

Dostoyevski, Fyodor 241, 242

Duke or Duchess 102, 107–08, 115, 119, 128, 135, 137, 153, 154, 156, 157,

CPSIA information can be obtained
at www.ICGtesting.com
Printed in the USA
BVHW04s0914040818
523431BV00010B/173/P